Praise fɔ

Transitio
Youth and Your
with Emotional or Behavioral Difficulties
An Evidence-Supported Handbook

"One of the most urgent of challenges in the field of special education involves trying to figure out how to help young adults with emotional or behavior difficulties move from high school into postsecondary education and employment settings. Clark and Unruh have taken on this challenge by providing the reader with an evidence-based framework and corresponding interventions that WILL better help these young adults attain productive postsecondary outcomes."

—Larry Kortering, Ph.D.
Professor, Special Education
Appalachian State University

"This timely and user-friendly handbook contains the latest information on evidence-based models and practices for young people and their families, educators and service providers, researchers, and administrators."

—Judith A. Cook, Ph.D.
Professor of Psychiatry
University of Illinois at Chicago

"The textbook provides a variety of easy-to-use, evidence-supported strategies. . . . I really liked the focus on practical examples and student voices that were presented throughout the handbook. This handbook will be a welcome addition to the field of secondary transition."

—David W. Test, Ph.D.
Professor
Department of Special Education and Child Development
University of North Carolina at Charlotte

"A very well-researched compendium of research, data, information, and best practices for those who are policymakers, academicians, and educators committed to ensuring successful adult outcomes for transition-age youth."

—**Lili Frank Garfinkel**
Coordinator, Juvenile Justice Project
PACER Center

"This book provides practitioners with a powerful, research-supported framework that helps at-risk youth successfully transition into adulthood. The authors have effectively eliminated the excuse that 'we just don't know what works with these kids.' Their contribution challenges us to fund programs that really do work; they have clearly demonstrated how these courageous young people can become resource producers rather than resource consumers!"

—**Peter Caproni, Ph.D.**
Psychologist
Miami, Florida

"Clark and Unruh have compiled a comprehensive and practical guide that reflects the very best of what we know works for supporting transition-age youth and young adults with emotional or behavioral difficulties. The authors possess a depth and breadth of experience that enables them to combine an honest treatment of the challenges involved in serving these youth with a hopeful view of what is possible when our services and supports are built upon a strong evidence base. This is the handbook you will not want to be without."

—**Erik Carter, Ph.D.**
Associate Professor of Special Education
University of Wisconsin–Madison

"While the handbook was written to address transition for students with EBD, many of the evidence-supported practices, implementation issues, and strategies to improve postschool transition outcomes are relevant and practical for all students with disabilities. The voices of the students throughout the handbook speak the realities and challenges of good transition planning practices. A great handbook for anyone interested in transition and improving the postschool lives of young adults with disabilities."

—**Ed O'Leary, Ed.D.**
Program Specialist
Mountain Plains Regional Resource Center
Logan, Utah

"This handbook has been long awaited by practitioners and researchers who collaborate with youth and young adults with mental health challenges. . . . Documents in useful detail the evidence that is currently available across several domains, including education, vocational rehabilitation, and mental health services."

—Nancy Koroloff, Ph.D.
Portland State University

"Compiles the collective wisdom accrued and honed over decades through efforts to develop and implement programs and policies to support youth in transition. Administrators, practitioners, young adults, and their families will find a well-articulated framework of principles and practices to guide future efforts. Successful efforts to support employment, education, and positive social engagement and stem the tide of substance abuse, incarceration, and homelessness will reap great benefits for our communities."

—Ann Vander Stoep, Ph.D.
Associate Professor
Department of Psychiatry and Behavioral Sciences
Department of Epidemiology
University of Washington

"The important work that has been compiled in this text will positively impact the post-school outcomes for our most vulnerable youth: young people with emotional and behavioral difficulties. The combination of research, evidence-based practices, and case studies is exactly what is needed to ensure that a community of professionals, family members, and young people join together to identify, develop, and provide services and support at both a large-scale and personal level."

—Cinda Johnson, Ed.D.
Assistant Professor
Special Education Program Director
Seattle University
Transition specialist, writer,
and mother of a daughter with bipolar disorder

"This book includes the importance of discovering and accepting mental illness as part of recovery for young people. It resonated with my own journey of bipolar disorder. This text reduces the stigma of mental health conditions for young people, provides information and resources, and does so by including authentic case stories."

—Linea Johnson
College student, mental health advocate,
speaker, and writer

"An outstanding, empirically based guide . . . The coauthors of each chapter include professionals as well as youth and family members who have wrestled with education and other service-delivery systems, providing credibility and insight not found in most texts addressing the transition of youth with emotional or behavioral difficulties."

—**Peter E. Leone, Ph.D.**
Director
National Center on Education,
Disability, and Juvenile Justice

"Offers us the tools we need to be a community of support . . . for helping youth with emotional disorders successfully transition to adulthood."

—**Linda Rosenberg, M.S.W.**
President/CEO, The National Council
for Community Behavioral Healthcare

Transition *of* Youth & Young Adults *with* Emotional or Behavioral Difficulties

Transition *of* Youth & Young Adults *with* Emotional or Behavioral Difficulties

AN EVIDENCE-SUPPORTED HANDBOOK

edited by

Hewitt B. "Rusty" Clark, Ph.D.
National Network on Youth Transition for Behavioral Health
Florida Mental Health Institute
College of Behavioral and Community Sciences
University of South Florida
Tampa

and

Deanne K. Unruh, Ph.D.
Secondary Special Education & Transition
College of Education
University of Oregon
Eugene

·P·A·U·L·H·
BROOKES
PUBLISHING Co.®

Baltimore • London • Sydney

Paul H. Brookes Publishing Co.
Post Office Box 10624
Baltimore, Maryland 21285-0624
USA

www.brookespublishing.com

Typeset by Integrated Publishing Solutions, Grand Rapids, Michigan.
Manufactured in the United States of America by
Versa Press, Inc., East Peoria, Illinois.

The individuals described in this book are composites or real people whose
situations are masked and are based on the authors' experiences. In most
instances, names and identifying details have been changed to protect
confidentiality. Real names and stories are used by permission.

Library of Congress Cataloging-in-Publication Data

Transition of youth and young adults with emotional or behavioral difficulties : an
evidence-supported handbook / edited by Hewitt B.
"Rusty" Clark and Deanne K. Unruh.
    p.   cm.
  Includes bibliographical references and index.
  ISBN-13: 978-1-55766-963-6 (pbk.)
  ISBN-10: 1-55766-963-5 (pbk.)
  1. Youth—Mental health services—United States. 2. Young adults—
Mental health services—United States. 3. Problem youth—Services for—United States.
4. Problem youth—Rehabilitation—United States.
I. Clark, Hewitt B.   II. Unruh, Deanne K.   III. Title.
  RJ503.T7195 2000
  362.198′92—dc22   2009025018

British Library Cataloguing in Publication data are available
from the British Library.

2013   2012   2011   2010   2009
10   9   8   7   6   5   4   3   2   1

Contents

About the Editors.. vii
Contributors... ix
Foreword   *Gary M. Blau and Diane L. Sondheimer* xiii
Acknowledgments.. xvii

**Introduction to Transition to Adulthood Issues
and the Evidence-Supported Handbook**
Understanding and Addressing the Needs
of Transition-Age Youth and Young Adults
and Their Families
Hewitt B. "Rusty" Clark and Deanne K. Unruh 3

Section I   **Challenges and Effective Transition Systems**

Chapter 1   The Service System Obstacle Course for
Transition-Age Youth and Young Adults
Maryann Davis, Melanie Green, and Cheri Hoffman 25

Chapter 2   Navigating the Obstacle Course:
An Evidence-Supported Community
Transition System
Hewitt B. "Rusty" Clark and Karen Hart............... 47

Section II   **Community Initiatives: Evidence-Supported
and Enduring Transition Programs**

Chapter 3   Partnerships for Youth Transition: Creating
Options for Youth and Their Families
DeDe Sieler, Spencer Orso, and Deanne K. Unruh 117

Chapter 4   High School and Community College
Partnerships with Vocational Rehabilitation
*K. Brigid Flannery, Lauren Lindstrom,
and Michael Torricellas* 141

Chapter 5   Serving Young Adults with Serious Mental
Health Challenges from Dependency
Programs and Community Settings
*Marc A. Fagan, Wayne Munchel, Isiah Rogers,
and Hewitt B. "Rusty" Clark*........................ 163

Chapter 6   Improving the Transition Outcomes of
Adolescent Young Offenders
*Deanne K. Unruh, Miriam G. Waintrup,
Tim Canter, and Sinjin Smith* 189

Chapter 7   More than Friends: Peer Supports for Youth
            and Young Adults to Promote Discovery
            and Recovery
            Lisa B. Galasso, Amy Arrell, Paul Webb,
            Samuel Landsman, David Holmes, Kimberly Frick,
            Luke Bradford Knowles, Crystal Fair-Judson,
            Rebecca Smith, and Hewitt B. "Rusty" Clark 209

Section III   Improving Practice, System, and Policy
Chapter 8   Prevention Planning: Collaborating with
            Youth and Young Adults to Reduce Risk
            Behavior and Related Harm
            Mason G. Haber, Hewitt B. "Rusty" Clark,
            and Ryan Parenteau 235
Chapter 9   Policy, Funding, and Sustainability: Issues
            and Recommendations for Promoting
            Effective Transition Systems
            Cheri Hoffman, Craig Anne Heflinger,
            Michele Athay, and Maryann Davis 263
Chapter 10 Collaborative Approach to Quality
            Improvement in Process, Progress, and
            Outcomes: Sustaining a Responsive and
            Effective Transition System
            Karyn L. Dresser, Peter J. Zucker,
            Robin A. Orlando, Alexandra A. Krynski,
            Gwendolyn White, Arun Karpur,
            Nicole Deschênes, and Deanne K. Unruh 291

**Section IV   Future Focus: Advancing the
             Transition Agenda**
Chapter 11 Future Focus: Practice, Program, System,
            Policy, and Research
            Deanne K. Unruh and Hewitt B. "Rusty" Clark 325

Index 345

About the Editors

Hewitt B. "Rusty" Clark, Ph.D., Director, National Network on Youth Transition for Behavioral Health, and Professor, Florida Mental Health Institute, College of Behavioral and Community Sciences, University of South Florida, 13301 Bruce B. Downs Boulevard, MHC 2332,Tampa, Florida 33612

Dr. Clark has developed and researched various innovative programs on youth with emotional and/or behavioral difficulties. His research interests and grants focus on evaluating the effectiveness of 1) individualized planning and interventions for children and youth with emotional and/or behavioral difficulties and their biological, adoptive, and foster families; and 2) preparation and facilitation of youth and young adults in their transition into employment and career, educational opportunities, and community-life functioning.

Dr. Clark and has published extensively, with 5 books and more than 125 professional publications to his credit. He has served as the lead guest editor for a *Special Issue on Transition to Adulthood Research*, published in the *Journal of Behavioral Health Services & Research* (2008, October). Dr. Clark is a board-certified behavior analyst, serves on various editorial boards for professional journals, and consults nationally and internationally.

When not conducting research and workshops, teaching, consulting, or developing programs on his topics of professional interest, Dr. Clark enjoys his avocations of sailing the Gulf of Mexico and other seas—and photographing wildlife. In fact, with his trip to the Antarctic, where he observed the penguins and other wildlife of the region, he has now been on all seven continents of the world.

Deanne K. Unruh, Ph.D., Senior Research Associate, Secondary Special Education & Transition (SSET), 204 Clinical Services Building, 5260 University of Oregon, Eugene, Oregon 97403

In addition to her work at the SSET, Dr. Unruh is Director of the Post-School Outcome Center at the University of Oregon (UO), with research expertise in high-risk adolescents involved in the juvenile justice system. She has received $6.1 million in research, model demonstration, and personnel preparation funding from the U.S. Department of Justice, Office of Juvenile Justice and Delinquency Prevention; the U.S. Department of Education, Office of Special Education Programs; and the Institute of Educational Sciences.

Dr. Unruh's research interests include 1) developing facility-to-community transition programming for adolescents involved in the juvenile justice system, 2) improving employability social skills for high-risk adolescents, and 3) developing employment-ready measures for adolescents with disabilities. Dr. Unruh contributes to the doctoral training in transition and research methods in the College of Education. She teaches the Program Evaluation doctoral research methods sequence within the UO College of Education. Prior to coming to UO, she was a teacher and administrator in alternative education schools for high-risk youth in urban settings for more than 12 years. During this tenure, Dr. Unruh was a certified trainer for the National Diffusion Network and trained state, district, and school staff nationwide on effective instructional strategies for working with at-risk youth.

When Dr. Unruh is not at work, her interests include acting on and advocating for food sustainability and equity. She is an avid gardener and grows most of the vegetables and fruits she eats year-round. Dr. Unruh also serves on the board of her local food bank, which distributes food, operates dining rooms for the homeless, educates individuals in food self-sufficiency, and supports community gardening to disseminate fresh, organic food to those in need within her county.

Contributors

Amy Arrell
Coordinator of Transition Age
  Services
The Bridge of Central Mass
4 Mann Street
Worcester, Massachusetts 01602

Michele Athay
Pre-Doctoral Fellow
Young Adult Coauthor
Vanderbilt University
PMB 151
230 Appleton Place
Nashville, Tennessee 37203

Tim Canter
Transition Specialist,
Springfield School District
  Community Transition Program
Lane Co. Juvenile Justice Center
John Serbu Youth Campus
2727 MLK Blvd
Eugene, Oregon 97401

Maryann Davis, Ph.D.
Research Associate Professor
Center for Mental Health Services
  Research
Department of Psychiatry
University of Massachusetts
  Medical School
55 Lake Avenue
Worcester, Massachusetts 01655

Nicole Deschênes, M.Ed.
Co-director
National Network on Youth
  Transition for Behavioral
  Health
Florida Mental Health Institute
College of Behavioral &
  Community Sciences
13301 Bruce B. Downs Boulevard
Tampa, Florida 33612

Karyn L. Dresser, Ph.D.
Director of Research and Program
  Practices
Stars Behavioral Health Group
7700 Edgewater Drive, Suite 658
Oakland, California 94621

Marc A. Fagan, Psy.D.
Associate Director of Child and
  Adolescent Programs
Thresholds
4101 North Ravenswood
  Avenue
Chicago, Illinois 60613

Crystal Fair-Judson
Peer Support Worker/
  Transitional Outreach
  Counselor
The Bridge of Central Mass
4 Mann Street
Worcester, Massachusetts 01602

K. Brigid Flannery, Ph.D.
Senior Research Associate/Associate
    Professor
Educational and Community
    Supports
University of Oregon
1571 Alder
1235 University of Oregon
Eugene, Oregon 97403

Kimberley Frick
Young Adult Coauthor
The Bridge of Central Mass
4 Mann Street
Worcester, Massachusetts 01602

Lisa B. Galasso, Ph.D.
Director of Mental Health Services
The Bridge of Central Mass
4 Mann Street
Worcester, Massachusetts 01602

Melanie Green
Mental Health Recovery Coordinator
Young Adult Coauthor
Clark County Department of
    Community Services
Post Office Box 5000
Vancouver, Washington 98666

Mason G. Haber, Ph.D.
Assistant Professor
Department of Psychology
University of North Carolina at
    Charlotte
9201 University City Boulevard
Charlotte, North Carolina 28223

Karen Hart, B.S.
Child, Youth, and Family Advocate
United Advocates for Children and
    Families
291 San Bernabe Drive
Monterey, California 93940

Craig Anne Heflinger, Ph.D.
Associate Dean for Graduate
    Education
Professor of Human and
    Organizational Development
Vanderbilt University
Peabody #90
230 Appleton Place
Nashville, Tennessee 37203

David Holmes
Peer Support Leader
Young Adult Coauthor
The Bridge of Central Mass
4 Mann Street
Worcester, Massachusetts 01602

Cheri Hoffman, Ph.D.
Fellow
Vanderbilt Center for Nashville
    Studies
1207 18th Avenue South
Nashville, Tennessee 37212

Arun Karpur, M.B.B.S., M.P.H.
Research Associate
Cornell University
Employment and Disability Institute
School of Industrial and Labor
    Relations
310 ILR Extension Building
Ithaca, New York 14853

Luke Bradford Knowles
Young Adult Coauthor
Genesis Club
274 Lincoln Street
Worcester, Massachusetts 01605

Alexandra A. Krynski,* M.Ed.
Transition Coordinator
Pittsburgh Public Schools
Pittsburgh Peabody High School
515 North Highland Avenue
Pittsburgh, Pennsylvania 15206

---

*Previously served as Youth Support Coordinator and then as Special Projects Coordinator for the System of Care Initiative with Allegheny County Department of Human Services, Office of Behavioral Health, in Pittsburgh, Pennsylvania.

Samuel Landsman, B.A.
Generalist Staff, Young Adult
    Services
Genesis Club
274 Lincoln Street
Worcester, Massachusetts 01605

Lauren Lindstrom, Ph.D.
Senior Research Associate/Associate
    Professor
Secondary Special Education and
    Transition Program
209 Clinical Services Building
5260 University of Oregon
Eugene, Oregon 97403

Wayne Munchel, LCSW
Director of Training, Los Angeles
    Region
Stars Behavioral Health Group
    (SBI IG)
1501 Hughes Way, Suite 150
Long Beach, California 90810

Robin A. Orlando, M.A.
Systems Integration Specialist
Allegheny County Department of
    Human Services
Executive Office
One Smithfield Street, Suite 400
Pittsburgh, Pennsylvania 15222

Spencer Orso
Young Adult Coauthor
Clark County Department of
    Community Services
Post Office Box 5000
Vancouver, Washington 98666

Ryan Parenteau
Young Adult Coauthor
Transition to Independence Program
359 Main Street, Suite 209
Haverhill, Massachusetts 01830

Isiah Rogers
Young Adult Coauthor
Thresholds
4101 North Ravenswood Avenue
Chicago, Illinois 60613

DeDe Sieler
Youth Program Manager
Clark County Department of Com-
    munity Services/Youth House
Post Office Box 5000
Vancouver, Washington 98666

Rebecca Smith
Young Adult Coauthor
Genesis Club
274 Lincoln Street
Worcester, Massachusetts 01605

Sinjin Smith
Young Adult Coauthor
Lane Co. Juvenile Justice Center
John Serbu Youth Campus
2727 MLK Blvd
Eugene, Oregon 97401

Michael Torricellas
Young Adult Coauthor
Eugene, Oregon 97403

Miriam G. Waintrup, M.Ed.
Senior Research Assistant
Secondary Special Education and
    Transition
University of Oregon
206 Clinical Services Building
5260 University of Oregon
Eugene, Oregon 97403

Paul Webb
Child/Adolescent Case Management
    Supervisor
Department of Mental Health
305 Belmont Street
Worcester, Massachusetts 01604

Gwendolyn White, M.S.W.
Director
System of Care Initiative
Allegheny County Department of
    Human Services
Office of Behavioral Health
Regional Enterprise Tower
425 Sixth Avenue, Third Floor
Pittsburgh, Pennsylvania 15219

Peter J. Zucker, Ph.D.
Vice President of Clinical Services
Stars Behavioral Health Group
    (SBHG)
1501 Hughes Way, Suite 150
Long Beach, California 90810

Foreword

As parents of transition-age youth, we know firsthand that this is both a unique and critical developmental stage in a young person's life. We know about the angst, experimentation, and boundary testing—and we also know about the joy, discovery, and the creation of new relationships. We bet that everyone reading this book either knows or knows of an adolescent or young adult who is in the transition-age group. It may be a personal connection or perhaps a professional connection as a mental health, child welfare, general and special education, juvenile justice, substance-abuse treatment, supported employment, or vocational rehabilitation professional. Let's face it—the transition to adulthood is simultaneously complicated and wonderful and, when the proper supports are in place, it can be a time of great growth and accomplishment.

For transition-age youth and young adults with emotional and/or behavioral difficulties (EBD), the journey is often prolonged and complex. The separation of child and adult mental health systems and the lack of sufficient and developmentally appropriate services and supports severely hamper these individuals' ability to become functional adults. Consequently, transition-age youth with EBD experience poorer long-term outcomes than do their peers. These include school dropout, under- and unemployment, contacts with the juvenile or criminal justice system, substance abuse disorders, early and unplanned pregnancy, and homelessness. We also know that 50% of all mental illnesses manifest themselves by age 14, and by the age of 24, that number increases to 75%. These findings reinforce the importance of focusing more attention and resources toward addressing the needs of this vulnerable population of young people.

The timing of this handbook could not be better—because it provides a significant contribution to advance the understanding of how to work with youth and young adults with EBD and their families. We think this handbook will educate, challenge, and inspire you—no matter your background or professional orientation. Clark and Unruh have designed and integrated the chapters of this handbook so as to provide the latest thinking and evidence about the most effective approaches for working with transition-age youth. The reader will find useful information for direct practice, developing and sustaining programs that work, involving the community, and creating policy that reflects the values and principles that drive a system of care approach. Most important, the handbook provides a research and evidence-supported framework for understanding what works in transition programs from the perspectives of youth, parents, service providers, and educators. The voices in this handbook are the voices of experience from having lived transition, developed transition programs, and/or researched them.

Several important themes emerge in this handbook. First, Clark and Unruh call for expanding the age range that constitutes the transition period. Expanding the age range underscores the importance of understanding that a myriad of youth and adult service systems have an integral role in helping young people reach their full potential. Examples include secondary and postsecondary education, the juvenile and criminal justice systems, vocational rehabilitation, employment and housing settings, and other services that are provided by both "child" and "adult" human service providers. The authors also bring attention to the importance of building social and economic capital with young people so that they can sustain their success beyond their involvement with human service providers by offering a number of innovative, practical, and successfully tested strategies.

If we, as a nation, are to effectively tackle the complexities of ensuring that our youth make a successful transition to adulthood, then we must be able to articulate the interconnectedness between policy and practice to ensure that providers who serve adults as well as those who serve children, youth, and families can deliver an array of relevant services and supports that provide continuity for a young person across time. We must also develop and use practice models that are developed in partnership with young people and families. Thus, this handbook is as important for the practitioner as it is for the agency administrator. It is as important for the youth coordinator as it is for the executive director of a family organization. Effectively addressing issues related to transition to adulthood is not a singular task—it is everyone's task. This handbook provides an effective roadmap to show how that can be done and the role each of us can play.

Implementing the recommended strategies from this handbook will require strong leadership at the policymaking level. Operating under the premise that transition is a process shared by all, we must aggressively look at how services are funded, encouraging policies that support the continuity of service from childhood into adulthood and requiring connections between child and adult service systems. Also, growing a knowledgeable workforce must involve strategies for hiring youth, young adults, and parents to be integral components in any service delivery approach. It is not enough to say we need youth and family involvement. Transition programs and systems must begin to show evidence of this commitment through a change in hiring practices. Equally important is the need to conduct extensive evaluation of transition models to assess effectiveness in terms of cost, training, and outcomes that contribute to the sustainability of the program.

We know that a systems of care approach works. We know that in order for communities to be successful in serving transition-age youth, they must incorporate a youth and family guided approach that reflects and honors the cultural makeup of the community being served. We also know that services and supports should not end simply because a child reaches 18 years of age. Clark and Unruh remind us with stark testimony and example after example that the population of transition-age youth and young adults has significant needs and can benefit greatly from effective practice supported by innovative policy focused on maintaining a quality, responsive, sustainable transition system. We encourage you to consider the practices, illustrations, and recommendations of this handbook and begin to integrate them into your work with your local, state, and federal partners to find ways to promote youth- and family guided approaches to working with transition-age youth and young adults and their families. Happy reading!

Gary M. Blau, Ph.D.,
Chief
and
Diane L. Sondheimer, M.S.N., M.P.H., C.P.N.P.
Deputy Chief
Child, Adolescent, and Family Branch
Substance Abuse
Mental Health Services Administration
Rockville, Maryland

Acknowledgments

We have been privileged to work with some of the most wonderfully insightful young adults throughout the development and preparation of this book. Over the years, youth, young adults, and parents challenged us to understand their experiences and perspectives. They, as well as other young people and parents, have contributed greatly to the authenticity of the chapters—enhancing the validity of our practitioner-oriented and policy recommendations. By coauthoring chapters, they have enriched the depth of this handbook and the lives of young people and families.

Of course, in an edited book, one cannot progress far without the active, wise, and dedicated efforts of the chapter authors. These practitioners, program managers, educators, young adults, researchers, parent advocates, and administrators are not, for the most part, the typical academic collaborators who are solicited to write chapters. These are individuals who were selected because they represent model programs and who are intimately involved in program development and operational activities for youth and young adults with emotional and/or behavioral difficulties (EBD). The lead author of each chapter deserves particular recognition for enduring the numerous requests for rewrites by the editors to ensure that this book provides the reader with a coherent and comprehensive perspective on the principles, practices, and system issues across chapters and the next steps needed to ultimately improve the adulthood outcomes of youth and young adults with EBD.

The development of this book was guided masterfully by several individuals at Paul H. Brookes Publishing Co., including Acquisitions Editor Sarah Shepke, Acquisitions Assistant Amanda Donaldson, and Senior Production Editor Leslie Eckard. Each of them was sensitive and flexible with us in the creation of this unique handbook.

Finally, we want to acknowledge you, the reader of this handbook. It is with your interest and curiosity in learning about and improving services for youth and young adults with EBD and their families that led you to pick up this book. We commend your initiative and we thank you in advance for taking what you learn and choosing to act tenaciously toward advancing the practices and policies for improving outcomes for young people with EBD.

—Hewitt B. "Rusty" Clark and Deanne K. Unruh

*We dedicate this book to the
youth and young adults and their family members
who have taught us so much from their experiences and perspectives
and whose voices have contributed so much
to the chapters in this handbook.*

Introduction to
Transition to Adulthood Issues
and the Evidence-Supported Handbook

Understanding and Addressing the Needs of Transition-Age Youth and Young Adults and Their Families

Hewitt B. "Rusty" Clark and Deanne K. Unruh

"As my life got bigger, my illness got smaller!"

—Young woman from Massachusetts

The transition road to adulthood typically includes some pleasurable straight-a-ways, thrilling curves, and treacherous, narrow sections with dangerous cliffs along the edge. Despite the advancement in GPS navigational equipment, GPS provides little help or safety to youth and young adults driving this transition roadway. Many diverse life changes and rights of passage to adulthood occur along this transition road. Leaving high school, obtaining and maintaining employment, developing different social networks, choosing postsecondary education or training options, being involved in intimate relationships that may lead to family commitments, building a career, and living independently are just a few of the life-defining developmental markers of adulthood functioning (Arnett, 2000; Cohen, Kasen, Chen, Hartmark, & Gordon, 2003; Shanahan, 2000). Navigating across these developmental markers is particularly daunting for young people with emotional and/or behavioral difficulties (EBD) as they leave childhood and children's services and enter adulthood, with or without the corresponding services they and their families may have relied on. They face the same challenges that all young people face during this transition period, yet they carry the added burden of a largely invisible disability (Armstrong, Dedrick, & Greembaum, 2003; Clark & Foster-Johnson, 1996; Vander Stoep et al., 2000; Wagner, Kutash, Duchnowski, Epstein, &

3

Sumi, 2005). Youth and young adults with EBD who have out-of-home placements (e.g., child welfare, runaway/homelessness, juvenile justice) or who are experiencing substance abuse problems and/or trauma are at even greater risk of not advancing well on these transition markers (Appleyard, Egeland, Dulmen, & Srofei, 2005; Bynner, 2005; Copeland, Miller-Johnson, Keeler, Angold, & Costello, 2007; Courtney et al., 2007; Courtney et al., 2005; Davis, Banks, Fisher, & Grudzinskas, 2004; Pecora et al., 2005; Wall & Kohl, 2007; White, O'Brien, White, Pecora, & Phillips, 2008).

The public and private service sector for these youth and young adults is often disjointed—lacking coordination of the multiple services needed to support a young person's successful trajectory to adulthood. Youth with EBD maturing into adulthood face the overwhelming task of navigating the treacherous pathways between child- and adult-serving agencies. Unfortunately, no unified public agency is designated to help these young people and their families move into adulthood (Davis, Geller, & Hunt, 2006; Lyons & Rogers, 2004; McMillen et al., 2004; Pottick, Bilder, Vander Stoep, Warner, & Alvarez, 2008). Although pockets of systemic collaboration can be found in some communities, typically, child- and adult-serving agencies are fragmented across eligibility requirements, service delivery methods, and philosophies of service (Clark, Deschênes, Sieler, Green, White, & Sondheimer, 2008; Davis & Koroloff, 2007).

The evolving evidence-supported practices and systemic strategies for improving the transition outcomes of youth and young adults (ages 14–29 years) with EBD is the focus of this handbook. We target the high-risk youth on the cusp of their developmental movement from adolescence to young adulthood. This handbook addresses transition issues specifically for youth and young adults with EBD by bringing together experts, family members, and young adults to clarify and address the broad spectrum of issues surrounding this topic, as well as making recommendations for evidence-supported solutions and policy reform—all of which are focused on more effectively serving these young adults and improving the outcomes for young people with EBD.

PURPOSE OF THIS EVIDENCE-SUPPORTED HANDBOOK

The purpose of this transition handbook is to

- Familiarize the reader with the characteristics of this population and the challenges they and their families face

- Provide knowledge on current system gaps in services provided to this population

- Describe the recommended practices for best serving the unique, individualized needs of these youth and young adults and their families within their cultural contexts

- Exemplify current evidence-supported practices in the context of collaborative community service systems along with strategies for oyotem improvement and sustainability

- Review the current status of research regarding the transition of these youth and young adults

- Provide perspectives through the voices of young people on barriers to transition and strategies that facilitate the transition to positive adult outcomes

- Provide a framework for quality improvement and evaluation strategies to improve and ensure that youth-guided services are provided

- Provide guidelines for the development, expansion, and sustainability of an evidence-supported system to facilitate the transition of these youth and young adults into greater self-sufficiency

- Discuss issues related to transition financing, policy, systemic reform, and advocacy

TARGET AUDIENCE FOR THIS TRANSITION HANDBOOK

As services for these young adults encompass both child- and adult-serving agencies, this handbook targets the wide audiences from both of these arenas, including practitioners, educators, administrators, and policy makers working in the following public and private sectors:

- Child and adult mental health

- Mental health transition-age youth and young adults (TAY) programs

- Traditional and alternative education high school programs, specifically transition-related educators

- Postsecondary education (e.g., community college, universities, and employment training agencies)

- Child welfare

- Juvenile justice and adult corrections

- Employment supports (e.g., vocational rehabilitation and Workforce Investment Boards)

- Substance abuse agencies

- Residential programs (e.g., mental health, independent living)

- Homeless and runaway shelters

- Children's systems of care

In addition, this handbook is relevant to private therapists, behavior analysts, psychologists, and psychiatrists who specialize in this age group. It is suited to inform community and natural support sources such as extended family members, recreation personnel, staff at faith-based organizations, and community leaders. Two additional important functions of this handbook are to 1) guide parents in understanding what service resources may be needed for their transition-age youth and young adults; and 2) guide advocates and policy makers in the reform of funding, systems, and policies at the local, state, and federal levels in order to align systemic infrastructures to support and sustain effective community transition systems.

DESIGN OF THE HANDBOOK
AND RELATED DEFINITIONAL ISSUES

Like our first transition to adulthood book released in 2000,[1] this handbook also includes the "voices" of young people and/or parents who serve as coauthors of every chapter. Invaluable lessons are learned from the perspectives and experiences of youth and young adults with EBD and their parents, and many of the lessons are reflected throughout this handbook.

Discussions with young people, parents, providers, administrators, and researchers in planning these works have brought us to understand the desire to minimize stigma associated with young people with EBD, their families, and others; and with the provision of services and supports. Our intent has been to use youth-friendly terms in referring to our focused population, so we refer to these individuals as *youth, young adults,* and *young people* rather than as *clients* and *consumers*. Gen-

---

[1]Clark, H.B. & Davis, M. (2000). *Transition to adulthood: A resource for assisting young people with emotional or behavioral difficulties.* Baltimore: Paul H. Brookes Publishing Co.

erally, we use the term *youth* to refer to those who are ages 14–17 years old; the term *young adult* to refer to those who are 18–29 years of age; and terms such as *young person, young persons,* and *young people* to refer to individuals falling within this entire age range.

We also have adopted the use of the term *emotional and/or behavioral difficulties* (EBD) in referring to these individuals' psychological, behavioral, or psychiatric challenges. The EBD term encompasses youth, 14–17 years old, with severe emotional disturbances (SED); young adults, 18–29 years old, with severe mental illness (SMI); and youth enrolled in high school with a special education diagnosis of emotional disturbance (ED) or behavior disorder (BD). We focus this book on young people whose difficulties result in significant functional impairment that begins prior to age 18. This purposeful emphasis was designed to capture the challenging tasks faced by these young people and their families in making a transition into adult roles.

Our discussions also identify the importance of addressing the systemic issues involved in the fragmented services young people with EBD and their families receive, and the complexities involved in traversing the huge chasm between child-serving and adult-serving systems. We do occasionally refer to the clinical diagnostic system (i.e., *Diagnostic and Statistical Manual of Mental Disorders, Fourth Edition, Text Revision* [DSM-IV-TR; American Psychiatric Association, 2000]) in order to more accurately describe the population (e.g., individuals with mood or anxiety disorders versus individuals with psychotic disorders) and to assist the reader in interpreting the progress and outcome findings from some of the published studies (Haber, Karpur, Deschênes, & Clark, 2008). For more information regarding definitional and population issues, see Chapter 1 and other articles in the literature (e.g., Armstrong, Dedrick, & Greenbaum, 2003; Pottick, Bilder, Vander Stoep, Warner, & Alvarez, 2008; Vander Stoep, Davis, & Collins, 2000).

In this handbook, we generally try to use the term *parent* to refer specifically to the biological or adoptive parent of a young person. However, in some usage, it may refer to the young person's role as a parent of his or her own children. In other words, the term *parent* is typically used to denote the legal guardian of a minor. We hope that it is clear from the context how the term is being used. The term *family* in our handbook generally refers to a youth's parents and siblings (biological, adoptive, or foster) and a young adult's "family of choice." This phrase refers to the fact that an emancipated young adult is more inclined to define *family* from his or her perspective, and the meaning of such may involve friends, gang members, biological parents, siblings, members of the extended family, a former foster parent, a girl- or boyfriend, the young person's own children, and/or any combination of these. Some young adults may use the term *family* to denote their affiliation with a spiritual, ethnic, or cultural group (e.g., Living Waters Church group, Hispanics, lesbian friends). Some of these terms (e.g., *youth, young person*) in chapters are at times used somewhat interchangeably in order to provide some variety for readers.

RESEARCH AND YOUTH AND FAMILY VOICE DEMONSTRATE UNMET NEEDS

The reason we and, more recently, other researchers have turned our attention to issues related to transition to adulthood is, in part, because on average, these youth and young adults with EBD demonstrate poorer long-term outcomes than almost all individuals with disabilities. Although many of our readers know this from their experience as a young person, a parent, or a service provider, the research findings speak very loudly to the severity of these poor outcomes and their long-term impact on young people, families, communities, and society at large (Armstrong, Dedrick, Greenbaum, 2003; Clark, Koroloff, Geller, & Sondheimer, 2008; Morrissey, Cuddeback, Cuellar, & Steadman, 2007; Vander Stoep, Davis, & Collins, 2000).

Cautionary Note When Comparing Data from Multiple Studies

Examining relevant transition-related outcomes is an essential activity as we target interventions based on the needs of youth and young adults as they move into adult roles. Table I.1, beginning on p. 14, provides a summary of the outcomes across some of the studies that document transition-to-adulthood outcome findings[2]. Before discussing the outcomes of these studies, it is important to note that readers should be cautioned with regard to the multiple methodological concerns of comparing outcomes across variant studies for this target population. First, the various outcomes measured (e.g., currently employed, secondary school completion) are defined differently across the studies, which means that the definition of each outcome may be slightly different for each study. We have only included studies that have somewhat similar definitions to lessen this concern. In addition, targeted populations in each of the studies differ. For example, the individuals in the studies summarized range from those having a severe psychiatric diagnosis to a special education diagnosis of "individuals with emotional distur-

---

[2] The authors would like to thank Scott H. Yamamoto, Special Education doctoral candidate at the University of Oregon, for the literature search and organization of the outcomes for young adults in Table 1.1. His diligence was greatly appreciated in assisting us in demonstrating the gaps individuals with EBD experience in their adulthood trajectory.

bance." Therefore, direct comparisons across outcomes should be viewed with caution. We have tried to be transparent in the definitions as much as possible in the table notes.

Overview of Transition Studies

Table I.1 is organized in columns with each representing a different study and/or comparison population of young adults. We summarize three primary service system-based studies along with two community-based studies from community programs. The service system studies included 1) the National Longitudinal Transition Study (NLTS) and National Longitudinal Transition Study-2 (NLTS2; Valdes, Williamson, & Wagner, 1990; Wagner et al., 1991; Wagner et al., 1993; Wagner, et al., 1992, http://www.NLTS2.org), 2) the National Adolescent and Child Treatment Study (NACTS) (Greenbaum & Dedrick, 1996; Kutash et al., 1995; Prange et al., 1992; Silver et al., 1992), and 3) the McGraw Center Study of adolescents with severe psychiatric impairments in Washington state (Vander Stoep, Taub, & Holcomb, 1994). We have provided a summary of both the original NLTS with the newly updated NLTS2 study to highlight the changes in outcomes in the decade between these two studies. In addition, to further highlight the differences of individuals with any special education diagnoses compared with youth who specifically have a special education diagnosis of emotional disturbance[3] (ED), we have included columns highlighting outcomes for both NLTS and NLTS2 across the averages for the total sample of individuals with disabilities compared with just those with an ED diagnosis. One community-based study, the Children in Community Study (CICS) (Cohen et al., 1993), compares young adults with and without psychiatric disorders in two counties in New York across the broad transition-to-adulthood domains of employment, secondary school completion, residence, and other high-risk behaviors (i.e., criminal involvement, early parenting). The second community-based study compares young adults with EBD and with a matched comparison group of nonclassified peers in Miami-Dade County in Florida on employment, post-secondary education enrollment, and incarceration Karpur, Clark, Caproni, & Sterner, 2005). Finally, the far right column provides a summary of the U.S. general population's outcomes as accessed through various federal agencies (e.g., U.S. Census Bureau, Federal Bureau of Investigation [FBI], National Institute of Mental Health [NIMH]).

---

[3] In the first NLTS study, the Individuals with Disabilities Education Act (IDEA) of 1990 (PL 101-476), diagnosis was labeled *Serious Emotional Disturbance*, and since this time, through IDEA reauthorization, the new label was defined as *Emotional Disturbance*, as noted in the newer NLTS2 study.

School Completion

Graduating from high school is a generally accepted right of passage into adulthood, and empirical evidence has demonstrated that individuals with a completion document achieve more positive adult outcomes than young adults with no completion document. These studies report that young people with EBD graduate from high school with rates ranging from 21% to 62% as compared with the general U.S. population, with a reported school completion rate of 79%. Of note, across the NLTS and NLTS2 studies, young adults with ED in the special education system have improved completion outcomes from 48% to 62% between study dates,[4] but even with this improved high school completion rate, young adults with ED still lag behind the average with all young adults with a special education diagnosis. These outcomes demonstrate that youth with EBD still struggle with school completion, and that school systems must be included in the transition system to ensure that young adults with EBD achieve positive outcomes.

Employment

Employment is an essential adult outcome to foster personal independence. Young adults with emotional difficulties represented in these studies report current employment rates ranging from 46% to 59%, again lagging behind the general population's employment rate of 62%. Surprisingly, current employment rates of youth with ED decreased from 48% in the first NLTS to 42% in NLTS2. Of course, it must be noted that employment rates are dependent on the overall economic outlook for the time in which the study was conducted, and these studies range across two decades with varying economic pictures. Keeping this in mind, it is still evident that employment skills are an essential component for inclusion in a transition-to-adulthood program and a necessary skill needed in adulthood. Employment-related strategies in both getting and maintain a job are included in all of the programs highlighted within this handbook.

Postsecondary Education Enrollment

Furthering educational goals beyond high school leads to long-term increases in wage rates for individuals and helps individuals meet their career goals. These educational opportunities vary for the career inter-

---

[4]Fully understanding and validating the high school completion percentages being reported between NLTS and NLTS2 would require a complete analysis of the two separate study periods regarding such factors as portion of students being classified ED, dropout rates for students classified as ED versus peers who were not classified, and proportion of students who would have qualified as ED but were placed in alternative/charter schools or in the juvenile justice system.

ests and needs and can include university, community college, vocational/technical training, or certification programs. Again, young adults with EBD are engaged in postsecondary education opportunities at a rate far lower than the general population reported in the U.S. Census Bureau (2007). For example, in the study summaries, young adults with EBD are engaged in educational opportunities between 4% and 31% as compared with their peers with no disabilities who are enrolled at rates between 33% and 49%. On a positive note, in examining trend data from the NLTS2 study, both students with disabilities and specifically young adults with EBD increased their rates of participation in postsecondary education as compared with those individuals in the original NLTS study conducted a decade earlier. Unfortunately, the enrollment percentages for young adults with EBD still lagged behind those of their peers with other disabilities. For example, the samples for the NLTS1 and NLTS2 for all disabilities increased their engagement rates in postsecondary education by 15 percentage points as compared with a dismal increase of 5 percentage points for young adults with EBD. Several chapters in this book address the challenges that young adults face in accessing postsecondary education opportunities and also the policy recommendations for such institutions. Even more important, Chapter 4 provides an evidence-supported program that advances young adults with EBD in furthering their educational goals through a community college program.

Residential Status

Current demographic trends demonstrate that in the general population, young adults are returning to or remaining in their family's residence for a longer period of time than in prior years (Settersten, Furstenberg, & Rumbaut, 2005). This rate, too, should translate into future rates of young adults with EBD living with family members. Rates of young adults with EBD living with family members in the studies summarized range from 43% to 68%, whereas young adults in the general population are reported at 65%. Again, the differences between the two NLTS studies do demonstrate an increase in young adults living with a family member, although young adults with ED still live independently at a lower rate than all individuals with disabilities. We would be remiss if we did not add that there are critical segments of this population, such as youth involved in the foster care system or youth leaving the juvenile justice system, which may not have the safety net of such families to provide housing stability (White, Havalchak, O'Brien, & Pecora, 2006). Therefore, transition services need to include housing support, if needed, along with other independent living skill development for this vulnerable population.

Additional Risk Factors

Prior research has documented that individuals with additional risk factors also demonstrate poorer adult outcomes than do individuals not experiencing multiple risks. Table I.1 summarizes the prevalence of four high-risk factors: 1) criminal involvement, 2) early parenting (Ventura, Abma, Mosher, & Henshaw, 2008), 3) co-morbidity of diagnoses, and 4) substance abuse. For each of these risk factors, higher rates of prevalence are reported for each of these factors for young adults with EBD than are reported in the general population. Young adults with EBD who experience these additional risk factors will undoubtedly require additional service access across multiple agencies and face additional challenges in their transition to adulthood.

USING THIS HANDBOOK
TO FORGE FUTURE EFFORTS

This evidence-supported handbook is designed to assist program personnel, educators, administrators, and other stakeholders in implementing programs and policies to address the priority needs of youth and young adults with EBD and their families to improve their outcomes on the developmental markers of adulthood. This handbook is organized into four sections, described in detail next. Briefly, Section I focuses on challenges in serving young people with EBD and describes programmatic strategies for implementing effective community transition systems. Section II provides examples of transition initiatives implemented in a local and/or state context. Section III provides a framework for programmatic, system, and policy issues. Finally, Section IV provides a synthesis of issues relating to serving young people with EBD and their families—and actions for program staff, administrators, policy makers, family members, young adults, and researchers to make for improving the adult outcomes of these young people. This handbook is designed to be user-friendly and to guide the work of practitioners, educators, transition specialists, peer associates, parent advocates, behavior analysts, program managers, administrators, and policy makers in their work at practice, program, and system levels. Each chapter is briefly described next.

Section I: Challenges in Serving Young People and Designing Effective Transition Systems

The first chapter in this section describes the recent service and policy research findings as well as practical field experience illustrating the continued gaps in services for young people with EBD and their families. The gap analysis illustrates the sources of problems contributing to these difficulties, including factors such as 1) deficit-based approaches, 2) stigma, 3) age-determined eligibility, 4) discontinuity between child and adult mental health, 5) lack of culturally competent services, 6) developmentally inappropriate services, 7) lack of funding streams, and 8) incompatible federal and state policies.

Chapter 2 provides the reader with an evidence-supported practice—referred to as the Transition to Independence Process (TIP) model—which has been refined substantially through application and research since our book *Transition to Adulthood* was published in 2000. The seven principles and associated practices of this community service system will be described as well as the transition domains of employment and career development, secondary and postsecondary education and training, living situations and supports, personal effectiveness and wellbeing, and community-life functioning. The TIP model is now considered an evidence-supported practice and is being implemented in dozens of communities across the nation.

Section II: Community Initiatives:
Evidence-Supported and Enduring Transition Programs

This section presents multiple examples of evidence-supported community transition programs, many of which are implementing the TIP model. Across the five chapters, illustrations of the implementation and operation of transition programs targeting youth and young adults with EBD, as well as their partnerships and practices that contribute to their success in serving these young people and their families, are provided. Multiple collaborative service sectors (e.g., adult mental health, education, vocational rehabilitation, juvenile justice, and community services) are used by each program, and therefore, the chapters will be useful to multiple care provider audiences. Each chapter provides evaluation data along with practical recommendations for replication and sustainability of each of the programs. Current or former program participants for each program serve as coauthors of these chapters.

Chapter 3 describes the development and sustainability of a countywide, youth-guided transition system for youth and young adults with EBD. This program was developed based on a countywide needs assessment targeting this population and is grounded in the TIP model. Chapter 4 illustrates the benefits for young people derived through a collaborative program between vocational rehabilitation (VR) and education. Two programs are highlighted. One program is a statewide collaborative effort between local school districts and vocational rehabilitation. The second program provides an example of a program collaboration with

Table I.1. Comparing young-adult outcomes across transitions studies (percentage)

	McGraw Study (Ages 18–22 years)	NACTS (Ages 18–22 years)	NLTS 1 (SED)	NLTS 1 (All disabilities)	NLTS 2 Wave 3 (ED)	NLTS 2 Wave 3 (All disabilities)	CICS PD (Ages 18–21 years)	CICS No PD (Ages 18–21 years)	Young adults with EBD in Miami-Dade	Non-classified young adults in Miami-Dade	U.S. general population
Secondary school completion	23	42	48	67	62	79	61	96	—	—	79[a]
Currently employed	46	52	48	62	42	55	59	78	51	62	62[b]
Post-secondary education	4	26	27	31	42	—	—	9	33	49[c]	
Residing with family	43	45	45	55	66[e]	73	68	74	—	—	65[d]
Recent police incidents/arrests/incarcerations[g]	37	22	58	30	53	26	24	10	12[g]	2[g]	22[f]
Pregnancy in young women	50	38	48	41	14	8[j]	29	10	—	—	12[h]
Comorbidity/multiple diagnoses	—	41[m]	24	2[l]	11	1[k]	9	NA	—	—	12[i]
Illegal drug use in past 30 days	—	—	—	—	36	17[o]	—	—	—	—	20[n]

NLTS 1, National Longitudinal Transition Study 1, 3 to 5 years out of school 1990; NLTS 2, National Longitudinal Transition Study 2, Wave 3–Parent/Youth Survey (2005a–g); CICS, Children in Community Study; NACTS, National Adolescent and Child Treatment Study; PD, psychiatric disorders; SED, serious emotional disturbance; ED, emotional disturbance; Young adults with EBD in Miami-Dade County, Florida, and Non-classified (without disabilities) young adults in Miami-Dade County were the two comparison groups in research evaluation of the Steps-to-Success Program (ages 18 to 22 years).

[a]Age group = 18–24 years (U.S. Census Bureau, 2007); Census Bureau and NLTS 2, Wave 3 measured "high school graduates."

[b]Age group = 18–24 years (U.S. Dept. of Labor, Bureau of Labor Statistics, 2007).

[c]Post-secondary education: In general population, "educational attainment" age group 18–24 years (U.S. Census Bureau, 2007); Miami-Dade County "enrollment in postsecondary education" (Karpur, Clark, Caproni, & Sterner, 2005); NLTS 2, Wave 3 "Out of secondary school youth has ever attended a postsecondary institution since leaving high school" (Parent & Youth Survey, 2005); NLTS 1 "Out of school 3–5 years; had ever attended postsecondary school" (1990); NACTS "had completed at least 1 year of college."

[d]Age group = 18–24 years (U.S. Census Bureau, 2007).

[e]Residing with parents, 18 or older.

[f]Percent arrest of 18–22 year-olds out of all age arrests in U.S. (FBI Arrests By Age, 2006); CICS measured "trouble with police"; McGraw and NACTS "arrests"; NLTS 1 and NLTS 2, Wave 3 "ever arrested"; Midwest Foster Care Study "arrested since last interview."

[g]The Miami-Dade County data is for percent incarcerated or on controlled release.

[h]Pregnancy rate, age group = 18–19 years (National Vital Statistics Reports – Centers for Disease Control & Prevention, 2004).

[i]NLTS 1 measured "parenting rates" among females; NLTS 2, Wave 3 measured "youth had or fathered any children" by disability category collapsed across both genders, and by females and males collapsed across disability category.

[j]National Institute of Mental Health (2008)–The Numbers Count: Mental Disorders in America (Retrieved from web site http://www.nimh.nih.gov/health/publications/the-numbers-count-mental-disorders-in-america.shtml#Intro); ages 18 and older.

[k]Multiple disabilities as primary disability for youth with IEP/504 Plan & primary disability of youth with ED who have other disabilities in NLTS 2 Wave 1 (2002).

[l]Students whose diagnosed primary disability was "multiply handicapped," and "any other disability" in addition to the primary disability of emotional disturbance in NLTS 1.

[m]Wave 1 (out of 7 waves).

[n]National Survey on Drug Use and Health, age group = 18–25 years (Substance Abuse & Mental Health Services Administration, 2006).

[o]Age group = 18 years or older.

local community colleges and VR to improve students' educational and career-related outcomes.

Chapter 5 provides an example of the application of the TIP model in two programs serving young adults with severe mental illness. One program is oriented on the TIP model and the other is moving toward full implementation of the TIP model. Chapter 6 describes a transition system serving youth involved with the juvenile justice system—featuring multiple agencies collaborating to target the unique needs of this population—as well as findings related to decreasing continued criminality and improving youth community adjustment outcomes at reentry.

Chapter 7, "More than Friends," was written with the input of five young adult collaborators representing two peer support/mentoring programs in the adult mental health arena serving metropolitan and rural areas.

Section III: Improving Practice, System, and Policy

In this section, we address recommendations for replication, fidelity of implementation, and sustainability of interventions along with program or policy development. Each chapter provides practical suggestions for the field from the synthesis of lessons learned from implementation of transition systems (as highlighted in Chapter 2 and Section II).

The co-occurrence of high-risk behaviors and situations is prevalent in this vulnerable population, causing additional service challenges. Chapter 8 provides a conceptual framework and procedures for working with young people in a developmentally appropriate process, and assisting the youth in recognizing risk behaviors and situations and the benefits of minimizing these in their lives through a prevention planning process. Chapter 9 explicitly addresses transition-related system gaps through strategic policy and funding reform to create a federal, state, and local infrastructure that could facilitate and sustain effective transition service systems for young people and their families.

Chapter 10 focuses on the strategies for continuing quality improvement of the responsiveness and effectiveness of transition systems. Descriptions of fidelity assessment probes, youth/young adult progress tracking instruments, and quality assurance processes are provided and their applications illustrated across different types of programs.

Section IV: Future Focus: Advancing the Transition Agenda

Chapter 11, the final chapter, summarizes and highlights current practice, program, system, funding, policy, and research issues. It also provides relevant agendas for future advocacy, policy and system reform, and research essential to enhancing collaboration across multiple systems (e.g., child welfare, mental health, and education) to ultimately improve transition outcomes for youth and young adults with EBD.

We, along with our contributing authors (including young adults, parents, practitioners, educators, researchers, and administrators), trust this handbook will inspire and guide readers to improve the provision of evidence-supported, developmentally appropriate, and effective supports and services for these youth and young adults and their families in communities throughout the country.

REFERENCES

American Psychiatric Association. (2000). *Diagnostic and statistical manual of mental disorders* (4th ed., text rev.). Washington, DC: Author.

Appleyard, K., Egeland, B., Dulmen, M.H.M., & Alan Sroufe, L. (2005). When more is not better. The role of cumulative risk in child behavior outcomes. *Journal of Child Psychology and Psychiatry, 46*(3), 235–245.

Armstrong, K.H., Dedrick, R.F., & Greenbaum, P.E. (2003). Factors associated with community adjustment of young adults with serious emotional disturbance: A longitudinal analysis. *Journal of Emotional & Behavioral Disorders, 11*(2), 66–76.

Arnett, J.J. (2000). Emerging adulthood: A theory of development from the late teens through the twenties. *American Psychologist, 55*(5), 469–480.

Bynner, J. (2005). Rethinking the youth phase of the life-course: The case for emerging adulthood? *Journal of Youth Studies, 8*(4), 367–384.

Clark, H.B., & Davis, M. (Eds.) (2000). *Transition to adulthood: A resource for assisting young people with emotional or behavioral difficulties.* Baltimore: Paul H. Brookes Publishing Co.

Clark, H.B., Deschênes, N., Sieler, D., Green, M., White, G., & Sondheimer, D. (2008). Services for Youth in Transition to Adulthood in Systems of Care. In B.A. Stroul & G.M. Blau (Eds.), *The system of care handbook: Transforming mental health services for children, youth, and families* (pp. 517–543). Baltimore: Paul H. Brookes Publishing Co.

Clark, H.B., & Foster-Johnson, L. (1996). Serving youth in transition into adulthood. In B.A. Stroul (Ed.), *Children's mental health: Creating systems of care in a changing society* (pp. 533–551). Baltimore: Paul H. Brookes Publishing Co.

Clark, H.B., Koroloff, N., Geller, J., & Sondheimer, D.L., (2008). Research on transition to adulthood: Building the evidence base to inform services and supports for youth and young adults with serious mental health disorders. *Journal of Behavioral Health Services and Research, 35*(4), 365–372.

Cohen, P., Cohen, C., Kasen, S., Velez, C.N., Hartmark, C., Johnson, J., et al. (1993). An epidemiological study of disorders in late adolescence and adolescence. I. Age- and gender-specific prevalence. *Journal of Child Psychology and Psychiatry, 34,* 851–867.

Cohen, P., Kasen, S., Chen, H., Hartmark, C., & Gordon, K. (2003). Variations in patterns of developmental transmissions in the emerging adulthood period. *Developmental Psychology, 39*(4), 657–669.

Copeland, W.E., Miller-Johnson, S., Keeler, G., Angold, A., & Costello, E.J. (2007). Childhood psychiatric disorders and young adult crime: A prospective, population-based study. *American Journal of Psychiatry, 164*(11), 1668–1675.

Courtney, M.E., Dworsky, A., Cusick, G.R., Havlicek, J., Perez, A., & Keller, T. (2007, December). *Midwest evaluation of the adult functioning of former foster youth: Outcomes at age 21*. IL: Chapin Hall Center for Children at the University of Chicago. Retrieved August 14, 2008, from http://www.chapinhall.org/content_director.aspx?arid=1355&afid=402&dt=1

Courtney, M.E., Dworsky, A., Ruth, G., Keller, T., Havlicek, J., & Bost, N. (2005) *Midwest evaluation of the adult functioning of former foster youth: Outcomes at age 19*. IL: Chapin Hall Center for Children at the University of Chicago.

Davis, M., Banks, S., Fisher, W., & Grudzinskas, A. (2004). Longitudinal patterns of offending during the transition to adulthood in youth from the mental health system. *Journal of Behavioral Health Services & Research, 31*(4), 351–366.

Davis, M., Geller, J., & Hunt, B. (2006). Within-state availability of transition-to-adulthood services for youths with serious mental health conditions. *Psychiatric Services, 57*, 1594–1599.

Davis, M., & Koroloff, N. (2007). The great divide: How public mental health policy fails young adults. In W.H. Fisher (Ed.), *Research on community-based mental health services for children and adolescents: Vol. 13*. Oxford, UK: Elsevier Sciences.

Greenbaum, P.E., & Dedrick, R.F. (1996). National adolescent and child treatment study (NACTS): Outcomes for children with serious emotional and behavioral disturbance. *Journal of Emotional & Behavioral Disorders, 4*(3), 130–146.

Haber, M., Karpur, A., Deschênes, N., & Clark, H.B. (2008). Predicting improvement of transitioning young people in the Partnerships for Youth Transition Initiative: Findings from a multisite demonstration. *Journal of Behavioral Health Services & Research. 35*, 4, 488–513.

Individuals with Disabilities Education Act (IDEA) of 1990, PL 101-476, 20 U.S.C. §§ 1400 *et seq.*

Karpur, A., Clark, H.B., Caproni, P., & Sterner, H. (2005). Transition to adult roles for students with emotional/behavioral disturbances: A follow-up of student exiters from Steps-to-Success. *Career Development for Exceptional Individuals, 28*, 36–46.

Kutash, K., Greenbaum, P., Brown, E., & Foster-Johnson, L. (1995). *Longitudinal outcomes for youth with severe emotional disabilities*. Paper presented at the eighth annual research conference: A System of Care for Children's Mental Health: Expanding the Research Base, Tampa, FL.

Lyons, J.S., & Rogers, L. (2004). The U.S. child welfare system: A de facto public behavioral health care system. *Journal of the American Academy of Child & Adolescent Psychiatry, 43*(8), 971–973.

Manteuffel, B., Stephens, R.L., Sondheimer, D.L., & Fisher, S.K. (2008). Characteristics, service experiences, and outcomes of transition-aged youth in systems of care: Programmatic and policy implications. *Journal of Behavioral Health Services & Research, 35*(4), 469–487.

McMillen, J.C., Scott, L.D., & Zima, B.T., Ollie, M.T., Munson, M.R., & Spitznagel, E. (2004). Use of mental health services among older youths in foster care. *Psychiatric Services 55*, 811–817.

Morrissey, J.P., Cuddeback, G.S., Cuellar, A.E., & Steadman, H.J. (2007). The role of Medicaid enrollment and outpatient service use in jail recidivism among persons with severe mental illness. *Psychiatric Services, 58*(6), 794–801.

National Institute of Mental Health. (2008). *The numbers count: Mental disorders in America.* Retrieved August 14, 2008, from http://www.nimh.nih.gov/health/publications/the-numbers-count-mental-disorders-in-america.shtml #Intro

National Longitudinal Transition Study-2, Wave 1–Student School Program Survey, Special Education. (2002). *Primary disability of youth with IEP/504 Plan: Overall and by primary disability category.* Retrieved August 25, 2008, from http://www.nlts2.org/data_tables/tables/7/NPR1D2brfrm.html

National Longitudinal Transition Study-2, Wave 3–Parent/Youth Survey. (2005a). *Behaviors of Youth (Combined Youth and Parent Items): Youth has reported being arrested in current or prior wave* [Online data table]. Retrieved August 6, 2008, from http://www. nlts2.org/data_tables/tables/12/np3U8a_J15afrm .html

National Longitudinal Transition Study-2, Wave 3–Parent/Youth Survey. (2005b. *Behaviors of Youth (Items Asked of Youth 18 or Older Only): Youth used any drugs in the past 30 days* [Online data table]. Retrieved August 6, 2008, from http://www.nlts2.org/data_tables/ tables/12/np3U5_Anyfrm.html

National Longitudinal Transition Study-2, Wave 3–Parent/Youth Survey. (2005c). *Characteristics of Youth (Items Asked of Parent Only): Where youth lives now* [Online data table]. Retrieved August 6, 2008, from http://www.nlts2.org/data_tables/tables/12/np3A6afrm.html

National Longitudinal Transition Study-2, Wave 3–Parent/Youth Survey (2005d). *Employment of Youth Out-of-Secondary School A Year or More (Combined Youth and Parent Items): Youth out of secondary school a year or more currently has a paid job outside the home* [Online data table]. Retrieved August 6, 2008, from http://www.nlts2.org/data_tables/tables/12/np3T7a_L7a_I2bfrm.html

National Longitudinal Transition Study-2, Wave 3–Parent/Youth Survey (2005e). *Household Characteristics (Combined Youth and Parent Items): Respondent reported that youth had or fathered any children in current or prior wave* [Online data table]. Retrieved August 25, 2008, from http://www.nlts2.org/data_tables/tables/12/ np3W2a_M4_everfrm.html

National Longitudinal Transition Study-2, Wave 3–Parent/Youth Survey. (2005f). *Secondary School Experiences (Combined Youth and Parent Items): If youth who is out of secondary school graduated from high school* [Online data table]. Retrieved August 6, 2008, from http://www.nlts2.org/data_tables/tables/12/np3S1a _D1k_ D2d_D3bfrm.html

National Longitudinal Transition Study-2, Wave 3–Parent/Youth Survey. (2005g). *Postsecondary Education at Any Institution* [Online data table]. Retrieved October 12, 2008, from http://www.nlts2.org/data_tables/tables/12/np3S3aS4a S5a_D4a1D4a2D4a3_everfrm.html

Pecora, P.J., Kessler, K.C., Williams, O'Brien, K., Downs, A.C., English, D., et al. (Revised 2005, March 14). *Improving family foster care: Findings from the Northwest Foster Care Alumni Study*. Seattle, WA: Research Services at Casey Family Programs. Retrieved August 14, 2008, from http://www.casey.org/NR/rd onlyres/4E1E7C77-7624-4260-A253-892C5A6CB9E1/375/CaseyAlumniStudy updated082006.pdf

Pottick, K.J., Bilder, S., Vander Stoep, A., Warner, L.A., & Alvarez, M.F. (2008). U.S. patterns of mental health service utilization for transition-age youth and young adults. *Journal of Behavioral Health Services & Research, 35*(4), 373–389.

Prange, M., Greenbaum, P., Silver, S., Friedman, R., Kutash, K., & Duchnowski, A. (1992). Family functioning and psychopathology among adolescents with severe emotional disturbances. *Journal of Abnormal Child Psychology, 20*, 83–102).

Settersten, R.A., Furstenberg, F.F., & Rumbaut, R.G. (Eds.) (2005). *On the frontier of adulthood: Theory, research and public policy*. IL: The University of Chicago Press.

Shanahan, M.J. (2000). Pathways to adulthood in changing societies: Variability and mechanisms in life course perspective. *Annual Review of Sociology, 26*, 667.

Silver, S., Duchnowski, A., Kutash, K., Friedman, R., Eisen, M., Prange, M., et al. (1992). A comparison of children with serious emotional disturbance served in residential and school settings. *Journal of Child and Family Studies, 1*, 43–59.

Substance Abuse and Mental Health Services Administration. (September 2007). *Results from the 2006 National Survey on Drug Use and Health: National findings* (Office of Applied Studies, NSDUH Series H-32, DHHS Publication No. SMA 07-4293). Rockville, MD. Retrieved August 6, 2008, from http://oas .samhsa.gov/nsduh/2k6nsduh/2k6Results.pdf

U.S. Census Bureau. (2007). *Educational attainment of the population, 18 years and over by age, sex, race, and Hispanic origin: 2007* [Data file]. Retrieved August 6, 2008, from http://www.census.gov/population/www/socdemo/education/ cps2007.html

U.S. Census Bureau. (2007). *Family Status and Household Relationship of People 15 Years and Over, by Marital Status, Age, and Sex: 2007* [Data file]. Retrieved August 6, 2008, from http://www.census.gov/population/www/socdemo/ hh-fam/cps2007.html

U.S. Department of Justice, Federal Bureau of Investigation. (2007, September). *Crime in the United States, 2006, Table 38–Arrests by Age* [Data file]. Retrieved August 6, 2008, from http://www.fbi.gov/ucr/cius2006

U.S. Department of Labor, Bureau of Labor Statistics: Labor Force Statistics from the Current Population Survey. (2007). *Employment status of the civilian noninstitutional population by age, sex, and race* [Data file]. Retrieved August 6, 2008, from http://www.bls.gov/cps/demographics.htm#age

Valdes, K., Williamson, C., & Wagner, M. (1990). *The national longitudinal transition study of special education students. Statistical Almanac: Vol. 3. Youth categorized as emotionally disturbed.* Menlo Park, CA: SRI International.

Vander Stoep, A., Beresford, S., Weiss, N.S., McKnight, B., Cauce, A.M., & Cohen, P. (2000). Community-based study of the transition to adulthood for adolescents with psychiatric disorder. *American Journal of Epidemiology, 152* (4), 352–362.

Vander Stoep, A., Davis, M., & Collins, D. (2000). Transition: A time of developmental and institutional clashes. In H.B. Clark & M. Davis (Eds.), *Transition to adulthood: A resource for assisting young people with emotional or behavioral difficulties* (pp. 3–28). Baltimore: Paul H. Brookes Publishing Co.

Vander Stoep, A., & Taub, J., (1994). Predictors of level of functioning within diagnostic groups for transition-age youth with affective, thought and conduct disorders. In C. Liberton, K. Kutash, & R.M. Friedman (Eds.) *The seventh annual research conference: A System of Care for Children's Mental Health: Expanding the Research Base.* (pp. 373–379). Tampa: University of South Florida, Louis de la Parte Florida Mental Health Institute, Research and Training Center for Children's Mental Health.

Vander Stoep, A., Taub, J., & Holcomb, L. (1994). Follow-up of adolescents with severe psychiatric impairment into young adulthood. In 6th Annual Research Conference Proceedings. *A system of care for children's mental health: Expanding the research base.* Tampa: University of South Florida, Florida Mental Health Institute, Research and Training Center for Children's Mental Health, 315–320.

Vander Stoep, A., Beresford, A.A., Weiss, N.S., McKnight, B., Cauce, A.M., & Cohen, P. (2000). Community-based study of the transition to adulthood for adolescents with psychiatric disorder. *American Journal of Epidemiology, 152*(4), 352–362.

Ventura, S.J., Abma, J.C., Mosher, W.D., & Henshaw, S.K. (2008, April 14). Estimated pregnancy rates by outcome for the United States, 1990–2004. *National Vital Statistics Reports, 56*(15). Hyattsville, MD: National Center for Health Statistics. Retrieved August 6, 2008, from http://www.cdc.gov/nchs

Wagner, M., Blackorby, J., Cameto, R., Hebbeler, K., & Newman, L. (1993, December). *The transition experiences of young people with disabilities: A summary of findings from the National Longitudinal Transition Study of special education students.* Menlo Park, CA: SRI.

Wagner, M., D'Amico, R., Marder, C., Newman, L., & Blackorby, J. (1992). *What happens next? Trends in postsecondary outcomes of youth with disabilities.* Menlo Park, CA: SRI International.

Wagner, M., Kutash, K., Duchonowski, A.J., Epstein, M.H., & Sumi, W. (2005). The children and youth we serve: A national picture of the characteristics of students with emotional disturbances receiving special education. *Journal of Emotional and Behavioral Disorders, 13*(2), 79–96.

Wagner, M., Newman, L., D'Amico, R., Jay, E.B., Butler-Nalin, P., Marder, C., & Cox, R. (1991, September). *Youth with disabilities: How are they doing? The first comprehensive report from the National Longitudinal Transition Study of special education students.* Menlo Park, CA: SRI.

Wall, A.E., & Kohl, P.L. (2007). Substance use in maltreated youth: Findings from the national survey of child and adolescent well-being. *Child Maltreatment, 12*(1), 20.

White, C.R., Havlicek, A., O'Brien, K., & Pecora, P. (2006). *Casey Family Programs Young Adult Survey, 2005: Examining outcomes for young adults served in out-of-home care.* Seattle, WA: Casey Family Programs.

White, C.R., O'Brien, K.O., White, J., Pecora, P.J., & Phillips, C.M. (2008). Alcohol and drug use among Alumni of foster care: Decreasing dependency through improvement of foster care experiences. *Journal of Behavioral Health Services & Research 35*(4), 419–434.

SECTION

I

Challenges and
Effective Transition Systems

The Service System Obstacle Course for Transition-Age Youth and Young Adults

Maryann Davis, Melanie Green, and Cheri Hoffman

"It's hard enough to work on my own stuff. When I turned 18 and had to figure out how to navigate all these new systems, it just made everything that much harder."

—Young woman from Washington State

In 1995, the Center for Mental Health Services of the Substance Abuse and Mental Health Services Administration (CMHS/SAMHSA) brought together a group of national experts on issues related to youth with mental health conditions and their transition to adulthood (Davis & Vander Stoep, 1996). During this meeting, these experts, including researchers, practitioners, policy makers, and family advocates, expressed concern about this group of young people and described their own observations or experiences in which they found inadequacies in service provision for these individuals. Davis and Vander Stoep (1997) reviewed the limited strands of research in the literature to summarize what was known about how well young adults fared during their transition into adulthood. The conclusions were alarming; in young adulthood, this group experienced high dropout rates, underemployment, poverty, homelessness, early pregnancy, and frequent trouble with the law. Around this time, Hewitt B. "Rusty" Clark published his cornerstone paper summarizing common features among programs that had been nominated as strong and innovative in working with this group (Clark, Unger, & Stuart, 1993). From that work, Dr. Clark expanded those findings into what is currently recognized as the only comprehensive framework for community systems working with transition-age youth and young adults: the Transition to Independence Process (TIP) model (Clark & Foster-Johnson, 1996; see also Chapter 2). These three publications (Clark & Foster-Johnson, 1996; Clark et al., 1993; Davis & Vander Stoep, 1997) mark the beginning of a growth period in the field of services for transition-age youth.

One of the consequences of the work done in this field since that time is an identification of many of this population's needs and a refinement of evidence-supported, if not evidence-based, practices. Development of good practice models is moot if they cannot be placed into service frameworks that support them. A review of the existing literature in 2005 (Davis & Koyanagi, 2005) allowed for extrapolation of the basic policy tenets that would support services consistent with the TIP model and research findings. Those tenets serve as a standard by which to judge progress. In this chapter we describe those policy tenets and use them as a basis from which to describe the literature on policy and system gaps. We begin by creating a picture.

Trystan is 20 years old and on his way to becoming an independent adult. When Trystan turned 18, he didn't feel like he was ready to end services with the therapist he had been seeing since he was 15, although this would be the time one would typically shift to an adult service provider. Trystan and his therapist were in the middle of doing some great work together, and both feared that ending the relationship early would hinder Trystan's progress. In addition, Trystan was attending an adolescent support group that was very beneficial to him. Fortunately, in the state where Trystan lives, public mental health centers are licensed by service, not by age. Trystan was able to continue working with his therapist until the time they both felt more comfortable with transitioning Trystan to another provider.

During this time, Trystan and his therapist not only continued to work on many of the things they had been exploring before but also became better prepared for his transition to adult services. Trystan and his parents toured a few of the adult service provider agencies in town, and Trystan was able to choose the one that he liked best. He was able to meet the therapist he would be working with. This allowed him to feel more comfortable about what was to come. Trystan was also able to continue with his support group, even for several months after he transitioned to his new therapist. Instead of the services he was used to abruptly ending on his 18th birthday, Trystan had the opportunity to wait until the time was right for him. He also knew what to expect rather than being tossed into an entirely different system without knowing anything about it.

Trystan's new therapist is part of the young adult team at his agency. He has specific training—and a personal interest— in assisting young people in the transition to adulthood. Trystan enjoys visiting his new therapist's office. The space was clearly designed to meet the needs of people his age. The atmosphere is fun and inviting, with funky furniture and art on the walls created by the youth that use the office. After Trystan meets with his therapist, he likes to stay and hang out for a while. Sometimes he spends time with other youth shooting pool or playing foosball. Other times he utilizes the computer lab to work on his resume, search for job leads, or surf the Internet. Trystan also attends a lot of the groups and classes offered at the center that teach young people about everything from budgeting to how to get a driver's license and also provide them with an opportunity to socialize and support one another.

The following section briefly describes the basic policy tenets, which are discussed more fully in Chapter 9 (Davis & Koyanagi, 2005).

Policy Tenet 1: Provide continuity of care from ages 14 or 16 to ages 25 or 30.
Stated simply, policies need to support continuation of beneficial services throughout the transition years, and service continuity should be based on the individualized needs of youth and young adults rather than on their chronological age category.

Policy Tenet 2: Provide continuous and coordinated care across the many systems that offer relevant services. System of care values (Stroul & Friedman, 1986) call for the continuity and coordination of services within and across children's systems. For transition-age youth, continuity and coordination needs to be extended to adult-serving systems as well (Clark, Deschênes, & Jones, 2000).

Policy Tenet 3: Provide developmentally appropriate and appealing services. It is important that transition support services address the unique developmental needs of this age group and tailor services to them (e.g., Davis & Vander Stoep, 1997; Vander Stoep, Davis, & Collins, 2000). In addition, policies need to support services that appeal to this group; otherwise, they will not engage in the services. These features are illustrated more fully in the TIP system guidelines in Chapter 2.

Policy Tenet 4: Promote a density of good services from which individualized service and treatment plans can be constructed. Individualizing services requires choice, which requires options. The absence of numerous good transition support programs can force young people to use suboptimal programs or reject services entirely.

Policy Tenet 5: Promote appropriate involvement of family. The parental role moves from a central position in early adolescence to a more peripheral one as young people mature and develop their own social networks and significant or marital relationships. Policies should provide the freedom for practitioners, young people, and family members to make decisions to best suit their circumstances.

Policy Tenet 6: Promote the development of expertise in professionals who work with this population. Because knowledge about this population and how to work effectively with it is still in its infancy, policies need to promote the establishment of evidence-based and evidence-supported practices with this transition-age group as well as the training and exchange of knowledge among practitioners working with them.

Trystan's story highlights features of some of the most basic policy tenets that promote strong transition support services (Davis & Koyanagi, 2005). Trystan experienced continuity of care (Policy Tenet 1) as he crossed an age threshold that marks the end of child services for most individuals. He was able to continue with the same program and therapist until he was ready for change (Policy Tenet 2). He was also able to access developmentally appropriate and appealing services (Policy Tenet 3); his existing services were developmentally appropriate and appealing, and as he moved into new services they were also tailored to the needs of his age group. In addition, he was able to choose from various services rather than just a single service for this age group (see Policy Tenet 4), and he and his parents went to see several of these programs together (see Policy Tenet 5).

GAPS IN SERVICE SYSTEMS
RELATED TO TRANSITION TO ADULTHOOD

Although much knowledge about services for transition-age youth and young adults has developed in the past 10 years, it is unclear whether our systems are positioned to support the implementation of this knowledge through interventions. In the remaining sections we use the policy framework addressed by the six tenets to evaluate the gaps in service systems documented in the literature.

Gaps in Age Continuity

Chloe is a high school senior who recently turned 18. She received mental health services at a child-serving agency for the past year and a half. She had a therapist who she really liked. She was also working with a vocational specialist on finding and keeping a job and was eager to get her first job.

When Chloe turned 18, however, her age made her ineligible for child services. Not only did she have to end her sessions with her therapist but also her diagnosis of oppositional defiant disorder was not one of the qualifying diagnoses for adult services. Chloe's therapist worked with her for 6 months to prepare her for the end of services, but when the time came, she wasn't ready.

She began slipping back into old habits and behaviors. She was deeply hurt and angered by having to end her sessions with her therapist. At school, Chloe started getting into arguments with teachers and engaged in a couple of physical altercations with other students. She was eventually expelled from school for her behavior and was too angry to pursue a general equivalency diploma (GED). Chloe's parents struggled with her behavior at home. They knew she needed help but were also concerned about the negative effect she was having on her younger siblings. They struggled with the decision of whether to allow Chloe to continue to live at home.

Chloe's parents knew that she had made great progress with her therapist. Neither Chloe nor they could understand why she couldn't continue services when it was clear that the services were a huge benefit to her. Chloe felt she somehow wasn't good enough to be allowed to continue and wondered what more she could have done. In reality, there was nothing Chloe could have done; the mental health system in which she was engaged had narrow diagnostic criteria for adult services and strict age cutoffs for children's services that left her out in the cold.

Age-Based Policies

Unfortunately, Chloe's experiences are all too common. Eligibility criteria for accessing services are different in child and adult mental health systems, and these systems have targeted their services at different populations, generally reflecting the differences between how the terms *serious emotional disturbance* and *serious mental illness* are defined. Other child-serving systems such as special education, child welfare, or juvenile justice also end their services at particular, but not the same, ages. Age is one of the characteristics that define who a system serves. Typically, age limits occur sometime during the transition to adulthood. This section describes some of those age-based policies. Some adult agencies serve those 16 and older, whereas others serve those beginning at age 18.

Federal Policies

Koyanagi and colleagues analyzed federal policies that affected transition-age youth with serious mental health conditions (Davis & Koyanagi, 2005; Judge David L. Bazelon Center for Mental Health Law, 2005). They identified 55 programs run by 20 or more different agencies in 9 departments of the federal government (e.g., the Chaffee Foster Care Independence Program, the Partnerships for Youth Transition Program). The 55 programs were different in purpose, target population, funding, and organization. Twenty-three programs had age-based eligibility rules, which resulted in an individual being eligible at one age but not consistently eligible through age 25. There were other age-related issues, as well. For example, 15 programs were for individuals of all ages, so youth had to compete with adults for services. Medicaid and Supplemental Security Income (SSI), which offer benefits to those of all ages, change eligibility rules at a certain age (change in Medicaid benefits occurs between ages 18–21 depending on the state; SSI, at age 18). Other programs require that an individual be a *legal adult*, whereas others target individuals who have left school.

One key federal mental health policy defines the target populations for federal Mental Health Block Grants funds. For children under age 18, the criteria are based on the definition of *serious emotional disturbance* (SED); for adults age 18 and older, they are based on the definition of *serious mental illness* (SMI) (*Federal Register, 58*(96), p. 29422). Davis and Koroloff (2006) analyzed these policies. The language of the two definitions is remarkably similar. Both require the presence of certain types of diagnoses (i.e., any diagnosis in the *Diagnostic and Statistical Manual of Mental Disorders* or equivalent and subsequent revisions that are not V-codes, substance use, and developmental disorders) and significant functional impairment. V-codes are used to describe factors influencing mental health status not attributable to mental disorder (e.g., occupational problem, bereavement, sibling relational problem). There is no explicit difference in the diagnostic criteria referenced in the two definitions. And, with the exception of the diagnosis of antisocial personality disorder, which cannot be assigned before age 18, all diagnoses that qualify for SED also qualify for SMI and vice versa. The only difference in terminology in the two definitions is in the delineation of functional impairment. For those under age 18, the focus is on age-appropriate skills (e.g., social, behavioral, cognitive, communicative, adaptive), whereas functioning is not tied to developmental considerations for those 18 and older and includes "basic daily living skills; instrumental living skills (e.g., maintaining a household, managing money, getting around the community, taking prescribed medication); and functioning in social, family, and vocational/educational contexts" (*Federal Register, 58*(96), p. 29422).

State Policies
We obtained and analyzed the population policies for child and adult state mental health systems for 45 states and the District of Columbia (Davis & Koroloff, 2006). *Eligibility criteria*, on the one hand, referred to a series of conditions that individuals must have in order to obtain services. *Target* or *priority population definitions*, on the other hand, typically identified a series of conditions that define who services are designed for and who has preferential access. One of the results of prioritizing populations is that groups who are not considered priority can be denied access or have access only to limited or inappropriate services. In this chapter, we refer to eligibility criteria and target/priority population policies as *population policies*.

Age   No state contributed one policy that applied to both child and adult mental health systems. The upper age limit in 69% of state child systems is 18, with all but 7% of the remaining states continuing to age 21.

Diagnosis   Policy analysis revealed that most states required a psychiatric diagnosis. The child and adult diagnostic requirements were aligned in 28% of states, with nonaligned states typically being more restrictive in adult requirements than in child requirements.

Functional Impairment   Most states also included a functional impairment requirement. In combination with diagnostic requirements, no state had aligned child and adult population policies. Thus, in each state, youth from the child mental health system could, on reaching the adult age, be denied adult services solely because their age changed and not because their service needs changed.

The number of youth negatively affected by these misaligned population policies is unknown. However, one report found that as many as one-third to one-half of adolescents receiving public mental health services did not go on to receive services in the adult system (Delman &

Jones, 2002). A report on Florida's Medicaid system showed that youth begin to drop off from services after the age of 15, with a steep 44% decrease in service penetration rates between ages 17 and 18. Enrollment rates declined in a similar trajectory, but service use declined at a higher rate, indicating that service access was lower for these youth as they reached the transition years (Stiles, Dailey, & Mehra, 2001).

Gaps Between the Child and Adult Mental Health Systems

As Brynn approached her 18th birthday, she and her parents worked with her care coordinator to prepare for her transition into adult mental health services. They had what appeared to be a solid plan in place, including setting up an intake appointment with the adult mental health agency across town so that there would be no lapse in her counseling or medication appointments. However, as Brynn's services in the adult system began, she and her parents noticed a complete change in the way these services were delivered.

Brynn's parents always knew that if Brynn felt she needed them, or her counselor thought it was important, they'd be informed of any issues. When Brynn began working with an adult provider, however, that communication stopped. Not only were Brynn's parents surprised but also Brynn was confused as to why her new counselor never brought up the possibility of their involvement. She knew she was supposed to be an adult now, but her former counselor wanted everyone to work as a team.

Brynn's teacher was also surprised to be excluded from the process. Brynn was a student in the special education program with an active individualized education program (IEP) and was not scheduled to graduate for at least another 2 years. Brynn's teacher had had frequent conversations with her child-system counselor previously. The two had shared insights and information about Brynn. This lack of communication with the new counselor made matters more challenging for Brynn's teacher— and in turn, for Brynn.

Brynn's story illustrates one of the ways in which child and adult mental health services differ in their general approach to intervention, with one emphasizing a broader system (family, other service systems, and community) and the other emphasizing the individual. This section explores differences between child and adult mental health services in detail.

Culture

In terms of intervention, there are several typical cultural differences between child and adult mental health systems. The first is the manner in which parental figures are involved. Stroul and Friedman (1986), in their seminal work defining system-of-care principles, focused on the importance of partnering with parents to provide appropriate intervention and supports for their child. Similarly, many interventions with strong research support for children or adolescents also work directly with parents to bring about improvements in their child's condition. However, family involvement is less emphasized in adult systems and in evidence-based practices for adults. Families often report being completely cut out of consideration in their young adult's care. Not only can young adults legally prevent clinicians from sharing their clinical information but also clinicians are less likely to suggest parental involvement. Thus, an adolescent's circumstances can rapidly change from having parents function as advocates and case managers to being expected to make all of his or her own decisions. There are no studies that describe how changes in the parent–child relationship during the transition should shape parental involvement.

Children with emotional and/or behavioral difficulties (EBD) are often involved in several systems at once, including juvenile justice, special education, child welfare, and mental health (described in Chapters 2, 3, and 9). Providers in these child service systems are typically aware of other systems' involvement and communicate and coordinate with them. Adult mental health is often insular, providing services such as vocational rehabilitation or drug treatment within the mental health system rather than partnering with other systems (Chapters 2 and 5). Communication across these systems can be minimal at best. Davis and colleagues (2005) measured relationships between organizations (e.g., mental health clinics, vocational programs) that served part or all of ages 16–25 in Clark County, Washington. Although this was a single case study (one county), it is likely representative of many counties across the country. Analysis of the patterns of communication among these organizations revealed a distinctive interconnected child system, a fairly disconnected adult system, and few organizations that communicated across the two systems. Given that youth were being referred from child to adult systems, the lack of communication is of concern. Moreover, lack of within-adult-system communication highlights a difference between child and adult systems that can add to the confusion and difficulty of the transition.

Last, one of the fundamental features of child systems is that they recognize and address developmental changes in youth, including age-graded services (e.g., preadolescents receiving different programs from adolescents), and practitioners with developmental training who incorporate developmentally appropriate approaches in their intervention, treatment, or services. Adult mental health systems are not developmentally informed in their practices. Adulthood is typically viewed as a single stage of the life cycle, with the exception of old age, in which individuals require services tailored to senior citizens. Furthermore, Davis (2003) found little recognition by adult mental health administrators that adult services not tailored for young adults would be inappropriate or rejected by young adults. The lack of a developmental perspective in adult mental health services likely contributes to the rarity of services for young adults within adult mental health systems, and contributes to a discontinuity in service approaches for those transitioning from adolescent to adult services. On the child system side, although shaped by developmental considerations, the absence of a focus on the imminent approach of legal adulthood in older adolescents can result in young adults who are less prepared for adult functioning than they would be had their transition to adulthood been adequately addressed. In essence, both child and adult mental health systems would benefit from emphasizing the unique developmental needs during the transition period.

Funding

Child and adult systems have many streams of funding from different levels of government and private sources. Many funding streams are age defined or limited and can add to the complexity of continuity and coordination among and between child and adult systems. States' major funding sources for public mental health are Medicaid, federal block grants, and state legislative funding. Most states allocate federal, state, and local funds separately for child and adult services. And, as described earlier, the policies of each state differ in terms of child and adult population requirements and services, which often define who these funds support or the age criteria for the funds set at the federal, state, or local level (Davis & Koroloff, 2006). As described in the previous section, Medicaid eligibility has different child and adult criteria. Several state mental health administrators (Davis, 2001) have noted that transition-age youth lose Medicaid coverage as adults even though they had qualified for Medicaid as minors due to their poverty level; this is because the adult poverty level criteria are stricter. This is exacerbated by many states having a more generous poverty level cutoff for children (e.g., households within 200% of federal policy level for children but 100% of poverty level for adults), and by the common situation that 18-year-olds often live with their families who have a household income that is too high to qualify.

The Community Mental Health Service Block Grant (funded through CMHS/SAMHSA) is a state formula grant program. Funds from the block grant may be used to provide services for individuals of all ages and can include any mental health and related support services needed. There is nothing in the block grant program that prevents states from using these funds to bridge the transition ages. Although most states allocate the funds separately to child and adult systems, a few states (e.g., Maryland), have specifically used these funds to improve transition services.

State and local funds typically round out the budgets for public mental health funding. Funding for transition-age programming and fragmentation of funding between child and adult systems were described as some of the most common barriers to the improvement of these services by adult mental health administrators in a national study (Davis & Hunt, 2005).

Finally, as examples of the challenge produced by separate child and adult funding, Davis (2008) found that of the seven local transition programs interviewed in depth, all of which offered age continuity and received some public mental health funding, six programs received funding *either* from child or adult mental health, not from both. Each program had to make their argument about why the child or adult mental health funder should be willing to allow their funding to go to individuals outside the age group they usually (and sometimes mandatorily) funded. Although this study did not systematically examine the number of transition programs that provide age continuity, these seven were the only ones that were identified based on previous interviews with each state's mental health authority in which all transition support programs were identified. That such programs appear to be quite rare may, in part, result from funding streams that are age defined.

Gaps within and Across Systems

Caleb is 20. He has experienced psychosis for almost 2 years. He and his doctor have been unable to find medication to adequately control his symptoms. When he was 19, Caleb was arrested on an assault charge. During a psychotic episode, he was confronted by a neighbor and the incident turned violent. The neighbor sustained some moderate injuries and Caleb spent a week in jail and was sentenced to 2 years' probation. During his time in jail, Caleb's psychotic episode continued and he was kept in isolation due to his behavior. A delay in the administration of his medications in jail worsened his condition. Once out of jail, Caleb's symptoms decreased and he met regularly with his psychiatrist to find the right medication regimen. The severity of his symptoms interfered with his ability to work, so he lived with his parents. Caleb's psychiatrist assured him and his parents that they would eventually find the right combination of medications and that Caleb would be able to regain control over his life.

The justice system interpreted Caleb's behavior very differently than did his psychiatrist and the mental health system. Caleb missed a scheduled meeting with his probation officer once during a severe psychotic episode. His father left a voicemail message for the probation officer canceling the appointment and describing the situation. However, the next time Caleb met with his probation officer, he was charged with a probation violation and sent to jail for one night for the missed appointment. According to the probation officer, if Caleb had a valid excuse for missing an appointment, he needed to call and speak for himself. Caleb was told that he was a grown man and he needed to start acting like it, not having his parents call to make excuses for him. This led Caleb to wonder whether or not his symptoms were real or if his parents and psychiatrist were just coddling him. Moreover, his parents worried that if his symptoms weren't brought under control, Caleb would be seen increasingly as breaking probation and as a risk to society in the eyes of the justice system.

Caleb's story highlights vast cultural differences between subsystems of the adult system. These differences may have been exacerbated by a lack of communication between the two systems regarding his condition. As described in Chapters 2–7 and 9, this group of young people is often involved in multiple systems at a given time. As shown in Figure 1.1, these systems split along child and adult lines. Indeed, most systems do not have both child and adult components; child welfare and special education have no adult counterpart, and substance abuse and vocational rehabilitation typically have no child or adolescent counterpart. Only mental health and justice systems typically have both child and adult components. Less is known from research about the complexity of the transition period caused by the presence of so many systems. Presumably, discontinuities across these systems can make for

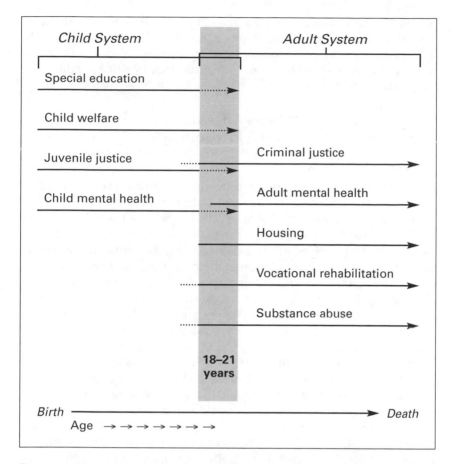

Figure 1.1. Public systems with which youth and young adults with emotional and/or behavioral difficulties (EBD) are involved are bifurcated into child and adult components that are separated by the ages of the individuals who can be served in the systems. Age separation generally occurs between ages 18–21. Dotted lines represent ages at which state practices often vary (e.g., most states end child mental health at age 18, though some continue to age 21), or when most youths at these ages are not served in this system (i.e., most special education students with EBD end their schooling at age 18 regardless of completion; a small proportion of 16-year-olds are handled in criminal justice).

services that are extremely fragmented and redundant and that ineffectively address a young person's needs. The typical issues of system fragmentation seen *within* the child and adult mental health systems are multiplied across these many systems when considering the needs of transition-age youth and young adults. Differing eligibility criteria (e.g., different definitions of SED in special education versus mental health), differing funding streams (e.g., local property taxes for education versus mostly state and federal funding for child welfare), and different cultures (e.g., very punitive approaches in corrections versus rehabilitation and recovery in adult mental health) abound to complicate smooth coordination and continuity across systems. In addition, these discontinuities can be disorienting to young people as they move within and between systems, and can cause poor or unappealing services and rejection of services.

Non–Mental Health Policies Affecting Transition Coordination and Preparation

Secondary Education

The primary policy governing transition coordination and support aimed at those with disabilities is the Individuals with Disabilities Education Improvement Act (IDEA) of 2004 (PL 108-446), which mandates transition planning and services for students in special education. Although the language of IDEA 2004 has many strengths in the area of transition issues, implementation of the policy lags far behind. Geneen and Powers (2006) identified that across the 12 transition areas in IEPs in which special education students ought to have goals, the average student's plan had fewer than 6. Wagner and Davis (2006) examined the transition plans of special education students in the primary disability category of emotional disturbance (ED) in comparison with students with other disabilities. With regard to students' goals for the period immediately following high school, more than two-thirds of students with ED had an employment-related goal, usually involving obtaining competitive employment. The primary goal for almost half of these students was receiving vocational training and attending a 2- or 4-year college. However, approximately two-thirds of these students were pursuing a course of study that school staff reported was merely fairly well or even less well-suited to their goals. These aspects of transition planning were similar for students with disabilities as a whole.

Justice System

The policies that most affect the transition to adulthood of youth who come into contact with juvenile and criminal justice systems are those that embrace a "Get tough on crime" approach that many states enacted in response to heightened fears about a wave of youth violence in the mid-1980s. These policies encouraged criminal prosecution of juveniles as adults (Travis & Visher, 2005) and tougher sentencing practices in juvenile court. On average, 7,500 juveniles are held in adult jails each day in the United States (Campaign for Youth Justice, 2007). The safety of juveniles is seriously compromised in adult settings (Campaign for Youth Justice, 2007). In addition, the practice of treating juveniles as adults does not appear to have any greater deterrence on future offending than standard juvenile practice, and may actually be worse (Centers for Disease Control and Prevention, 2007). In addition, the more severe juvenile court sentencing can be at odds with the goals of rehabilitation, resilience building, and reintegration that are necessary for the successful transition to adulthood for a young person in the juvenile correctional system. The emphasis on punishment over rehabilitation has shifted support away from areas that can ease the transition to adulthood for juvenile offenders such as drug treatment, educational support and planning, mental health services, job training and placement, and assistance with housing (Altschuler, 2005).

Having a criminal record, particularly one including nontrivial charges, can greatly restrict access to several avenues that are critical for young adult development and functioning; formal regulation or simply common practice can limit access to areas such as public housing, college loans, Medicaid, and employment. Individuals in detention or corrections settings lose Medicaid coverage, according to federal statutes. Public housing authorities commonly bar those with felony charges from living in public housing. Overall then, justice system policies continue to punish individuals far beyond the period of their formal sentence and well into their life trajectories.

Gaps in Effective, Developmentally Appropriate, and Appealing Services

Miles is 19. He's a high school graduate, and is struggling with the symptoms of his anxiety disorder. Miles's therapist recommended that he attend the adult hospital diversion program at her mental health center. The program consisted of education and support groups offered throughout the day as well as individual support from staff. On Miles's first day, he walked through a crowd of adults smoking outside the door. He checked in and filled out paperwork, then was told he had some free time before the first group. Miles sat on one of the couches and looked around. Everyone looked older. Two women who looked to be about 40 sat and talked. A group of similarly middle-aged men sat around a table, not looking at or speaking to anyone. A number of other individuals were scattered across couches, sound asleep.

On surveying this environment, Miles's anxiety rapidly increased. Not only was the place nothing like the support program he attended before but he also began to fear that the people he saw around the room were a glimpse of what was awaiting him later in life. The situation did not improve across the day. He felt out of place, and there was no one else his age. He found the groups disappointing; they were boring and depressing. People just sat around doing nothing during the excessive amounts of free time. Miles was used to support programs where they played games and where there were activities that gave him a chance to get his emotions out. He was used to chatting with other youth his age and listening to music during breaks. Whereas the adult program was meant to serve individuals 18 and older, it was not developmentally appropriate for young adults. Miles did not return to the program.

Whenever anyone seeks mental health treatment, it needs to be appealing enough to engage the individual, effective, and age appropriate. In Miles's case, the program was insufficiently appealing because it was age inappropriate. Its efficacy was irrelevant because Miles dropped out. Standard, one-size-fits-all adult services are typically age appropriate for 30- to 60-year-olds because their developmental changes are minimal. In contrast, the transition age is all about development and change. Youths also become legally emancipated and can reject services, thus *developmentally appropriate* implies that services will be appealing enough that young folks are willing to engage in them of their own volition. Developmentally appropriate services modify their approaches as youth mature to fit their biopsychosocial maturational changes. For example, services need to appropriately involve parents, friends, and significant others or spouses across the marked developmental changes in the roles that these individuals can play in supporting a youth's treatment progress (refer to Chapter 2).

Another example is the need to provide age-appropriate psychopharmacological approaches. Physicians typically provide different medications for adolescents than they do for adults for conditions such as major depressive disorder (Cohen, 2007), first-episode psychosis (Weiden, Buckly, & Grody, 2007), or bipolar disorder (Smarty & Findling, 2007). The transition from adolescent to adult psychopharmacological approaches should be based on research specifically examining how medications should be modified at these ages.

The Research Base

What does research tell us about gaps in developmentally appropriate and effective services for transition-age individuals? First we need to know what developmentally appropriate and effective practices are; then we need to know about gaps in those practices.

What Are Developmentally Appropriate and Effective Services?
One of the biggest gaps in our service systems is the lack of a scientific
answer for what developmentally appropriate and effective services are
for transition-age youth. The National Institute of Mental Health
(NIMH) is the federal government's organization for conducting and
funding research on mental health treatment and services. In 2006, the
NIMH issued a request for applications for "research aimed at refining
and testing innovative interventions and service delivery models for
youth with severe mental illnesses . . . who are transitioning to adulthood" (http://grants1.nih.gov/grants/guide/rfa-files/RFA-MH-07-051
.html). The rationale for issuing the request for applications was that the
NIMH recognized that no evidence-based interventions exist that span
the transition ages (see U.S Department of Health and Human Services,
2006). Typically, we scientifically test whether an intervention works
through an established process called clinical trials. This process includes clearly describing the intervention in detail (through a manual),
applying that intervention to one group of individuals and comparing
their outcomes with those of another group or groups of individuals
that are not treated with that intervention. The most rigorous way to
compare the groups is to randomly assign each study participant to the
experimental or other intervention group (essentially deciding which
group the study participant is assigned to by a flip of a coin). Increasingly demanding features of randomized clinical trials are typically
added to each subsequent trial, which increases the level of confidence
in the effectiveness of the intervention (e.g., the first trial is with a small
group of individuals to make sure it is safe; the second trial is with a
larger group). As an intervention passes each step of rigorous testing, it
is labeled accordingly. The higher levels of testing allow an intervention
to be labeled *probably efficacious* and, at the highest level, *well established*
(Burns & Hoagwood, 2002). Clark, Koroloff, Geller, and Sondheimer
(2008) provided a recent collection of research designs, methodologies,
and findings related to transition-to-adulthood research.

The few interventions that met with success in clinical trials and included this age group do not include the entire transition-age range
(e.g., Multisystemic Therapy for antisocial behavior in juveniles;
Henggeler et al., 1992) or have not specifically examined efficacy with
the transition-age portion of the age group (e.g., supported employment for adults; Becker & Drake, 2003). Thus, our systems currently
have no practices that meet the standards for *probably efficacious* or *well
established* to put forth for transition-age youth as a group. Evidence-
supported approaches described in this volume and elsewhere (e.g.,
Clark, Deschênes, et al., 2008; Hagner, Cheney, & Malloy, 1999; Karpur,
Clark, Caproni, & Sterner, 2005; Wagner & Davis, 2006) do exist that are

consistent with research findings about transition-age youth character-istics (e.g., the functional areas in which they often struggle). We use these as the current standards of age-appropriate and effective practices to answer the question, "How available are they?"

Youth Voice

Current guidelines for services for transition-age youth and young adults require the use of *youth voice* to shape practice (see Chapters 2, 3, and 7). Youth voice refers to having meaningful input. The extent to which youth voice currently shapes interventions and services for transition-age youth is unknown. However, there has been obvious growth in the involvement of youth voice at the federal level and in for-mal consumer lead advocacy organizations focused on youth (Mata-rese, McGinnis, & Mora, 2005). However, youth voice organizations are not nearly at the level of being readily available to inform state policy or services in most states. Given that the parent empowerment and ad-vocacy movement of the 1980s and 1990s led to the successful establish-ment of such organizations in every state, this is a standard by which to compare the youth voice movement in the future.

Tailored Practices

There is no research that describes the extent to which evidence-supported transition-age youth service approaches are available. Two studies examined the presence of any transition support services in state mental health systems (Davis, 2001; Davis, Geller, & Hunt, 2006). State child and adult mental health administrators were interviewed in 2001 and 2003 regarding transition services in their state mental health system. One quarter of the child and one half of the adult state mental health systems offered no transition services, and few provided any kind of transition service in more than one site. Most types of transition services were available in fewer than 20% of states. These findings indi-cate that transition support services of any type are lacking across the United States' public mental health systems.

SUMMARY AND CONCLUSIONS

Returning to the policy tenets described at the beginning of this chapter and further described in Chapter 9, we can see that they are not in com-mon practice or are currently unmeasured. Perhaps, above all, this chapter highlights the need for research in several areas: 1) a scientifi-cally rigorous approach to interventions for transition-age youth, 2) an examination into services currently available for youth and young adults with EBD both within mental health and in other child- and adult-service systems, 3) investigation of appropriate family involvement in services or interventions during the transition years, and 4) assessment of the knowledge base among practitioners and policy makers about this age group and their strengths and needs. Although the task of this chapter has been to describe what we currently know about gaps in our policies and service systems for this population, this description allows us to target our efforts. Significant progress has been made from 2000 to 2008, the knowledge base is growing, and strategies for implementing best practice transition services and systems are described in the remaining chapters of this book.

REFERENCES

Altschuler, D.M. (2005). Policy and program perspectives on the transition to adulthood for adolescents in the juvenile justice system. In D.W. Osgood, E.M. Foster, C. Flanagan, & G.R. Ruth, (Eds.), *On your own without a net: The transition to adulthood for vulnerable populations.* IL: The University of Chicago Press.

Becker, D.R., & Drake, R.E. (2003). *A working life for people with severe mental illness.* New York: Oxford University Press.

Burns, B., & Hoagwood, K. (2002). *Community treatment for youth.* Oxford University Press.

Campaign for Youth Justice. (2007). *Jailing juveniles: The dangers of incarcerating youth in adult jails in America.* Washington, DC: Author. Retrieved January 23, 2008, from http://www.campaignforyouthjustice.org/Downloads/National ReportsArticles/CFYJ-Jailing_Juveniles_Report_2007-11-15.pdf

Centers for Disease Control and Prevention. (2007). *Morbidity and mortality weekly report: Recommendations and reports: Effects on violence of laws and policies facilitating the transfer of youth from the juvenile to the adult justice system.* Atlanta, GA: Author. Retrieved January 23, 2008, from: http://www.cdc.gov/mmwr/pdf/rr/rr5609.pdf

Clark, H., Deschênes, N., & Jones, J. (2000). A framework for the development and operation of a transition system. In H.B. Clark & M. Davis, (Eds.), *Transition to adulthood: A resource for assisting young people with emotional or behavioral difficulties* (pp. 29–51). Baltimore: Paul H. Brookes Publishing Co.

Clark, H.B., Deschênes, N., Sieler, D., Green, M.E., White, G., & Sondheimer, D.L. (2008). Services for youth in transition to adulthood in systems of care. In B.A. Stroul & G.M. Blau (Eds.), *The system of care handbook: Transforming mental health services for children, youth, and families* (pp. 517–544). Baltimore: Paul H. Brookes Publishing Co.

Clark, H.B., & Foster-Johnson, L. (1996). Serving youth in transition into adulthood. In B.A. Stroul (Ed.), *Children's mental health: Creating systems of care in a changing society* (pp. 533–551). Baltimore: Paul H. Brookes Publishing Co.

Clark, H.B., Koroloff, N., Geller, J., & Sondheimer, D.L. (2008). Research on transition to adulthood: Building the evidence base to inform services and supports for youth and young adults with serious mental health disorders. *Journal of Behavioral Health Services and Research, 35*, 4.

Clark, H., Unger, K., & Stewart, E. (1993). Transition of youth and young adults with emotional/behavioral disorders into employment, education, and independent living. *Community Alternatives International Journal of Family Care, 5*, 21–46.

Cohen, D. (2007). Should the use of selective serotonin reuptake inhibitors in child and adolescent depression be banned? *Psychotherapy & Psychosomatics, 76*(1), 5–14.

Davis, M. (2001). *Transition Supports to Help Adolescents in Mental Health Services.* Alexandria, VA: National Association of State Mental Health Program Directors.

Davis, M. (2003). Addressing the needs of youth in transition to adulthood. *Administration and Policy in Mental Health, 30*, 495–509.

Davis, M. (2008). *Pioneering transition programs: The establishment of programs that span the ages served by child and adult mental health.* Rockville, MD: U.S. Department of Health and Human Services, Substance Abuse and Mental Health Services Administration, Center for Mental Health Services.

Davis, M., Geller, J., & Hunt, B. (2006). Within-state availability of transition-to-adulthood services for youths with serious mental health conditions. *Psychiatric Services, 57*, 1594–1599.

Davis, M., & Hunt, B. (2005). *State adult mental health systems' efforts to address the needs of young adults in transition to adulthood.* Rockville, MD: U.S. Department of Health and Human Services, Substance Abuse and Mental Health Services Administration, Center for Mental Health Services.

Davis, M., Johnsen, M., Starrett, B., Koroloff, N., & Sondheimer, D. (2005). *Where are bridges needed? Relationships between youth and adult services before strengthening the transition system: Report on the interrelationships of agencies in a Center for Mental Health Services Partnerships for Youth Transition grant.* Rockville, MD: U.S. Department of Health and Human Services Substance Abuse and Mental Health Services Administration, Center for Mental Health Services.

Davis, M., & Koroloff, N. (2006). The great divide: How public mental health policy fails young adults. In W.H. Fisher (Ed.), *Community based mental health services for children and adolescents* (Vol. 14, pp. 53–74). Oxford, UK: Elsevier Sciences.

Davis, M., & Koyanagi, C. (2005). *Summary of Center for Mental Health Services youth transition policy meeting: National experts panel.* Rockville, MD: U.S. Substance Abuse and Mental Health Services Administration, Center for Mental Health Services.

Davis, M., & Vander Stoep, A. (1996). *The transition to adulthood among adolescents who have serious emotional disturbances: At risk for homelessness.* Delmar, NY: National Resource Center on Homelessness and Mental Illness.

Davis, M., & Vander Stoep, A. (1997). The transition to adulthood for youth who have serious emotional disturbance: Developmental transition and young adult outcomes. *The Journal of Mental Health Administration, 24*(2), 400–427.

Delman, J., & Jones, A. (2002). *Voices of youth in transition: The experience of aging out of the adolescent public mental health system in Massachusetts: Policy implications and recommendations.* Dorchester, MA: Consumer Quality Initiatives, Inc.

Geenen, S.J., & Powers, L.E. (2006). Transition planning for foster youth. *Journal for Vocational Special Needs Education, 28*(2), 4–15.

Hagner, D., Cheney, D., & Malloy, J. (1999). Career-related outcomes of a model transition demonstration for young adults with emotional disturbance. *Rehabilitation Counseling Bulletin, 42,* 228–242.

Henggeler, S.W., Melton, G.B., & Smith, L.A. (1992). Family preservation using multisystemic therapy: An effective alternative to incarcerating serious juvenile offenders. *Journal of Consulting & Clinical Psychology, 60*(6), 953–961.

Individuals with Disabilities Education Improvement Act (IDEA) of 2004, PL 108-446, 20 U.S.C. §§ 1400 *et seq.*

Judge David L. Bazelon Center for Mental Health Law. (2005). *Moving on: Analysis of federal programs funding services for transition-age youth with serious mental health conditions.* Retrieved November 30, 2008, from http://www.bazelon.org/publications/movingon/index.htm

Karpur, A., Clark, H.B., Caproni, P., & Sterner, H. (2005). Transition to adult roles for students with emotional/behavioral disturbances: A follow-up study of student exiters from a transition program. *Career Development for Exceptional Individuals, 28*(1), 36–46.

Matarese, M., McGinnis, L., & Mora, M. (2005). *Youth involvement in systems of care: A guide to empowerment.* Washington, DC: Technical Assistance Partnerships, American Institutes of Research.

Smarty, S., & Findling, R.L. (2007). Psychopharmacology of pediatric bipolar disorder: A review. *Psychopharmacology, 191*(1), 39–54.

Stiles, P.G., Dailey, K., & Mehra, S. (2001). The transition from adolescence to adulthood on Medicaid: Use of mental health services. Submitted to the Florida Agency for Health Care Administration by the Louis de la Parte Florida Mental Health Institute. Tampa, FL: University of South Florida.

Stroul, B., & Friedman, R. (1986). *A system of care for severely emotionally disturbed children and youth.* Washington, DC: CASSP Technical Assistance Center.

Travis, J., & Visher, C.A. (2005). Prisoner reentry and the pathways to adulthood: Policy perspectives. In D.W. Osgood, E.M. Foster, C. Flanagan, & G.R. Ruth (Eds.), *On your own without a net: The transition to adulthood for vulnerable populations.* Chicago: University of Chicago Press.

Twamley, E.W., Jeste, D.V., & Lehman, A.F. (2003). Vocational rehabilitation in schizophrenia and other psychotic disorders: A literature review and meta-analysis of randomized controlled trials. *Journal of Nervous and Mental Disease, 191,* 515–523.

U.S. Department of Heath and Human Services. (2006, September 11). *Refining and testing mental health interventions and services for youth with mental illness who are transitioning to adulthood (R01)* [Request for applications]. Retrieved November 30, 2008, from http://grants.nih.gov/grants/guide/rfa-files/RFA-MH-07-050.html

Vander Stoep, A., Davis, M., & Collins, D. (2000). Transition: A time of developmental and institutional clashes. In H.B. Clark & M. Davis (Eds.), *Transition to adulthood: A resource for assisting young people with emotional or behavioral difficulties* (pp. 3–28). Baltimore: Paul H. Brookes Publishing Co.

VanDenBerg, J.E., & Grealish, E.M. (1996). Individualized services and supports through the wraparound process: Philosophy and procedures. *Journal of Child and Family Studies, 5*(1), 7–21.

Wagner, M., & Davis, M. (2006). How are we preparing students with emotional disturbances for the transition to young adulthood? Findings from the National Longitudinal Transition Study–2. *Journal of Emotional and Behavioral Disorders, 14,* 86–98.

Weiden, P.J., Buckley, P.F., & Grody, M. (2007). Understanding and treating "first-episode" schizophrenia. *Psychiatric Clinics of North America, 30*(3), 481–510.

Navigating the Obstacle Course

An Evidence-Supported Community Transition System

Hewitt B. "Rusty" Clark and Karen Hart

"Having someone in my life who I feel truly cares about me and believes in me has been the biggest help in my transition."

—Young adult from California

This chapter provides an overview of an evidence-supported transition system developed and researched to address the challenges faced by youth and young adults with emotional and/or behavioral difficulties (EBD) and their families. In the Introduction to this handbook, we provide data that illustrate the types of poor outcomes that are typical for many youth and young adults with EBD across transition indicators of employment, postsecondary education, independent living, criminal involvement, and substance use. In Chapter 1, data are presented to illustrate the barriers that put this particular population at significantly greater risk for school failure, involvement with correctional authorities, dependency on social services, substance use, and poor postsecondary progress across employment, independent living, and career-oriented education. Chapter 1 also vividly describes how fragmented the service systems are during the transition period for these young people and their families; and even when services are available, the quality of these are typically judged to be extremely poor.

Lead author note: I would like to express appreciation and gratitude to my dear friend and colleague Nicole Deschênes for her creativity, wisdom, and diligence in our efforts to evaluate, refine, and disseminate the TIP model to serve youth and young adults with EBD and their families.

Fortunately, some agencies, communities, and states are taking it upon themselves to examine ways to improve the progress and outcomes for transition-age young people with EBD (from 14 through 29 years of age). Those of us at the National Network on Youth Transition for Behavioral Health (NNYT) have been amazed at the level of dedication and perseverance that some agency and community stakeholders have demonstrated through their efforts to transform fragmented services into a transition system tailored to the needs and goals of these young people.

This chapter describes the Transition to Independence Process (TIP) model and its principles and practices. The TIP model is the only evidence-supported practice that has been shown to be effective in improving the outcomes of youth and young adults with EBD. Our program development and research efforts have been guided by the voices and perspectives of young people, parents, and practitioners in the field. Four outcome studies conducted by our research team at NNYT and two other outcome studies conducted by other researchers demonstrate improvement in real-life outcomes for these young people with EBD (e.g., Clark, Pschorr, Wells, Curtis, & Tighe, 2004; Haber, Karpur, Deschênes, & Clark, 2008; Hagner, Cheney, & Malloy, 1999; Koroloff, Pullmann, & Gordan, 2008). The implementation of the TIP model across various communities' sites are illustrated in Section II of this book.

TRANSITION TO INDEPENDENCE PROCESS (TIP) MODEL

TIP System Definition

The TIP model was developed for working with youth and young adults (14–29 years old) with EBD to 1) engage them in their own futures planning process; 2) provide them with developmentally appropriate, nonstigmatizing, culturally competent, and appealing services and supports; and 3) involve them and their families and other informal key players in a process that prepares and facilitates them in their movement toward greater self-sufficiency and successful achievement of their goals related to relevant transition domains (i.e., employment/career, educational opportunities, living situation, personal effectiveness and wellbeing, and community-life functioning). The TIP system is operationalized through seven guidelines and their associated practices that drive the work with young people and provide the framework for the program and community system to support these functions (Clark, Deschênes, & Jones, 2000; Clark & Foster-Johnson, 1996). These

Table 2.1   The Transition to Independence Process (TIP) system guidelines

1. Engage young people through relationship development, person-centered planning, and a focus on their futures.
2. Tailor services and supports to be accessible, coordinated, appealing, nonstigmatizing, and developmentally appropriate—and building on strengths to enable the young people to pursue their goals across relevant transition domains.
3. Acknowledge and develop personal choice and social responsibility with young people.
4. Ensure a safety net of support by involving a young person's parents, family members, and other informal and formal key players.
5. Enhance young persons' competencies to assist them in achieving greater self-sufficiency and confidence.
6. Maintain an outcome focus in the TIP system at the young person, program, and community levels.
7. Involve young people, parents, and other community partners in the TIP system at the practice, program, and community levels.

Note: Refer to Appendix 2.1 at the end of this chapter for the complete listing of the guidelines and their associated practice elements.

TIP system guidelines synthesize the current research and practice knowledge base for transition facilitation with youth and young adults with EBD and their families. The seven guidelines are listed in Table 2.1, and a complete listing of these guidelines and their associated elements is provided in Appendix 2.1 of this chapter.

Independence and Interdependence

Originally, the lead author of this chapter had planned to name the model the Transition to *Interdependence* Process (TIP) system. Instead, the youth and young adults who were collaborating with him at some sites wanted the emphasis to be on *independence*, something they could relate to more directly. Their points were well taken, and clearly the TIP system promotes greater self-sufficiency and independence. However, the concept of interdependence is central to working effectively with young people. This concept nests the focus of independent functioning (e.g., budgeting money, maintaining a job) within the framework of young people learning that there is a healthy, reciprocal role of supporting others and receiving support from others (i.e., social support network for emotional, spiritual, and physical support). The TIP model is designed to develop understandings and competencies within young people regarding both of these concepts.

Transition Facilitators

To ensure the continuity of planning, services, and supports, the TIP system is implemented by *transition facilitators* who work with young people; their parents; family members; and other informal, formal, and community supports.

- The term *transition facilitator* is used to emphasize the function of facilitating the young person's future, not directing it.
- The role is that of a *proactive* case manager—but no one wants to be a "case" and no one wants to be "managed."
- Different sites and service systems use similar terms, such as *transition specialist, resource coordinator, transition coach, TIP facilitator, transition mentor, service coordinator,* or *life coach.*
- The role of transition facilitators with young people, their parents, family members and other informal and formal key players, and community representatives will be described in detail throughout this chapter and illustrated throughout this handbook.

TIP Core Practices

The TIP system guidelines provide the framework by which the transition facilitators work with young people and the other key players in their lives. The transition facilitators are also provided competency training in TIP core practices to facilitate young people's abilities in making better decisions as well as improving their progress and outcomes. The transition facilitators use the following core practices:

- Strength discovery and needs assessment
- Futures planning
- Rationales
- In-vivo teaching
- Social problem solving
- Prevention planning on high-risk behaviors and situations
- Mediation with young people and other key players

Practice Model

The TIP system is a practice model, meaning that it can be delivered by personnel within different service delivery platforms such as case management or in a team format (e.g., Assertive Community Treatment [ACT]). Transition facilitators are at the heart of the TIP practice model. For a transition facilitator to actively engage and facilitate young people and their key support players, each should be serving 15 or fewer youth and young adults. In one national study across several TIP sites, the ratio of facilitators to young people at different community sites ranged from 1:9 to 1:13 (Clark, Karpur, Deschênes, Gamache, & Haber, 2008).

The TIP model also provides for the use of other evidence-supported interventions to address critical clinical needs of individual young people. Many young people have co-morbidity with severe mental health conditions and substance use and may require specialized interventions in addition to the TIP futures focus context (Bender, Springer, & Kim, 2008). Other targeted clinical interventions might be Motivational Interviewing (Miller & Rollnick, 2002; Rollnick & Miller, 2008; Wagner, 2009); Structured Psychotherapy for Adolescents Responding to Chronic Stress (SPARCS/DBT; The National Child Traumatic Stress Network, 2008); Aggression Replacement Therapy (ART; Glick, 1996; Goldstein, Glick, & Gibbs, 1998); behavior analysis functional assessment and interventions; and Wellness Recovery Action Plan (WRAP; Copeland, 2002, 2007).

APPLICATION OF THE TIP MODEL

This chapter describes the TIP system guidelines and associated practices, illustrates their application through examples, and presents supporting research. Although the seven TIP system guidelines will be described sequentially, it is important to understand that the TIP system is an integrated process with a young person, his or her informal key players (e.g., parents, relatives, friends, spouse), and formal key players (e.g., therapist, teacher, supervisor). Thus, the transition facilitators and others working with youth and young adults need to apply the guidelines and core practices on an individualized basis, addressing the priorities, needs, and wishes of each young person to facilitate his or her goal planning and accomplishments.

1. Engage Young People Through Relationship Development, Person-Centered Planning, and a Focus on Their Futures

Many young people with EBD have learned not to trust adults or to bond with others (e.g., a youth who has had 12 out-of-home placements). Personnel working with these youth and young adults need to build relationships (Blase & Fixsen, 1989; Hines, Merdinger, & Wyatt, 2005), and involve young people in an informal, flexible, futures planning process driven by the individual interests, dreams, needs, strengths, and cultural and familial values. The TIP system uses a person-centered planning approach driven by a strength-discovery assessment of the young person and the young person's ecological situation.

Use a Strength-Based Approach with Young People, Their Families, and Other Informal and Formal Key Players

Individuals tend to develop and grow based on their particular interests, aspirations, and strengths (Rapp, 1998). To enhance the young person's motivation during the transition process, an ongoing strength-discovery approach is used that focuses on learning about the young person's likes, dislikes, competencies, talents, needs, resources, and dreams. This strength-based approach is used with a young person, his or her parents, and other key players to 1) learn each of their perspectives, 2) increase the likelihood that they will view the youth in a more optimistic light, and 3) maximize the likelihood of them assisting the young person with some aspect of his or her transition. This is a powerful approach that often yields active involvement on the part of the young person and those around him or her; a sharp contrast to what typically occurs with deficit-based assessments that constantly revisit the young person's impairments, problems, and/or pathologies (Nelson & Pearson, 1991). However, this is not to suggest that the young person's needs and those of the family are ignored. Through the strength-discovery process, assessments, and records, the transition facilitator learns of the needs of the young person and his or her family.

A strength-discovery assessment is a process for creating a profile of the young person's personal and ecological resources (e.g., natural support system), needs, and wants; as well as exploring his or her dreams and aspirations across the domains of employment and career, educational opportunities, living situation, personal effectiveness and well-being, and community-life functioning. A strength-discovery approach is not a one-interview event, but rather an evolving profile of the young person and his or her situation that occurs through informal conversations over time.

The strength-discovery approach provides the basis for an initial profile and subsequent revisions as more is learned about the young person and his or her circumstances, needs, aspirations, and those of the informal key players. The approach also allows for the use of the previously untapped and unsolicited resources of the young person and those of the family and other members of his or her natural support system. A strength-based approach is empowering—it creates a sense of personal accomplishment; contributes to satisfying relationships with family members, peers, and adults; and contributes to resiliency in personal, social, and academic arenas during times of adversity and stress (Cox, 2006; Epstein & Sharma, 1998; VanDenBerg & Grealish, 1996).

A personnel training module titled, *Strength Discovery and Needs Assessment Process for Working with Transition-Age Youth and Young Adults* is available through our TIP web site (http://tip.fmhi.usf.edu). This module can assist transition facilitators and other personnel working with young people and their families in conducting developmentally appropriate assessments. The strength-discovery assessments, as was previously stated, are best achieved through informal conversations with young people, parents, and other informal and formal key players who the young person wants to involve or who are essential to the success of this youth.

Build Relationships and Respect
Young Persons' Relationships with Family
Members and Other Informal and Formal Key Players

One of the most essential functions of the transition facilitator and others who work with these young people is relationship development. The initial and ongoing strength-discovery conversations provide a growing understanding of a young person's interests and strengths, which provide the transition facilitator with the basis for discussions and activities with the young person that contribute further to relationship development. Also, frequent compliments, smiles, and social praise for appropriate behavior—along with minimal criticism—will contribute greatly to the building and strengthening of the relationship. It is also important for a transition facilitator to have the ability to genuinely focus on positive aspects of a youth's characteristics (e.g., persistence, speaking up, self-advocacy), which often requires the reframing of a youth's behavior (e.g., being rebellious with adults may reflect youth's attempt to advocate for himself). The transition facilitator can assist the relationship development process further by being clear, consistent, honest, and flexible.

Recognizing that the young person probably has existing relationships or past relationships with informal and formal key players (e.g., parent, aunt, girlfriend, soccer coach, or minister) that would benefit the young person, efforts should be given to the possibility of further nurturing and/or rekindling these relationships. Nurturing relationship development between the young person and existing or past supports may contribute greatly to the young person's future success, since this network of supports may continue when formal key players are terminated. Exploring with the young person and others these possible supports and ways of strengthening them may prove helpful in targeting relationships that would be particularly beneficial to the young person. The transition facilitator's goal in developing a relationship with a young person is not to detract from his or her other valued supports but to enable the facilitator to work more effectively in understanding and guiding the young person with an eye toward the future. Such guidance may take the form of assisting the young person in strengthening and appreciating his or her support system as well as assisting members of that support system in providing healthy and helpful assistance to the youth.

Facilitate Futures Planning and Goal Setting

Person-centered planning has assumed major importance in special education and is becoming an important tenet of intervention strategies targeted towards youth and young adults' transitioning to adulthood (Corbitt & Paris, 2002; Kincaid, 1996; Malloy, Cheney, Hagner, Cormier, & Bernstein, 1998; Nerney, 2004). A person-centered planning approach assists young people in their goal planning and the development of means to achieve those goals across the transition domains of employment and career, educational opportunities, living situation, personal effectiveness and wellbeing, and community-life functioning.

Considerations on Futures Planning

To be developmentally responsive to youth and young adults with EBD, planning must be approached to maximize the engagement of the young person in the process and commitment to his or her outcomes. For most older youth and young adults, this translates into listening to their voices as to who they want to plan with as well as realizing this may only be one or two people and may vary by topics and over time. Young people are in a mode of *discovery,* and as such need to try things out and then proceed with their plans or make adjustments based on their experiences. Young people are not keen on waiting for weeks or months to gather people together before their plans can be adjusted. Again, to be developmentally responsive to these young people, we need to have a youth-friendly planning process in which they can make adjustments easily and in a timely fashion. The following paragraphs describe aspects of more traditional person-centered planning and contrast it with the more developmentally appropriate planning strategies that more effectively engage most youth and young adults with EBD.

Traditional Person-Centered Planning Teams

In a traditional person-centered planning approach, a number of people identified as significant by the parent and young person, such as other family members, friends, school teachers, therapist and athletic coaches, are brought together to help the young person dream, plan, and ultimately achieve his or her goals. Ideally, planning is done and decisions are made in partnership *with* the young person, not *for* him or her. The preparation and facilitation of these youth team meetings are often very involved and challenging because of 1) the youth's lack of interest in having a team of people knowing about him or her, 2) lack of motivation on the part of the young person and others to stay involved, 3) difficulty of getting other team members to shift to more of a strength and future orientation, and 4) the youth's inability to remain attentive and engaged in a process that will not always feel positive to him or her. Some of these challenges can be minimized through pre-meeting preparation work with the young person—as well as separate pre-meeting preparation with each member of the team regarding the purpose of the meeting; the need to keep a strength-based approach; and the need to listen to the young person, recognize the young person for his or her contributions, and maintain a futures perspective.

It would seem that the traditional person-centered team planning process would be ideal; this planning approach has been shown to be an excellent model for *wraparound*, a family-driven process (Walker & Bruns, 2006; Walker, Bruns, & Penn, 2008). However, most older youth and young adults are adamant that they do not want to meet with a large group of adults. Youth often lack interest in having a team of people getting to know them and their business. Even with good facilitation, group meetings can often turn ugly, with someone airing a youth's "dirty laundry." Young people can often fall into *teenage repertories,* or appear to be agreeable but then leave with no commitment to the plan. It is often difficult to maintain the motivation, attention, engagement, and the strength approach required of a young person and others to make this process work for the young person.

TIP Model Futures Planning Solution

Based on research and experience with our sites and other sites we have worked with across the nation, we recommend that the planning process be a very flexible one with the young person. The planning for a given topic, need, or goal that a young person has would be done with one or more "planning partners" with whom he or she would feel most comfortable and supported for this discussion. The young person and his or her planning partners would then make the "necessary connection(s)" that would help to advance his or her progress related to the topic, need, or goal.

The recommendations for futures planning with youth and young adults with EBD are outlined next.

Planning Partners

- *Planning partners* are selected by the young person.

- He or she might choose *different* key players to serve as *planning partners* for *different* topics, needs, or goals.

- Often, a young person may want to only involve him- or herself and one or two key players (e.g., transition facilitator, parent, friend) to serve as *planning partner(s).*

Necessary Connections

- The young person's topic/need/goal determines who is a *"necessary connection"* (e.g., probation officer, vocational rehabilitation counselor, community college instructor) for him or her to make progress on this topic, need, or goal.

- The young person and transition facilitator or other *planning partner* would contact, plan, and/or negotiate with the *necessary connection(s)* regarding any actions or issues that have evolved from this planning process.

    The following are examples of working with planning partners and necessary connections:

- When planning on issues related to finishing high school, it may be important for the youth, transition facilitator, and parent to meet as the planning partners because the parent will be considered the legal entity to negotiate with the school guidance counselor (i.e., necessary connection), even if the parent wants the transition facilitator to join him or her.

- A young adult woman has finally gotten off of street drugs and is now trying to function at her new job, but she wants to try to stabilize on a psychotropic medication that she now thinks could be helpful. However, she doesn't want to go back on the same medication that the psychiatrist had prescribed previously because it made her feel nauseated and often very tired. The young woman doesn't feel confident that she alone can deal with the psychiatrist adequately, and is planning with the transition facilitator (i.e., planning partner) to assist her in assertively discussing these issues with the psychiatrist (i.e., necessary connection).

- When planning for a technical school training program, the young adult and the transition facilitator might serve as the planning partners, with the two of them approaching the vocational rehabilitation services councilor (i.e., necessary connection) with a proposal for attending an automobile mechanics training program (e.g., young adult will need tuition, tools, books).

Rationales for TIP Futures Planning

The rationale for the *planning partners* and *necessary connections* are as follows:

- To engage youth and young adults, we need to approach them with developmentally appropriate and appealing assessment and planning processes.

- Youth voice and choice need to guide the process.

- As mentioned previously, young people are in a mode of "discovery" more than "recovery." As such, they need to try things out and then adjust their plans to meet their new interests, goals, and needs.

- Planning and revamping plans need to be done frequently with young people to be relevant to their current interests and progress or difficulties.

- The planning partners can be responsive and timely in working with the young person, whereas a large group would not be able to meet frequently enough to keep up with the young person's agenda.

- The involvement of the young person in the planning and decision-making process is a key element to the success of his or her transition to adulthood (Bullis & Benz, 1996; Bullis & Fredericks, 2002; Clark & Davis, 2000; Wehmeyer & Lawrence, 1995). Indeed, when their transitions are self-determined, youth and young adults are more committed to the process, take greater ownership of outcomes, and adjust to their new situations in a more personally meaningful and enduring way (Field & Hoffman, 1998).

- Unless the young person "owns the plan," it will not be followed.

Keeping Informal and Formal Key Players in the Loop

- Alanzeo, a 17-year-old African American youth, might not want to do his initial planning directly with his probation officer about the community service situation; he might rather just work with the transition facilitator. However, the probation officer does hold some powerful contingencies over the youth, such as determining the community service assignments or drug testing regiments. Alanzeo wants a different community service assignment—one that would be after school (rather than before) and is more in line with his interests in becoming a carpenter. He works with the transition facilitator (i.e., planning partner) on this plan and then they meet to negotiate with the probation officer (i.e., necessary connection).

- Although Alanzeo does not want to do this initial planning with his aunt and uncle with whom he now lives, the transition facilitator has helped him come to understand that life can run more smoothly for him if he'll keep his legal guardians at least informed of his plans and goals (if not, involve the guardians in some of the planning).

Bottom Line on Futures Planning

The take-home points that older youth and young adults have taught us regarding futures planning is that it usually works best 1) on an informal basis with the young person, 2) when it occurs in the presence of only those people who the young person selects regarding a given topic, and 3) when there is active follow-up to assist the youth in accomplishing the goals. For our planning to be relevant to young people, it needs to align with the "discovery mode" of their developmental level. A young woman might want to become a veterinarian until, on a job shadowing, she learns that it will require 7 years of college—but she has also learned that there is a 2-year veterinarian assistant course program that she now wants to explore.

Futures Planning Applications with Youth Under 18

Transition facilitators and other transition program personnel also need to understand that in most states, the parents are legally responsible for the actions of their daughter or son until the child reaches the age of 18. Thus, it is imperative that the transition facilitators know their legal and ethical responsibilities to families and set clear ground rules with the youth regarding the limits of confidentiality. The transition facilitators also do well to assist the youth in understanding the benefits to the youth of involving parents or other family members in relevant aspects of the planning process.

For more guidance on the application of futures planning and for related materials, please refer to the personal training modules on Strength Discovery and Futures Planning (both available through the TIP web site at http://tip.fmhi.usf.edu).

Include Prevention Planning for
High-Risk Behaviors and Situations as Necessary

At times, youth and young adults place themselves in high-risk situations or engage in behaviors that put themselves and others at risk. If it is evident that a pattern of risk is evolving, it is advisable to conduct prevention planning with the young person.

Behavior analysis research has demonstrated the value of data in making decisions regarding appropriate treatments (Neef & Iwata, 1994)—and this characteristic has become most evident since the 1990s with the advent of functional analytic and functional assessment perspectives (Horner, 1994; Iwata, Dorsey, Slifer, Bauman, & Richman, 1994; Repp & Horner, 1999). The functional approach of behavior analysis calls for a pre-intervention assessment of environmental conditions that serve to maintain a specified behavior, and then uses assessment information to devise an intervention plan tailored to meet the circumstances and needs of the individual. The term *functional assessment* refers to the "process of gathering information that can be used to maximize the effectiveness and efficiency of behavioral support" (O'Neill et al., 1997, p. 3). Two of the primary outcomes of a functional assessment are 1) identification of the consequences that maintain the target behavior, which leads to inferences about the function or payoff of the behavior for that individual; and 2) identification of the antecedent conditions (situations, person) that help predict when a target behavior is more likely to occur and when a target behavior is less likely to occur.

When attempting to address high-risk behaviors or situations that youth and young adults engage in or experience, it is often helpful for us to understand the function or payoff of the behavior for them when formulating strategies to minimize their high-risk types of behaviors that may place them in harm's way. The application of this functional approach will be illustrated more fully under TIP Guideline 5, and the prevention planning process will be described and illustrated in Chapter 8.

Engage Young People in Positive Activities of Interest

One of the most effective strategies to reach youth and young adults is to assist them in becoming engaged with activities of interest to them. These activities of interest (e.g., bicycling, basketball, book clubs, working at a veterinarian's office) may set the occasion to 1) capture the young peoples' attention and enthusiasm; 2) remove them from boring or risky situations (e.g., hanging around drug-infested streets after school); 3) expose them to peers and/or adults who model more socially appropriate behavior; and 4) expose them to prompts, models, and contingencies from which new skills (e.g., conversational skills, a basketball hook shot) can be developed and reinforced. The engagement in such activities may also lead to the development of new, informal key players who may improve personal, social, and community outcomes for the young person.

Respect Cultural and Familial Values and Young Persons' Perspectives

For the TIP facilitators to serve these young people adequately, they need to be *culturally competent,* meaning they must demonstrate sensitivity and responsiveness to individual variation in gender, ethnicity, sexual orientation, social class, and other unique orientations and needs of each transition-age youth or young adult and his or her family. Having parents actively involved in the planning process can also be extremely beneficial in integrating important ethnic and familial cultural priorities into transition planning and futures orientation (Harper et al., 2006; Hernandez & Isaacs, 1998; Isaacs, Hopkins, Hicks, & Wang, 2008).

Although teenagers and parents are always a challenging mix, parents (or other family members or guardians) typically represent an essential element for the future success of these youth and young adults (Ryndak, Downing, Lilly, & Morrison, 1995). Often, young people have quite different ideas about their futures from those held by their parents. Sometimes transition facilitators are able to bring these ideas closer together by working in partnership with both the young person and their parents. At other times, however, all that transition facilitators can accomplish is assisting parents in understanding the developmental processes that their youth will need to experience and the level of support that will be helpful to the young people.

Young people have their own *youth cultures* that are more like exclusive clubs that are largely closed to adults. However, even though we, as adults, might not be able to keep up with the hottest scenes in hip hop, rap music, handshakes, and text-messaging language, we can still show an interest in what they like about an artist's music or the meaning of a particular song. Youth cultures are not only about ethnicity; rather, they are linked more to the *discovery* mode that is a part of this developmental period for transition-age young people. Thus, a young person's dominant cultural influence for a period of time might be that of a peer group, movie actress, gang, foster care history, and/or sexual identity (lesbian, gay, bisexual, transgender, intersex, and/or questioning community [LGBTIQ]; Gamache & Lazear, 2009).

In order to engage older youth and young adults, we must be open to their discovery mode while working with them on understanding the benefits and/or risks associated with their choices and behaviors. This is a delicate balance, but an important one in engaging young people and assisting them in staying healthy and safe and progressing toward adult roles that they might value.

2. Tailor Services and Supports to Be Accessible, Coordinated, Appealing, Nonstigmatizing, and Developmentally Appropriate—and Building on Strengths to Enable the Young People to Pursue Their Goals Across Relevant Transition Domains

Facilitate Young Persons' Goal Achievement Across Relevant Transition Domains

The TIP system is comprehensive in scope, encompassing three major setting-based domains—*employment/career, educational opportunities, and living situation*—as well as two domains that are relevant across all aspects of life—*personal effectiveness and wellbeing* and *community-life functioning* domains (see Figure 2.1 and Appendix 2.2). These five transition domains are shown in Figure 2.1 and are used with young people in this format because these are the arenas that seem to capture young people's attention and spark their interest in their futures.

The transition facilitator's function as a coach is to guide young people through the planning and goal-setting processes as well as help them navigate the rough waters involved in pursuing their

Figure 2.1.   The five transition domains. The three setting domains of *employment, education,* and *living situation*—and the *personal effectiveness and wellbeing* and *community-life functioning* domains shown in this figure—are useful in capturing young people's attention and their focus on their futures. The last two domains encompass several subdomains that are relevant to success in each of the other domains. Refer to Appendix 2.2 of this chapter for a complete listing of the transition domains, subdomains, and their elements.

goals across the transition domains. A complete outline of the transition domains, sub-domains, and their components is provided in Appendix 2.2.

Tailor Services and Supports to Be Developmentally Appropriate, Addressing the Needs and Building on the Strengths of Young People, Their Families, and Other Informal Key Players

The TIP system provides and facilitates a comprehensive array of community-based service and support options within each of the transition domains to accommodate the strengths, needs, and life circumstances of each young person. For example, in the employment domain, it is helpful if a system creates access to a range of work opportunities with varying levels of support available, including practicum and paid work experience (e.g., apprenticeships), transitional employment, supported employment, and competitive employment (Baer, 2003; Bond et al., 2003). Similarly, in the domain of personal effectivenes and well-being, supports and services may be needed by some young people to address behaviors that may limit their choices and options (e.g., managing anger, disagreeing appropriately, accepting constructive feedback) in home, school, and work settings.

Not every youth or young adult wants assistance across all of the transition domains or requires all of the services and supports related to a given domain. The objective within the TIP system is to meet the particular transition needs and priority goals of the young person, customizing the supports and services to the individual's needs and resources rather than basing them on preexisting program requirements. In other words, the type and intensity of supports and services provided during the transition process must match the priority needs and goals of the young person and his or her resources and settings. Albin, Lucyshyn, Horner, and Flannery (1996) referred to this approach in the design of interventions as *contextual fit*. The transition facilitator may also need to provide or connect the youth with a diverse set of interventions and supports (e.g., a relevant informal key player) to match emergent or current needs and goals (e.g., employability skills associated with maintaining a job, anger management, social problem-solving skills, self-advocacy, self-management of medications).

Ensure that Services and Supports Are Accessible, Coordinated, Appealing, and Nonstigmatizing

Although the administrators of a transition program may think that the program and its components provide continuity for young people and their families, these attributes of a system must be judged from the eyes of the beholders, that is, the young

"I don't want to attend a program where a bunch of old people sit around smoking and talking about their stuff."

person and his or her informal key players. Continuity refers to the extent to which relevant and timely supports and services are accessible to a young person and provided in a coordinated fashion. All too often there is no continuity across services. Similarly, a young person's perspective is needed to assess if a service is appealing and nonstigmatizing (Biddle & Gowen, 2009).

Jody's teacher is advocating that she be placed in special education. Her psychiatrist has just increased her medication for attention deficit/hyperactivity disorder (ADHD) despite the fact that it leaves her nauseated throughout the day. Her foster care caseworker is seeking to have Jody removed from her foster home of 4 years to be placed in a residential facility because she does not seem to be doing well in the foster home or in school, and Jody's mental health specialist at an adult mental-health day program where Jody goes after school wants her to attend more consistently.

Clearly, there is no continuity for Jody across the services being provided or planned. Not only are each of the providers functioning independently but also the services are not all accessible (e.g., Jody's foster mother states, "I can't always leave the other children in the afternoon to drive Jody to the mental health program") nor developmentally appropriate, appealing, and nonstigmatizing (e.g., Jody says, "I don't want to attend a program where a bunch of old people sit around smoking and talking about their stuff").

To ensure access to needed community resources and to create opportunities across all of the transition domains, collaborative links must be established at the young person's level and at the system level. At the young person's level, the TIP system has to assume responsibility to link the young person and his or her family to the resources, services, and supports that are appealing and appropriate to their changing needs and goals. Note that when a young person judges a support or service to be appealing, it probably would also be considered nonstigmatizing from his or her perspective.

At the system level, links are required with a broad array of child- and adult-serving systems. The development of networks of individuals and organizations to assist in working with a young person is also the responsibility of the TIP system. These efforts must include reaching out to ethnic communities so that culturally relevant supports are available to individuals who require them. Recommended approaches to developing these system-level collaborations are discussed and illustrated in Chapters 1 and 10, as well as the chapters in Section II of this handbook. Other resources related to the benefits and development of community collaborations at the transition level are Benz (2002); Certo and colleagues (2003); Clark, Deschênes, and colleagues (2008); and other documents available through the TIP web site (http://tip.fmhi.usf.edu) and the NNYT web site (http://nnyt.fmhi.usf.edu).

Balance the Transition Facilitators' Role with that of the Young People, Their Parents, and Other Informal and Formal Key Players

As was stated previously, the transition facilitators are at the heart of the TIP system—working with the young people, their parents, other family members, other informal and formal key players, and community representatives. The TIP facilitators work with young people to create an array of informal and/or formal key players and services to facilitate achievement of the young persons' goals across relevant transition domains. From the young person's perspective, access to a transition facilitator should maximize continuity between services that are being provided by different providers (e.g., school, vocational rehabilitation, mental health) and the supports being provided by parents and other informal key players. The TIP model encourages linking young people to informal supports within their home, work, school, and community environments whenever possible (Clark & Davis, 2000; Clark & Foster-Johnson, 1996). For example, a mentor might be hired to work with a young adult who needs to be guided away from a drug-involved peer group and into more community-acceptable leisure-time activities. Later, this role might be shifted to a cousin or an uncle with whom a relationship is being renewed, or even to a new friend with whom the young person has connected within the activity setting. Youth and young adults should be taught to identify and develop use of informal supports in their lives.

Transition facilitators collaborate first and foremost with the young people with whom they work and secondarily with an array of informal and formal key players and community representatives who are relevant to these young people and their transition needs (see Table 2.2). As mentioned earlier, the term *transition facilitator* is used to emphasize the function of *facilitating* the young person's future, not directing it. (Refer

Table 2.2.   Informal and formal key players and community supports who may be helpful collaborators with transition facilitators

Informal key players	Formal key players	Community supports
Parents and siblings	Case managers, support coordinators	Mentors from community organizations
Extended family members	Teachers, guidance counselors	Employers, supervisors, co-workers, and co-worker mentors
Friends	Employment specialists, job coaches	
Roommates and co-workers	Job developers	Spiritual leaders
Intimate partner, spouse, or life partner	Vocational rehabilitation specialists	Recreation specialists from Parks Departmet or YMCA
	School integration specialists	
	Postsecondary education liaisons	
	Behavior specialists, applied behavior analysts, mental health counselors, and therapists	
	Psychologists and psychiatrists	
	Physicians and other health care professionals	

Note: Some individuals listed as community supports or formal key players may come to serve as an informal key player depending on their relationships and roles with the young person.

to Program Manuals on the TIP web site for sample position descriptions for the transition facilitator and TIP program supervisor.)

3. Acknowledge and Develop Personal Choice and Social Responsibility with Young People

Developmentally, these youth and young adults are at a level at which they will be making decisions regardless of whether we think they are ready to do so. Thus, we need to design our service system and practices to accommodate this reality. Certainly, all of the guidelines and practices contribute to this approach (e.g., futures planning)—and this third guideline describes two other features of the model that are extremely helpful in working with these young people.

Encourage Problem-Solving Methods, Decision Making, and Evaluation of Impact on Self and Others

Life comes with a continuing stream of problems—or opportunities when reframed. Using social problem-solving and decision-making methods can be particularly helpful tools for young people and for those who work with them.

One social problem-solving method that can be modeled and taught to young people is *SODAS* (Situation, Options, Disadvantages, Advantages, Solution). Figure 2.2 illustrates the components of this relatively simple method. The first step involves working with the young person in describing as clearly as possible the current *situation*. With the situation defined, a brainstorming process is undertaken to generate as many *options* (i.e., approaches, actions) to the situation as possible. This process of generating options should be judgment free, not eliminating or refuting any of the options that the young person or you put on the table.

The next steps involve listing all of the likely *advantages* and *disadvantages* for the young person related to each option. Once this is accomplished for each of the options, the young person may be better able to make an informed decision. The choice that the young person makes represents a *solution*. The arrows on Figure 2.2 illustrate the reality that every *solution* (i.e., actions taken or not) then creates a new *situation*, which may or may not need to be problem solved.

This problem-solving method can set the occasion for improved decision making and self-evaluation of the impact of the young person's actions on self and others. Thus, SODAS can be a valuable teaching tool for working with young people—and a tool that many young people begin to adopt as a method for approaching simple and complex social problem situations that come their way.

We have developed a personnel training module to assist staff and supervisors in learning the SODAS method. The module is titled, *A Social Problem-Solving Process for Working with Transition Age Youth and*

S   Situation

O   Options (brainstorming)

D   Disadvantages*

A   Advantages*

S   Solution

*Likely advantages and disadvantages associated with each option.

Figure 2.2.   SODAS (**S**ituation, **O**ptions, **D**isadvantages/**A**dvantages, **S**olution) problem-solving method. The arrows illustrate the reality that every *solution* (i.e., actions taken or not) then creates a new *situation*, which may or may not need to be problem solved.

Young Adults: The SODAS Framework. The module is available through the TIP web site, and arrangements can also be made for competency training on this method and the other six core practices that are essential to the TIP model (core practices: strength discovery and needs assessment, futures planning, rationales, in-vivo teaching, social problem solving, prevention planning on high-risk behaviors and situations, and mediation with young people and other key players).

Balance One's Work with Young People Between Two Axioms

Seasoned transition facilitators operate by two axioms that guide their ongoing coaching, teaching, counseling, and relationship development in their work with youth and young adults:

1. Maximize the likelihood of the success of young people.

2. Allow young people to encounter natural consequences through life experience.

Guided by these axioms, facilitators use mentoring, functional assessment, teaching of skills, contingency contracting, counseling, humor, coaching, and problem solving to maximize the likelihood that the youth will succeed. The facilitators also recognize the powerful role that life experience plays in teaching young people through their successes and failures. It may be that Elyse has gone through two social skills training groups, but it is only after being fired from her fourth job that she displays any receptivity to learning how to follow instructions and to problem solve with authority figures. Similarly, it could be that Hector "fires" us and only after experiencing the street drug scene for a few months does he return to ask, "What's this about your being able to help me get a job?"

Sometimes life's natural consequences can come through lighter experiences as well. Gianna was delighted to have secured a summer job as a clerk in a small gift and snack shop in a hotel lobby in Orlando. On her third day, after serving a customer a hot dog, he asks her, "Where are the condiments?" A bit startled by the question, she answered, "You'll have to get those at a drugstore." As the customer smiled and explained what condiments were, she had to laugh about not knowing the difference between a condiment and a condom.

4. Ensure a Safety Net of Support by Involving a Young Person's Parents, Family Members, and Other Informal and Formal Key Players

Each of us benefits by having a support network around us. As youth and young adults are seeking their own identity, they may not always value the relationships of those who have been there for them. Transition facilitators work with young people on understanding the benefit of maintaining and expanding their social support network and the reciprocal nature of relationships.

Involve Parents, Family Members, and Other Informal and Formal Key Players

A young person's parents, members of the extended family, and other informal key players may be extremely rich resources in identifying youth strengths, helping the youth plan for success, contributing to the youth's safety net, and advocating for the youth. For many young people, their survival and success are related directly to a parent, aunt, girlfriend, or spouse who hung in there with them over time.

Parents, Family Members, or Other Informal Key Players May Need Assistance in Understanding this Transition Period or May Need Services/Supports for Themselves

Everyone understands that the adolescent period can be challenging but may not understand all of the biological, neurological, social, and physical changes that define this period and beyond. Transition facilitators can assist parents and other informal players greatly by being supportive listeners to the experiences that they have had with their young person and providing some additional insight into this developmental period where appropriate.

Some family members or other informal key players may also need supports or services for their own situations (e.g., unemployment, housing, drug abuse). The transition facilitators should guide them to relevant natural, formal, or community resources. Both of these previously described functions are not the exclusive role of the transition facilitators. For example, some transition sites have created parent-to-parent supports or parent/family specialists to assist family members with these issues.

Assist in Mediating Differences in the Perspectives of Young People, Parents, and Other Informal and Formal Key Players

It is common for youth and parents to have quite different perspectives about their short- and long-term goals. Transition facilitators often assist in mediating these differences between parents and the young person, enabling the youth to pursue his or her interests and maximize the level of support possible from parents and other informal key players.

Mediation topics can range from curfew time on the weekends to approaches for dealing with substance use.

We have developed a personnel training module for guiding personnel in a mediation method. The module is titled *Mediated Social Problem Solving with Young People and Other Key Players* (refer to TIP web site).

Facilitate an Unconditional Commitment to the Young Person Among His or Her Key Players

VanDenBerg and Grealish (1996) defined *unconditional commitment* as never denying services because of extreme severity of disability, being willing to change services as the needs of the child and family change, and never rejecting the child or family from services. Although the TIP site recognizes that young people 18 years or older may refuse service, transition facilitators must remain creative and determined to stick with them to the extent possible, adjusting services and supports to meet these individuals' changing needs. Furthermore, a careful analysis of when and why youth refuse services may lead to a change in facilitation and service delivery strategies.

Create an Atmosphere of Hopefulness, Fun, and a Future Focus

Unconditional commitment is a powerful expression of the TIP staff's hopefulness and positive affirmation of the young person's worth and merit (Deschênes & Clark, 1998). This feature of hopefulness, fun, and future is manifested by staff encouraging young people, speaking respectfully, involving youth and parents as partners, respecting youth's choices, and sharing a sense of humor. The strength-discovery and goal-planning processes also set the tone for a futures focus.

5. Enhance Young Persons' Competencies to Assist Them in Achieving Greater Self-Sufficiency and Confidence

Two essential ingredients for the long-term success of youth and young adults are having meaningful relationships and the social and life skills that enable these individuals to negotiate the obstacle course of their life pathway. This fifth guideline focuses on the importance of our role in assisting youth and young adults to learn competencies that will be relevant to them and their goals.

Utilize Information and Data from Strength Discovery and Functional Assessment Methods

Assessment information can be collected through numerous methods concerning a young person's knowledge and skills related to the transition domains (i.e., employment and career, educational opportunities, living situation, personal effectiveness and wellbeing, and community-life functioning). Some of these methods rely on direct observations of discrete behaviors (e.g., functional behavior analysis [Miltenberger, 2004; O'Neill et al., 1997]); other methods use interviewing or behavioral checklists with the target individual and those around him or her (e.g., Transition Planning Inventory [Clark & Patton, 1997]), and other skill assessment methods use a combination of the two strategies (e.g., functional behavior assessment [Hieneman et al., 1999; Liberman, 2008; O'Neill et al., 1997]). Functional assessment assists transition facilitators in understanding the possible "function" that a behavior is serving for a young person. For example, Katrina, a 16-year-old girl, may be running away from a group home to escape the coercive interactions with staff or running to the reinforcers of being with her siblings who are at a foster home or to the reinforcers of access to her friends or street drugs. Using functional assessments and function-based interventions with Katrina and 13 other youth who had high rates of runaway behaviors from foster care placements, we demonstrated that these individually tailored interventions reduced their runaway behaviors and increased their days in safer settings (Clark, Crosland, et al., 2008).

Through strength discovery and functional assessment, the transition facilitator is learning about the strengths, needs, interests, social support systems, and possible functions that behaviors serve for the young person. Armed with this type of information, the transition facilitator and his or her team can formulate hypotheses as to how to best support the young person toward choices that might prove more beneficial to him or her. Consider the example of Juan.

Juan, a 21-year-old young man, may be refusing to take his prescription medications for his bipolar diagnosis to avoid or escape the aversive side-effects that he experiences on his current medications, or to experience the reinforcing feelings he has when he is "in control" and self-medicating with alcohol and marijuana. Juan's transition facilitator has learned through strength conversations with him and others, review of records, and observations when visiting him at his apartment and work settings that since Juan went off his medications and began self-medicating on alcohol and marijuana, he is spending most of his free time alone in his own bedroom of his apartment and is not meeting up with his friends after work. Juan is also on the verge of losing his job for showing up intoxicated on two recent occasions and being verbally aggressive with a co-worker. His job is in line with what he wants to do in the future, and it enables him to have this apartment placement and keep his "cool" but old car operating.

The transition facilitator and her team of facilitators came up with several hypotheses about Juan:

1. He would be devastated by the loss of his job and the possible consequences of losing his apartment and car.

2. Juan had functioned rather well on an earlier prescription medication that did not seem to have the side-effects of the new drug prescribed by a new psychiatrist.

3. He wants to be in charge of his own life.

4. He would like to reconnect with two of his friends with whom he played sports activities.

5. He would possibly respond well if a young adult mentor who has lived a similar situation and the transition facilitator were to talk with him to help him understand the possible consequences of his current behavior and the possibility of stabilizing on the previous medication that might enable him to advance his job and career possibilities and access his friends and leisure-time activities.

They would also talk with Juan about whether he would want to resume seeing a therapist who he had found extremely helpful in the past. These hypotheses assist the transition facilitator in formulating strategies for working more effectively with Juan to improve the likelihood of his improving his transition outcomes.

Some traditional and standardized types of assessment can be helpful. One cautionary note is that because most young people have not had sufficient experience in various work, school, and living situations, traditional paper and pencil assessments typically yield limited information. Furthermore, even if the instruments have been standardized, it is unlikely that they would have been standardized on young people, particularly those with EBD (Bullis, Tehan, & Clark, 2000).

The initial intake and continuing strength discovery is extremely valuable in learning about a young person's interests, background, dreams, knowledge, and skills related to each of the transition domains (Corbitt & Paris, 2002). Based on the transition facilitators' professional training and experience, they may be able to use clinical records and psychiatric evaluations to further inform their work with young people and the challenges they present on the mental health, health, or substance abuse fronts. A supervisor needs to provide transition facilitators with guidance as to their role as coaches versus therapists with their young adults. Sometimes it is also helpful for the transition team to be able to call on consultants (e.g., psychologist, nurse, psychiatrist, behavior analyst, youth's therapist) for particular expertise as necessary.

Some sites find it helpful to use additional structured assessments such as the Ansell-Casey Life Skills Assessments (ACLSA; Nollan, Horn, Downs, & Pecora, 2002). There are parallel assessments for different age ranges, with the 13- to 15-year-olds being served by the ACLSA III and the young people 16 years or older being served by ACLSA IV. This system is web-based, available free of charge, and has some language options (e.g., English, Spanish, French). The ACLSA is based on a youth report and/or a caregiver (i.e., interested party who has observed the youth extensively) report on what the youth or young adult knows (e.g., "I know how to wash clothes." "I know how to use the bus system"). If a young person and a caregiver both complete an assessment, it is likely that the skill profiles for the youth from the two perspectives will vary. ACLSA advocates that the young person, the interested party, and the case worker use the two profiles to discuss where there are agreements and discrepancies across their perspectives on the youth's life skills (Nollan et al., 2002; http://www.caseylife skills.org/pages/whatis.htm). The Casey Family Programs also provides a web-based assessment focused on transition-age youth and young adults who are in foster care, emancipated, or in an aftercare program. This is referred to as the Chafee Assessment and is available on the organization's web site: http://www.chafee.org.

Some sites are finding one of the transition versions of the Child and Adolescent Needs and Strengths (CANS; Lyons, Uziel-Miller, Reyes, & Sokol, 2000) to be helpful to them. The transition versions are known as the Adult Needs and Strength Assessment–Indiana (ANSA–Indiana version, http://ibhas.in.gov) and the Adult Needs and Strength Assessment-Transition Version (ANSA-T, http://www.praedfoundation .org).These assessment tools may prove useful in the initial version and in some of the ongoing transition planning activities.

The strength-discovery and functional assessments provide transition personnel with an understanding of not only a young person's interests and resources but also how he or she functions in real-life situations and settings. This information and the associated hypotheses that evolve from these data can be very helpful in the transition planning and tailoring of supports and services. For a description and sample forms related to these types of assessment methods as applied to vocational settings, refer to a book edited by Bullis and Fredericks (2002), *Vocational and Transition Services for Adolescents with Emotional and Behavioral Disorders: Strategies and Best Practices*—paying particular attention to the chapter by Corbitt and Paris (2002) and several by Nishioka (2002a, b, c, d).

Teach Meaningful Skills Relevant to the Young Person Across Transition Domains

Competence in a variety of skills is necessary for successful entry into the workplace and independent community living. In a TIP system, skill development refers to teaching skills in community settings that will equip youth and young adults with the competencies to meet the demands they encounter in their schooling, work, and community settings and in their social relationships. The identification and development of skills is aided by functional assessments, instructional efforts, and curriculum activities focusing on teaching these necessary skills (e.g., budgeting of personal earnings, completion of job applications, anger management, vocational skills) in a context that is meaningful and relevant to the young person (Bullis, Nishoka-Evans, Fredericks, & Davis, 1993; Dunlap, Kern-Dunlap, Clarke, & Robbins, 1991; Horner, Sprague, & Flannery, 1993; Kopelwicz, Liberman, & Zarate, 2006; O'Neill, et al., 1997; Unger, 1994). For teaching to be most meaningful for a young person, it should be delivered on an individual basis. It is less likely that a group training format will serve a young person in a fashion that will be adequately focused or timely for him or her; however, small group training sessions are used at many transition sites for particular skill development (e.g., Aggression Replacement Therapy [ART]) by certified trainers. Another example for which small group sessions might work well occurs at some sites that enlist young adult peer associates to conduct employability modules for one to four young people who want to know how to complete job applications or prepare for job interviews.

Use In-Vivo Teaching Strategies in Relevant Community Settings

In-vivo teaching refers to conducting instruction and coaching of the youth or young adults in the relevant natural community settings of home, school, work, and community to develop or assist in the generalization of relevant skills to the appropriate people and settings (Liberman, 2008, Liberman, Glynn, Blair, Ross, & Marder, 2002). Although most young people with EBD would not find it appealing to have a "job coach" coming onto a work site with him or her, there are ways to accomplish in-vivo teaching through natural supports that are already a part of the worksite (e.g., co-worker mentors). Cellular technologies also hold promising practice for prompting through voice mail or texting a note on the use of skills, securing feedback on how the use of the skill went, and staying connected with these mobile youth and young adults.

Creative teachers and independent living specialists can make their classroom instruction more community relevant to students by 1) bringing real-life stimulus materials and situations into their classrooms (e.g., set up student bank accounts), 2) building on young people's preferences and interests in the assignments, and 3) providing youth with effective individualized instruction to teach skills that are relevant to their daily lives. Researchers have found that youth taught with these instructional strategies tend to increase their ability to acquire the necessary skills, become more motivated to learn new skills, generalize learning to other settings, and decrease their problem behaviors (Dyer, Dunlap, & Winterling, 1990; Elliott, Sheridan, Gresham, & Knoff, 1989; Foster-Johnson, Ferro, & Dunlap, 1992; Kopelwicz, Liberman, & Zarate, 2006; Liberman et al., 2002; Van Reusen & Bos, 1994). Such strategies can also lead to increased graduation rates for these youth (Frank, Sitlington, & Carson, 1991).

Practice opportunities experienced in real-life environments are particularly important for young people with EBD because many of them have had extremely poor experiences related to traditional classroom instruction (Bullis & Fredricks, 2002; Wehman, 2006). In a community-based instruction model, teachers and other transition practitioners work in collaboration to teach selected academic, vocational, and functional life skills in natural community environments such as work sites, schools, homes, shopping malls, recreation areas, and vocational/technical training settings. Community-based learning may also be a means by which students can earn high school credits toward graduation while acquiring relevant experience (Cheney, Hagner, Malloy, Cormier, & Bernstein, 1998).

Transition facilitators and other personnel working with transition-age youth and young adults need to be effective teachers along with classroom educators, behavior specialists, counselors, case managers, foster parents, and mentors. As teachers, they need to be able to create or recognize opportunities to teach. This component of teaching is illustrated through a staff training series that the lead author of this handbook conducted for a newly formed team of five seasoned case managers, members of a transition team formed in a large metropolitan area to serve young adults with serious mental health conditions (i.e., minimum of three psychiatric hospitalizations in lifetime and at least one within the past year). This consultant spent extensive time in the field shadowing case managers and the young adults with whom they worked during activities in community settings. One of the many occasions that exemplified the need to recognize opportunities to teach came when Martha (a case manager) picked up Rhonda from school to go to a doctor's appointment. Rhonda had missed one of her periods and was concerned that she might be pregnant. Martha conducted some good counseling and problem solving, and incorporated some humor to soften some of the sensitive issues while driving to the doctor's office. As they walked into the six-story medical complex, Martha found the building directory and the doctor's suite number, negotiated their way through security, led Rhonda to the elevator, punched the fourth- floor button, and after finding the doctor's suite, announced that Rhonda was here for her appointment.

What a lost opportunity to assess and teach Rhonda how to negotiate a large medical or business complex to obtain required services. These in-vivo opportunities are ideal for assessing an individual's competencies and for providing highly effective teaching. Rhonda's team of case managers talked independence but often missed important opportunities to assess and/or teach community-relevant skills. After some mini-workshops on this issue, additional field shadowing, and coaching across the case managers they became much more effective teachers.

In their teaching or coaching role, transition facilitators create practice opportunities through simulated situations (e.g., behavioral rehearsal), as well as in natural situations and settings. Facilitators, through their relationship with young people, can serve to reinforce their use of new skills and progress on goals. Skill acquisition and maintenance requires that young people are reinforced in the use of these skills (in appropriate situations) through social praise, recognition, tangible reinforcers, and natural consequences in community settings (Blase, Jaeger, & Fixsen, 1988; Liberman, 2008). When teaching encompasses these types of maintenance or generalization strategies (e.g., practice in a variety of settings with various people and situations present, gradually phasing out training from natural settings, booster training sessions), the acquisition of new skills occurs, and the use of these skills over time and across settings is enhanced (Kazdin, Bass, Siegel, & Thomas, 1989; Lochman, 1992).

The acquisition and generalization of new skills can also be facilitated through the use of *rationales* (Blase & Fixsen, 1989; Blase, Jaeger, & Fixsen, 1988). *Rationales* assist young people in bridging their behavior and the natural consequences they are likely to encounter. As Figure 2.3

illustrates, rationale statements can link the likelihood of positive natural consequences following appropriate behavior or the likelihood of negative natural consequences following inappropriate behavior.

The following are some examples of rationale statements:

- "If you learn to greet people appropriately, you can use this skill on your job interview and it will be more likely that you will get the job."

- "When you cheat in class, you are likely to get caught and may lose your place on the wrestling team."

- "When you let your parents know where you are so they do not worry about you, they will be more likely to trust you and let you do more things on your own."

- "If you engage in unprotected sex, you may become pregnant or get AIDS or other STDs. I care about you and your future success. Perhaps you might want to make an appointment with a public health nurse to learn more about safe sex, abstinence, and birth control?"

- "When you are able to manage your anger, it is more likely that you will be able to keep this new job and a regular paycheck coming in."

Personnel working with young people should use rationale statements to help link their behaviors and choices to likely outcomes of *benefit* or *risk* to them. The facilitators should not expect that rationales will change behavior immediately. *Consequences* change behavior. Rationales do provide a brief, real-life reason for working with the young person on a particular new or replacement skill, converting statements from nagging to a reason that is more likely to be seen as relevant to the youth because it describes possible benefit or risk for him or her.

Rationales also assist young people in understanding the negative natural consequences that their inappropriate behaviors create for them. Rationales assist youth and young adults in making more informed and hopefully wiser choices over time. Rationales are even more meaningful to youth when they are personal to them (i.e., individualized to match their interests and goals). Thus, strength discovery leads to more meaningful rationales, as does soliciting the types of benefits or risks through discussion with the young people. We have devel-

Appropriate behavior >>>>likely>>>>**Positive natural consequences**
Inappropriate behavior >>>>likely>>>>**Negative natural consequences**

Figure 2.3.   Rationale statements link the likelihood of positive natural consequences following appropriate behavior or the likelihood of negative natural consequences following inappropriate behavior.

oped a personnel training module (available on the TIP web site) to assist personnel in learning the use of rationales. The module is titled, *Developing and Using Rationales for Working with Transition Age Youth and Young Adults*.

Develop Skills Related to Self-Management, Problem-Solving, Self-Advocacy, and Self-Evaluation of the Impact of One's Choices and Actions on Self and Others

In working with youth and young adults, we are assisting them in becoming empowered to address and advocate for solutions to issues related to their rights, their needs, and the provision of essential services and supports. Transition facilitators need to work with the young person to teach and encourage self-determination and self-advocacy. Self-determination involves skills such as choice clarification, decision making, goal setting, self-monitoring, self-evaluation, and assertiveness. The facilitators and other personnel involved with young people provide frequent opportunities for them to express their preferences through choices, clarify possible benefits and risks associated with their choices, make decisions, and advocate for themselves. An important goal is that young people learn to speak on their own behalf and to gradually assume responsibility for their own futures.

6. Maintain an Outcome Focus in the TIP System at the Young Person, Program, and Community Levels

Focus on a Young Person's Goals and the Tracking of His or Her Progress

The five guidelines previously discussed involve processes that can assist youth and young adults in achieving successful outcomes across the transition domains (refer to Table 2.1 and Appendix 2.1). For each transition goal established by the young person, written, measurable objectives should be established to track progress on individualized goals and successes over time. For example, Sasha, at 15½ years old, may be interested in getting an after-school or weekend job at a veterinarian's office. She and her planning partners may establish four related goals to be completed by the time she is 16 and eligible to work: 1) Sasha will be able to complete job applications with 100% accuracy for all essential information across four different forms of applications; 2) Sasha will be able to correctly recognize and label the 25 most common types of dogs and cats from pictures and from viewing them at pet stores; 3) Sasha will complete three consecutive role-play interviews and two in the field using at least 90% of the interview components; and 4) Sasha will secure at least two interviews at veterinarians' offices or other pet-related settings. It will help Sasha greatly if she can see her progress on her goals weekly and make adjustments if having difficulties or setbacks.

Although most agencies have their own treatment planning forms, many site personnel have found it helpful to adopt or adapt the TIP Transition Planning Form (http://tip.fmhi.usf.edu) or use the web-based TAPIS Goal Achiever (Karpur, Clark, Deschênes, & Knab, 2007), which is described more fully in this chapter and in Chapter 10.

Evaluate the Responsiveness and Effectiveness of the TIP System

The TIP system's effectiveness should also be assessed. Table 2.3 provides an overview of TIP system objectives that reflect the types of goal areas that individuals are working on and the transition domain outcomes that the TIP system is attempting to achieve. Assessing key progress and outcome indicators (based on the young adult's outcomes in the five transition domains) can help measure the effectiveness of the TIP system. For example, aggregation of data regarding individuals' employment goals allows for determination of the percentage of young people who have 1) part-time and full-time jobs, 2) earnings over a particular wage per hour, 3) employer-paid benefits, and 4) jobs that are on desired career tracks. These types of key outcome indicators, if tracked over an extended period of time, can provide stakeholders and policy makers with valuable information on the responsiveness and effectiveness of the TIP system as being implemented at their site.

The Transition to Adulthood Program Information System (TAPIS; Clark, Karpur, Deschênes, & Knab, 2007; Karpur et al., 2007) has been developed as a web-based progress follow-along instrument. The TAPIS has two major components: 1) the TAPIS Goal Achiever, and 2) the TAPIS Progess Tracker. The TAPIS Goal Achiever is used with young people in assisting in the setting and tracking of their own individualized goals. For each goal there can be several tasks and/or strategies to accomplish the goal, as well as other information that youth and their transition facilitators might find helpful toward the accomplishment of their goals (e.g., person responsible for task completion, target date, and objective indicators of progress). The TAPIS Goal Achiever provides the young person with an indication of the progress that he or she is making on the individualized goals; and also the young person, transition facilitator, and the program supervisor can see on what proportion of goals he or she is making progress or has completed over the past 6 months.

Table 2.3. Transition to Independence Process (TIP) system objectives across the transition domains

The Transition to Independence Process (TIP) system aims at achieving better transition outcomes across the domains of employment, education, living situation, personal effectiveness and wellbeing, and community-life functioning. Here are some examples of possible goal areas that youth and young adults might set for themselves:

EMPLOYMENT
- Engages in employment exploration and experience (e.g., job shadowing, practicum, apprenticeships)
- Improves employment stability (e.g., staying employed, planned changes versus firings and walkouts)
- Makes employment and career advancement (e.g., wage per hour increases over time, promotion, career-track type positions versus entry-level jobs only, benefits available and increase over time)

EDUCATION
- Completes high school or general equivalency diploma
- Explores career options (e.g., interviewing people in careers, library explorations and web searches on careers, visiting community trade schools and colleges)
- Pursues postsecondary education or training (e.g., enrollment, certificates and/or degrees)

LIVING SITUATION
- Lives in home-type living arrangements (e.g., settings such as apartment, house, college dorm versus group home or residential facility)
- Improves stability in housing location (e.g., planned moves versus evictions and fleeing to avoid rent)
- Increases stability in living with a preferred person(s)
- Feels safe with respect to location and roommates (e.g., feels safe in neighborhood at 10 p.m.)
- Decreases use of restrictive placements (e.g., number of days in crisis unit, treatment center, jail)

PERSONAL EFFECTIVENESS AND WELLBEING
- Enjoys positive relationships with peers, coworkers, and other informal supports
- Maintains contacts with family and/or relatives (frequency and satisfaction)
- Develops and maintains a primary intimate relationship (i.e., stability over time and satisfaction)
- Demonstrates assertiveness, conflict-resolution, and problem-solving with others
- Copes with daily stress
- Maintains balanced diet, exercise, and rest

(*continued*)

Table 2.3. *Continued*

- Manages risk situations and risk behaviors (e.g., avoiding or decreasing substance abuse, violence, criminal activities, sexually transmitted diseases, teen or unwanted pregnancies, injecting illegal drugs)
- Decreases use of public aid support over time (e.g., Temporary Assistance for Needy Families [TANF], food stamps, Medicaid, general assistance, housing subsidy)
- Accesses and uses preventative and necessary medical and dental services
- Maintains and self-manages prescribed medications (e.g., adheres to the prescription such as taking the medication with food and knowing possible side effects)

COMMUNITY-LIFE FUNCTIONING
- Engages in leisure time and recreational activities
- Locates needed or interesting resources in the community (e.g., recreational activities, bicycle paths, emergency room, libraries, free concerts or events)
- Attends or volunteers with community organizations, activities, support groups, spiritual supports
- Utilizes mobility recourses (e.g., bicycle, buses, walking, light rail) to gain access to community environments of relevance
- Uses daily living skills to function in living environment and other relevant community environments (e.g., meal preparation, budgeting, managing personal income, securing driver's license, filing income taxes, initiating utilities on one's apartment)

Note: These examples are aligned with the Transition to Adulthood Program Information system (TAPIS) Progress Tracker and the individualized goals that a young person might be working on within the TAPIS Goal Achiever. (See Guideline 6 and Chapter 10 for more information regarding TAPIS.)

The data from the TAPIS Goal Achiever can also be aggregated across young people to provide the team and program with a sense of credit for progress they are making with their young people. For example, the team and supervisor, and their community funding entity, might want to know information such as, "Of the young people who have not been employed over the past 6 months, what percentage have engaged in job shadowing; have met competencies in preparation of their resumes, job applications, or interviewing skills; or have participated in practicum work experience?" These types of questions can also be gathered related to prerequisite activities related to exploring or preparing for postsecondary career training or college, or to address questions related to the combined transition markers of either preparing for postsecondary work and/or school/training.

The second major component of TAPIS is the TAPIS Progress Tracker. The purpose of the progress tracker is to assess and track, on a quarterly basis, a young person's progress and/or difficulty in transition across the five transition domains: employment and careers, education, living situation, personal effectiveness and wellbeing (sub-domains), and community-life functioning (sub-domains) (see Appendix 2.2). The TAPIS is designed to assist transition facilitators and program supervisors in the provision of an effective transition to adulthood program. TAPIS yields reports relevant to personnel at each level of their work in an attempt to ensure that the effective services and supports are being provided to youth and young adults to advance their progress toward adulthood functioning. It also enables personnel to query their data to address questions such as, "Over the past 12 months, what percent of youth have graduated from high school? What percent of young adults are working and/or enrolled in postsecondary education (e.g., college or vocational/technical career training)? What percent of young people with previous criminal involvement at the 18-month assessment are no longer involved with such? What percent of young people at the 12-month assessment are reporting that their mental health or substance abuse conditions are not interfering, or only minimally interfering, with their functioning in their personal relationships, schooling, and/or working?"

TAPIS is more fully described in Chapter 10 and on the TIP web site (http://tip.fmhi.usf.edu), and as a web-based instrument on the Mosaic Network web site (http://www.mosaic-network.com).

The type and depth of assessment and tracking that an organization wants to pursue will determine which of the instruments and methods the organization might want to adopt. We find that most transition sites are leaning in the direction of using one of the following instruments: Transition Follow-Along Checklist (Bullis & Fredericks, 2002); Ansell-Casey Life Skills Assessment; Casey Family Program Chaffee Assessment; or TAPIS (Clark et al., 2007; Karpur et al., 2007; http://www.mosaic-network.com).

Use Process and Outcome Measures
for Continuous TIP System Improvement

Unless the TIP guidelines and practices are incorporated adequately, individual and systemic outcomes will never be achieved. Thus, measures of process implementation for system improvement assist stakeholders by providing a periodic check of the TIP system's responsiveness in the provision of quality services and support.

One of the important quality improvement processes involves the use of a *Case-Based Review*. The purposes of this process are twofold:

1) inform and enrich the transition team's work with specific young people; and 2) set the occasion to enhance the knowledge and competencies of the transition facilitators and other program personnel in the application of the TIP guidelines and practices, aiming to improve the progress and outcomes of youth and young adults with EBD and their families. The Case-Based Review process should be conducted with your transition site personnel only. This would not include the young person and other stakeholders. This is an educative process to enhance competency of the transition facilitators and other transition personnel, in a setting where they can share their difficulties, frustrations, efforts, and requests for assistance; celebrate their successes; and explore alternative ways of assisting the young person. The Case-Based Review sets the occasion to examine, in depth, two or three young people every 2 weeks. Selecting a youth or young adult for an in-depth Case-Based Review should be based on the current needs of the young person as well as how this young person might further inform your transition team's knowledge and competencies.

In preparation for a Case-Based Review, the transition facilitator completes a Descriptive Outline of a Transition-Age Young Person. A Descriptive Outline provides a brief written summary of a young person, highlighting such things as his or her strengths, challenges related to his or her transition, his or her goals, and the progress or barriers associated with each. The Descriptive Outline should provide as much specific quantitative information as is available regarding progress on goal achievement (e.g., charts, graphs, numerical information).

In addition to Case-Based Reviews, the Descriptive Outline can be used by transition facilitators and other transition-related personnel in case consultations for the purpose of problem solving, planning, coordinating, and celebrating successes. Some programs use this form for a shorthand documentation of a young person's progress on a monthly basis. The Descriptive Outline can then provide the basis for quarterly and/or biannual summaries and, when written up as a brief young person study, it can serve as one level of program evaluation illustrating progress, continuing program or systemic barriers, and highlighting program successes. The *Case-Based Review Administration Manual and Descriptive Outline* are available under the Personnel Training section of the TIP web site.

The NNYT team has also developed a Transition Program Fidelity Assessment Protocol for assisting sites in determining their strengths and weaknesses in the delivery and array of supports and services for youth and young adults with EBD and their families (Deschênes, Herrygers, & Clark, 2008). Chapter 10 illustrates additional quality assurance measures and processes in using data for continuing quality improvement. For more information on these quality assurance instruments, please visit the NNYT web site (http://nnyt.fmhi.usf.edu) and the TIP Model web site (http://tip.fmhi.usf.edu).

7. Involve Young People, Parents, and Other Community Partners in the TIP System at the Practice, Program, and Community Levels

Maximize the Involvement of Young People, Family Members, and Other Informal and Formal Key Players and Relevant Community Representatives

As has been illustrated through the previous six guidelines, transition facilitators and others working with youth and young adults should respect and encourage young people's connections with their informal, formal, and community support persons. Although certain formal key players (e.g., counselor, case manager) may wish to remain connected with a young person for extended periods, all too often, funding or other eligibility criteria limit this formal linkage. Whatever can be done to assist young people in maintaining and extending their positive informal and community supports will be invaluable on a long-term basis (Clark & Crosland, 2008; Courtney & Dworsky, 2006).

Tap the Talents of Peers and Mentors

Peer mentors and other natural mentors can often relate to young people and share experiences with them that parents and other formal providers cannot communicate as effectively. Peers and mentors can be tapped in many creative ways. TIP systems that hire peer mentors and peer associates to work collaboratively with transition facilitators report that, typically, this arrangement is extremely beneficial for both the mentors and those young people with whom they are working.

Peer support groups can be valued by peers and can vary greatly in their formation, operation, and purpose. Some peer support groups are formulated and operated by peers with little guidance from formal personnel, whereas others are co-managed by the peers and program personnel. The purposes of peer support groups range from recreation club and community-life success to postsecondary school achievement and career achievement. An example of one peer support group was the

Employment Achievement Recognition Group that was formed by two peer mentors and the young people. The purpose of the group was to provide a monthly meeting during which young people who were employed or were seeking employment could come together to celebrate successes, learn about employment-related issues, and support each other. Membership in this group was voluntary and included young people who had already "graduated" from the program and were out in the employment sector as well as young people seeking to secure their first job or find a new position. The meetings were typically held in the basement of a church and occurred over a dinner that was provided by the church; the meal was prepared by some church members and young people who volunteered to assist in the meal preparation and clean-up. (Each member of the group had to assist with grocery shopping, meal preparation, and/or clean-up at least once every four meetings.) The young people also established a chair and vice chair position to organize and run the meetings. The chairperson secured suggestions for topics and identified members or outside speakers to present. Many youth and young adults have suggested that they benefited greatly from the support, guidance, and fun that this peer support group provided.

For a complete description of a peer support program, please refer to Chapter 7. Also, for a more structured version of a vocational support group, refer to Nishioka (2002e).

Some TIP system sites are using mentors to personally guide young people in settings relevant to their goals (Linnehan, 2003; Westerlund, Granucci, Gamache, & Clark, 2006). College mentors in postsecondary educational and training settings, roommate mentors in an apartment setting, and co-worker mentors in employment settings are a few examples. Mentors may be paid or unpaid. Many employees and supervisors have served as mentors in the work place—teaching and guiding young people in becoming acquainted with different types of jobs, workplace expectations, and the social aspects of the setting. Examples have included nursing home facilities and conference hotels in which 15–25 young people are working, each being mentored by a co-worker across jobs ranging from housekeeping and food service to maintenance and bookkeeping. In large work sites such as these, typically there is an employment specialist on site to coordinate the program to ensure that 1) young people are receiving the exposure and guidance in areas of interest to them; 2) young people are learning necessary employability and job skills; 3) co-worker mentors are provided individualized guidance on how to work effectively with their particular young person; 4) all parties know when to seek assistance; and 5) the pairings are proving to be safe and helpful. An employment specialist coordinator might be a program employee, an employee of the company, or jointly funded by the company and the program.

Partner with Young People, Parents, and Others in the TIP System Governance and Stewardship

The greater the sense of ownership that young people, parents, and others have in the TIP system, the more likely it is that the system will be valued and have a positive impact. The involvement of young people and parents in the governance (e.g., participation on management boards as a community partner, in decision making, in advisory committee roles) of a community TIP site increases the likelihood that the system will be tailored to their needs and their cultural, familial, and developmental values and perspectives (West, Fetzer, Graham, & Keller, 2000). A typical side effect of this involvement is *ownership* (Hatter, Williford, & Dickens, 2000).

Advocate for System Development, Expansion, and Evaluation—and for Reform of Funding and Policy to Facilitate Implementation of Responsive, Effective Community Transition Systems for Youth and Young Adults and Their Families

Parents and young people can often bring more clout to bear on an issue with policy makers than program and school administrators from human service and educational sectors. Some program and research professionals are coming to understand the importance of partnering with parent advocates on many fronts (e.g., planning of community programs, design of research and evaluation, testifying before legislative bodies). For example, at a state legislative hearing, a researcher can present research findings regarding the need and effectiveness of a program, and the advocate can give the issue a human face and clout ("I represent a state advocacy organization of 1,900 families").

The voice of youth and young adults with EBD are also resonating in communities and states and nationally. In some communities, the young adults are destigmatizing mental health problems and educating the public through their "speaker bureaus." In some states the voices of youth and young adults have convinced legislators to reform policy and expand funding to enable agencies and communities to develop or expand transition services and systems. At the national level, Youth M.O.V.E. (Motivating Others through Voices of Experience) was recently formed by and for youth and young adults to build national, state, and local advocacy for quality and effective transition service systems for them and their families (Matarese, Carpenter, Huffine, Lane, & Paulson, 2008).

Those of us working as practitioners, educators, program managers, administrators, and in other stakeholder roles would do well to assist in nurturing and supporting advocacy organizations such as Youth M.O.V.E., the National Federation of Families for Children's Mental Health, and the National Alliance on Mental Illness.

ESSENTIAL FEATURES FOR THE IMPLEMENTATION AND SUSTAINING OF THE TIP MODEL

The TIP model is considered to be an evidence-supported practice based on six published studies that demonstrate improvement in real-life outcomes for youth and young adults with EBD. (Please refer to the Theory and Research section on the TIP web site). Agencies and communities seeking to develop or enhance their service systems for transition-age youth and young adults and their families may want to consider implementing the TIP system. The NNYT serves as the purveyor of the TIP model and works with agencies and communities across the nation on the implementation of the TIP model. We also work with communities, states, and federal entities on examining their infrastructure (e.g., policy and funding) to enable agencies and communities to better serve this population of transition-age young people—and in some communities and states, to orient practitioners and stakeholders to the critical needs of these young people and their families and strategies to be considered in addressing these needs.

As a way of summarizing the TIP model, we are providing two Appendices that bring together all of its features. Appendix 2.3 summarizes the essential elements of the TIP model and Appendix 2.4 provides the organizational features that define the TIP model framework. Agency, community, and state stakeholders interested in learning more about the TIP system may find it helpful to review these tables and to examine the other resources available through our TIP and NNYT web sites (http://tip.fmhi.usf.edu; http://nnyt.fmhi.usf.edu). Also, as you continue to read this handbook you will learn more about the application of the TIP system in various communities and with various adaptations to accommodate the unique features of the service delivery system or the particular young people being served (e.g., youth aging out of the foster care system, young adults with co-morbidity of severe mental health conditions and substance use). The voices and actions of youth and young adults will be particularly evident in the chapters in the next section of this handbook. You'll see their role in assisting the planning, implementation, and sustaining of these transition programs and systems.

REFERENCES

Albin, R.W., Lucyshyn, J.M., Horner, R.H., & Flannery, K.B. (1996). Contextual fit for behavioral support plans: A model for "goodness of fit." In L.K. Koegel, R.L. Koegel, & G. Dunlap. *Positive behavioral support: including people with difficult behavior in the community* (pp. 81–98). Baltimore: Paul H. Brookes Publishing Co.

Ansell-Casey. (2003). *Ansell-Casey Life Skills Assessments*. Retrieved June 1, 2004, from https://www.caseylifeskills.org/default.htm

Baer, R. (2003). Supporting the employment of people with serious mental illness. In D.P. Moxley & J.R. Finch (Eds.), *Plenum Series in Rehabilitation and Health* (pp. 363–377) New York: Springer.

Bender, K., Springer, D., Kim, J.S., (2008). Treatment effectiveness with dually diagnosed adolescents: A systematic review. *Brief Treatment and Crisis Intervention. 6*(3), 177–205.

Benz, M. (2002). Building school and community partnerships. In M. Bullis & H.D. Fredericks (Eds.) (2002), *Vocational and transition services for adolescents with emotional and behavioral disorders: Strategies and best practices* (pp. 13–30). Champaign, IL: Research Press.

Biddle, L., & Gowen, L.K. (2009, Winter). Stigma and the cycle of avoidance: Why young people fail to seek help for their mental distress. *Focal Point: Research, Policy, & Practice in Children's Mental Health 23*(1), 26–28.

Blase, K.A., & Fixsen, D.L. (1989). *Preservice workshop manual for interdependent living services*. Calgary, Alberta: Hull Child and Family Services.

Blase, K.A., Jaeger, D., & Fixsen, D.L. (1988). *Preservice workshop manual for first choice parenting (treatment foster care)*. Calgary, Alberta: Hull Child and Family Services.

Bond, G.R., Becker, D.R., Drake, R.E., Rapp, C.A., Meisler, N., Lehman, A.F., et al. (2003). Implementing supported employment as in evidence-based practice. In R.E. Drake & H.H. Goldman (Eds.). *Evidence-based practices in mental health care* (pp. 29–38). Washington DC: American Psychiatric Association.

Bullis, M., & Benz, M. (1996). *Effective secondary/transition programs for adolescents with behavioral disorders*. Arden Hills, MN: Behavioral Institute for Children and Adolescents.

Bullis, M., & Fredericks, H.D. (2002). *Vocational and transition services for adolescents with emotional and behavioral disorders: Strategies and best practices.* Champaign, IL: Research Press.

Bullis, M., Nishoka-Evans, V., Fredericks, H.D., & Davis, C. (1993). Identifying and assessing the job-related social skills of adolescents and young adults with emotional and behavioral disorders. *Journal of Emotional and Behavioral Disorders, 1*(4), 236–250.

Bullis, M., Tehan, C.J., & Clark, H.B. (2000). Teaching and developing improved community life competencies. In H.B. Clark & M. Davis (Eds.), *Transition to adulthood: A resource for assisting young people with emotional or behavioral difficulties* (pp. 107–131). Baltimore: Paul H. Brookes Publishing Co.

Certo, N.J., Mautz, D., Smalley, K., Wade, H.A., Luecking, R., Pumpian, I., et al. (2003). Review and discussion of a model for seamless transition to adulthood. *Education and Training in Developmental Disabilities, 38*(1), 3–17.

Cheney, D., Hagner, D., Malloy, J., Cormier, G., & Bernstein, S. (1998). Transition to adulthood for students with serious mental illness: Initial results of Project RENEW. *Career Development for Exceptional Individuals, 21*(1), 17–31.

Cipani, E., & Schock, K.M. (2007). *Functional behavioral assessment, diagnosis, and treatment: A complete system for education and mental health settings.* New York: Springer.

Clark, H.B., & Crosland, K. (2008). *Social and life skills development: Preparing and facilitating youth for transition into adult roles. Achieving permanence for older children and youth in foster care.* New York: Columbia University Press.

Clark, H., Crosland, K., Geller, D., Cripe, M., Kenney, T., Neff, B., & Dunlap, G. (2008). A functional approach to reducing runaway behavior and stabilizing placements for adolescents in foster care. *Research on Social Work Practice. 18*(5), 401–409.

Clark, H.B., & Davis, M. (Eds.). (2000). *Transition to adulthood: A resource for assisting young people with emotional or behavioral difficulties.* Baltimore: Paul H. Brookes Publishing Co.

Clark, H.B., Deschênes, N., & Jones, J. (2000). A framework for the development and operation of a transition system. In H.B. Clark & M. Davis, (Eds.), *Transition to adulthood: A resource for assisting young people with emotional or behavioral difficulties* (pp. 29–51). Baltimore: Paul H. Brookes Publishing Co.

Clark, H.B., Deschênes, N., Sieler, D., Green, M.E., White, G., & Sondheimer, D.L. (2008). Services for youth in transition to adulthood in systems of care. In B.A. Stroul & G.M. Blau (Eds.), *The system of care handbook: Transforming mental health services for children, youth, and families* (pp. 517–544). Baltimore: Paul H. Brookes Publishing Co.

Clark, H.B., & Foster-Johnson, L. (1996). Serving youth in transition to adulthood. In B.A. Stroul (Ed.), *Children's mental health: Creating systems of care in a changing society* (pp. 533–552). Baltimore: Paul H. Brookes Publishing Co.

Clark, H.B., Karpur, A., Deschênes, N., Gamache, P., & Haber, M. (2008). Partnerships for Youth Transition (PYT): Overview of community initiatives and preliminary findings on transition to adulthood for youth and young adults with mental health challenges. In C. Newman, C. Liberton, K. Kutash, & R. M. Friedman. (Eds.), *The 20th Annual Research Conference Proceedings: A System of Care for Children's Mental Health: Expanding the Research Base* (pp. 329–332). Tampa, FL: University of South Florida. The Louis de la Parte Florida Mental Health Institute, Research and Training Center for Children's Mental Health.

Clark, H.B., Karpur, A., Deschênes, N., & Knab, T.J. (2007). Transition to adulthood program information system: Progress tracker on progression to adulthood roles (Version 1.0). Tampa, FL: Louis de la Parte Florida Mental Health Institute, University of South Florida.

Clark, G.M., & Patton, J.R. (1997). Transition planning inventory: Administration and resource guide. Austin, TX: PRO-ED.

Clark, H.B., Pschorr, O., Wells, P., Curtis, M., & Tighe, T. (2004). Transition into community roles for young people with emotional behavioral difficulties: collaborative systems and program outcomes. In D. Cheney (Ed.) *Transition of secondary approaches for positive outcomes* (pp. 201-226.). Arlington, VA: The Council for Children with Behavioral Disorders and The Division of Career Development and Transition, Divisions of The Council for Exceptional Children.

Clark, H.B., Unger, K.V., & Stewart, E.S. (1993). Transition of youth and young adults with emotional/behavioral disorders into employment, education, and independent living. *Community Alternatives: International Journal of Family Care, 5*(2), 19–46.

Copeland, M.E. (2002). *Wellness Recovery Action Plan: A system for monitoring, reducing and eliminating uncomfortable or dangerous physical and emotional difficulties.* West Dummerston, VT: Peach Press.

Copeland, M.E. (2007). *About mental health recovery & WRAP.* Retrieved April 17, 2009, from http://www.mentalhealthrecovery.com/aboutus.php

Corbitt, J., & Paris, K. (2002). Intake and preplacement. In Bullis, M., & Fredericks, H.D. (Eds.), *Vocational and transition services for adolescents with emotional and behavioral disorders: Strategies and best practices* (pp. 31–54). Champaign, IL: Research Press.

Courtney, M.E., & Dworsky, A. (2006). Early outcomes for young adults transitioning from out-of-home care in the USA. *Child & Family Social Work, 11*(3), 209–219.

Cox, C.F. (2006). Investigating the impact of strength-based assessment on youth with emotional or behavioral disorders. *Journal of Child and Family Studies, 15*(3), 287–301.

Deschênes, N., & Clark, H.B. (1998). Seven best practices in transition programs for youth. *Reaching Today's Youth: The Community Circle of Caring Journal, 2*(4), 44–48.

Deschênes, N., Herrygers, J., & Clark, H. B. (2008). The development of fidelity measures for youth transition programs. In C. Newman, C. Liberton, K. Kutash, & R. M. Friedman. (Eds.), *The 20th Annual Research Conference Proceedings: A system of care for children's mental health: Expanding the research base* (pp. 333–338). Tampa: University of South Florida. The Louis de la Parte Florida Mental Health Institute, Research and Training Center for Children's Mental Health.

Dunlap, G., Kern-Dunlap, L., Clarke, S., & Robbins, R.F. (1991). Functional assessment, curricular revision, and severe behavior problems. *Journal of Applied Behavior Analysis, 24*(2), 387–397.

Durand, V.M., & Hieneman, M. (2008). *Helping parents with challenging children: Positive family intervention.* New York: Oxford University Press.

Dyer, K., Dunlap, G., & Winterling, V. (1990). Effects of choice making on the serious problem behaviors of students with severe handicaps. *Journal of Applied Behavior Analysis, 23*(4), 515–524.

Elliott, S.N., Sheridan, S.M., Gresham, F.M., & Knoff, H.M. (1989). Assessing and treating social skills deficits: A case study for the scientist-practitioner. *Journal of School Psychology, 24*(2), 197–222.

Epstein, M.H., & Sharma, J.M. (1998). *Behavioral and emotional rating scale: A strength-based approach to assessment.* Austin, TX: PRO-ED.

Field, S., & Hoffman, A. (1998). Self-determination: An essential element of successful transitions. *Reaching Today's Youth: The Community Circle of Caring Journal, 2*(4), 37–40.

Foster-Johnson, L., Ferro, J., & Dunlap, G. (1992, November). *Does curriculum affect students' behavior?* Paper presented at the 37th Annual Conference of the Florida Educational Research Association, Winter Park, FL.

Frank, A.R., Sitlington, P.L., & Carson, R.R. (1991). Transition of adolescents with behavior disorders: Is it successful? *Behavioral Disorders, 16*(3), 180–191.

Gamache, P., & Lazear, K.J., (2009). *Asset-based research and a public health approach to addressing the needs of lesbian, gay, bisexual, transgender, questioning, intersex, and two-spirit (LGBTQ12-S) youth and families.* Tampa, FL: University of South Florida, Louis de la Parte Florida Mental Health Institute, Research and Training Center for Children's Mental Health.

Glick, B. (1996). "Aggression Replacement Training in Children and Adolescents." *The Hatherleigh Guide to Child and Adolescent Therapy 5,* 191–226.

Goldstein, A.P., Glick, B., & Gibbs, J.C. (1998). *Aggression Replacement Training: A Comprehensive Intervention for Aggressive Youth.* Champaign, Ill: Research Press.

Haber, M., Karpur, A., Deschênes, N., & Clark, H.B. (2008). Community-based support and progress of transition-age young people with serious mental health problems: A multi-site demonstration. *Journal of Behavioral Health Services and Research, 35,* 4.

Hagner, D., Cheney, D., & Malloy, J. (1999). Career-related outcomes of a model transition demonstration for young adults with emotional disturbance. *Rehabilitation Counseling Bulletin, 42*(3), 228–242.

Halpern, A.S., & Fuhrer, M.J. (Eds.). (1984). *Functional assessment in rehabilitation.* Baltimore: Paul H. Brookes Publishing Co.

Harper, M., Hernandez, M., Nesman, T., Mowery, D., Worthington, J., & Isaacs, M. (2006). *Organizational cultural competence: A review of assessment protocols (Making children's mental health services successful series, FMHI pub. No.240-2).* Tampa, FL: University of South Florida, Louis de la Parte Florida Mental Health Institute, Research & Training Center for Children's Mental Health.

Hatter, R.A., Williford, M., & Dickens, K. (2000). Nurturing and working in partnership with parents during transition. In H.B. Clark & M. Davis (Eds.), *Transition to adulthood: A resource for assisting young people with emotional or behavioral difficulties* (pp. 209–228). Baltimore: Paul H. Brookes Publishing Co.

Hernandez, M., & Isaacs, M.R. (1998). *Promoting cultural competence in children's mental health services.* Baltimore: Paul H. Brookes Publishing Co.

Hieneman, M., Presley, J., Gayler, W., Nolan, M., De Turo, L., & Dunlap, G. (1999). *Facilitator's guide: Positive behavior support.* Tallahassee: Florida Department of Education, Division of Public Schools and Community Education, Bureau of Instructional Support and Community Services.

Hines, A.M., Merdinger, J., & Wyatt, P. (2005). Former foster youth attending college: Resilience and the transition to young adulthood. *American Journal of Orthospsychiatry, 75*(3), 381–394.

Horner, R.H. (1994). Functional assessment: Contributions and future directions. *Journal of Applied Behavior Analysis, 27*(2), 401–404.

Horner, R.H., Sprague, J.R., & Flannery, K.B. (1993). Building functional curricula for students with severe intellectual disabilities. In R. VanHouston & S. Axelrod (Eds.), *Effective behavioral treatment* (pp. 47–71). New York: Plenum.

Isaacs, M.R., Hopkins, V.H., Hicks, R., & Wang, E.K.S. (2008). Cultural and linguistic competence and eliminating disparities. In B.A. Stroul & G.M. Blau (Eds.). *The system of care handbook: Transforming mental health services for children, youth, and families* (pp. 301–328). Baltimore: Paul H. Brookes Publishing Co.

Iwata, B.A., Dorsey, M.F., Slifer, K.J., Bauman, K.E., & Richman, G.S. (1994). Toward a functional analysis of self-injury. *Journal of Applied Behavior Analysis, 27*(2), 197–209.

Karpur, A., Clark, H.B., Deschênes, N., & Knab, J.T. (2007). Transition to Adulthood Program Information System (TAPIS). In C. Newman, C. Liberton, K. Kutash, & R.M. Friedman, (Eds.), *The 19th Annual Research Conference Proceedings: A system of care for children's mental health: Expanding the research base* (pp. 255–260). Tampa, FL: University of South Florida, the Louis de la Parte Florida Mental Health Institute, Research and Training Center for Children's Mental Health.

Kazdin, A., Bass, D., Siegel, T., & Thomas, C. (1989). Cognitive-behavioral therapy and relationship therapy in the treatment of children referred for antisocial behavior. *Journal of Consulting and Clinical Psychology, 57*(4), 522–535.

Kincaid, D. (1996). Person-centered planning. In L.K. Koegel, R.L. Koegel, & G. Dunlap (Eds.), *Positive behavioral support: Including people with difficult behavior in the community* (pp. 439–465). Baltimore: Paul H. Brookes Publishing Co.

Kopelwicz, A., Liberman, R.P., & Zarate, R. (2006). Recent advances in social skills training for schizophrenia. *Schizophrenia Bulletin, 32*(S1), S12–S23.

Koroloff, N., Pullmann, M., & Gordon, L. (2008). Investigating the relationship between services and outcomes in a program for transition age youth. In C. Newman, C. Liberton, K. Kutash, & R.M. Friedman (Eds.), *The 20th Annual Research Conference Proceedings: A System of Care for Children's Mental Health: Expanding the Research Base.* Tampa, FL: University of South Florida, The Louis de la Parte Florida Mental Health Institute, Research and Training Center for Children's Mental Health, 326-329.

Liberman, R.P. (2008). *Recovery from disability: Manual of psychiatric rehabilitation.* Washington, D.C.: American Psychiatric Publishing.

Liberman, R.P., Glynn, S., Blair, K.E., Ross, D., & Marder, S.R. (2002). In vivo amplified skills training: Promoting generalization of independent living skills for clients with schizophrenia. *Psychiatry, 65*(2), 137–155.

Linnehan, F. (2003). A longitudinal study of work-based, adult-youth mentoring. *Journal of Vocational Behavior, 63*(1), 40–54.

Lochman, J. (1992). Cognitive behavioral intervention with aggressive boys: Three-year follow-up and preventive effects. *Journal of Consulting and Clinical Psychology, 20*(3), 426–432.

Lyons, J.S. (2004) *Redressing the emperor: Improving our children's public mental health system.* Westport, CT: Praeger Publishers.

Lyons, J.S., Uziel-Miller, N.D., Reyes, F., & Sokol, P.T. (200). The strengths of children and adolescents in residential settings: Prevalence and associations with psychopathology and discharge placement. *Journal of the Academy of Child and Adolescent Psychiatry, 39,* 176–181.

Malloy, J., Cheney, D., Hagner, D., Cormier, G.M., & Bernstein, S. (1998). Personal futures planning for youth with EBD. *Reaching Today's Youth: The Community Circle of Caring Journal, 2*(4), 25–29.

Matarese, M., Carpenter, M., Huffine, C., Lane, S. & Paulson, K. (2008). Partnerships with youth for youth-guided systems of care. In B.A. Stroul & G.M. Blau (Eds.), *The system of care handbook: Transforming mental health services for children, youth, and families* (pp. 275–300). Baltimore: Paul H. Brookes Publishing Co.

Miller, W.R., & Rollnick, S. (2002). *Motivational Interviewing: Preparing People to Change.* Second Edition, NY: Guilford Press.

Miltenberger, R.G. (2004). *Behavior modification principles and procedures* (3rd ed.). Belmont, CA: Wadsworth/Thomson Learning.

The National Child Traumatic Stress Network: Structured Psychotherapy for Adolescents. *Responding to Chronic Stress (SPARCS/DBT).* (2008). *Sparcs Fact Sheet.* Retrieved April 17, 2009, from http://www.nctsnet.org/nctsn_assets/pdfs/promising_practices/SPARCS_fact_sheet_3-21-07.pdf

Neef, N.A., & Iwata, B.A. (1994). Current research on functional analysis methodologies: An introduction. *Journal of Applied Behavior Analysis, 27*(2), 211–214.

Nelson, C.M., & Pearson, C.A. (1991). *Integrating services for children and youth with emotional and behavioral disorders.* Reston, VA: Council for Exceptional Children.

Nerney, T. (2004). *The promise of self-determination for persons with psychiatric disabilities.* Retrieved April 08, 2009, from http://www.centerforself-determination.com/quality.html

Nishioka, V. (2002a). Job development and placement. In M. Bullis & H.D. Fredericks (Eds.), *Vocational and transition services for adolescents with emotional and behavioral disorders: Strategies and best practices* (pp. 55–68). Champaign, IL: Research Press.

Nishioka, V. (2002b). Job training and support. In M. Bullis & H.D. Fredericks (Eds.), *Vocational and transition services for adolescents with emotional and behavioral disorders: Strategies and best practices* (pp. 69–90). Champaign, IL: Research Press.

Nishioka, V. (2002c). Behavioral interventions. In M. Bullis & H.D. Fredericks (Eds.), *Vocational and transition services for adolescents with emotional and behavioral disorders: Strategies and best practices* (pp. 91–122). Champaign, IL: Research Press.

Nishioka, V. (2002d). Tracking student progress. In M. Bullis & H.D. Fredericks (Eds.), *Vocational and transition services for adolescents with emotional and behavioral disorders: Strategies and best practices* (pp. 123–138). Champaign, IL: Research Press.

Nishioka, V. (2002e). Vocational support groups. In M. Bullis & H.D. Fredericks (Eds.), *Vocational and transition services for adolescents with emotional and behavioral disorders: Strategies and best practices* (pp. 159–172). Champaign, IL: Research Press.

Nollan, K.A., Horn, M., Downs, A.C., & Pecora, P.J. (Eds.). (2002). *Ansell-Casey Life Skills Assessement (ACLS) and Life Skills guidebook manual* (rev. ed.). Seattle, WA: Casey Family Programs.

O'Neill, R.E., Horner, R.H., Albin, R.W., Sprague, J.R., Storey, K., & Newton, J.S. (1997). *Functional assessment and program development for problem behavior: A practical handbook* (2nd ed.). Belmont, CA: Wadsworth Publishing Co.

Praed Foundation. (1999). *Adult Needs and Strength Assessment: ANSA Manual. An information integration tool for adults with behavioral health challenges* (Version 2). Canada: University of Ottawa.

Rapp, C.A. (1998). *The strengths model: Case management with people suffering from severe and persistent mental illness.* New York: Oxford University Press.

Repp, A.C., & Horner, R.H. (1999). *Functional analysis of problem behavior: From effective assessment to effective support.* Belmont, CA: Wadsworth Publishing Co.

Rollnick, S., & Miller, W.R. (2008). *Applications of Motivational Interviewing.* New York, NY: Guilford Press.

Ryndak, D., Downing, J., Lilly, J.R., & Morrison, A. (1995). Parents' perceptions after inclusion of their children with moderate or severe disabilities. *Journal of The Association for Persons with Severe Handicaps, 20*(2), 147–157.

Shogen, K., Wehmeyer, M., Reese, M., & O'Hara, D. (2006). Promoting self-determination in health and medical care: A critical component of addressing health disparities in people with intellectual disabilities. *Journal of Policy and Practice in Intellectual Disabilities. 3*(2), 105–113.

Unger, K. (1994). Access to educational programs and its effect on employability. *Psychosocial Rehabilitation Journal, 17*(3) 117–126.

U. S. Department of Education. (2001). *Twenty-second annual report to Congress on the implementation of Public Law 101-476: The Individuals with Disabilities Education Act.* Washington, DC: Author.

VanDenBerg, J., & Grealish, M. (1996). Individualized services and supports through the wraparound process: Philosophy and procedures. *Journal of Child and Family Studies, 5*(1), 7–21.

Van Reusen, A.K., & Bos, C.S. (1994). Facilitating student participation in individualized education programs through motivation strategy instruction. *Exceptional Children, 60*(5), 466–475.

Wagner, C. (2009, March). *Motivational interviewing: Resources for clinicians, researchers, and trainers.* Mid-Atlantic Addiction Technology Transfer Center, Motivational Interviewing Resources, & LLC Motivational Interviewing Network of Trainers (MINT) Inc. Retrieved April 17, 2009, from http://www.motivationalinterview.org/

Walker, J.S., & Bruns, E.J. (2006). The wraparound process: Individualized, community-based care for children and adolescents with intensive needs. In J. Rosenberg & S. Rosenberg (Eds.), *Community mental health: Challenges for the 21st century* (pp. 47–57). New York: Routledge.

Walker, J.S., Bruns, E.J., & Penn, M. (2008). Individualized services in systems of care: The wraparound process. In B.A. Stroul & G.M. Blau (Eds.), *The system of care handbook: Transforming mental health services for children, youth, and families* (pp. 127–154). Baltimore: Paul H. Brookes Publishing Co.

Wehman, P. (2006). *Life beyond the classroom: Transition strategies for young people with disabilities.* Baltimore: Paul H. Brookes Publishing Co.

Wehmeyer, M.L., & Lawrence, M. (1995). Whose future is it anyway? Promoting student involvement in transition planning. *Career Development of Exceptional Individuals, 18*(2), 68–84.

West, T.E., Fetzer, P.M., Graham, C.M., & Keller, J. (2000). Driving the system through young adult involvement and leadership. In H.B. Clark & M. Davis (Eds.), *Transition to adulthood: A resource for assisting young people with emotional or behavioral difficulties* (pp. 195–208). Baltimore: Paul H. Brookes Publishing Co.

Westerlund, D., Granucci, E., Gamache, P., & Clark, H.B. (2006). Effects of peer mentors on work-related performance of adolescents with behavioral/learning disabilities. *Journal of Positive Behavior Interventions, 8*(4), 244–251.

Transition to Independence (TIP) Model Guidelines and Associated Practice Elements

1. **Engage young people through relationship development, person-centered planning, and a focus on their futures.**

    *   Use a strength-based approach with young people, their families, and other informal and formal key players.

    *   Build relationships and respect young persons' relationships with family members and other informal and formal key players.

    *   Facilitate futures planning and goal setting.

    *   Include prevention planning for high-risk behaviors and situations as necessary.

    *   Engage young people in positive activities of interest.

    *   Respect cultural and familial values and young persons' perspectives.

2. **Tailor services and supports to be accessible, coordinated, appealing, nonstigmatizing, and developmentally appropriate—and building on strengths to enable the young people to pursue their goals across relevant transition domains.**

    *   Facilitate young persons' goal achievement across relevant transition domains (refer to Figure 2.1 & Appendix 2.2).

        —Employment and career

        —Educational opportunities

Sources: Clark & Foster-Johnson (1996), Clark, Unger, & Stewart (1993), and Clark et al. (2000).

—Living situation

—Personal effectiveness and wellbeing

—Community-life functioning

- Tailor services and supports to be developmentally appropriate; addressing the needs and building on the strengths of young people, their families, and other informal key players.

- Ensure that services and supports are accessible, coordinated, appealing, and nonstigmatizing.

- Balance the transition facilitators' role with that of the young persons, their parents, and other informal and formal key players.

3. **Acknowledge and develop personal choice and social responsibility with young people.**

- Encourage problem-solving methods, decision making, and evaluation of impact on self and others.

- Balance one's work with young people between two axioms:

  —Maximize the likelihood of the success of young people.

  —Allow young people to encounter natural consequences through life experience.

4. **Ensure a safety net of support by involving a young person's parents, family members, and other informal and formal key players.**

- Involve parents, family members, and other informal and formal key players.

- Parents, family members, or other informal key players may need assistance in understanding this transition period or may need services/supports for themselves.

- Assist in mediating differences in the perspectives of young people, parents, and other informal and formal key players.

- Facilitate an unconditional commitment to the young person among his or her key players.

- Create an atmosphere of hopefulness, fun, and a future focus.

5. **Enhance young persons' competencies to assist them in achieving greater self-sufficiency and confidence.**

    - Utilize information and data from strength discovery and functional assessment methods.

    - Teach meaningful skills relevant to the young people across transition domains.

    - Use in-vivo teaching strategies in relevant community settings.

    - Develop skills related to self-management, problem-solving, self-advocacy, and self-evaluation of the impact of one's choices and actions on self and others.

6. **Maintain an outcome focus in the TIP system at the young person, program, and community levels.**

    - Focus on a young person's goals and the tracking of his or her progress.

    - Evaluate the responsiveness and effectiveness of the TIP system.

    - Use process and outcome measures for continuous TIP system improvement.

7. **Involve young people, parents, and other community partners in the TIP system at the practice, program, and community levels.**

    - Maximize the involvement of young people, family members, and other informal and formal key players and relevant community representatives.

    - Tap the talents of peers and mentors:

        —Hire young adults as peer associates to work with transition facilitators and young people (with possible functions such as mentoring, counseling, public education, and/or youth leadership development).

        —Assist young people in creating peer support groups and youth leadership opportunities.

        —Use paid and unpaid mentors (e.g., co-worker mentors, college mentors, apartment roommate mentors).

- Partner with young people, parents, and others in the TIP system governance and stewardship.

- Advocate for system development, expansion, and evaluation—and for reform of funding and policy to facilitate implementation of responsive, effective community transition systems for youth and young adults and their families.

Transition Domains and Subdomains

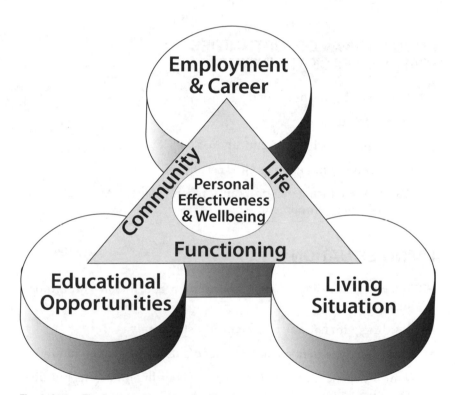

Figure A2.2. The five transition domains. The three setting domains of *employment, education,* and *living situation*—and the *personal effectiveness and wellbeing* and *community-life functioning* domains shown in this figure—are useful in capturing young people's attention and their focus on their futures. The last two domains encompass several subdomains that are relevant to success in each of the other domains.

Refer to Chapter 2 for more on the transition domain illustration.

EMPLOYMENT AND CAREER

- Competitive employment site

- Work experience, paid or unpaid, at competitive or entrepreneurial worksite (e.g., apprenticeship with employee serving as coworker mentor)

- Supported employment (e.g., paid placement at competitive worksite with formal support, such as a job coach)

- Transitional employment opportunities, paid or unpaid, at a non-competitive worksite placement

EDUCATIONAL OPPORTUNITIES (CAREER-TRACK TRAINING)

- Bachelor's degree or beyond

- Associate's degree

- Vocational or technical certification

- High school completion or GED certificate

- Workplace educational programs where placement is related to school/college enrollment

LIVING SITUATION

- Independent residence (e.g., living in an apartment with a roommate)

- Residing with natural, adoptive, or foster family

- Other family situation (e.g., girlfriend's family, extended family)

- Semi-independent living (e.g., service coordinator assists but does not live on-site)

- Supported living (e.g., supervised apartment with live-in mentor or on-site support staff at apartment complex)

- Group home or boarding home

- Restrictive setting (e.g., crisis unit, residential T center, detention center

PERSONAL EFFECTIVENESS AND WELLBEING

Interpersonal Relationships: Family, Friends, and Mentors

- Relationship development and maintenance of friendships
- Balance of independence and interdependency with family members
- Dating skills and development/maintenance of intimate relationships
- Maintenance of relationships with mentors and informal key players

Emotional and Behavioral Wellbeing

- Create reciprocal relationships with others
- Expression of care and concern for others
- Social skills (e.g., positive feedback to others, acceptance of negative feedback, self-monitoring, self-evaluation)
- Assertiveness skills and conflict resolution skills
- Coping with stress and ability to relax
- Management of anger and moods
- Spiritual wellbeing
- Self-management of psychotropic medications and side-effects
- Manage use of alcohol and drugs
- Avoid physical confrontations and criminal activities
- Avoid danger to self and others

Self-Determination

- Social problem solving (e.g., generate alternative options, make informed decisions)
- Set goals and develop plans for achieving such

- Evaluate one's progress in achieving goals
- Accept one's strengths and limitations
- Advocate for one's rights and positions

Communication

- Express one's ideas and feelings through speaking and listening
- Reading and writing skills for learning, fun, and communication
- Knowledge of information sources (e.g., use of library, authorities, Internet communications, and other resources)
- Study and learning skills for gaining and applying new information
- Cyberspace safety (e.g., revealing personal information, meeting contacts in person, use of credit cards online)

Physical Health and Wellbeing

- Health care and fitness (e.g., balance diet, physical activity)
- Recognizing when to see a physician
- Self-management of over-the-counter and prescription medications and possible side effects
- Knowledge of sexual functioning and birth control (e.g., prevention of sexually transmitted diseases and unwanted pregnancies)
- Ability to access medical and dental services

Parenting

- Health of mother for the prenatal fetus (e.g., balance diet, physical activity, adequate sleep, no smoking)
- Recognizing when to see a physician for prenatal and postnatal care
- Young adult male supports girlfriend/spouse in promoting the health of the mother and baby
- Young adult male and female assuming responsibility for rearing the children (e.g., care and discipline, behavioral parenting practices, providing home setting, finances)

COMMUNITY-LIFE FUNCTIONING

Daily Living

- Self-care
- Maintenance of living space and personal possessions
- Money management
- Cooking and nutrition
- Maintenance and security of personal and financial documents
- Safety skills (e.g., avoid dangerous situations, prevent victimization)

Leisure Activities
- Entertaining one's self
- Activities with others
- Creating indoor and outdoor activities of interest and fun
- Places of entertainment and fun
- Safe and healthy activities (e.g., cyberspace safety precautions, safe routes for walking, biking, and driving at different times of the day, choice of friends)

Community Participation
- Mobility around the community
- Access and use of relevant community agencies and resources
- Citizenship responsibilities, knowledge of basic rights and responsibilities
- Community social support (e.g., peer groups, community organizations)
- Access to legal services
- Cultural and spiritual resources

Essential Practice Elements of the Transition to Independence Process (TIP) Model

TIP System Guidelines

- These principles or guidelines drive the youth-friendly, stigma-free, culturally sensitive, developmentally appropriate, and effective work by the transition facilitators with

  —Youth and young adults

  —Their families, other informal key players, and formal key players

- Review the seven TIP System Guidelines on Table 2.1 and Appendix 2.3.

- The TIP model is considered to be an evidence-supported practice based on six published studies that demonstrate improvement in real-life outcomes for youth and young adults with emotional and/or behavioral difficulties (EBD). Refer to the TIP web site: http://tip.fmhi.usf.edu, *"Theory and Research Summary of the TIP Model."*

Transition facilitators use seven core practices to enhance the effectiveness of their work with youth and young adults:

1. Strength discovery and needs assessment
2. Futures Planning
3. Rationales
4. In-vivo teaching
5. Social problem solving (SODAS)
6. Prevention planning process on high-risk behaviors
7. Mediation with young people and other key players

Transition domains: Youth and young adults are encouraged to establish and pursue their own goals across relevant transition domains and subdomains.

- Employment

- Education and career development

- Living situation

- Personal effectiveness and wellbeing

    —Interpersonal relationships

    —Emotional and behavioral wellbeing

    —Self-determination

    —Communications

    —Physical health and wellbeing

    —Parenting

- Community-life functioning

    —Daily Living Skills

    —Leisure Activities

    —Community Participation

Futures Planning Process with youth and young adults involves a youth-driven planning process.

- Planning Partners

    —*Planning partners* are selected by young person.

    —He or she might choose *different* key players to serve as *planning partners* for *different* topics, needs, or goals.

    —Often a young person may want to only involve him- or herself and one or two key players (e.g., transition facilitator, parent, friend) to serve as planning partner(s).

- Necessary Connections

    —Young person's topic/need/goal determines who is a *necessary connection(s)* (e.g., probation officer, vocational rehabilitation counselor, community college instructor) for him or her to make progress on this topic, need, or goal.

—Young person and transition facilitator or other *planning partner* would contact, plan, and/or negotiate with the *necessary connection(s)* regarding any actions or issues that have evolved from the planning process.

Targeted clinical interventions may be needed for some youth and young adults with EBD within the TIP system framework. The primary goal is to engage young people in continuing to make progress on their goals across relevant transition domains.

- At times, targeted clinical interventions such as the following might be required—these are most useful when the young person is interested and willing to participate in the therapeutic or treatment process:

    —Structured Psychotherapy for Adolescents Responding to Chronic Stress (SPARCS/DBT; The National Child Traumatic Stress Network, 2008), Motivational Interviewing (Miller & Rollnick, 2002; Rollnick & Miller, 2008; Wagner, 2009), Behavior Analysis Functional Assessment & Treatment, Substance Abuse Treatment, Aggression Replacement Therapy (ART; Glick, 1996; Goldstein, Glick, & Gibbs, 1998), Wellness Recovery Action Plan (WRAP; Copeland, 2002).

    —Appropriate referrals and follow-along supports should be provided so as to maintain the young person in his or her transition process (or re-engage the young person back into the transition process as soon as feasible).

Essential Organizational Features of the TIP Model

The transition program or system has a clearly stated mission and is

- Community-based in the provision of services and supports

- Meets all of the specified Essential Elements

- Actively develops and maintains an array of developmentally appropriate, appealing services and supports for youth and young adults

  —Directly through the transition program or system and/or

  —Available through partner agencies or other community resources

- Committed to youth and young adult voice and participation in all aspect of the program/system

The TIP model is a community-based system where the provision of services and supports follows the young person across relevant settings:

- Young people are served, to the extent possible, in nonstigmatizing settings (e.g., program co-located with a career center or YMCA, meet young person at Burger King, walk in the park, "windshield time" with youth while transporting to job interview).

- Facilities and services are as accessible and youth-friendly as possible (e.g., career center or YMCA is located on convenient bus route).

- Transition facilitators work with youth and young adults at times that are workable for them (e.g., after school, before afternoon work shift, on Saturday).

The TIP System is an evidence-supported model for the following population:

- Serves youth and young adults with emotional and/or behavioral difficulties (EBD)

- Encompasses the terms of

  —Youth under 18 years of age who have "severe emotional disturbances (SED)"

  —Young adults over 18 years of age who have "severe mental illness (SMI)"

  —Some transition sites also serve youth and young adults at risk of EBD, but might not fully meet the diagnostic classification for SMI

- Transition age usually encompasses the entire period from 14 years through 29 years of age.

  —Some transition sites only target a segment of this age range (e.g., 17–21, 18–25, 16–29 years of age)

- Target population for the program is clearly specified.

  —Potential referral agencies and community partners understand the referral process.

  —Appropriate outreach efforts are made to reach youth and young adults who need services and supports in line with the program mission.

Selection of personnel to serve as transition facilitators:

- Typically, personnel have at least a bachelor's degree in behavioral or social science fields with experience in working with youth and young adults with EBD

- Preference given to transition facilitator candidates to create cultural diversity within the team that maximizes the likelihood that young people will relate to them comfortably (e.g., ethnicity, linguistics, sexual orientation, previous histories such as gang involvement)

- Essential that all transition program personnel demonstrate

  —Professionalism (e.g., respect for others, responsive to corrective feedback, tolerant of other points of views, willingness to learn new skills)

—Care for and an enjoyment in being around youth and young adults

—Ability to not personalize everything

—A sense of shared, appropriate humor

- Transition facilitator candidates will need to possess good relationship and coaching skills and will need to be willing to refine these and learn other interactional and practice skills as needed to be effective in engaging and facilitating youth and young adults with EBD. The qualitative interactional skills include

—Soliciting youth's input throughout interactions

—Acknowledging youth's input (active listening)

—Remaining nonjudgmental

—Using a pleasant and steady voice tone (avoid lecturing)

—Expressing enthusiasm where appropriate

—Matching facial expressions/eye contact/body language

—Expressing empathy, concern, care, and/or encouragement

—Offering assistance, as appropriate

—Setting limits and expectations, as necessary

—Using positive, descriptive praise.

Role of transition facilitators:

- The transition facilitator works with young people to assist them in planning and achieving their goals across all relevant transition domains.

- The transition facilitator is providing or brokering individually tailored services and supports to best meet the needs and goals of each young person.

- The facilitators coach the young people, teach skills, and guide social problem solving, and they also need to recognize when to involve a young person with a professional with particular expertise (e.g., trauma therapist, behavior analyst, psychologist, DBT therapist, psychiatrist).

- It is important that the team of transition facilitators and program supervisor have available, at least on a consultative basis or through a partner agency basis, professional expertise that the team can tap as necessary (e.g., psychologist, behavior analyst, psychiatrist, job developer, peer partner, housing specialist).

Youth, young adults, and families have a voice in the program and system:

- Their voice brings a "youth" and/or "parent" perspective, culture, and ownership to the process and program.

- Offer peer mentor or peers support roles (e.g., encourage paid positions for peer mentors to work with transition facilitators with young people).

- Serve on planning, advisory, and governing committees, possibly participate on interviewing and hiring of transition facilitators, and possibly serve on advocacy groups.

- If not a member of the program staff, the parent or young person should be compensated for his or her time and participation.

Ratio of young people to transition facilitators does not exceed 15 to 1:

- One study across five community transition sites showed that one site had a ratio of 9 to 1 and another site 13 to 1, with the other three falling within this range.

- Factors such as the following may necessitate requiring a lower ratio of young people per facilitator: travel time for service delivery; severity level of EBD; degree of risk versus stability in their home, school, and/or employment placements; availability of developmentally appropriate, appealing, and effective supports and services in the community.

Levels of the TIP system coaching. TIP services and supports for each young person may progress throughout the four levels of coaching outlined:

- *Initial Assessment and Planning:* Typically completed within the first 3–8 weeks of the assignment to the TIP team.

- *Active Coaching Status:* Average of 9 months after the initial assessment—with a typical range from 4–24 months.

- *Maintenance Coaching Status:* Average of 10 months following the active coaching status—with a typical range from 4–48 months.

- *Follow-Along Status:* Ongoing, with young person and/or informal key players maintaining services/supports as required in the community.

- NOTES:

    —The Initial Assessment and Planning Level is focused on engaging the young person through strength discovery/functional assessment and relationship development—and then developing an initial transition plan.

    —The flow across these levels of supports is highly individualized. A young person may move across these levels and then may return to a previous coaching status for a period of time. Also, these estimates have not been scientifically validated.

Transition program supervisors utilize personnel training and coaching to support the competencies of the transition facilitators, including

- Office-based supervision and coaching

- Field-based supervision and coaching

- Team based training and coaching

    —Pre-service training

    —In-service training

- Case-Based Review for Continuing Personnel Competency Enhancement:

    —Sets the occasion for the transition facilitators and the program supervisor to

    Review the extent to which the TIP guidelines and practices are being applied

    Brainstorm ways to facilitate the young person's progress and adjustment, and celebrate success of a young person

    Recommend that the team examine two or three young people's cases in depth every couple of weeks.

The TIP model usually operates from either of these two organizational platforms:

- Case management platform where young people are "assigned" to a transition facilitator

- ACT model type platform where all of the young people are served by the team of transition facilitators

Most transition programs use a case management platform to launch their services and supports.

The transition program establishes quality improvement and program evaluation methods and utilizes these for continuing enhancement of the program. To do this, they

- Periodically and systematically collect feedback from young people who are being, or have been, served by the transition program on the responsiveness and effectiveness of the personnel and services

- Track the progress and outcomes of each young person across his or her individualized goals and across all of the transition domains

- Provide feedback loops of relevant data from the above two items so that administrators, program managers, supervisors, frontline personnel, and other stakeholders involved with the transition program will be able to use these findings to improve the quality and effectiveness of their program and associated services and supports

Quality Assessment and Continuous Quality Improvement (QA and CQI) coordinators at the agency or community level can assist in compiling program services and outcome data as well as help guide documentation to comply with local, state, and federal regulatory standards.

The transition program/system is managed and funded to ensure that it has the capacity to support the above Essential Practice Elements and Organizational Features.

- The transition program/system is demonstrated to be responsive to the needs, interests, and goals of the youth and young adults.

- Flexible funds are available to support the young person's needs and goals when the use of categorical funding is not feasible.

- Community resource development is an ongoing effort

    —Identifying relevant services and community resources (e.g., community asset mapping)

—Maintaining information regarding these resources and arranging access to them (e.g., web site for transition program personnel, website for young people to identify resources relevant to them)

- Management and fiscal features of the program/system are transparent (e.g., parents and young adults serve on the Community Steering Committee, which has access to program data and budget/expense data).

- Recognize and maintain affiliation with the National Network on Youth Transition for Behavioral Health (NNYT) Purveyor of the TIP model for implementation and sustaining of the transition system with fidelity to the model.

Community Initiatives

Evidence-Supported and
Enduring Transition Programs

Partnerships for Youth Transition

Creating Options for Youth and Their Families

DeDe Sieler, Spencer Orso,
and Deanne K. Unruh

"Growth . . . that's a really powerful word in my life. . . . It took me awhile to see this for myself, but when I did, it was AWESOME!"
—Spencer Orso, young adult coauthor

The young people involved in the development of the transition system in Clark County, Washington, selected the program name as *Options: Your Power, Your Right, Your Choice.* The mission of the Options Program is the following:

> To help all youth and families move from isolation to connection. We strive for a seamless system of care in Clark County that better supports transition-age youth and young adults with emotional and/or behavioral difficulties (EBD) and their families in developing healthy autonomy.

The Options transition system was built on the framework of the Transition to Independence Process (TIP) model and incorporated supported employment, both of which are best practices recognized by the Substance Abuse Mental Health Services Administration (SAMHSA). The young people served by the Options program are at a dynamic point in their lives wrought with change, expectations, challenges, and

Author note: A special note of appreciation to the Options transition personnel whose brilliance, dedication, and belief in young people enabled us to develop this transition system—and to those youth and young adults who taught us so much along the way.

opportunities. Options is not a program solely created to assist a young person's transition into the adult mental health system, but is one that helps youth successfully transition into adulthood (Clark & Foster-Johnson, 1996; see also Chapter 2).

The Options program is jointly administered by the Clark County Department of Community Services and Columbia River Mental Health Services, a community-based nonprofit mental health services agency. These two lead entities and their partners undertook the planning, development, and implementation of their transition system under the Partnerships for Youth Transition (PYT) initiative funded by SAMHSA and U.S. Department of Education. (For more information, please refer to Clark et al., 2008; http://nnyt.fmhi.usf.edu).

Throughout this chapter, a young woman and co-author of this chapter, Spencer Orso, shares features of her personal story as a way of illustrating the role and impact that the Options transition system has had on her, but also it shows the profound impact and setbacks that can occur because of mental health challenges and other circumstances. We could have invited another young adult to tell a story that highlighted more consistent progress over time, but Spencer's story reveals the dark side as well as the up side of the transition experience within Options. Spencer is a gifted young adult who is willing to reveal her challenges, difficult times, progress, setbacks, and the impact that the Options transition system has had on her life. Spencer shares her experiences to provide a flavor of the many complexities involved in engagement, goal setting, and achievement in the context of profound mental health challenges and raw emotions as a participant in the Options program.

POPULATION SERVED

The target population served through Options transition system interventions is youth and young adults and their families whose needs are greater than can be met with clinical interventions alone. Typical referrals include young people who display especially challenging and persistent EBD and those with pervasive neurological disorders that cannot be satisfactorily resolved through standard clinical interventions.

The youth population served by the Options transition system meets the following eligibility/admission criteria:

1. Transition-age youth and young adults (ages 14–25 years) meeting the criteria of a *Diagnostic and Statistical Manual of Mental Disorders-IV-TR* (American Psychiatric Association, 2000) diagnosis and living

in Clark County, Wahington (youth who are participants in the program prior to age 22 are eligible for program services through age 25)

2.   Residence in out-of-home placements or at imminent risk of out-of-home placement

3.   Voluntary consent to participate. (In Washington State, youth can direct their own mental health care at age 13.)

In addition, family members of participating youth are involved at the family members' and youths' discretion.

IDENTIFICATION AND ENROLLMENT

Youth identification for enrollment in services during the initial development of this model program was a two-phase process. The original program model identified youth with existing wraparound teams as the recipients of the transition services. During the community strategic planning meetings that involved youth and young adult participants, a very strong message was conveyed from young people and community providers that the program needed to be available to youth without existing wraparound teams. In fact, many individuals felt that youth without wraparound teams would be in greater need of transition services than those who were already connected with a support system.

The Options Community Steering Committee agreed to introduce referrals into the program in two phases. In Phase I of enrollment, the referrals were accepted from agencies that served youth and families through a wraparound process. In Clark County, that meant referrals initially came from one of the following two programs:

1.   Connections, a program of the Clark County Juvenile Justice Department, which incorporates the wraparound model and serves 100 youth probationers with EBD and their families by connecting them with appropriate interventions and resources

2.   Catholic Community Services, a nonprofit mental health provider, which provides intensive support services for youth who have severe and enduring emotional, behavioral, or neurobiological disorders and who are involved in multiple systems or are already placed in out-of-home settings and require exceptional support in order to return to the community and their home

The intention of this graduated process was to allow the Options program personnel the time to strengthen the skills acquired during training and to increase system capacity at a reasonable and manageable pace. Additional time also allowed the Options program personnel to establish and demonstrate that their services enhanced rather than duplicated existing community services.

Phase II of the referral process was initiated 1 year after Phase I. To help ensure that the program was broadly accessible, referrals were expanded in Phase II to come from a wide array of agencies (e.g., schools, child welfare, adult mental health), private parties, and youth who self-refer themselves to the program.

ENGAGEMENT AND DISCHARGE

The initial strategic planning for the Options program strongly identified that youth-driven services needed to be an integral component of the program. All services (e.g., initiating and/or ending services) are determined by the youth. The discharge criteria states that the decision to leave the program must be made by the youth or young adult in a statement (verbal or written) to the transition specialist or the Options program coordinator.

This policy is often difficult to manage because interpreting the actions of youth who are not fully engaged in the program is often complicated. Many of our youth and young adults are disenfranchised, hard to reach, and difficult to keep engaged. Often we have needed to question whether an individual youth's lack of engagement was a choice not verbalized. The transition specialist's role is to make every attempt to engage the youth, using as many creative strategies as necessary. We regularly discuss this issue in team meetings. Options is not a "three no-shows and you're out" program, and time with youth and young adults is not routinely scheduled on a standard 50-minute billable hour.

The Options program's belief in youth voice is practical, and sometimes tested, in both youth engagement and program discharge. Youth who come to our program have current and historical circumstances requiring us to be careful about how we engage and disengage our services with them. Initiation into Options, unlike more formal intake processes, requires us to meet youth "where they are at" in their development, circumstances, and locations—often meeting youth creatively in the community (e.g., skate parks, coffee shops, shelter settings, shopping malls, juvenile detention centers, under bridges, on the basketball court).

Many prospective program participants have experienced multiple services that youth have deemed inadequate for their needs. We therefore allow time (sometimes months) to build a relationship of trust and model our youth focus and commitment to youth voice. Multiple and varied attempts to engage the youth and young adults over this period allows the service-wary youth to understand our program's service model. Others are initially more receptive to receiving assistance and support for setting, working toward, and eventually accomplishing their goals. Options works with individuals in their own time frame for engagement, progress, and fading from our services and supports.

We know, however, that youth and young adults may well get frustrated, "fire" us, and begin to disengage from services, so we are careful to allow each individual a way to work through his or her frustrations and build a stronger relationship with the transition specialists—if, ultimately, that is the desire of the young adult. We are respectful of the young adult's choice to leave the program as well, but we also provide easy access to return with no negative consequences. In considering discharge we look at the relationship, supports, resources, and, when possible, how to celebrate successes that were made while in the program before closure. The youth and young adults determine whether they want to continue in the program.

Spencer's Story

I guess I would start off with the death off my father. For me, this is where my life went "wrong." My father had committed suicide 5 days before my freshman year of high school. Although I had been in the mental health system for more than 6 years prior to my father's death, my emotions and behaviors were very mild, only affecting my ability to stay within the mainstream school system. I showed a lack of respect for authority and displayed mild disruptive behavior. But when my dad died, I felt worthless and unwanted. Those feelings led me to shut down with the people close to me. I could show only one emotion . . . RAGE! I made it seem like I hated everything and everyone around me and wanted nothing more to do with life.

My freshman year was so hard. I had missed over a third of the year sleeping in and skipping classes. Detention seemed more like my homeroom class. Although I was able to maintain about a 3.5 GPA by doing a ton of make-up/extra credit work, I never really got to experience high school life. My anger, behaviors, and the wall I built around myself got in the way of my connecting on any front. Before my dad's death, I don't think I had ever really experienced depression. During my freshman year, death seemed like the best option for me. Three weeks before the 1-year anniversary of my dad's death, I got myself in a situation that ended in the loss of my virginity via rape. The next day I attempted suicide for the first time. I was in a very dark place and I didn't know how to cope. I lost all self-control and broke down.

I started my sophomore year in high school with an attitude that got me sent back to a special education school. My attitude also landed me in trouble with the law for the first time. I was charged with a felony assault on a police officer. I had a real issue with authority at that point. I had completely lost control and I could not see any hope. My probation work began with a juvenile justice/mental health–targeted team called Connections, focused on community integration. Looking back now, I can say I owe a lot to each member of my probation team for being determined to help me be successful and for believing in me, even in my deepest and darkest time. They tried many different ways to help me improve but still [held] me accountable for my actions despite my mental illness.

The relationship with my mother was definitely affected by my actions and my pain over the loss of my father. At some point I believe she gave up and lost faith in me. We were constantly fighting and I felt at times a sense of loss of self-control with her. This had led me to spend some time in a youth shelter. While I was there, I met Samuel, who would become not only one of my greatest advisors but also one of my closest friends.

In my conversations with Samuel, he continued to urge me to join a program my probation team had suggested to me on several occasions. Options, I was told, was set up to be dedicated to the successful transition of youth into adulthood. When probation had first mentioned Options, I guess the thought of joining anything scared me, but Samuel helped me to see that my life was going nowhere fast, and if I chose to continue down the road I was traveling, it would more than likely end in my destruction. With his support, when I left the shelter, I agreed to meet with Kate, a woman who would become my transition specialist at Options. I was surprised both when I walked into the Youth House, because it was actually a house, and when I met Kate, she showed such kindness and respect toward me and really seemed to sincerely want to know me and my interests and dreams. Nevertheless, it was a struggle for me in the beginning. I really didn't participate much in the program. I would meet with Kate now and then to talk and try to sort out ideas for my future. I still felt very alone with my sadness, rage, depression, and anger. I wouldn't allow myself to fall fully into Options or allow others into my life. This decision didn't allow me to really reap the benefits of Options when I first enrolled.

Around this same time, I found myself falling into the habit of self-mutilation. I would cut myself every day and pretty much enjoyed every minute of it. This all changed when I met Russ, who also worked at the Options Youth House. I found myself suddenly coming down to talk with him several times a week. He revealed some personal stuff and he ended up being the first person I told about my cutting. With help from Russ and Kate, I was finally willing to go into therapy. It was during this time that I found myself breaking down emotionally, which led to me spending 3 weeks in a crisis hospital unit. I was 16 when I went into the hospital. It was there that I got my albatross of diagnoses—bipolar II borderline personality disorder, major depression, and posttraumatic stress disorder. They started me on medications and released me with a court order to seek mental health treatment for 6 months.

OPTIONS IS FRAMED BY THE TIP MODEL

The Options transition system is structured on the TIP model and its seven guidelines (Chapter 2). The transition specialists and other Options personnel work with youth and young adults on their priority needs and goals across the transition domains of employment and career educational opportunities, living situations, personal effectiveness and wellbeing, and community-life functioning. An example of working with a youth or young adult who wants to pursue employment involves some or all of the following:

- *Employment interests:* Through strength discovery the Options transition specialists learn about a youth's interests, strengths, resources, and needs across all the transition domains, including that of employment and career.

- *Assessment of strengths, interest, and needs:* The job developer and transition specialists assess the youth's interests, strengths, and needs to determine if the young person might want to explore the work arena, secure a job, or attend postsecondary schooling/training related to building a career. For example, the young person may want a "survival" job for immediate cash or might want to pursue an associate's degree at the community college for a career in nursing. Often, youth explore many options and try various job interests until they find something that fits. Sometimes job shadowing can be a valued experience to let a young person gain a sense of the type of work and setting before having to make any kind of commitment.

What a young person experiences and learns during job explorations and placements will probably influence his or her future job and career interests, decisions, goals, and choices.

- *Facilitating goal setting and goal achievement:* The transition specialist or job developer helps the young adult to set an employment goal and identify the steps to achieve this goal, realizing that goals may change frequently as they do with all young adults at this age. The job developer builds connections with local employers and organizations to create an array of employment-related opportunities for young people. The array should cross types of work as well as types of exposure and placements (e.g., job shadowing, volunteering, practicum placements, apprenticeships, part-time or full-time competitive employment). The job developer works with the young person and the transition specialist in matching the young adult to the job opportunity, anticipating what types of employment supports might be needed for this young adult, establishing an employment agreement with the business enterprise, and introducing the young adult and the transition facilitator to the employer. With some young adults, these steps are streamlined because the young adult does not need all of these supports or is too concerned about the stigma associated with having an employer know about his or her connection with a transition program. However, the stigma issue has been minimized in our community because Options became known as much for its employment placement activities as its other services. Once the young person is in placement, the job developer assumes more of the role in supporting the young adult in the progress and challenges associated with the work domain. The job developer also maintains connections with other employment services and supports such as Workforce Investment Act (WIA) and the Department of Vocational Rehabilitation (VR) so that these can be tapped as needed. The job developer and transition facilitators are careful to allow the young adult to assume as much responsibility for securing the job opportunity and related supports as possible. The decision on whether to have the job developer or the transition facilitator provide the primary support related to a given young person and work site was made based on the types of supports needed and the relationship with the young person and the employer.

- *Youth-focused family and staff support:* The Options transition program personnel and families act as a safety net of support, hope, and encouragement. A young person needs an ally who provides unconditional support and opportunities for the youth to explore strengths in both personal and work life.

- *Teaching relevant skills:* Options assists young people in achieving greater independence by teaching and coaching them on relevant skills such as employability, goal setting, ability to follow complex instructions, and self-advocacy. For some youth and young adults, this may take the form of building employment readiness skills such as interviewing, resumé writing, or conducting a job search. For others it may involve teaching the young adult to be assertive in negotiating an equitable work schedule or appropriately resigning from a job so that relationships are maintained for future references. To support a young adult in developing new competencies requires using teachable moments to reinforce self-advocacy skills instead of "do-for-them" moments. The concept of natural consequences of the youth's choices is integral to a youth's experiential learning. Options also provides the corollary to this by providing unconditional support to the youth regardless of the consequence of a decision.

- *Evaluation and support:* We support youth and young adults in the periodic resetting of their goals and in the pursuit of goal attainment. Options tracks successes and accomplishments through appropriate documentation, encouragement, and accolades for achievement.

- *Peer mentors and other natural mentors:* Former Options young people serve as mentors to current Options youth in learning various skills such as interviewing, job searching, or community mobility. In other instances, the job developer might work with the employer to pair the young person with a co-worker who is interested in helping to mentor him or her in learning the work and understanding the setting expectations.

CULTURALLY APPROPRIATE PRACTICES TO ACCOMMODATE YOUTH DIVERSITY

People vary—so does good practice. Options is driven by a set of TIP principles and aligned practices that allow our personnel to adjust strategies to serve youth and young adults with various diversities. These diversities take the form of ethnicity, language, sexual orientation, cognitive functioning, disabilities (e.g., hearing impaired), background of street life, homelessness, out-of-home placement, and criminal involvement, as well as varying youth culture. The tailoring of services and supports for one young person will look very different from those for another young person.

The range and depth of diversity varies widely across the United States. The Options transition system is situated in an area of the country where ethnic and racial diversity is relatively low. However, the region has experienced recent rapid growth with sizeable increases in the variety of minority cultures, languages, and ethnicities. Experience or circumstances may also create a group of young people who have a common characteristic outside of the norm. Our community analysis identified serious gaps in services for individuals aging out of foster care and for court-involved youth, particularly those who were also living in poverty. These populations present us with the challenge of engaging youth who are part of disenfranchised subcultures and who are frequently distrustful of mental health and other public or private social service systems. In such circumstances it is imperative that program personnel demonstrate flexibility, resourcefulness, and respectful persistence in gaining a youth's trust.

After my experience in the crisis hospital unit, I found myself engaging in Options more fully and starting to make a lot of progress in my transition. I was able to get my GED (the "Good Enough Diploma"). That was a big moment for me. I was always told that if I didn't walk with my graduation class, I was nothing and would never amount to anything. It was scary at first. I wasn't very big on tests. But Options helped me through it. One of the team even took me to an arcade the morning of my last test to help me relax. It was great! I left feeling confident and I passed my test with flying colors! From there, I proceeded to enroll in college. Talk about a milestone! I guess I would describe college as BIG and SCARY! I didn't know anyone because I was 2 years ahead of my high school class. I went there hoping to one day achieve a master's degree in Theater Arts. I was determined. It was a big confidence booster when I got an A on my first English paper. That paper ended up being the first time I openly talked about my dad's death . . . it made my instructor cry. But as those first weeks went by, I found it becoming harder and harder to study and make it to class. I fell back into a state of depression and refused all sources of help, despite Kate's ongoing attempts to reach out to me.

In July of 2005, I committed my second felony. I was 17. Things weren't looking very good for me. This time around, I was court ordered into mental health treatment for 1 year. That didn't do much but piss me off.

To be quite honest, until about March, 2007, I hadn't really invested anything in my life. The

"The program has its up and downs, its good qualities and its not so good. But . . . hey, sounds like a youth to me!!"

only place and people who made me feel included were those from the Options program. I wouldn't call myself a success just yet, but I can say that Options has been a huge positive in a field of negative over the last few years. The program has its up and downs, its good qualities and its not so good. But . . . hey, sounds like a youth to me!! The fact that my transition specialist has gotten my mother and me speaking civilly suggests that there's a lot of hope for Options and the young people with whom the team members work. I am beginning to see what I want out of life. The clarity I find, I most definitely have to thank Options for. I've learned new skills and a lot about myself. Little by little, I learned not to be afraid to be me. At least with Options, people seemed to like the real me. Though the depression did not go away, when I was at the Youth House, I guess I could see my way out of it.

BUILDING COMMUNITY PARTNERSHIPS

The community planning process we used in the development of the Options transition system brought child- and adult-serving agency personnel and other community representatives together in a way that transformed the community. The resulting network has provided mutual benefits to the greater service community and its capacity to serve young people and their families. Our transition system has oriented more providers to adopt TIP principles in their work with youth and young adults. The partnerships have also provided the Options team with access to an array of consultants who have expertise and extensive experience in addressing the diverse needs of young people across varied groups.

TRANSITION PROGRAM PERSONNEL ROLES

The Options team is composed of transition specialists, a job development specialist, a mental health therapist, and a part-time program coordinator. Originally, an employment specialist was provided, but we found that after supplying employment training to transition specialists, they could provide employment services as well as services and supports needed across the other transition domains. The job development functions were found to be critical and so this position was maintained. The Options team members share many roles and cross-train when appropriate to provide coordinated and continuous support services for each young adult and their informal and formal key players. The multidisciplinary nature of the team composition ensures that a sufficient number of transition specialists, experiences, and expertise are consistently available to young people.

Team members work with youth and young adults with varying intensity levels for the types of support so no one team member is intentionally working with all youth who require intensive service levels. The Options team does not function as a crisis response team. This was a deliberate decision made by the Options Community Steering Committee in the initial design of the transition system. Crisis response is handled through the existing countywide crisis system that includes a crisis line, crisis mobilization team, and hospital support. We decided it was important to fully employ and not duplicate an existing and strong crisis response system.

Role Clarity

Role clarity of transition program personnel is maintained by ongoing discussion to support each staff member in complimentary roles as outlined in position descriptions. As some elements of work are found to not fit or be clearly identified in existing position descriptions, ongoing discussion to clarify roles and responsibilities specific to a young person are essential for program operation.

Role clarity is enhanced with clear decision-making authority. The Options team determines the scope and level of authority required for a variety of decisions within the program, helping team members to understand the parameters to make choices in various circumstances that personnel may encounter. A horizontal management structure creates an atmosphere of teamwork but is focused by a clear understanding of when to seek guidance from the program coordinator and additional information or approval on particular issues.

The principles of the TIP model serve as the framework for the moment-to-moment and day-to-day decision making as the Options team members work with the young people, their family members, and other key players in their lives. The Options Program Operations Manual provides the mission statement, logic model, belief statements, procedures, and forms that personnel use in their work. However, it is having a shared vision, operating principles, effective practices, and belief statements that are transformative in the team's work with the young people, their family members, and the community.

One of the TIP model guidelines focuses on the importance of assisting young people in building supportive people into their lives who may prove to be with them for a lifetime (e.g., re-nurturing one's relationship with an aunt, maintaining friendships, developing an intimate relationship). Another part of Spencer's story helps to illustrate how the Options transition facilitators are primarily interested in helping their young people connect with supportive people in one's family and community to develop possible "connections for life."

> I think the support I got from Options helped me in my attempt to integrate into a church and its young adult group that I wanted to explore. I started volunteering at the church and gained a lot of experience. I also met my now good friend and mentor, Greg. I think he respected my involvement in Options due to all the support I got there and my marked growth. *Growth*...that's a really powerful word in my life. Greg and others continued to comment on the amazing growth they have seen in my life over the past year and a half. It took me awhile to see this for myself, but when I did, it was AWESOME!

SETTINGS AND ENGAGEMENT

Engagement with the young people in the Options program takes place in the community. Sometimes it occurs in cars while giving youth rides to and from work; on prospective and current work sites during employment coaching; or at skate parks, coffee shops, and other gathering places throughout the community. As important as these natural community settings are, there is one central hub of activity to which all other services are in some way tethered. This center of activity is known as the Youth House.

An environment that supports positive morale and wellbeing, is developmentally appropriate, and is accessible for both young persons and staff is an important component in the facility design. This environment allows youth to feel comfortable and welcome and includes a neutral zone where one's disabilities and differences, as well as attending judgments and assumptions, do not enter into the setting. Environments such as a mental health clinic can subliminally fasten a label to the inhabitants—the Clark County Youth House is established free of such barriers and stigmas.

By Youth, for Youth

The Youth House is a Victorian period house located in mixed-use urban area of older homes, including some retail and office spaces. Public transportation is nearby to support a young adult's access. The building is owned privately by several community members and is leased to the county to house a number of youth-related programs. In addition to Options, the Youth House includes the following independent but complementary activities and youth-related groups:

- TeenTalk, a "warm line" staffed by trained young people who lend a listening ear and nonjudgmental support to their peers

- The Clark County Youth Commission, an official advisory group to the Clark County Board of County Commissioners

- The Clark County Peer Education program, which focuses on substance abuse prevention. The Youth House setting supports the work and spirit of youth and staff through

  —*Décor and culture of the house:* It creates a comfortable, relaxed, but well-maintained setting attuned to youth and young adults.

  —*Structure:* The Youth House is not a drop-in center, but a place that subtly reminds people of the power of intention. The walls boast awards and photos of accomplishments of the program and youth served. Rooms are set up for meetings and learning. The first-floor library is filled with books, videos, and other material selected by the young people themselves. Computers and resources are available to the young adults for e-mail, job searches, and other success-plan related activities.

- The Youth House Bylaws and Business Plan, developed jointly by youth and adults, outline how the house is to be used.

- *Access to staff:* The entire Options team is housed here as well as the Clark County Youth staff responsible for the daily operations of the previously mentioned groups.

Over the years, Options has given me many opportunities to participate in youth- and young-adult driven events. I was able to meet different county officials and have my voice heard by them. I have been able to lead many youth meetings and speak at conferences with various county officials, and I have served on a review board for Portland State University. I have learned a lot about myself, others, and how I can interact in ways that help me develop relationships that are meaningful in my life.

IMPACT OF OPTIONS

The impact of programs can be evaluated in many ways—some at the quantitative level, some at the qualitative level, and some mixed methods tapping the strengths of both. As part of our evaluation we have used both sources of information to refine and adjust implementation of the overall Options transition system. Findings from our evaluation allow us to adjust and guide our work with young adults, their family members, and other key players.

A research team from Portland State University has assisted us collaboratively in establishing a continuous quality improvement system including evaluative progress and outcomes of youth and young adults. Options outcome measures demonstrated that, over a 9-month period, young people demonstrated significant improvements in the proportion advancing in educational engagement and reduced criminal-justice involvement (Koroloff, Pullmann, & Gordon, 2008). Also, a positive correlation was achieved between the hours of employment services provided by Options transition specialists and the likelihood of a young person being employed.

A cross-site evaluation of the five community Partnerships for Youth Transition (PYT) sites (including the Clark County PYT site) was conducted by the National Network on Youth Transition for Behavioral Health at the University of South Florida (Clark, Karpur, Deschênes, Gamache, & Haber, 2008). The following progress indicators were assessed initially (90-day period prior to entry) and then every 90 days thereafter (i.e., quarterly) over a 1-year period: 1) employment status, 2) graduation from high school and/or enrollment in postsecondary education; 3) high school dropout; 4) mental health interference; 5) drug or alcohol use interference; and 6) criminal system involvement. The findings demonstrated improvement over time across each of the six variables, and a trend analysis revealed that these improvements were statistically significant for the first five of these. Although involvement in the criminal justice system showed a decrease over time, the trend analysis was not statistically significant. These initial findings from the outcome studies on the Options transition system and the PYT cross-site analysis were very encouraging and contributed to a growing body of literature suggesting that TIP model programs can improve outcomes with youth and young adults across the transition domains of employment and career, postsecondary education and vocational training, living situation, personal effectiveness and wellbeing, and community-life functioning. For more information, please visit the Theory and Research section of the TIP system web site: http://tip.fmhi.usf .edu.

LESSONS LEARNED

The community of Clark County has a very strong vision and practice of individually tailored, community-based services. The development and implementation of the Options transition system in our community was eased by

- Policies and practices supporting the *belief that people can get better* (versus a more medical model of illness)

- *Systems support* through prior funding through a SAMHSA System of Care grant had provided incentive for agency collaboration, which meant that people were already to some degree out of their silos and establishing relationships

- *TIP model* provision of a system framework for the Options program, as well as the practice guidelines and personnel competencies required for developmentally appropriate work with youth and young adults and their families

- *Social network analysis* and *resource mapping* showing points of strength and gaps that existed specifically within the transition system

- *Champions:* Every community needs people who will be champions of a cause. We were fortunate in our community to have those individuals at the policy, program, and practice levels who are committed to transforming the system to advance the provision of tailored services and supports of populations in need.

Our Options transition system experiences, in particular our youth and families, have taught us many things across the course of our time together. We are sharing the following lessons with the anticipation and hope that every community can learn from our failures, challenges, and successes.

Lesson 1: Challenge your community, transition team, and yourself to allow and embrace true youth voice and youth-driven supports and services. The importance of youth voice in the planning, implementation, and ongoing evaluation of the program and services is invaluable. Reflecting over past years, the Options program would not be what it is today without the insight and direction provided by youth and young adults in the program. In many community planning processes, a common error that stakeholders make is to design programs based on what is perceived as needed and what will work best without involving the most crucial stakeholder—the youth and young adults. We found it critical to initiate youth involvement from the very beginning of the planning process. Asking for active involvement in program development from those who will be most affected will, in the end, engage the young people based on their unique perspectives. Instilling youth voice from the beginning will infuse a sense of ownership from young adult participants. Gathering youth voice takes a major time commitment due to the active lives of the youth and young adults whose schedules may not coincide with a professional's work schedule. Professionals who come to the table to assist with the design and implementation may be genuine and compassionate but are still (in the majority of circumstances) being paid to do what they do—it is a part of their expected work schedule. Young people may be driven to participate by how they are responded to or how participation will benefit them. If they feel their contributions are taken seriously and are helping to create and guide overall program/service options, they will participate, as they are compelled to make a difference both in the immediate and distant future. However, it is important that young people are not provided expectations that whatever they say in a committee meeting will be fully adopted; rather, youth are guided in the process for collective decision making on committees and other advisory group decision-making bodies.

One of the most passionate and heartfelt thoughts about the need for a community to listen to its youth and young adults comes from Spencer Orso:

When a kid says it's hard to go on, listen; don't be so quick to disregard it. Some of the things I've learned in my very few years have taught me to listen and not judge. It sucks when you're alone and no one seems to want to listen. As the days, then years, go by, things seem to get clearer. When a child has

"When a child has something horrible on their mind all day every day, it gets very hard for them to function. What can you do? Here's the answer: LISTEN!!!"

something horrible on their mind all day every day, it gets very hard for them to function. What can you do? Here's the answer: LISTEN!!! Never just forget. All a youth really needs sometimes is just someone compassionate enough to hear him or her. When something goes wrong in their life, a youth's first response is "Where's my help?" If they never have that listening ear, their response is "What the hell am I supposed to do?" Everybody needs someone. The leaders in the community need to step up and lead the fight. Let the youth know that they have somewhere to go, someone to talk to.

Lesson 2: Services and supports must be developmentally and culturally appropriate and appealing. As a community truly embraces and celebrates the value of youth voice, they will also understand the significance of services and supports that are developmentally and culturally appropriate and appealing to youth and young adults (TIP Guideline 2). We find evidence of this in how we operate the Youth House and our service guidelines for maintaining young adult engagement. A young person involved in the initial design of the program in Clark County stated, "Even if you present it (the transition program) as something new, but it is just more of the same, we will not come!" This statement was a powerful challenge to the community.

Lesson 3: Barrier busting is an essential part of building and maintaining an effective transition system. The standard operating procedures at an agency, county, region, or state level may represent some of the major barriers to implementing effective supports and services for transition-age youth and young adults. For example, in the establishment of services for Options, a barrier to accessing mental health services was the age-determined funding mechanisms. Funding was delineated into pre- and post-18-years-of-age categories where youth would have to change therapists and maybe even provider agencies at 18 years of age. This procedure proved not to be in accordance with state law, since it had been reformed several years earlier but had gone unnoticed or ignored by local system administrators and providers. Thus, there was not a legal or regulatory requirement forcing a young person involved in the children's mental health system to move to the adult mental health system on their 18th birthday. The end of an intervention service or therapeutic relationship is now based on youth and family preference and/or a clinical and relational decision, not a birth date.

Another example related to barrier busting is the agency that required that only agency vehicles could be used to transport individuals. This resulted in the three agency vehicles, which were 8- and 12-passenger vans, being booked fully during the week for medical and other types of required appointments and on the weekends for recreational outings. Even if these vans had been available, the transition-age youth and young adults were not about to be "caught dead" in one of those vans. After a great deal of advocacy by young adults, personnel, and other stakeholders, the agency determined that it could sell its fleet of vans, require personnel to maintain an appropriate level of auto insurance, and pay personnel a fair mileage rate for transporting individuals in their own cars without increasing the agency's expenditures all that much. The personnel in the child, adult, and transition programs were much more comfortable with this arrangement versus the hassles they were having in accessing an available van in working order under the previous agency policy and procedure. The transition-age youth and young adults were now being served in an appealing way that allowed for the individual tailoring of services and supports that they needed and wanted.

Program administrators will do well to question existing operating procedures, regulations, rules, and policies of their agency, community, county, and state. It may be that some rules are "myths" that are not grounded in reality or that need to be reformed and are going to require barrier busting to ensure that an effective transition services system can be established and sustained.

Lesson 4: We realized that our initiative was about a successful transition into adulthood versus a successful transition into adult services. As our community began the strategic planning process for this program, the term *transitioning youth* was understood by many to mean transitioning a young person from child-serving systems to adult-serving systems. The unspoken and unintentional assumption was that youth would not recover from the need for ongoing mental health support. As the steering committee continued to openly discuss the real meaning of *transitioning youth,* it was clear that not all youth want or need to move into adult services. Although this may seem less than earth shattering at face value, what we recognized as a community was that it was our responsibility to assist young people with the *successful transition into adulthood,* and for some youth that would mean tapping into adult services, but this must not be taken as a given. This common realization among all involved in the program design process clearly moved this program to a different level of energy and creativity—in alignment with the TIP model.

Lesson 5: As with all relationships, the contemplative period is critical. The *contemplative period* is the phase in which young people get to know the program and transition specialists in order to make well in-formed decisions about whether or not to actively participate in the program. During the contemplative period, people spend time get-ting to know each other, there is a testing of boundaries, and young people watch to see if the transition specialists and other program personnel are "talking the talk and walking the walk." For some youth and young adults, this program may be their first introduc-tion to unconditional commitment. The transition specialists must be willing to meet the youth where they are in their lives. The ideal circumstance is to not have the formal intake and paperwork be considered as a part of the contemplative process. Although this ideal is not always possible, depending on the funding require-ments involved, it is highly desirable. The work done during the contemplative period ultimately leads to the most critical compo-nent in the engagement process for young people and eventually the development of a respectful and trusting relationship.

Lesson 6: Program personnel must understand and function in the capacity of an ally. The transition specialists who perform work commonly characterized as *proactive* case management must recognize that their duties are much more than that. The *Options* team often de-scribes their role with youth and young adults as one of being an *ally,* a term that originated with Bruce Anderson, co-founder of Community Activators. An *ally* is described as any person who finds him- or herself in a position to support or guide another while he or she is making changes in life. The transition specialists need to understand that the most critical time for the testing of a true ally is when a young person's world feels like it is crashing down. It is at that very point that an ally never leaves the side of the person they are supporting and in fact places energy into ensuring that the world is welcoming for the young person and that they use their strengths to move them forward out of the difficult challenges.

Carl is my current transition specialist and a real character. I don't think I will ever be bored around him. I've learned that I have someone who genuinely wants to see me succeed and as-sists me in pursuing my interests and goals at my pace. I can say that even when my depression reappears, Carl won't give up. He sees now what an invalidating environment I live in. Carl really seems like he enjoys working with me, even when I seem to make it impossible. I like that. I want to say also that for the first time I am willingly attending therapy. Carl and Yoda (my nickname for my Buddhist-like therapist) [are] a good team. Although they have respected my wishes to not speak openly to each other about what the other is working with me on, the two services are exactly what I need right now—they both are listening to me and tailoring their supports to best help me. I am a year away from my last suicide attempt. It feels good to know that I have Carl and Yoda in my corner sacrificing for my success. I see that Carl is really invested in me to continue with therapy. Sometimes it's hard for me though, particularly when I am going through a lot of family struggles, but Carl has continued to be there for me. Sometimes, just him picking me up and chatting, planning around goals, and/or problem solving has helped a lot. With his guidance, I have been able to make a clear plan for my life. I feel as though I am growing to trust his opinion on things. Yoda has helped as well. I know I haven't been his nicest client and probably have inserted my foot in my mouth when it comes to him . . . quite often. Being able to lean on my therapist, though, I believe is why I am still alive. He has an amazing ability to help me understand what he is saying. He's got so much knowledge but still seems approachable. I kind of figure that's pretty hard to pull off in his profession. He's got me doing this DBT (dialectical behavioral therapy) thing. I have to say, it's pretty darn cool. It's like I am learning new coping skills every day. I know without Options help, I would never have met Yoda or have gotten on a path to establishing a future for myself.

Lesson 7: Do not ignore the data. This is a very easy lesson to articulate, but much more difficult to live. Whether one loves or fears data, they are a must! Collect, analyze, present, discuss, and use data to guide decisions. Data can help decision makers remain objective in work that can become very emotionally overpowering. Information from a well-developed and active quality improvement system can greatly assist transition specialists, transition facilitators, and stakeholders in adjusting aspects of the transition system to strengthen services and celebrate system features that are functioning well. The data will also assist transition specialists, their young people, and their parent advocates in telling the story to the rest of the community, and when possible, to legislators and other policy makers (refer to Chapter 10).

Lesson 8: Understand both adolescent brain development and the culture associated with adolescence and young adulthood. To be truly culturally competent, the transition personnel must be clear in their philosophical beliefs around young people and the issues of discovery and recovery for this developmental age group. Training and coaching of transition personnel regarding these cultural and developmental topics are priorities (Chapter 2).

Lesson 9: Develop a strong framework in which to conduct your work. Clark County undertook an extensive strategic planning process with the community. During this process, elements for a very strong, clear and concise logic model for *Options* surfaced. The logic model served as a reference on multiple occasions during the planning stages—primarily as a guide and framework to maintain program planning and design while juggling the desires and interests of the multiple stakeholders involved. As the program design strengthened and implementation began, it was the guiding principles of both the TIP model and supported employment that provided the structure around which the work occurred. Without this strong framework, the risks associated with trying to create a transition system that could be all things to all people would have been a reality, and the result might have been a messy, ineffective program. Having a strong framework kept the program responsive to its most important constituents—youth and young adults—and focused on their progress and outcomes.

CONCLUSION

The Options program leadership and transition specialists have had the distinct pleasure of sharing their experiences with others over the past several years. We hope that this chapter and the entire book prove helpful to you in understanding both the importance of this work and the ways of approaching youth and young adults that make it more likely that they will be engaged in a process that improves their progress and outcomes. We have found the work with transition-age youth and young adults to be the most transformative initiative that we have ever undertaken in our county. It has had a profound impact on youth, young adults, family members, provider agency personnel, administrators across various child- and adult-serving systems, and other community stakeholders.

Options has been there for most, if not all, my major milestones in transition. Makes you kind of see what sort of unique and pivotal part of this whole community, not just with the youth, Options has become. It makes me almost thankful that I had my emotional breakdown that led to my first crime. (Focus, please, on the word *almost*.)

> *"We believe that our life experiences brought us to this work for a reason that is magnificent."*
> —The Options Team

Each person who I have worked with from Options led me through different seasons of my life. Kate, along with Russ, helped me out of my "shut down" and [to] learn to feel again. The Options personnel have helped me find my voice, believe in myself, and assert my independence as well as helped me learn new skills and also see and value my own special talents and supports around me. Carl has helped me build a direction for where I want to go and how to create a path to get there. I can't stress enough how much I've learned and grown with Options. I would most likely be dead if this program didn't exist. I hope one day to do a lot of things. I hope one day to feel okay with myself. The thing is . . . I have hope and a sense of a future. To many more adventures. . . .

Salud, Spencer

REFERENCES

American Psychiatric Association. (2000). *Diagnostic and statistical manual of mental disorders* (4th ed., text rev.). Washington, DC: Author.

Clark, H.B., Deschênes, N., Sieler, D., Green, M.E., White, G., & Sondheimer, D.L. (2008). Services for youth in transition to adulthood in systems of care. In B.A. Stroul & G.M. Blau (Eds.), *The system of care handbook: Transforming mental health services for children, youth, and families* (pp. 517–544). Baltimore: Paul H. Brookes Publishing Co.

Clark, H.B., & Foster-Johnson, L. (1996). Serving youth in transition into adulthood. In B.A. Stroul (Ed.), *Children's mental health: Creating systems of care in a changing society* (pp. 533–551). Baltimore: Paul H. Brookes Publishing Co.

Clark, H.B., Karpur, A., Deschênes, N., Gamache, P., & Haber, M. (2008). Partnerships for Youth Transition (PYT): Overview of community initiatives and preliminary findings on transition to adulthood for youth and young adults with mental health challenges. In C. Newman, C. Liberton, K. Kutash, & R.M. Friedman (Eds.), *The 20th annual research conference proceedings: A system of care for children's mental health: Expanding the research base* (pp. 329–332). Tampa, FL: University of South Florida, The Louis de la Parte Florida Mental Health Institute, Research and Training Center for Children's Mental Health.

Koroloff, N., Pullmann, M., & Gordon, L. (2008). Investigating the relationship between services and outcomes in a program for transition aged youth. In C. Newman, C. Liberton, K. Kutash, & R.M. Friedman (Eds.), *The 20th annual research conference proceedings: A system of care for children's mental health: Expanding the research base* (pp. 326–329). Tampa, FL: University of South Florida, The Louis de la Parte Florida Mental Health Institute, Research and Training Center for Children's Mental Health.

High School and Community College Partnerships with Vocational Rehabilitation

K. Brigid Flannery, Lauren Lindstrom,
and Michael Torricellas

> *"For me personally, I had no interest in the typical college experience. I have always found the standard educational process frustrating. The vocational rehabilitation program gave me the skills to go and get the employment that I would now need to have without having to spend 2 years in college. The personal attention and hands-on experience that the [college] program gave me helped me progress quickly. For more than a year now I have been employed, working as a salesman and office assistant for a local company. I can honestly say that I would never have been able to perform this type of work before I received the personal training that the program gave me."*
> —CWST graduate

Successful transition from high school to adult roles is a process that requires coordinated efforts and shared responsibility among education and other adult-service agencies (Clark, 2007; Johnson, Stodden, Emanuel, Luecking, & Mack, 2002; Timmons, 2007). The Individuals with Disabilities Education Act Amendments of 1997 (PL 105-17) and the 1998 Rehabilitation Act Amendments (PL 105-220) both promote a shared vision for youth with disabilities to transition from high school to meaningful postschool employment or postsecondary training opportu-

Preparation of this manuscript was supported, in part, by a federal grant from the U.S. Department of Education, Rehabilitation Services Administration (#H235M010108) and an Interagency Agreement from Oregon's Office of Vocational Rehabilitation Services. Opinions expressed herein are the authors' and do not necessarily reflect the position of the U.S. Department of Education, and such endorsements should not be inferred.

nities. These two pieces of federal legislation share common language and clear expectations, defining transition services as a coordinated set of activities for a student designed within an outcome-oriented process that promotes movement from school to postschool activities (Individuals with Disabilities Education Act Amendments of 1997 (PL 105-17) Institute on Rehabilitation Issues [IRI], 2002).

Legislative mandates do not automatically translate to new, improved, or more effective service delivery models, however, especially for individuals with emotional and/or behavioral difficulties (EBD) (Clark & Foster-Johnson, 1996; Vander Stoep, Davis, & Collins, 2000). A recent report summarizing the need for coordinated services across education and rehabilitation agencies concluded, "There is a compelling need to strengthen transition programs and to coordinate services to youth with disabilities among secondary transition programs, postsecondary services for students with disabilities, and vocational rehabilitation agencies" (Lamb, 2007, p. 4).

Youth with EBD often present more complex challenges to the education and rehabilitation service delivery system given their low high school graduation rates, poor postschool employment outcomes, and overall lack of job stability (Clark, Pschorr, Wells, Curtis, & Tighe, 2004; FitzGibbon, Cook, & Falcon, 2000; Wagner, Newman, Cameto, Garza, & Levine, 2005). Postsecondary education may be a critical piece of the puzzle for these youth, since participation in postsecondary training has been linked to higher participation in the labor force and higher wages (Day & Newburger, 2002; Gilmore & Bose, 2005; Ryan, 2005). National as well as state employment data have indicated that the current workforce demands some level of post–high school training in order to enter living wage employment (Turner, 2007).

Individuals with disabilities who enroll in some level of postsecondary education are employed at twice the rate of those with only a high school diploma (Getzel, Stodden, & Briel, 2001; Gilmore & Bose, 2005). However, postsecondary participation rates for individuals with disabilities are still quite low compared with their same-age peers (Gilmore & Bose, 2005;Wagner et al., 2005). Those who do enroll typically participate in traditional academic programs rather than pursuing short-term postsecondary education and training opportunities. One viable but underused option may be occupationally specific, short-term training programs that are offered at many community colleges nationwide (Flynn, 2002; Grubb, 1996). These programs have different labels, but they share several core characteristics, including 1) a focus on specific occupations, 2) a curriculum that can be completed within 1 year or less, and 3) hands-on instruction and/or worksite-based training. The employment focus of these community college programs also aligns well with the mission and outcomes of vocational rehabilitation (IRI, 2002), and provides an ideal service-delivery structure to meet the needs of youth with EBD.

The purpose of this chapter is to describe two educational programs that have established partnerships with state vocational rehabilitation agencies in order to create more effective transition services and improve employment outcomes for individuals with disabilities. Both programs offer services in school settings and employ high school or community college personnel to provide employment and transition services. Although these programs were not designed specifically for individuals with EBD, they have successfully served these youth exiting the K–12 school system as well as adults with mental health and psychosocial disabilities (Benz, Lindstrom, & Latta, 1999; Flannery, Slovic, Benz, & Levine, 2007). Both programs use a set of key features to drive service delivery. These features are based on best practice literature and include many of the critical components that have been developed and field tested by the Transition to Independence model (Clark et al., 2004; Karpur, Clark, Caproni, & Sterner, 2005, see Chapter 2). By promoting collaboration, providing individualized services, and offering specific training in employment skills, individuals who complete these programs are more likely to enter higher wage, higher skill employment opportunities after leaving high school or postsecondary training (Benz, Lindstrom & Yovanoff, 2000; Flannery, Yovanoff, Benz, & McGrath Kato, 2008).

MODEL PROGRAMS

Program Development: Partnerships Between Education and Vocational Rehabilitation

Vocational rehabilitation is a federal agency that provides vocational counseling and employment services to more than 1 million individuals with disabilities in the United States (Lamb, 2007). Services are individualized based on strengths, abilities, and interests, and may include vocational evaluation, counseling, work adjustment, education and vocational training, job placement, and post-employment assistance (IRI, 2002). Although rehabilitation agencies typically focus on adults with disabilities, youth with documented disabilities can also receive these services beginning in high school, providing an opportunity for coordinated and comprehensive services across the transition years and bridging the gap from youth to adult focused services.

The Youth Transition Program (YTP) and the Career Workforce Skills Training (CWST) program were both developed in collaboration with Oregon's Office of Vocational Rehabilitation Services (OVRS) to improve employment outcomes for individuals with disabilities. The YTP serves high school youth in transition, whereas the CWST serves a wide range of individuals with disabilities who enroll in community college short-term training programs. Both programs support jointly funded employment and transition specialists who provide comprehensive, individualized career and transition services; referrals to additional support services; and enhanced high school or community college services. In addition, the University of Oregon has a contract to provide training, technical assistance, and evaluation support for local high school, community college, and VR staff implementing the programs statewide.

Youth Transition Program

The Youth Transition Program (YTP) is a comprehensive transition program for youth with disabilities operated collaboratively by the Oregon Office of Vocational Rehabilitation Services, the Oregon Department of Education, the University of Oregon, and local school districts statewide in Oregon. The YTP was initially developed in seven high schools in 1990 under the auspices of a federal grant. The program currently operates in more than 120 high schools in Oregon and is funded through a combination of state and local funds from participating education and rehabilitation agencies (Benz et al., 2000).

Participants

YTP serves youth and young adults with disabilities who need additional support beyond the services typically offered though the general or special education program to achieve their secondary and postsecondary employment and continuing education goals (Benz, Lindstrom, Unruh, & Waintrup, 2004). YTP youth are representative of all youth with disabilities nationally with respect to gender and primary disability categories; however, the majority of youth in the program experience a number of additional individual, family, or school system barriers such as poor academic skills, limited social and independent living skills, negative job experiences, and low levels of family involvement or support (Benz et al., 1999). More than 50% of youth currently served through the YTP live in low-income families, and 15% ($n = 239$) have a primary disability of EBD (Lindstrom, Lichtenstein, & McGrath-Kato, 2006).

Pattern of Services

The YTP provides services to youth beginning in their junior or senior year of high school and continuing into the early transition years. In each participating school district, YTP services are provided jointly by a transition specialist and a local vocational rehabilitation counselor. The transition specialist is funded through a collaborative arrangement whereby one third of the salary is paid through school district funds and two thirds are paid through matching VR funds. All students in the program receive a comprehensive pattern of service designed to address a broad array of transition needs. Specific services provided are described in the section that follows.

Screening and Referral to Vocational Rehabilitation

Transition specialists and VR counselors work as a team to identify potential YTP students and assist them in the process of determining eligibility for rehabilitation services. Transition specialists typically collect existing information from school records and gather new information from youth and families to facilitate a collaborative decision-making process regarding eligibility determination (Benz et al., 1999).

Individualized Transition Planning Focused on Postschool Goals and Self-Determination

All youth in the program participate in a strengths-based planning process to identify long-range hopes and dreams and needed supports to achieve these goals. Individualized goals are documented through special education individualized education programs (IEPs) and VR Individualized Plans for Employment (IPEs). Transition specialists also help coordinate plans with relevant community agencies, such as mental health or child welfare agencies.

Instruction in Academic, Vocational, Independent Living, and Personal Social Skills

Instruction is individualized and provided across a variety of high school and community-based settings. YTP youth also receive supports to either obtain appropriate secondary completion documents (e.g., high school diploma, general equivalency diploma [GED]) or to stay in and complete high school (Benz & Lindstrom, 2000). One young woman in the program commented on the value of this type of individualized academic support within the high school, "I don't think I would have graduated from high school if it weren't for the YTP staff. They kept me going."

Employment and Career Development Services

All YTP youth move through a structured process of career exploration to develop and refine appropriate and meaningful career goals. In local communities, YTP staff also create a variety of approaches to assist in building vocational skills. These approaches include 1) peer support groups such as job clubs, 2) opportunities for job shadowing or group industry tours, 3) school-based enterprises and student-run businesses to provide paid work experiences within school environments, and 4) individual job placements in community employment settings (Benz et al., 1999; Lindstrom, Benz, & Johnson, 1996).

Support Services

YTP transition specialists typically provide case management and intensive one-to-one support to address each student's individualized transition needs. Depending on the goals outlined in the individualized plan, VR counselors also provide additional vocational assessments, funding for transportation, and specialized clothing, equipment, or tools to assist youth in succeeding on a job placement. In addition to these vocational needs, many youth are provided with additional referrals to address independent living, mental health, substance abuse, or legal issues. Transition specialists help youth gain access to and follow through with these services, serving as a bridge across multiple and complex service systems that can often be overwhelming for youth with EBD. The YTP builds a framework of support across many domains, offering comprehensive services to youth who would otherwise fall through the cracks of the service delivery system. One young man who had recently graduated from the program commented on the importance of these support services: "They [YTP staff] were always there for me . . . problems over home, whatever. I mean they would stop anything. They would have stacks of papers and I would go in and say "I have a problem," and they would just talk about it."

Follow-Up Support

Another unique element of the YTP is the provision of follow-up support services. Transition specialists offer follow-up supports for 1 year after program exit to assist in maintaining positive outcomes in employment and/or postsecondary training programs. Follow-up services include regular contacts to document progress as well as the provision of additional support services or referrals as needed (Benz et al., 1999).

Career Workforce Skills Training

In 1998, Oregon's Office of Vocational Rehabilitation Services (OVRS), one Oregon community college, and the University of Oregon started a unique partnership. This partnership was developed to provide enhanced services to OVRS consumers so that they could successfully participate in community college programs and acquire targeted, occupation-specific skills in order to enter career-related employment. Individuals from these organizations met regularly to strategize the systemic changes that would need to occur to include individuals from OVRS in a short-term training program called Occupational Skills Training (described in more detail later). These meetings led to the development of 1) a process for referral, 2) a description of present services that could be offered to students with disabilities, and 3) a description of new services needed. Similar to the YTP model, the college provided funds to match the federal vocational rehabilitation funds available to Oregon. These funds (college and federal match) allowed the college to hire an employment specialist to provide services beyond those typically available in the college short-term training programs (e.g., navigating the college systems, completing the college application and financial aid process, linking to campus supports, job search) and also to collaborate with the local OVRS branch staff.

By 2003, four community colleges were participating in the model and the partnership became known as the Career Workforce Skills Training project (CWST). Individuals participating in the CWST project: 1) are OVRS clients who have, as part of their Individual Plans for Employment (IPEs), developed a mutually agreed upon skill-training goal with their VRS counselor; and 2) have agreed that a short-term training program is the appropriate learning environment to achieve their IPE goals.

Participants

Although the community college programs participating in CWST primarily serve adults, as a result of the partnership CWST employment specialists also work with local high schools to better prepare students for these college programs. Many youth with disabilities are beginning to enter CWST at the end of their senior year of high school. From 2003 through 2007, the average age of CWST participants was 37.5 years (range 17–66 years) with 22% (164) of participants 25 years of age or younger. The participants in CWST had a variety of identified disabilities. The most commonly identified disability categories were cognitive, psychosocial, and mobility/orthopedic, with 29% ($n = 215$ of 745) of all participants identified as having a psychosocial disability (e.g., schizophrenia, anxiety disorder, mental illness). Most of the participants had more than one disability.

Pattern of Services

The CWST partnership added services to the existing college short-term training programs so that OVRS consumers could be successful. The

CWST partnership began by using an existing college short-term training program, the Occupational Skills Training Program, originally developed to return injured workers to the workforce. The program allows for development of training plans for a wide range of occupations, and is driven by the labor market and student interests. These programs do not have a specific content focus (e.g., automotive, clerical), but provide services across many career areas (e.g., pharmacy technician, saddle maker, shipping and receiving, administrative assistant) that do not provide other certificate or degree programs. Over the past 5 years, the project has expanded to assist students in any of the short-term training programs in the participating college campuses. All students participating in the partnership receive the following services:

Assistance in Identifying a Career Goal that Matches the Student's Interests, Strengths, and Abilities

As many of the participants have neither been in the workforce nor received adequate career exploration earlier in life, the vocational rehabilitation counselors and students often work with the college employment specialist to determine career direction, explore available labor market data, and identify limitations that could hinder successful program completion. Two students commented about the role the CWST program played in clarifying career goals. As one student remembered, "My career goal when I first came, I don't remember what it was but I have changed it a lot. . . . But my career goal now is I'm trying to do office work." Another student shared the importance of a strength-building model when he said, "Well, at the time I couldn't figure out what I wanted. I would go from one subject to another. I had to figure out what I can do with my limitations."

A Short-Term Training Plan that Includes Occupationally Specific On-the-Job Training and Related Classroom Instruction

Because many of the students are not traditional learners, the use of hands-on instruction is critical. When asked during an interview if there was anything about the program that had been especially helpful, one student commented,

> Yeah; for me, I would have to say the actual co-op, the training sites. . . . I learn better that way. I'm not a real learner from books; that's difficult for me. I have always struggled to remember what I read, but I quickly learn from personal experience. Show me something and you only have to show me once.

Even when taking courses, students often comment on the value of the hands-on learning. For example, when talking about his automotive training classes, one student said,

> *"I'm not a real learner from books; that's difficult for me. I have always struggled to remember what I read, but I quickly learn from personal experience. Show me something and you only have to show me once."*

> A lot of it is lab work. I mean maybe 1 or 2 hours of classes and the rest is spent in the lab. It's so great. I know how to MIG weld and assembly weld and how to bang on the fender and get the dents out.

Thus, the starting place for determining course work and learning objectives are the skills and knowledge associated with the specific career area. The employment specialist first locates a community business or organization that is relevant to the student's career goal and is willing to provide on-site training. The site supervisor in the community business works collaboratively with the employment specialist to identify the required learning outcomes and develop a curriculum plan (e.g., occupational-specific and job-related skill-based learning objectives, related courses) for the CWST student.

Whenever possible, these learning outcomes are met on the training site, but some additional coursework may be required. This may be specific occupational-related coursework or other academic instruction (e.g., communication, human relations, computation) recommended by the training site or required by the college program. The employment specialists also network with relevant community college staff to identify courses relevant to the student's career goal and skill level as well as to develop alternate plans for skill acquisition. For example, if the student is interested in becoming a pharmacy technician, the employment specialist talks with the health occupations program faculty about relevant courses within that department.

Progress Monitoring of Each Student

Each student's plan is monitored to ensure adequate progress toward completion of the specific training objectives and required coursework. Students complete a monitoring form and often log a journal entry each week. The training site supervisor completes a monthly evaluation form documenting the student's progress toward objectives as well as information on the acquisition of employability skills. These are reviewed to identify areas of need for the student.

Support Services Necessary to Assist
Students to Master Their Training-Related Objectives
Support services include individualized feedback and role playing; course selection to maximize financial aid awards and minimize potential negative impact of dropping or failing courses; assistance with requesting alternative or course substitutions to maximize learning style; and support in communicating with instructors regarding assignments, attendance, and utilization of campus supports. For individuals with psychosocial disabilities, the employment specialists have found that although these individuals may require a longer time in the program, the key to success is knowing the disability and related issues in order to develop an appropriate training site and providing the needed supports. CWST employment specialists often provide additional troubleshooting at the training site and develop different sites for individuals if an initial placement falls through. Throughout the process, the employment specialist works closely with the OVRS counselor to identify additional community supports and services needed, such as anger management or mental health counseling. In addition, OVRS counselors provide ongoing counseling and support services including medication funds and monitoring to ensure that the individual is stable and ready to work. When asked to identify the most important aspects of the program, one CWST student described the value of the employment specialist and his attitude as a critical service:

> A lot of people come into this program that have had negative experiences. I'm here because my place (of employment) shut down. You know, I don't have a job. So it's hard to find people that are upbeat and want to lift you up and help you. I think that is a key thing.

Upon completion of the learning objectives identified in the student's curricula at the training site, job search and follow-up services are available as needed. These services are designed to assist the individual in obtaining and maintaining employment. Follow-up services include resumé development, interview role plays, and identification of potential job openings. As one student remembered, "[The employment specialist] helped me with resumés; she helped me try to find job contacts. I mean she would look and say 'Hey, did you see this one?'"

Another student also described the services: "[The employment specialist] helped me set up a portfolio so I could take that to work. And he helped me look for some job possibilities."

Program Impact: Empirical Evidence

Youth with EBD face multiple barriers in making the transition from high school to competitive employment, postsecondary education, and other adult roles (Clark & Foster-Johnson, 1996; Vander Stoep et al., 2000; Wagner & Cameto, 2004). However, programs such as YTP and CWST can ameliorate many of these poor outcomes by providing coordinated services; specific vocational training; and individualized, ongoing support to address emotional and behavioral issues. Since the mid-1990s, a number of studies have been conducted documenting the effectiveness and impact of the YTP and CWST. Young adults completing the programs have consistently earned higher hourly wages and are more likely to be engaged in either employment or career-related postsecondary education upon exiting high school (Benz et al., 1999; Benz et al., 2000; Flannery et al., 2008; Horne & Hubbard, 1995).

Youth Transition Program

Since 1990, the YTP has provided direct services and VR access to more than 8,000 students with disabilities (Lindstrom et al., 2006). The postschool outcomes for youth with disabilities participating in the YTP have been very encouraging. Based on data from our most recent reporting period (July 1, 2005–June 30, 2007), YTP students have an 83% high school completion rate, and 75% of participants are engaged in either competitive employment or career-related postsecondary training at exit from the program. In addition, the employment outcomes for program participants are substantially higher than a national sample of youth with disabilities who have exited high school (Wagner et al., 2005). Table 4.1 compares employment rates, average hourly wages, and average hours worked per week for a national sample of youth with disabilities in the National Longitudinal Transition Study-2 (NLTS2; http://www.NLTS2.org), all YTP youth, and the subset of YTP youth who are identified as having EBD. Outcomes for youth with EBD are slightly lower than the entire YTP sample but are still substantially higher than those of the national comparison group.

Table 4.1.   Employment outcomes: National control group compared with Youth Transition Program (YTP) participants (all disabilities and emotional and/or behavioral difficulties [EBD])

Type of sample	Employment rates	Hourly wages	Average hours per week
National sample: All disabilities*	42.5%	$7.30	28.9
YTP: All disabilities (n = 638)	62%	$9.23	34
YTP: Youth with EBD (n = 133)	60%	$9.08	33

*Source: From Wagner, M., Newman, L., Cameto, R., Garza, N., & Levine, P. (2005).

Career Workforce Skills Training

Between 2003 and 2007, CWST served 745 participants; 206 are still receiving active services. Table 4.2 compares employment rates, average hourly wages, and average hours worked for all CWST participants and the subset of CWST participants who were identified with a psychosocial-related disability. It also includes the average wage and hour data for all OVRS clients for 2006.

An earlier study of CWST at one community college compared outcomes for individuals who dropped out of the program with those who completed it (Flannery et al., 2008). This study demonstrated that the completion of the skills training program improves employment outcomes in the areas of wages, hours worked, and quarters worked. The data also indicated that those individuals who completed their program fared significantly better in terms of wages, hours worked, and quarters worked than those who were employed but did not complete their program. The conclusion that the outcomes of youth and young adults with EBD can be improved through individually tailored, developmentally appropriate services and supports has also been supported by a growing body of research (Clark et al., 2004; Hagner, Cheney, & Malloy, 1999; Karpur et al., 2005).

Table 4.2. Comparison of employment and certificate outcomes for Career Workforce Skills Training (CWST) Program participants: All categories, those with psychosocial disabilities, and Oregon's Office of Vocational Rehabilitation Services (OVRS) participants

	Certificate rates	Employment rates	Wages	Average hours per week
CWST: All disability categories (2003–2007) (N = 745)	44%	37%	$10.47	32
CWST: Psychosocial disability category (2003–2007) (N = 214)	33%	35%	$10.85	32
Oregon's Office of Vocational Rehabilitation Services (OVRS): All disabilities (2006)			$10.02	30

Special Features and Suggestions for Replication

YTP and CWST offer a unique set of program features that have consistently produced positive outcomes for youth with EBD and adults with psychiatric disabilities and mental health needs. In this section, we briefly summarize some of the key system level features present in both programs that have contributed to their success.

Program Infrastructure and Collaboration

Qualified Personnel
YTP and CWST services are provided by a variety of educational personnel; however, the jointly funded transition or employment specialists and the OVRS counselor are the key players in service delivery. These specialists have the skills to work with individuals with disabilities and the knowledge of resources on the high school or college campus. In addition, specialists are able to learn about, utilize, and connect to different campus and community-based support agencies (e.g., career center staff, school-to-work specialists, mental health specialists, anger management classes) within each region, and creatively pull these various supports together to help students overcome challenges in order to complete their training programs and launch possible careers. YTP high school transition specialists must be familiar with high school graduation requirements, career exploration strategies, and job placement skills, whereas the CWST employment specialists need up-to-date knowledge about the inner workings of the community college, program requirements, and workforce. The OVRS counselor needs to have basic vocational counseling and guidance skills; however, those who have been most effective enjoy working with youth and young adults (YTP), are able to collaborate in the delivery of services, think differently about how services might be provided, and are often willing to try again when a first attempt for a postschool option does not come to fruition.

Collaborative Funding
As mentioned earlier, individuals in these programs receive the standard educational services that any individual with a disability would be able to access. The unique and *value-added* services provided through YTP and CWST are primarily offered by the jointly funded transition or employment specialist. By using school district and community college dollars as matching funds, OVRS is able to generate additional federal matching dollars, which in turn support the ongoing service delivery model. High schools, community colleges, and OVRS all benefit from

this matching funding arrangement (Benz & Lindstrom, 2000; Timmons, 2007).

Outreach, Communication, and Networking

To implement these collaborative services requires outreach, communication, and networking by the specialists with the OVRS counselor, the employer, educational staff, educational support services, and community resources. The specialists are critical because they provide initial program information; connect with students throughout the program; and offer follow up and ongoing communication with the OVRS counselor, employer, and educational staff. In addition, the specialist or the OVRS counselor provides outreach to the community to arrange appropriate services as varied as mental health, drug counseling, child care services, or dental work. When unforeseen problems arise that require immediate attention in order to keep a student on track either academically or on a training site/employment setting, the specialists are also available to problem solve with the student and the OVRS counselor to develop needed plans for support.

Flexibility and Adaptability

Both of these models operate within many different community contexts, educational infrastructures, and staffing patterns. This requires them to be able to respond to and build from the community and educational contexts. In order to maintain flexibility but also systematically expand and sustain the services of these models, each has developed a set of features to guide program development (Benz et al., 2004; Flannery et al., 2007; Flannery et al., 2008). The ongoing success of the students in these programs is dependent on coordinated efforts between local OVRS branch managers and counselors, educational staff, the students, and other stakeholders (e.g., disability services, career centers, local community training sites) to put these features in place in a manner that makes sense in their community.

In the CWST program, the features are rated yearly on their status of implementation by all stakeholders, and the results are used to develop an action plan delineating responsibilities across organizations, to make necessary adjustments to support students also served by the OVRS system, and to document programmatic changes over time. The written action plan identifies activities, roles and responsibilities, and timelines to increase the success of vocational rehabilitation clients enrolled in these programs. YTP teams also conduct periodic internal performance reviews, responding to feedback from school, rehabilitation, and community stakeholders.

Technical Assistance/Support

Local CWST and YTP programs are supported through training and technical assistance offered by the University of Oregon. Experienced technical assistance providers are assigned to specific sites and provide ongoing assistance through e-mail, telephone, and regular on-site visits. Both projects also bring educational and rehabilitation staff together for ongoing professional development. CWST staff facilitate regular cross-site meetings, whereas the YTP network offers statewide and regional trainings. These events have been critical to allow information sharing and problem solving across programs (Lichtenstein, 2006).

In addition to training and technical assistance, all YTP and CWST sites participate in a structured system of program evaluation. With input from participating colleges, districts, and OVRS, the University of Oregon staff developed a database system for performance monitoring and ongoing evaluation. In order to receive OVRS funding, each of the participating districts and the community college are expected to meet a set of performance benchmarks (see Table 4.3).

The University of Oregon team provides support to the colleges, school districts, and affiliated rehabilitation branches to review progress and make needed program modifications on a regular basis. State and regional OVRS administration and participating college and high school sites also receive quarterly performance reports relevant to their individual benchmarks. One of the challenges of preparing youth for the transition from high school to the community is that educators can no longer focus only on what goes on within the four walls of the high school. Professionals must understand and promote linkages between high school and post-school partners such as vocational rehabilitation, developmental disability services, local community-based support agencies (e.g., mental health), and postsecondary training programs (Clark & Davis 2000; Johnson et al., 2002). To respond to these complex needs, CWST technical assistance staff have formed local workgroups of college staff, high school district staff, and community members interested in transition of youth with disabilities. The purpose of these workgroups is to build and exchange knowledge in order to influence and improve outcomes for youth with disabilities. Technical assistance staff as well as local YTP and CWST staff participate and have been able to use this forum for professional development and ongoing problem solving.

Student-Focused Services

In addition to these system-level features, CWST and YTP are both highly responsive to individual student needs. These models are both

Table 4.3.   Benchmarks and database elements developed by the University of Oregon for performance evaluation and ongoing evaluation of the Youth Transition Program (YTP) and Career Workforce Skills Training (CWST) Program

Program	Benchmarks	Database areas
YTP	OVRS application: Participants who complete an application for OVRS services and have an identified vocational goal Individual Plan for Employment: Participants who participate in the development of an IPE Engagement: Participants who are engaged in either employment or career-related postsecondary training at exit, 6 months, and 12 months	Demographic information (e.g., date of birth, gender, ethnicity) Disability information Barriers at entry (individual, school, and family barriers) Supports at entry Employment status (e.g., job title, hours/wage/benefit information) VR closure status and date Postsecondary education status (types of training program hours enrolled)
CWST	Project participants who obtain a completion document (state certificate or local college award) Project participants who enter employment in their IPE area Employed project participants who maintain employment for 90 days	Demographic information (e.g., date of birth, gender, ethnicity, residence status, financial support) Disability information Case referral (e.g., referral source, VR eligibility status) Barriers (e.g., lost multiple jobs, prior arrest, absenteeism history) Education (e.g., educational background, placement test information) Training (e.g., program, IPE goal, college services, coursework, support services, training site information including start/stop date and hours) Exit (e.g., employer, hrs/wage/benefit information, employment date, drop date and reasons dropped) Follow-up (employment status, employer, hrs/wage/benefit information)

strength based, and the specialists have learned to not consider any disability label as a barrier to success. Instead, YTP and CWST staff work closely with participants to enhance their skills and seek out employment settings that build on individual strengths, interests, and preferences. The specialists also work to consider the cultural characteristics of the individual and family when selecting the type of training site or services to be provided (Lichtenstein et al., 2008) Finally, the programs provide a comprehensive array of services, addressing multiple transition needs (Benz et al., 2004). The following case study illustrates the power of this type of collaborative service delivery model.

Jared is a tall, energetic young man who likes to talk and joke. He grew up living with his mother. She was divorced from Jared's father, remarried, and has been separated from Jared's stepfather for several years. Jared's disabilities were not diagnosed until he reached adolescence. In middle school he started showing serious behavior problems—conflicts with peers, impulsive acting out, temper outbursts, noncompliance with teachers and other authority figures, truancy, and fighting. When Jared was in 7th grade, he was diagnosed with attention deficit disorder and behavior conduct disorder and became eligible for special education services. He was placed into a self-contained classroom for students with behavioral disabilities and was supported with ongoing counseling by a private therapist.

When Jared entered high school, his participation in mainstream classes increased to 80% of his course schedule. The next year, however Jared's noncompliant behavior increased to such a degree that his mother encouraged him to drop out of high school and enroll in the community college's high school completion program. After enrolling at the college, Jared fell into the wrong crowd of students and began abusing alcohol. That spring, he was admitted to a residential alcohol and drug treatment center.

Jared's case manager at the drug and alcohol program was aware of the YTP available through the local school district. He contacted the YTP staff regarding Jared's need for after care and support. Instead of going immediately back into a high school setting, Jared went to work at a local grocery store. He was referred and found eligible for vocational rehabilitation services. At his intake meeting, Jared stated that his career goal was to join the Marines. His VR counselor noted in the case files that the military "may be an unrealistic avenue for him to pursue. However this will be explored as a possible option." Jared's transition specialist and VR counselor helped Jared develop a transition plan that included employment, continuing education, job training, assistance with obtaining a driver's license, and ongoing mental health counseling.

The YTP transition specialist grew to be someone that Jared looked up to and trusted very much. She developed and provided on-the-job training and intervention support for Jared over the duration of his employment at the grocery store. His transition specialist also assessed his learning style. She concluded, "Once Jared understands the cause-and-effect nature of the task, he will accomplish it. If he doesn't see meaning in it, he'll check out." The best approach to motivate him, in her opinion, was to spend time talking through issues and giving Jared lots of space to manage and monitor his own behavior. For example, the transition specialist developed a behavioral assessment checklist that he could use to rate his own behavior on a daily basis. During that time, Jared was also continuing his substance abuse prevention follow-up and was applying the social coping skills he learned in group sessions to his own interactions with peers and coworkers.

As part of his transition plan, VR paid for Jared to reenroll in the community college's high school completion program. (At that time, the local community college did not have a CWST program, which could have been an ideal place for Jared to obtain additional vocational skills training.) YTP staff and the alcohol and drug counselor felt that the community college, with support from program staff, was a better educational environment for Jared than his former high school. His teacher noted, "Schools tend to reintegrate people into the same old environment, which is to put them back into the same role. You don't do that. You use the community." Six months after reenrolling in the community college program, Jared became the first student with a behavioral disability from his school district to graduate successfully from the college's high school completion program.

As Jared was nearing the completion of his vocational and educational goals through the YTP, he applied for and was accepted into the U.S. Marines. In May of what would have been his senior year in high school, Jared started basic training. At first his transition into the Marines was difficult. His mother, the YTP specialist, and the VR counselor all wrote to Jared to encourage him and give him emotional support. Jared completed boot camp and attended advanced training in the Marine Corps. Jared has since served two tours of duty in the Middle East, reenlisted in the Corps, and is presently awaiting a promotion that will catapult him into becoming a recruiter. He is also married and has two young children.

Seven years after leaving the YTP, Jared sent a brief letter to the school staff who had supported him. He wrote,

Well I reckon it's update time. Mary and I just went over 6 years of marriage and in May I will have been in the Marines for 7 years. In July I will be going to Recruiting school. There is a good chance that I will be selected for Staff Sergeant this year. Other than that, not much is new! How is the YTP Program? I hope everything is well. Tell those young ones that if they put their minds to it, they can do anything.

Jared is typical of many students with EBD who face myriad obstacles to completing their educational and post-school goals. His story underscores the importance of acknowledging a youth's vision and allowing the student's self-identified needs and goals to drive the transition planning process. In addition, professionals from education, rehabilitation, and mental health agencies all combined resources to assist Jared along his chosen path. By providing a framework of supports along with flexibility to meet individualized needs, programs such as YTP and CWST are able to help youth successfully make the transition from high school to adult roles in the community.

REFERENCES

Benz, M., & Lindstrom, L. (2000). *Helping youth with disabilities realize hopes and dreams: Oregon Youth Transition Program decade report, 1990–2000.* Eugene: Secondary Special Education and Transition Program, University of Oregon.

Benz, M., Lindstrom, L., & Latta, T. (1999). Improving collaboration between schools and vocational rehabilitation: The Youth Transition Program model. *Journal of Vocational Rehabilitation, 13,* 55–63.

Benz, M., Lindstrom, L., Unruh, D., & Waintrup, M. (2004). Sustaining secondary and transition programs. *Remedial and Special Education, 25*(1), 39–50.

Benz, M., Lindstrom, L., & Yovanoff, P. (2000). Improving graduation and employment outcomes of students with disabilities: Predictive factors and student perspectives. *Exceptional Children, 66,* 509–529.

Clark, H.B. (2007). Transition to Independence Process (TIP) system: Lighting the way to independence for youth and young adults. *Theoretical and research underpinnings.* Retrieved July 8, 2007, from http://tip.fmhi.usf.edu/

Clark, H.B., & Davis, M. (Eds.). (2000): *Transition to adulthood: A resource for assisting young people with emotional or behavioral difficulties.* Baltimore: Paul H. Brookes Publishing Co.

Clark, H.B., & Foster-Johnson, L. (1996). Serving youth in transition into adult-hood. In B.A. Stroul (Ed.), *Children's mental health: Creating systems of care in a changing society* (pp. 533–551). Baltimore: Paul H. Brookes Publishing Co.

Clark, H.B., Pschorr, O., Wells, P., Curtis, M., & Tighe, T. (2004). Transition into community roles for young people with emotional/behavioral difficulties: Collaborative systems and program outcomes. In D. Cheney (Ed.), *Transition issues and strategies for youth and young adults with emotional and/or behavioral difficulties to facilitate movement in to community life* (pp. 201–226). Arlington, VA: Council for Exceptional Children.

Day, J.C., & Newburger, E.C. (2002). The big payoff: Educational attainment and synthetic estimated of work-life earnings. Population Report. Washington DC: U.S. Census Bureau. Retrieved October 18, 2006, from http://www .census.gov/prod/2002pubs/p23-210.pdf

Fitzgibbon, G., Cook, J.A., & Falcon, L. (2000). Vocational rehabilitation ap-proaches for youth. In H.B. Clark & M. Davis (Eds.), *Transition to adulthood: A resource for assisting young people with emotional or behavioral difficulties* (pp. 75–89). Baltimore: Paul H. Brookes Publishing Co.

Flannery, K.B., Slovic, R., Benz, M., & Levine, E. (2007). Priorities and changing practices: Vocational rehabilitation and community colleges improving workforce development programs for people with disabilities. *Journal of Vocational Rehabilitation, 27,* 141–151.

Flannery, K.B., Yovanoff, P., Benz, M., & McGrath Kato, M. (2008). Improving employment outcomes of individuals with disabilities through short-term training. *Career Development for Exceptional Individuals, 31,* 26–26.

Flynn, W.J. (2002). *More than a matter of degree: Credentialing, certification, and community colleges.* Carlsbad, CA: National Council for Education and Training. (ERIC Document Reproduction Service No. ED467853)

Getzel, E., Stodden, R.A., & Briel, L. (2001). Pursuing postsecondary education opportunities for individuals with disabilities. In P. Wehman (Ed.), *Life beyond the classroom: Transition strategies for young people with disabilities* (pp. 246–260). Baltimore: Paul H. Brookes Publishing Co.

Gilmore, D.S., & Bose, J. (2005). Trends in postsecondary education: Participa-tion within the vocational rehabilitation system. *Journal of Vocational Rehabilitation, 22*(33–40).

Grubb, W.N. (1996). *Working in the middle.* San Francisco, CA: Jossey-Bass.

Hagner, D., Cheney, D., & Malloy, J. (1999). Career-related outcomes of a model transition demonstration for young adults with emotional disturbance. *Rehabilitation Counseling Bulletin, 43,* 228–242.

Horne, R.L., & Hubbard, S. (1995). *The Youth Transition Program: Case study re-port.* Washington, DC: National Institute for Work and Learning, Academy for Educational Development.

Individuals with Disabilities Education Act (IDEA) of 1990, PL 101-476, 20 U.S.C. §§ 1400 *et seq.*

Individuals with Disabilities Education Act Amendments (IDEA) of 1997, PL 105-17, 20 U.S.C. §§ 1400 *et seq.*

Individuals with Disabilities Education Improvement Act (IDEA) of 2004, PL 108-446, 20 U.S.C. §§ 1400 *et seq.*

Institute on Rehabilitation Issues. (2002). *Investing in the transition of youth with disabilities to productive careers.* Hot Springs: University of Arkansas.

Johnson, D., Stodden, R., Emanuel, E., Luecking, R., & Mack, M. (2002). Current challenges facing secondary education and transition services: What research tells us. *Exceptional Children, 68*(4), 519–531.

Karpur, A., Clark, H.B., Caproni, P., & Sterner, H. (2005). Transition to adult roles for students with emotional/behavioral disturbances: A follow-up study of student exiters from Steps-to-Success. *Career Development for Exceptional Individuals, 28*(1), 36–46.

Lamb, P. (2007). Implications of the summary of performance for vocational rehabilitation counselors. *Career Development for Exceptional Individuals 30*(1), 3–12.

Lichtenstein, D. (2006, May). *Balancing fidelity and adaptation through the technical assistance process: Oregon's Youth Transition Program.* Poster session presented at Society for Prevention Research Conference. San Antonio, TX.

Lichtenstein, D., Lindstrom, L. & Povenmire-Kirk, T. (2008) Promoting multicultural competence: Diversity training for transition professionals. *Journal for Vocational Special Needs Education.* 30 (3). 3- 15[MSOffice1].

Lindstrom L., Benz, M., & Johnson M. (1996). Developing job clubs for students in transition. *Teaching Exceptional Children, 28*(2), 16–23.

Lindstrom, L., Lichtenstein, D., & McGrath-Kato M. (2006). *Oregon Youth Transition Program: 1989–2006 fact sheet.* Report prepared for U.S. Department of Education, Office of Special Education and Rehabilitation Services.

Rehabilitation Act Amendments of 1998, PL 105-220, 29 U.S.C. §§ 701 *et seq.*

Ryan, C.L. (2005). *What it's worth: Field of training and economic status in 2001 household economic studies.* U.S. Census Bureau. Retrieved June 15, 2007, from http://www.census.gov/prod/2005pubs/p70-98.pdf

Timmons, J. (2007). *Models of collaboration and cost sharing in transition programming.* Information brief from the National Center on Secondary Education and Transition. Minneapolis, Minnesota. Retrieved Feb. 4, 2009, from http://www.ncset.org

Turner, B. (2007, February). *Where will the jobs be?* Paper presented at Oregon Association of Vocational Special Needs Personnel Conference, Hood River, Oregon.

Vander Stoep, A., Davis, M., & Collins, D. (2000). Transition: A time of developmental and institutional clashes. In H.B. Clark & M. Davis (Eds.), *Transition to adulthood: A resource for assisting young people with emotional or behavioral difficulties* (pp. 3–28). Baltimore: Paul H. Brookes., Publishing Co.

Wagner, M., Newman, L., Cameto, R., Garza, N., & Levine, P. (2005). *After high school: A first look at the postschool experiences of youth with disabilities. A report from the National Longitudinal Transition Study-2 (NLTS2).* Menlo Park, CA: SRI International.

Wagner, M., & Cameto, R. (2004). *The characteristics, experiences and outcomes of youth with emotional disturbances: A report from the National Longitudinal Transition Study-2* (NLTS2). Menlo Park, CA: SRI International.

Serving Young Adults with Serious Mental Health Challenges from Dependency Programs and Community Settings

Marc A. Fagan, Wayne Munchel,
Isiah Rogers, and Hewitt B. "Rusty" Clark

*"Just because I have a mental illness or whatever, doesn't mean that's all
I am. People here get that. I've got a lot more going on. I'm working; I'm
going to school. No one before in my old residential programs thought I
could do that. And now I know I can do things on my own, and I know
there's people who actually listen to what's important to me."*
   —Young woman from Thresholds Young Adult Program, Chicago

Since the inceptions of the Thresholds Young Adult Program (YAP) and
the Village Transition-Age Youth (TAY) Academy, our efforts to create
and refine programs to serve young adults have been compared with
building a whitewater raft—while rafting! These subsequent years of
program development have been marked by continual adaptation and
improvisation while negotiating the turbulent rapids. Through these
rough waters, both Chicago, Illinois', YAP and Long Beach, California's,
TAY have careened into successes and failures on their way to providing best practices for young adults with emotional and/or behavioral
difficulties (EBD).

Author note: Special recognition goes to Christine Schmidt, Psy.D., for her superior ed-
iting contributions to this chapter.

PROGRAM DESCRIPTIONS

Thresholds Young Adult Program

Thresholds YAP is a transition program that serves 16- to 21-year-olds who have been diagnosed with a severe mental illness (SMI). Most young adults in the program are referred from the child welfare, school, or mental health residential service systems across Illinois. Thresholds is well known for its adult-based services, but over time it recognized a need for specialized supports and services for transition-age older youth and young adults. Since YAP became its own entity within Thresholds, it has grown to provide

- Individually tailored case management

- Supported employment

- Therapy

- Psychiatric and medical services

- Therapeutic high school

- Supported continuing education

- Supervised dormitory and supported apartment housing

Thresholds YAP's mission is "To engage and empower young adults in their journey toward recovery through individualized, developmentally appropriate services and supports designed to achieve members' maximum capacity for independence as they transition to adulthood." YAP is funded through the state child welfare system and other state entities to provide services to young adults with SMI until they are 21 years of age, at which point they are expected to engage in adult-based services or independence—whether they are ready or not. As illustrated in Figure 5.1, the majority of young adults entering our program arrive with a strong correlation to histories of exposure to institutional settings and mental health services. YAP embraces the Transition to Independence Process (TIP) system framework, and has adapted its practices as the program strives for full TIP implementation.

The Village Transition-Age Youth Academy

TAY Academy is a psychosocial rehabilitation/intensive case-management program in greater Long Beach, California. The TAY Academy

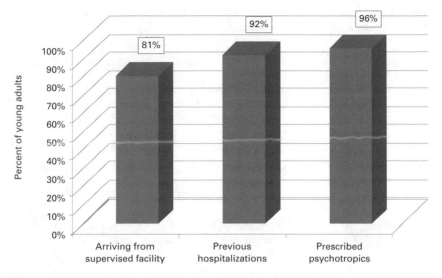

Figure 5.1.   Thresholds Young Adult Program (YAP) young adult intake data (*n* = 27; Fiscal Year 2006–2007).

also adopted many features of the TIP model. Its mission is identified as "mentoring young adults with SMI in discovering their strengths and accomplishing their goals in careers, relationships, homes, and wellness in the Long Beach community." The program's orientation could be characterized as a "Get a Life" program. This means young adults (18–26 years old) learn how to

- Develop and maintain supportive relationships

- Find and participate in educational and employment opportunities

- Secure safe shelter/housing

- Manage their illnesses, addictions, disabilities, and health

- Apply new skills and build on their own strengths

TAY and YAP: Similarities and Differences

As is evident from the previous descriptions, the TAY and YAP program initiatives have many common features between themselves and with the TIP system. The foremost differences between the TAY and YAP programs are outlined in Table 5.1 and are discussed next.

Table 5.1.   Comparison between Young Adult Academy (YAP) and Transition-Age Youth (TAY) programs

Transition program	YAP	TAY
Target age and population	16–21 Youth and young adults with serious mental illness (SMI)	18–26 Young adults with serious mental illness (SMI)
Primary funding source	Child welfare	Mental health
Orientation	Child/adolescent systems reaching up to adult-based supports	Adult systems reaching down to child/adolescent systems
Housing	Transitional and supported housing included	Supports for community housing
Specialized array of child-care services	Specialized program for young women with SMI who have child care needs for infants/toddlers	———

Length of Stay

TAY has the benefit of working with the young adults past 21 years of age, thus mentoring them to achieve more of their transition goals while navigating rougher and wilder parts of the transition river. Because YAP is largely supported by state child and adolescent funding entities, YAP services are limited for young people after age 21. However, the adult service personnel at Thresholds and other providers are also being trained to better serve YAP individuals as they leave and require ongoing mental health services and supports.

Program Orientation

TAY was created with the intention of adapting adult mental health systems for the young adults requiring services. Rooted in the child and adolescent service system, YAP was established to bridge services for the oldest young people with SMI preparing to leave the child welfare arena. Despite differences in orientation, both programs boast expertise in bridging the gap between the adolescent and adult service arena. The TIP Model has brought both programs to strengthen the focus on transition to adulthood functioning across all of the relevant transition domains.

Housing Options

On the housing front, TAY operates similarly to adult mental health providers, assisting young adults to find their own housing in the community. The array of housing options may encompass scattered-site apartments, supported housing, transitional housing, residential treatment facilities, or homeless shelters depending on the needs and circumstances of the young adults at the time. In contrast, YAP's services include transitional or supported housing in dormitory and apartment settings, with staff support for almost all young people entering the program as a part of their bundled services. YAP also has a specialized program for young women with SMI who have infants or toddlers and need access to the housing array, child care, and child and parenting development services.

Target Populations

Both the TAY Academy and Thresholds YAP have been predominately shaped by three main—but not separate—groupings of young adults with serious mental health challenges. These are the following:

- Young people who are referred with extensive histories of outpatient and residential mental health services

- Youth who have survived severe abuse or neglect and who are aging out of the foster care/child welfare system

- Young adults experiencing their first and/or early onset of mental illness who are showing severe and persistent symptoms that may be lifelong

The various diagnoses across these groups are often multiple and murky. Common childhood mental health diagnoses, including conduct disorders, mood disorders, attention-deficit/hyperactivity disorders, and severe emotional disturbances do not translate into the adult mental health lexicon, thus creating additional system barriers. The ubiquitous presence of drug and alcohol use, abuse, or dependence is a confounding overlay. In fact, more than 60% of TAY Academy's young adults are diagnosed with co-occurring disorders. Anecdotally, our programs are observing higher rates of co-occurring cognitive disturbances, developmental delays, and learning disabilities. Many staff also struggle with understanding emerging symptoms that look distinctly like personality disorders (Axis II), such as antisocial and borderline personality disorder. The symptoms of these disorders, however, may be more appropriately characterized as a correlate to the relational neglect many of our young adults experienced through childhood.

Although multiple diagnoses are the norm of the Thresholds YAP and TAY Academy service populations, the most common denominator of these various subpopulations is the indelible impact of trauma and its potential exacerbation of mental illness for young adults. However, the diagnosis of posttraumatic stress disorder (PTSD) does not seem to adequately categorize or describe this group. Van der Kolk (2005) has proposed the useful concept of developmental trauma disorder. According to his theory, there is a distinct difference between typical PTSD, which frequently is caused by a singular, traumatic event that often afflicts adults (disasters, injury, losses), and developmental trauma disorders, which are induced by prolonged exposure to interpersonal trauma in young and/or elementary-age children. The badly damaged attachment experiences of these children and youth often result in a persistent distrust of caregivers. Youth reenact their traumas, causing great disruption and anguish in their lives and in the lives of their caregivers and communities. Much of our programs' continuing evolution has been influenced by trying to provide transition services that address the complex needs of this developmentally traumatized group.

Progress and Outcomes

By providing services and supports dedicated specifically to the young adult population, both TAY Academy and Thresholds YAP have experienced significant progress over time. According to TAY's fiscal year 2006–2007 data, young adult incarceration was reduced by 42%, whereas young adult employment increased by 35% and the number of days worked also increased by 56% from the previous year.

According to YAP intake data for fiscal year 2005–2006, young adults averaged 10.4 years of education, whereas none of the admitted young adults had prior work experience. In 2005–2006, Thresholds YAP began working with the National Network on Youth Transition for Behavioral Health (NNYT) to orient its personnel to the TIP model, with a goal to achieve full TIP model implementation over the next several years. As shown in Figure 5.2, over a 3-year period, young adults in the YAP have increased in terms of number graduating from high school from our YAP special education school while also decreasing in terms of incidents of arrests. The percentage of young people with job starts varied over 3 years, but the most recent year showed the largest percent of young adult involvement with employment. As can be seen in Figure 5.3, young adults in YAP spent an average of 16.9 days in the hospital during 2005–2006. The average number of days in the hospital per young adult has dramatically decreased over the subsequent years to

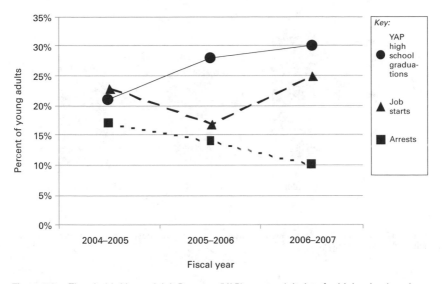

Figure 5.2.   Thresholds Young Adult Program (YAP) young adult data for high school graduations, job starts, and arrests.

approximately 11 days in 2007–2008 as Thresholds has converted more and more of its program components to the TIP system. These data trends are encouraging and are supported by the Clark, Pschorr, Wells, Curtis, and Tighe (2004) study as well as other published research findings on the TIP model outcomes.

Building the Boat While Whitewater Rafting

It is very encouraging that on local, state, and federal levels, policy makers are starting to become aware of both the needs of youth in transition and the best-service practices for these youth. The growing awareness of these young adults' needs and the subsequent but slowly expanding funding has allowed our programs to adapt more of the TIP model (see Chapter 2) into our work with young adults with mental illness.

After years of consistently "building the boat while whitewater rafting," many staff express a sense of confidence and understanding about our ability to navigate the turbulent rapids. They have started to integrate and learn from the evolving best practices and research. The more sophisticated we have become in matching our level of supports, energy, and interventions to the fidelity of our program models, the more the young adults have benefited. Nola's story exemplifies some of the young adult successes.

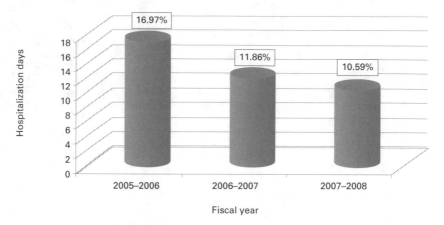

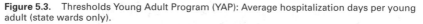

Figure 5.3.   Thresholds Young Adult Program (YAP): Average hospitalization days per young adult (state wards only).

Nola is now a 27-year-old student aide employed by the TAY Academy. Nola enrolled in TAY when she was 21 years old. She personifies the dramatic journey that is often associated with the TAY experience—living through ecstatic highs and horrible lows, but always demonstrating an indomitable courage to keep trying. Nola recounts holding at least 17 jobs in 7 years. She was fired by many employers, punched at least one boss, threw plates, and stormed out of jobs. Nola has lived in numerous housing situations of various types, including low-income motels, apartments, her car, friends' houses, and currently a HUD-subsidized apartment. She has been homeless, incarcerated, and assaulted. Nola has railed against the mental health system and TAY staff. She has vacillated between refusing and accepting medications and therapy, and she never seemed to be satisfied. At one point in her tenure as a TAY client, she tore down a "DO NOT ENTER" sign posted outside a staff room. This sign currently hangs on her apartment wall. Nola did not complete her journey of growing up at 26 years old, yet it's the arbitrary date one is expected to graduate from TAY. Since recently graduating from TAY, she currently receives services from TAY's parent program, the Village, for adults 25 and older. Now that she has also successfully joined the staff at the TAY Academy and has begun making "good trouble," she comments how, "These new TAY students need a lot of love, but with high expectations and ongoing coaching."

Lessons Learned: How to Navigate the Rapids

"These new TAY students need a lot of love, but with high expectations and ongoing coaching."

Through assimilation of evidence-supported practices, listening to our young adults, and much trial and error, our programs have created some significant strides in services for young adults. For the remainder of the chapter, we humbly share some of these failures and successes while illustrating some of our program adaptations and best practices that have evolved from our lessons learned across the topics of mental illness, engagement, service delivery, and housing.

MENTAL ILLNESS—DISCOVERY VERSUS RECOVERY

Tanya grew up in child welfare and lived in residential facilities the majority of her life. Growing up with many other teens who also had EBD, she never felt she was different from her peer group. When Tanya began the YAP program, she was one of only a few to graduate from high school on time and to attend community college. Despite her relative success, Tanya continued to struggle with diffuse rage, anxiety, and paranoia related to increased auditory hallucinations. It wasn't long before Tanya started to require more frequent hospitalizations, resulting from an increase in suicidal and homicidal ideations. Most of her difficulties involved attacking peers after even mild teasing. She stopped attending classes, spent more time in dangerous areas of the city, and slept more of the day. Tanya had surprising insight into worldly affairs and human nature, but she had little insight into her mental illness. As a result, Tanya refused medication, avoided discussing her wellness in therapy, and strayed from positive connections with peers in her program.

At 19 years of age, Tanya had an outburst at the program and was picked up by the police for walking naked down the street, which finally prompted her to discuss with her therapist how she did not always feel "herself." Over time, Tanya started to better acknowledge her strengths, limitations, and interests, which helped her rediscover some of her talents and again start to pursue some of her education goals.

As if adolescence isn't turbulent enough, the challenge of identity development and transitioning to adulthood is complicated by the presence of a mental illness. For many of our young adults, the presence of EBD continues to evolve across years. By the time young people reach early adulthood, discernable signs of serious mental illness emerge, including bipolar disorder, personality disorders, major depression, and schizophrenia. Close to 12% of young adults within the age range of 18–25 were reported in 2001 to have a serious mental illness (SAMHSA, 2002). This is the highest prevalence among any age group and is approximately double that of the general population (see also http://www.stopstigma.samhsa.gov).

Diagnosing Mental Illness

Many of the childhood psychiatric disorders are qualitatively different than the psychiatric disorders of adulthood. As a child develops, so do their symptoms, making it difficult for practitioners to reliably diagnose a child or adolescent at any one given point in time. Often, children and teens are described as having *emotional behavioral disorders* or *serious emotional disturbances* (SED) (U.S. Department of Health and Human Services, 1999). These labels do not represent a specific diagnosis; rather, they describe youth "under the age of 18 with a diagnosable mental health problem that severely disrupts their ability to function socially, academically, and emotionally" (U.S. Department of Health and Human Services, 1999).

The murky waters of diagnosis are perhaps best illustrated by the high prevalence of youth in care who are diagnosed with bipolar disorder. As we get to know the young adults in our programs, however, we find that many of them do not meet criteria for the adult diagnosis. Although there is controversy about the diagnosis of bipolar disorder in childhood, it is our experience that this psychiatric classification seems to be a catch-all for youth who have complicated histories of trauma and maltreatment in addition to complicated symptom pictures. Although pervasive symptoms of anxiety, mood dysregulation, and rage may have origins in developmental trauma disorders, such symptoms are at times erroneously viewed through the lens of mood disorder.

By the time youth enter TAY Academy or Thresholds YAP, it is not unheard of for them to have more than 10 different documented diagnoses, and in the case of YAP, young people enter with an extensive history of hospitalizations (e.g., young people with YAP intakes averaged 11.4 hospitalizations prior to entering in fiscal year 2005–2006). As youth move into young adulthood and enter our programs, the clinical picture starts to become clearer; symptoms become more consistent, yielding to a more accurate diagnosis, followed by a more accurately prescribed method of care. At YAP, the cornucopia of diagnoses for our young people falls into four main categories (schizophrenia/schizoaffective, major depression, bipolar, posttraumatic stress disorder), and one "other" category, as evidenced in Figure 5.4.

The adult model of care emphasizes *recovery* from mental illness. The concept of recovery implies that an individual had a disruption in their somewhat normal functioning, and that they are striving to return to the life and work trajectories they had before the onset of mental illness. In contrast, our young adults have typically endured EBD throughout the entirety of their lives, influenced by histories of neglect, abuse, and multiple placements that characterize developmental trauma disorders. In fact, nearly 50% of children in the child welfare system as a result of abuse or neglect are considered to have a significant EBD (Burns et al., 2004).

Although the manifestation of symptoms may change over a young adult's development, the serious mental health concerns in childhood and adolescence do not often disappear upon adulthood (Davis & Hunt, 2005). A study by Kim-Cohen and colleagues (2003) illustrated this continuum, in which 75% of adults with a psychiatric diagnosis at 26 years old had a documented diagnosis at 18 years old. Furthermore, 50% of the 26-year-olds had documented diagnoses at the age of 15 (Davis & Hunt, 2005).

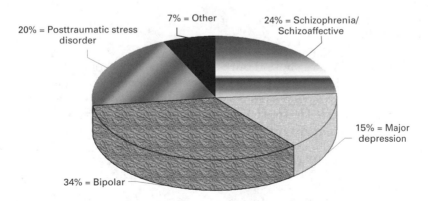

Figure 5.4. Breakdown of Thresholds Young Adult Program (YAP) young adults with Axis I diagnoses (*n* = 55).

Denying Mental Illness

The realization that difficulties (related to mental illness) are becoming more severe and will likely be present for life is an overwhelming one for a hopeful adolescent, much less for the adolescent who has little hope left. Out of necessity, our youth have developed an array of survival tactics that reflect their determination and resiliency. It is no wonder that, unlike most adults at Thresholds or The Village, the young adults rebel against and often refuse to accept having mental illness. One young adult said it best: To do so means to give up the fight for a normal life. "No one wants to go to a symptom management group because no one wants to sit around and admit that we have symptoms that need to be managed."

The malleability, resilience, and "fight" that many of our most traumatized and disadvantaged youth display are beneficial in another way. A young person's natural maturation process, coupled with these protective factors, can sometimes positively alter the trajectory of mental health symptoms (Schilling, Aseltine, & Gore, 2007).

A multitude of studies have focused on the need for specific services geared toward young adults to address their unique mental health needs during this crucial period of change. Solid mental health services are vitally important for preventing a deterioration of existing mental health, as well as preventing the development of new symptoms of mental illness (Clark & Foster-Johnson, 1996; Davis & Hunt, 2005). These studies have also emphasized that addressing and treating mental health and substance abuse issues should be within the context of assisting the young people to "get a life."

Discovery

At YAP and TAY, we support our young adults in the concept of *discovery* as a prelude to *recovery*. In all aspects of life, our young people are just beginning the process of discovering who they are, thereby increasing their identity development and self-knowledge as young adults. Discovery of their areas of interest, work that they might want to experience, and relationships they find supportive are all part of this process. Each young adult increasingly begins to discover that there are times when he or she is well and times when he or she is not so well. As they progress in self-knowledge, young adults often will identify

"No one wants to go to a symptom management group because no one wants to sit around and admit that we have symptoms that need to be managed."

more and more of what works best for them in order to stay well and function across the transition domains. Whereas parents, guardians, and state funders expect us to help our young adults realize that they have a mental illness, we see our job in supporting young adults in self-discovery at their own pace. Shifting from a deficit and illness model to a strengths-based, resiliency, discovery model allows us to better align our goals of lifetime wellness with the goals of our young adults we serve.

FACILITATING ENGAGEMENT

One of my first encounters at YAP involved a psychiatric appointment for a young man, Nathan, with a former staff psychiatrist. Although he was working part time at YAP, the staff psychiatrist's practice was overwhelmingly geared toward older adults. The doctor was conditioned to a very rigid schedule constructed ahead of time, thus leaving very little room for drop-ins. He also spent very little time out of his office working with the staff, getting to understand the culture of the program, or engaging with the young people away from the confines of his desk. Nathan's caseworker, Callie, described the story to me in detail.

Nathan wearily approached the door to the doctor's office with Callie by his side, appearing as though he might collapse and fall asleep at any minute. Callie tapped on the closed door and the doctor asked who was there. Callie answered for him, "Nathan's here for his appointment." The doctor, with his door remaining closed, replied, "I'm sorry; your appointment was 6 minutes ago. I'll see you next week." After voicing some choice expletives, Nathan stormed down the hallway, ripping posters off the wall, throwing chairs, and threatening to kill the psychiatrist and anyone who got in his way.

Attempting to play behavioral Sherlock Holmes, I met with Callie and other staff to find out from where the outburst originated. Apparently, the day began with Nathan refusing to get out of bed. Following numerous requests by Callie, Nathan finally emerged from his room stating that he would go if he could get some cigarettes on the way. Despite hearing voices and experiencing intense mood fluctuations, Nathan had refused to see the psychiatrist for about 4 months prior to this appointment. Agreeing to come to this ap-

> *"I'm sorry, your appointment was 6 minutes ago. I'll see you next week."*

pointment was a big step for him. Callie drove, and they arrived early to the building. While she parked the car, the caseworker left Nathan by the psychiatrist's door. In the meantime, Nathan got bored and decided to go the gym across the hall to shoot some hoops, fully expecting Callie to get him when it was time for his appointment. When Callie saw him in the gym, she expressed her frustration over Nathan not staying put. Her slight, though emotional, reaction triggered Nathan's anxiety and he responded by storming outside the building, swearing, and pulling out a cigarette to calm himself down. After some coaxing, Callie was able to reengage Nathan and convince him to attend the appointment. The psychiatrist's insensitive refusal to see Nathan clearly served as the final trigger, exciting in Nathan a fury of pent-up anger and frustration regarding not only the day in question but also despair over an illness that signified a lack of control over his thinking, feelings, and behaviors.

Engaging in a Future Focus

As our young adults approach independence, they find themselves at a confusing and scary crossroad. Given their collective histories of neglect, abuse, and emotional dysregulation, many of our young people still require the adults in their lives to function as their "external brain." This support and guidance becomes even more crucial when we consider the difficulty inherent in coping with a mental illness. As a natural corollary of the child welfare system, child mental health, and residential facilities, many of our young adults are unaccustomed to making decisions or managing many critical aspects of their lives.

Years of relatively little personal choice or decision-making power have left young adults transitioning out of these systems to fend for themselves, independent from adequate support or guidance. Ironically, this premature transition happens earlier for young adults in care who really need the supports. The general young adult population does not become fully engaged in careers, housing, and permanent intimate relationships until their late twenties or early thirties, as the economic realities of our society have shifted dramatically over the past several decades (Davis & Hunt, 2005). Moreover, our young adults have repeated experiences in which their world, uninformed about their history or their mental illness, responds callously, not at all unlike the aforementioned psychiatrist at YAP. Through their struggles, our young adults remind us that not only is there a learned helplessness of ownership over their transition but also this learned helplessness takes some time to unlearn. By embracing the TIP model guideline of engaging in a future focus, both YAP and TAY staff have developed strategies to increase young adult ownership over their goals toward self-discovery and adulthood.

Converging on Natural Engagement and Opportunities

The balance between motivating young adults to take part in their transition without pushing too hard is consistently difficult. It is easy for caseworkers, parents, coaches, and others to do things *for* the young adult when they are not motivated. In Nathan's example, the caseworker had many teachable moments that she could have taken advantage of:

- Allowing Nathan to make and keep track of the scheduled appointment

- Taking the bus instead of driving

- Apprising Nathan about the possible benefits to him of this visit to this psychiatrist for medical review—and the necessity of being on time due to the psychiatrist's back-to-back appointments

- Allowing Nathan to announce his own presence at the door

Callie clearly had the best of intentions. Simply, she attempted to remove all barriers for Nathan in an effort to help him get the assistance he so clearly needed. She did so, however, at the expense of engaging Nathan in the planning and organizing of his own life. In order to help our young adults succeed, we must provide them with the opportunity to practice taking initiative over their lives within the context of trusting relationships with their staff, mentors, family, and other key players. In doing so, we neither carry them on our backs nor turn them away at the door.

A pattern of tardiness or skipping appointments is not always equated with a lack of interest or motivation. (Just take notice at how many times young adults want your attention the one time you *do not* have time for them.) Young adults in our programs are rarely adamant about making their psychiatry appointments on time, much less their therapy groups, classes, or work. Appointment books do not fly off the shelf at our local store. Regardless, it is important to not give up on engaging young adults in activities and being flexible with teachable moments that will benefit their transition. As Clark expressed in Chapter 2, seasoned transition personnel operate by the following two axioms that guide their daily coaching, teaching, counseling, and relationship development practices in the field: 1) Maximize the likelihood of the success of young people, and 2) allow young people to encounter natural consequences though life experience.

Transition personnel, guided by these axioms, use mentoring, teaching of skills, contingency contracting, counseling, expectation-setting, problem solving, cajoling, and encouragement to maximize the likelihood that their youth will succeed. The facilitators also recognize the powerful role that life experience plays in teaching young people through their successes and failures. It may be that a young woman has gone through two social skills training groups, but it is only after being fired from her fourth job that she displays any receptivity to learning how to follow instructions and to problem solve with authority figures.

Program Strategies

We have noticed that most staff members are not prepared for the lack of motivation they encounter when working with young adults. For example, early on at Thresholds YAP we unexpectedly received a bounty of Chicago Cubs tickets available for an afternoon game. Although staff were excited to present what they perceived to be a fun activity for the young adults, not a single one ended up taking a ticket. There were many excuses: "You're not buying food for us, too," "I'm too tired," "The Cubs suck," "It's too hot (76 degrees)," and "It's too cold (76 degrees)." Understandably, the anxiety level rises intensely for staff members who cannot help but wonder how they will possibly get their young adults to stick with a group, school, or a job when they cannot even get them excited about a fun group activity.

We have found several strategies that are effective in facilitating engagement. At TAY, building relationships between young adults and staff is seen as a foundational task. Effective services are compromised unless rapport, trust, and a sense of connection are established. Through this connection, along with flexibility, empathy, and some targeted and effective cheerleading, we begin to engage the young adults in activities and services that they see as relevant to them on an individual basis. At TAY, we assign young adults to shared caseloads to maximize the opportunities for bonding with multiple staff from diverse backgrounds. We also conduct daily mobile outreach to young peoples' residences, places of work, school, or on the street to sustain contact with young adults who are unengaged, severely impaired, or new to being young adults.

At YAP, engagement means seizing the interests of the young adult as early as possible. Staff have the most success when they focus on discovering a young adult's strengths and interests early on, and then quickly help him or her pursue relevant activities that build on those strengths. Too often, we see examples of a young adult finally deciding that he or she is ready to go back to school only for the individualized education program (IEP) process to be delayed, resulting in the frustrated young adult changing his or her mind.

Early engagement also has the distinct effect of shifting a program's culture. Upon intake or preplacement visits, young adults are always looking to identify how they will fit in among their peers and what the program norms are (e.g., Do staff take an interest in my needs? What's the best way to get the attention I want? Do most of my peers work, go to school, or hang around the program causing trouble?). If a new young adult notices that most of his or her peers are involved in relevant activities, it's more likely that staff can engage him or her to follow suit in working on relevant activities toward his or her own unique transition goals. A program culture of young adult voice and peer mentors can greatly facilitate the engagement process.

SERVICE DELIVERY: "TWO'S A COUPLE, TEN'S A NIGHTMARE"

We stacked up old checkbooks, calculators, and grocery lists. We collated the 8-week curriculum we had spent hours tweaking, refining, and adjusting to fit the needs of our young adults. After retrieving the afternoon group snacks (our faithful motivator), we confidently stepped into the room of 10 familiar young adult faces, begrudgingly milling around the table.

Basic Allowance Budgeting 101 began with what was intended to be a discussion and subsequent consensus about basic group rules, thus compelling two of the members to stomp out of the group in disgust. Despite the minor disruption, the group was off to a decent start. Half of the group members followed the directions on how to use their checkbooks to deduct monthly costs from their allowance. Positive participation was short-lived, however, as two members then pulled out their cell phones, gabbing loud enough to demand attention. Soon, two others had their heads down, clearly on their way to an afternoon siesta. All the while, one group co-leader was attempting to give some individual assistance to James, who had significant delays in simple math. Another group member interrupted his phone call to sarcastically exclaim, "You graduated high school and you can't even add!?" Of course, several seconds later we found ourselves in the midst of separating James and his instigator. Shortly thereafter, as we tried to elicit cooperation to pick up the snacks scattered across the carpet, the three members who had successfully completed their budgeting task stated, "F— this" and strolled off to the corner store.

Shifting Program Paradigms

Although the previous example illustrates a rather extreme case of "when good groups go bad," a culmination of similar experiences did indeed highlight some serious flaws in our approach to serving these young adults. We concluded that the main source of disruption was due to the dearth of individually tailored supports and services. This group was full of young adults with not only different agendas but also different developmental needs and goals. Those who knew how to do the budgeting task were clearly uninterested, which led to disruption. Those who struggled did not get the attention they needed, or worse, were mocked and ridiculed by peers.

Thus, in all aspects of our work at YAP, we started to implement the TIP model to incorporate effective strategies for teaching skills that are relevant to the young person. We began to understand the essential guideline of engaging the young people and working with them to determine their interests and strengths, and then assisting them in developing their individually tailored goals and supports. This caused our staff to adjust how we used our psychoeducational groups, clinical staffings, team meetings, and other mainstays of the former program.

Consider Eric's story.

Eric was interested in learning more-advanced means of cooking meals. After adamantly denying cooking assistance, canned food started to wear on him. Rather than forming a cooking group, the transition team helped Eric think about a few recipes he would like to try out. His caseworker offered to do the grocery shopping with him on Tuesday afternoon, while the staff at his residence arranged to be available on Wednesday evening to assist him with the preparation. Eric agreed that if things went well, he'd get together with another friend in the program who had previously offered to open his eyes to some new delicacies.

In contrast to our evolving TIP practices, YAP's licensing representatives initially insisted on the program mandating a bundle of group therapy and psychoeducational sessions for the young adults. We have since educated key players at the licensing and funding level that, rather than a canned schedule of groups, applying the same interventions on a one-to-one level or very small group level increases young adults' interest and skill acquisition. Because not all youth need to learn the same skills or learn in the same manner, individually tailoring the skills increases youths' interest, engagement, and goal acquisition even more.

One Program Does Not Fit All

Most young adults growing up in residential facilities have spent years in a regiment of attending school by day and then returning to the residential unit to a schedule of after-school groups. For many years, their lives have also been dictated by a level system. A teen's path on the road to young adulthood in child welfare is about as similar to the real world as MTV's reality series *The Real World*. Isiah, a former YAP young adult, explained that, during the years he was growing up in residential facilities, staff attempted to help the residents lead a normal life but it felt nothing like normal to him. There was no separation between the peers with whom he lived and the peers with whom he attended school, thus leaving him with few social connections outside of his residential placement. The only job he began and maintained was within the residential program. Until 20 years of age, Isiah's entire life was encompassed by points and level systems that dictated his institutional engagement. He described how behaviors and accomplishments each day translated into points. Those points determined which of seven levels he was on. Once Isiah made it to level three, he was able to spend some supervised time outside of the residential unit. On the higher levels, he then could have some free time on his own. However, Isiah said he rarely made it to the higher levels, and thus, until he moved to YAP, he was rarely allowed free time outside of his residential placement.

The reinforcement and skill acquisition benefits of well-designed and monitored point and level systems are documented as evidence-based practices (Fixsen & Blase, 2004). However, it has also been shown that these motivational systems need to operate in the context of a humane and quality program arena that focuses on the relationship with the youth and teaching of relevant skills if it is to be effective (Wolf, Kirigin, Fixsen, Blase, & Braukmann, 1995). All too often, residential programs come to serve themselves, building rules and contingencies as a staff tool to manage group behavior, with little or no regard to the individualized needs of the young person. During his first 20 years, Isiah had experienced all too many of these types of programs and had little life experience, skills, or confidence to show for it. Thus he was not used to the relative freedoms he experienced upon transitioning out, or how to take control and structure his life without these external contingencies. Isiah had not been given any opportunity to experience discovery.

Moving from Artificial to Natural Reinforcers

Recognizing the need to assist our young adults in learning how to structure their own goals and progress during transition, our programs work hard on slowly decreasing the use of contrived points and level systems while increasing natural reinforcers for positive progress. The TAY Academy uses an incentive-based class module structure as part of the program. These twice-a-day modules are designed for young adults who lack basic life skills and can benefit from developing mental health coping strategies. Participation in *relevant* modules is reinforced by TAY "bucks," which are redeemable for food or drinks or can be saved for larger, future purchases to introduce a delay of gratification.

YAP facilitates various group skill development and therapeutic activities (e.g., Dialectical Behavior Therapy (DBT), Aggression Replacement Training [Goldstein, Glick, & Gibbs, 1998]) based on a young person's needs and interests. Participation, skill acquisition, and generalization are reinforced by YAP bucks. At the YAP monthly auction, young adults can bid with their YAP bucks for items such as CDs, snacks, hygiene products, games, clothes, or school supplies while practicing their learned skills.

Combining extrinsic motivators and natural consequences that benefit one's transition to independence is a great way to help young adults learn new skills, gain self-efficacy, and promote further engagement in the planning and achievement of their goals. When staff hope to increase a particular transition skill at the dorm, such as waking up in time for school or work, they might arrange a contingency such as presenting a favorite breakfast and providing rides for all of the young adults who get up on time. We also use rationales to assist young people in linking their behavior and choices with likely natural benefits or risks for themselves (Clark, Chapter 2). Instead of building an all-encompassing group level system, we use targeted incentives paired with natural consequences until the young adult acquires and generalizes the competency. After all, even adults (like these writers) can be motivated by reinforcers such as a favorite coffee or breakfast to help them wake up for work in the morning.

We are doing a disservice to our young adults if we shield them from the natural consequences inherent in their achievements or setbacks. In the end, when young people transition into a community apartment and they disturb their neighbors late at night, a landlord is not simply going to adjust their "level" status. Therefore, our transition personnel are always using the two axioms of maximizing a young person's likelihood of success while still allowing him or her to encounter natural life consequences. They then assist the young person in brushing off the dust and getting refocused on his or her goals.

HOUSING: "FROM NURSING HOME TO FRATERNITY"

I can recall more than a few parents who experienced their most severe anxieties over housing options for their son or daughter with emerging mental illness. For young adults who do not have adequate family support, housing is not only more critical but also more difficult to obtain. Unlike most young adults, those with mental illness are less likely to have an income to secure an apartment, less likely to obtain an educational loan, and less likely to have family assistance to help with rental payments. Furthermore, young adults coming from restrictive child welfare and other residential facilities are often ill-prepared for the independent living skills necessary for adult life. As children and early adolescents, they are used to having abundant staff support, meals prepared and presented to them, a strict schedule of chores, few visitors, and multiple restrictions on their free time outside of their living arrangement. Isiah suggested that most of these types of restrictions and dependency-building features of his placements extended well into late adolescence, substantially hindering his discovery, learning, and development of relationships and self-sufficiency.

The Needs/Housing Incongruence

On leaving child welfare or their family's home, inadequate preparation at such an early age often forces young adults to be housed in more restrictive placements than necessary, such as group boarding homes, nursing homes, or residential treatment facilities. Although most of our young adults do not require this highly institutionalized level of care, these restrictive facilities, homelessness, correctional facilities, and shelters become the fall-back realities for those without the skills and resources to live in the community.

Most states have large adult residential facilities or group homes. Though these options do provide some on-site staff and services, they are typically oriented to serve older adults and are still rather institutional. As a result, these placements deny young people the ability to actively prepare for their transition to adulthood roles. In our experience, many young people run away from these kinds of arrangements because they are not developmentally appealing; in other words, the average age of the folks living there are 10 to 20 years older than our young adults (Clark et al., 2008). Nell, a 21-year-old girl from YAP, told us that the adult residential option scared her, making her think that if she were to move there, she would end up "crazy" just like them. Following several visits to adult group homes, Stephen, 1 year younger than Nell, stated that the adult residents "Don't do a whole lot. They're never as active as me."

Once the young adult leaves or is kicked out of these settings, he or she often bounces between family, friends, and homelessness—while his or her mental health concerns intensify, gang involvement may occur and substance abuse typically exacerbates. Around 30 years of age, young adults on this trajectory typically end up again entering the criminal system or the mental health system.

Recognizing this dynamic, the best option is to allow young adults to gain developmentally appropriate life skills in the community while they still have the safety net of our programs to do so. Our programs have developed, or are linked to, an array of community-based living arrangements and supports to best match the young adult's needs and interests—and facilitate relevant learning and community-life functioning.

Tailoring Housing to Build Community-Living Skills

The TAY Academy has experimented with several different housing configurations for young adults, each providing progressively greater levels of independence. For young adults in TAY with the most serious needs, on-site 24/7 supervision is generally required to build skills and provide necessary structure. Focused on developmentally appropriate, normative housing, the TAY Academy established TAY Dorm. TAY Dorm's aim is to replicate a less-stigmatized, group-congregate setting while delivering housing supervision and structure for those requiring such.

Those who are at Thresholds YAP are also provided various levels of supervised and semi-independent housing until 21 years of age, thus affording young people the time and space to build life skills at their own pace and their own capacity. In our most supervised level of YAP housing, 10 to 12 young adults live in a male or female, dorm-style, three-flat building in the community. This housing arrangement, with its staff ratio of four young adults to each staff member, is a hybrid between a traditional group home and a college dorm setting. Even with the system's requirement that these facilities meet the definition of supervised housing, we work with each young adult to assume as much responsibility and autonomy as possible. Our experience with housing options also suggests that reducing the number of young adults living under one roof improves relationship development and individualized coaching of transition-based living skills.

Although YAP is contracted to provide high levels of staff oversight, we have attempted to make the setting as dorm-like as possible. In order to better accommodate a young person's transition to adulthood and community living, YAP has since developed a Hub Apartment Living model. This model demonstrates a transitional living arrangement that provides young adults with an effective mix of substantial independence along with tailored supports. The Hub model typically consists of six rented apartments in a larger community apartment building—five apartments for young adults and one apartment staffed 24/7. The young adults are responsible for the upkeep of their own apartment, which includes managing their cooking, cleaning, shopping, budgeting, and safety. They are subject to the rules of the landlord, yet because YAP is the provider agency, our Hub staff work with the young adults in planning, coaching, and supporting them to maintain their living situation and achieve their goals across relevant transition domains. Young adults who have experienced this Hub Apartment Living arrangement report that it provides them with the best balance of independent living and relevant, comfortable, engaging supports.

As the young adult moves closer toward 21 years of age, we facilitate their selection of an independent community apartment or other housing arrangement for them to maintain once they leave YAP. Staff from YAP, in conjunction with personnel from the adult mental health system, provide individualized transition services in order to provide a smooth transition over the service gap.

The YAP program could not have accomplished the implementation of this housing array nor the adoption of more and more of the TIP model without a growing shared vision by the leadership and other dedicated personnel in the Illinois Department of Child and Family Services (DCFs). The partnership with DCFs and other state and local agencies has proven to be essential to the progress we are making to improve the quality of services for young people and their life outcomes.

Allowing Young Adults a Choice and a Chance

Over the years, our programs have weathered plenty of arguments around housing. Many practitioners and administrators insist that young adults with mental illness are too "severe," and thus require the most restrictive of adult-based housing and services. Our programs' approach has been to establish an array of housing options and supports, and to individually tailor these as best we can to a young person, realizing that he or she may need other arrangements over time. A recent example can be illustrated by Sierra's experience while living at YAP.

Sierra was considered to be one of YAP's most successful young adults. She has excelled in learning and applying independent living skills, actively setting goals, and working to accomplish them. Now 19, she is a recent graduate of a mainstream education high school and is looking to pursue a job and eventually continue on to higher education. Sierra had been expressing a strong desire to move from our dorm facilities into her own apartment. While YAP staff assisted her in pursuing this goal, her child welfare representatives continued to focus on her mental illness and argued to keep her protected from the community. Her state child welfare representatives insisted that YAP staff instead pursue adult guardianship for Sierra and start paperwork to institutionalize her into adult-based residential care. Understanding that adult-based care will always be there, but that this chance to try supported independence is time-limited, Sierra's transition team finally resolved to follow Sierra's voice. Recently, she has been allowed a chance to maximize her success in a Hub apartment with individually tailored supports.

YOUNG ADULT VOICE: "TELL ME HOW YOU *REALLY* FEEL"

If we continue to limit youths' opportunities throughout their young adulthood, they will be denied the opportunity to live productively in the community and the ability to change the course of their lives. We have found that the more fully we implement the TIP model across our programs and apply the right mix of discovery, coaching, choice, and teaching, the better prepared our young adults are for successful community living at their maximum capacity.

As we review our lessons learned at Thresholds YAP and TAY Academy, it is no surprise that the greatest lessons we learn are from the young adults themselves. In 2008, there was a growing array of opportunities for young adults to have a voice on a large-scale basis within Illinois, other states, and nationally. As our young adults participate in local, state, and national forums, they illuminate how important it is to be involved and even lead to the decisions that directly affect their lives. They want us to know that their mental illness and troubled histories do not define them. They want to let program staff and parents know not to baby them or do everything for them. Instead, we need to allow young adults the freedom to experience discovery (e.g., natural consequences of their successes and mistakes) and to provide a safety net from which to learn from these experiences and recover from their poorer choices.

Some of the young adults who are closer to adulthood want to teach their lessons to the current young adults in our programs. The young people grow from and cherish peer mentorship and student aide opportunities (see Chapter 7). As peer mentors, they want to coach and share with other young adults their experiences and lessons learned. They want to

"You need to learn what to expect. If you're not learning what to expect when you're a teenager, it will hit you right in the face as an adult . . . you need to learn how to be an adult before you become one."

share that, in hindsight, the adults who worked with them actually *do* know what they are doing, and despite all of the grief they give adults it is hard to sever the relationship that has been there for them over time and trouble. Most of all, they want to tell other young adults to take advantage of support, growth, and discovery opportunities available within TIP-oriented programs such as ours. Isiah might have stated it best when he said, "You need to learn what to expect. If you're not learning what to expect when you're a teenager, it will hit you right in the face as an adult . . . you need to learn how to be an adult before you become one."

REFERENCES

Burns, B., Phillips, S., Wagner, H., Barth, R., Kolko, D., Campbell, Y., et al. (2004). Mental health needs and access to mental health services by youths involved with child welfare: A national survey. *Journal of the American Academy of Child and Adolescent Psychiatry, 43*(8), 960–970.

Clark, H., Crosland, K., Geller, D., Cripe, M., Kenney, T., Neff, B., & Dunlap, G. (2008). A functional approach to reducing runaway behavior and stabilizing placements for adolescents in foster care. *Research on Social Work Practice. 18*(5), 421–428.

Clark, H.B., & Foster-Johnson, L. (1996). Serving youth in transition into adulthood. In B.A. Stroul (Ed.), *Children's mental health: Creating systems of care in a changing society* (pp. 533–552). Baltimore: Paul H. Brookes Publishing Co.

Clark, H.B., Pschorr, O., Wells, P., Curtis, M., & Tighe, T. (2004). Transition into community roles for young people with emotional behavioral difficulties: Collaborative systems and program outcomes. In D. Cheney (Ed.), *Transition of secondary approaches for positive outcomes* (pp. 201–226.). Arlington, VA: The Council for Children with Behavioral Disorders and the Division of Career Development and Transition, Divisions of the Council for Exceptional Children.

Davis, M., & Hunt, B. (2005). State efforts to expand transition supports for young adults receiving adult public mental health services. Rockville, MD: Substance Abuse and Mental Health Services Administration, Center for Mental Health Services.

Fixsen, D.L., & Blase, K.A. (2004). The evidence bases for the Teaching-Family Model. Retrieved March 15, 2009, from http://www.fpg.unc.edu/~nirn/resources/detail.cfm?resourceID=4

Goldstein, A.P., Glick, B., & Gibbs, J.C. (1998). *Aggression Replacement Training(r): A comprehensive intervention for aggressive youth.* Champaign, IL: Research Press.

Kim-Cohen, J., Caspi, A., Moffitt, T.E., Harrington, H., Milne, B.J., & Poulton, R. (2003). Prior juvenile diagnoses in adults with mental disorder: Developmental follow-back of a prospective-longitudinal cohort. *Archives of General Psychiatry, 60*(7), 709–717.

Schilling, E.A., Aseltine, R.H., & Gore, S. (2007). Adverse childhood experiences and mental health in young adults: A longitudinal survey. *BMC Public Health, 7*(30). Retrieved September 5, 2007, from http://www.biomedcentral.com/1471-2458/7/30

Substance Abuse and Mental Health Services Administration (SAMHSA). (2002). *Results from the 2001 National Household Survey on Drug Abuse: Volume I. Summary of national findings* (Office of Applied Studies, NHSDA Series H-17, DHHS Publication No. SMA02-3758). Rockville, MD. Author.

U.S. Department of Health and Human Services. (1999). *Mental health: A report of the Surgeon General.* Rockville, MD: U.S. Department of Health and Human Services, Substance Abuse and Mental Health Services Administration, Center for Mental Health Services, National Institutes of Health, National Institute of Mental Health.

Van der Kolk, B. (2005). Child abuse and victimization: Treating complex trauma in children and adolescents. *Psychiatric Annals, 35*(5), 374–378.

Wolf, M.M., Kirigin, K.A., Fixsen, D.L., Blase, K.A., & Braukmann, C.J. (1995). The Teaching-Family model: A case study in data-based program development and refinement (and dragon wrestling). *Journal of Organizational Behavior Management, 15*(1/2), 11–68.

Improving the Transition Outcomes of Adolescent Young Offenders

Deanne K. Unruh, Miriam G. Waintrup,
Tim Canter, and Sinjin Smith

While incarcerated and asked about his future goals, one young man responded:

"To me it's to be a good father. Get married and have a good life. Not do drugs, not do alcohol. Have a good job. It doesn't matter if it's paying as long as it's steady. Get my own house. Get on my feet. Pay off bills. Get off parole. Have a happy family. There's part of me in that dream and I want to help people like me.

— Adolescent involved in the juvenile justice system

The goals of young people involved in the juvenile justice system do not differ from the goals of other young adults, yet the trajectory to adulthood is much more difficult. Youth involved in the juvenile justice system often exhibit additional risk factors such as drug use and mental health issues that provide additional challenges to their passage to achieving adult outcomes.

Annually in the United States, more than 2.2 million juveniles are arrested, with more than 110,000 juveniles incarcerated in juvenile correctional facilities (Snyder & Sickmund, 2006). Not only are these adjudicated adolescents at increased risk of committing future crimes (Bullis, Yovanoff, Mueller, & Havel, 2002; McCord, 1992) but they are also at risk of not becoming healthy, productive adults. Alarmingly, between 65% and 70% of these individuals have at least one diagnosable mental health disorder and, of even more concern, 60% of these youth meet the criteria for three or more diagnoses. In addition, young women involved in the juvenile justice system, who demonstrate internalizing behaviors more often than boys, are also at higher risk for mental health diagnoses, at a rate of approximately 80% (Shufelt & Cocozza, 2006).

Juvenile criminal behaviors also strain the resources of our legal and justice systems, burden victims and their families, and increase costs for medical and social services (Cohen, 1998). Young adults' continued criminality jeopardizes stable employment, career, and living options—increasing personal costs associated with not reaching their adult potential. States report average recidivism rates of nearly 55% for individuals who have exited a correctional facility for at least 12 months (Snyder & Sickmund, 2006). These long-term societal costs of continued criminality are a concern for our nation's economy. The costs of incarcerating an adolescent can be greatly reduced by implementing interventions targeting prescriptive, evidence-informed practices that decrease continued criminality. The implementation of evidenced-based practices were found in the state of Washington to reduce the need for future prison beds, thus saving money for state and local taxpayers and contributing to lower crime rates for their state (Aos, Miller, & Drake, 2006).

In intervention planning, youth with disabilities—predominately youth with EBD—in the juvenile justice system often are overlooked in the implementation of and adherence to special education transition policies and regulations (Leone, Meisel, & Drakeford, 2002). Mental health screening has only recently and with varying degrees of success been universally administered in youth correctional systems (Skowyra & Cocozza, 2007). As a result, the reentry outcomes for formerly incarcerated youth with disabilities are dismal compared with peers with and without disabilities (Bullis, Yovanoff, & Havel, 2004), and longitudinal studies suggest that many youth displaying criminal behavior will manifest continuing problems—at least to some degree—in their work, school, and family endeavors as adults (McCord, 1992).

Unruh and colleagues (in press), in a qualitative study of factors influencing the community adjustment process in young offenders, found a constellation of both risk and protective factors that influence a successful transition into the community post release from a youth correctional facility. This study identified how an individual's self-regulation and the subsequent relationships between peers and families influence the community adjustment status of individuals leaving closed custody (Unruh, Povenmire-Kirk, & Yamamoto, in press).

Service coordination for this population is difficult as these youth shift from child-centered social service agencies to adult-oriented agencies, often at the same time as leaving a secured correctional setting and returning to the community. This transition from a correctional setting, which is complicated and difficult, may result in diminished or ineffectual service provision (Vander Stoep, Davis, & Collins, 2000). Young offenders with EBD face individual barriers to success, and service coordination for these youth is characterized by additional fragmentation and service gaps for these youth transitioning into adulthood (see Chapter 1).

On a positive note, formerly incarcerated youth with disabilities who were working or going to school during the first 6 months of release were 3.2 times *less likely* to return to custody and 2.5 times *more likely* to remain working or enrolled in school 12 months after exiting the correctional facility (Bullis et al., 2002). In other words, findings from this research indicated that youth who became engaged in work and/or school soon after release to the community fared better in their transition than those who did not become engaged. Therefore, employment and further education immediately after exiting closed custody may serve as protective factors to reduce recidivism and improve postschool outcomes in the lives of formerly incarcerated adolescents with EBD.

Other factors influencing service models include the implementation of culturally appropriate and gender-specific services as integral elements for programming for this population. Unruh and Bullis (2005) identified a set of risk factors for young women offenders compared with male offenders. These factors are important for understanding service planning based on the individual needs of the young person. For instance, young women are statistically *more likely* to have a history of running from home or residential placement, suicide risk, and abuse (physical, sexual, or neglect) than are their male counterparts. On the other hand, young women are *less likely* be retained in a grade, to be unable to maintain a job, or to have externalizing behaviors such as ADHD than their male peers (Unruh & Bullis, 2005).

Acknowledging these multiple challenges for developing a sustainable community-based service model for juvenile offenders with EBD, representatives of the Oregon Department of Education (ODE), Oregon Youth Authority (OYA), and the University of Oregon (UO) initiated planning in May of 1998 to address these issues in working with youth with a special education or mental health diagnoses. The working session established the framework for a multiagency project centered on developing a collaborative process serving incarcerated youth with disabilities (the majority with EBD) as they transitioned from a long-term correctional setting into the community.

PROJECT STAY OUT

The purpose of this chapter is to describe the development, implementation, and essential features of and lessons learned from a multiagency state collaboration that has evolved into its current form, named *Project STAY OUT*—Strategies Teaching Adolescent Young Offenders to Use Transition Skills. A preliminary project—*Project SUPPORT*—was initiated in 1999 as a statewide service effort managed by the Oregon Department of Education, Oregon Youth Authority, Oregon Office of Vocational Services (VR), and the University of Oregon.

Governance Structure

An ongoing strategic planning process at both administrative and service levels was developed to administer the project and foster its sustainability within the existing education and correctional systems. A state management team consisting of the three state agencies (VR, ODE, and OYA) and the evaluation team of the University of Oregon met monthly to review project progress and to discuss new administrative or legislative changes affecting project services. In early 2008, the management team for STAY OUT was then expanded to include individual representation from the state's Workforce Investment Board (WIA) along with staff from the Department of Human Services in the Addiction and Mental Health Department.

Project SUPPORT was funded initially through matching funds from the three state agencies who formed a cooperative agreement to manage the disbursement of the funds. With the initiation of Project STAY OUT, a localized funding model was developed with guidance from the state agency advisory committee. To embed project services within the local communities, a sustainable funding process was defined within existing state fiscal structures through the use of state school funds. The initial start-up funds through grant dollars provide an opportunity for the development of the collaborative relationships across local agencies and project services and enable funding strategies to be implemented. Local Partnership Agreements are developed providing guidance and identifying responsibilities of each agency. To sustain ongoing funding, Project STAY OUT uses the Average Daily Membership (ADM) generated by the youth served within the project who still are eligible for state school funds to maintain the transition specialist position in youth enrolled in WIA who receive education and employment-related support. Eligibility for state school funds in Oregon includes any youth who has not received a regular high school diploma through the age of

19 for students without individualized education programs (IEPs) and the age of 21 for students with a special education diagnosis. School districts also have the discretion to expand general education student's access to education through the age of 21 with district policy. Since the transition specialists are ESD or school district employees and provide transition services to support a youth's educational goals and develop employability skills, their services meet the criteria for project youth to qualify for the state school support. This funding strategy allows for the project to employ the existing state school funding model in order to sustain the project across time.

Project STAY OUT's Service Delivery Model

The project's service delivery model was developed from existing evaluation literature of programs for youth with EBD (e.g., Bullis & Cheney, 1999; Bullis & Fredericks, 2002; Clark & Davis, 2000), and juvenile corrections (e.g., Altschuler & Armstrong, 1991). In addition, we relied on and used recommendations from the field to address system barriers for transition coordination (Bridgeo, Davis, & Florida, 2000; Cheney, Hagner, Malloy, Cormier, Bernstein, 1998; Clark, Deschênes, & Jones, 2000; Unruh & Bullis, 2005; Unruh, Gau, & Waintrup, 2008). The outcomes of students studied previously clearly pointed to the importance of engaging youth in work and/or school in the 12-month period immediately following exit from a correctional facility (Bullis, Yovanoff & Havel, 2004). Using this evidence, the planning team determined that the project services offered to each participant must be initiated while the individual is in the correctional facility to ensure that services are accessed immediately on exiting custody. The service delivery model's cornerstone relies on a transition specialist (TS), who works closely with facility treatment and education staff along with the parole officer (PO) to ensure that appropriate services are ready for the youth to access upon his or her release from custody.

Four regions, both rural and urban, were selected across the state as pilot sites. These regions participated in an initial needs assessment to define existing barriers and supports present within the regions to initiate the project. A fifth region was added in the second year and statewide coverage was achieved in the latter half of 2001. From 2001 through 2004, nine TSs provided Project SUPPORT services to youth across Oregon. In addition, two more transition specialists were added to population-dense regions with funding through a model demonstration grant from the Office of Special Education Programs (OSEP) of the U.S. Department of Education. In 2004, the Oregon Department of Education, in a change of administration, eliminated funding for the project and only the two urban regions, Lane (Eugene/Springfield) and Multnomah (Portland) Counties, maintained TS positions through grant funding that ended in September 2008. The Lane County TS was maintained by school district funding, relying on the funding model just described. The Oregon Youth Authority had maintained interest in recreating SUPPORT through developing a localized funding model; therefore, in 2008, the University of Oregon and OYA collaboratively received a grant from the Office of Juvenile Justice and Delinquency Prevention through the U.S. Department of Justice to develop a localized funding model for the project. This genesis resulted in the project's name change to STAY OUT, and as of December, 2008, two new regions in Oregon were once again initiating project services.

Essential Features of Service Delivery

The purpose of Project STAY OUT is to provide incarcerated youth with either a designated special education disability and/or a mental health disorder with prerelease training and coordinated planning to support a transition into the community. Program goals are to increase a participant's engagement in employment and/or school enrollment (high school/postsecondary) and decrease rates of recidivism.

The service delivery model components for this intervention are structured around features identified as effective for youth with EBD and include 1) strategies to enhance self-determination skills, with services focused on the unique needs, interests, strengths, and barriers of the youth; 2) competitive employment; 3) flexible educational opportunities; 4) social skill instruction; and 5) immediate service coordination (Bullis & Cheney, 1999) to develop a positive social network in the community. These components are aligned with the TIP guidelines discussed in Chapter 2. We will briefly describe each of the components included in the service delivery model and provide examples of themes that were captured when conducting a needs assessment of barriers and supports to the community adjustment process for young adults leaving the youth correctional facility. Many of the themes identified by the young adults interviewed are interconnected, as will be illustrated by the quotes.

Enhanced Self-Determination Skills

In asking individuals leaving the youth correctional facility about what their needs will be when returning to the community, a theme emerged related to the self-determination or self-regulation of the individual. As one youth put it, "It's on me; I either do it [be successful in the commu-

nity/not recidivate] or not."
The project works to develop
a youth's ability to become
an advocate for him- or her-

> *"A lot of us, if we really get bored, we just don't have nothing to do, we look for negative things to do."*

self along with support in developing and consistently practicing problem-solving skills. These skills need to be developed and practiced while the youth is in the facility—but more important—they need to be transferred to the community.

Competitive Employment

A paid work environment is essential because it allows the youth to participate in an applied setting and experience the natural consequences—both negative and positive—of being employed. In addition, being involved in work also increases the amount of time the young adult will be engaged in positive activities and not return to negative behaviors within the community.

This theme was expressed in the needs assessment:

> [My] job keeps me busy. A lot of us, if we really get bored, we just don't have nothing to do, we look for negative things to do. So anything, work, extracurricular, going to the gym, lifting weights, to keep our minds on positive stuff. . . .

In addition, the youth are concerned about the stigma of being involved in the juvenile justice system and worry about the employer's perceptions of this stigma. For example, one youth shared, "If [they] see somebody that's marked *felony* on their sheet [job application]; then they're going to pick the person that's not got it." Training the youth in appropriate ways to disclose being involved in the juvenile justice system and role playing various scenarios is helpful for youth getting ready to enter the job market. (For further information on job development strategies for youth involved in the juvenile justice system, see Waintrup & Unruh, 2008.)

Flexible Educational Opportunities

Typically, youth leaving the youth correctional facility are at the age that they have either received their high school diploma or GED in the correctional setting or they have too few credits, so that it would take an inordinate amount of time to earn a high school diploma. This means that oftentimes, a traditional public school setting is not an appropriate educational placement. In addition, many of the traditional school settings are not welcoming to youth wanting to reenroll; often these youth were not successful in school prior to incarceration and are not looking forward to returning to a place where they had no success prior to being incarcerated. Educational opportunities need to focus on the needs, academic levels, and interests of each individual in mind in order for the young adult to get a high school diploma or a GED if he or she left the correctional setting without one. If a youth has received a diploma, then various vocational training, certification, or postsecondary education options should be explored.

Social Skill Instruction

Youth who had been institutionalized were concerned about the ability to be able to function in the community. As one youth described it, "I'm not going to learn how to live here [institution], I'm going to learn how to be institutionalized."

This theme also extends into supporting the youth to develop appropriate social interaction skills for the various environmental settings in which he or she may interact—the workplace, school, home, with peers, and so forth. Each of these settings requires a different set of social skills to successfully maneuver between the various relationships within and across these settings.

Immediate Access to Service Coordination

The first 6 months after leaving the correctional setting are the most critical for preventing a return to either juvenile or adult corrections. Immediate access to services on leaving the youth correctional setting is essential, specifically, accessing health care after exit, for youth who may be taking various medications. In addition, many youth with EBD leaving the youth correctional facility may require multiple service agencies to be involved in their lives. These agencies may include the juvenile justice agency, mental health services, alcohol and other drug treatment services, vocational rehabilitation or workforce investment agency, and housing. Coordinating all of these possible services takes a great amount of organization, aside from other time commitments related to employment and going to school. Service coordination can be daunting to an individual, and support in planning, navigating across agencies, and maintaining schedules is an important skill learned in program services.

Development of Positive Social Networks and Independent Living Skills

As young adults adjust to being in the community, key obstacles in their path can include returning to their former negative peer network coupled with drug use. When asked to describe one barrier to successful transition, one young adult noted, "Making new friends, 'cause I've had the same friends since I was 12; I've been doing the same thing for a long time. It's going to be pretty difficult for me to have to make such a drastic change." An essential feature of this program is to support the youth in developing positive social networks in the community and their families, then. Often, positive networks are developed naturally when a young adult starts a new job or enrolls in a different school or vocational setting. Friends may develop from these new settings in which the youth is interacting. If these positive networks do not develop, project services may be targeted that encourage the youth to participate in positive extracurricular activities in the community (i.e., the gym, hobbies, volunteer opportunities, faith-based organizations.)

Individuals will need support in developing independent living skills. One youth offender described his concerns about his skills in this area,

> [I will need help] making my own food and like, just going outside, being in public, job applications . . . just simple things. They're going to be hard . . . like even doing my own clothes; it's going to be hard 'cause I haven't done it in a long time.

Often, these young people exit the facility at a much older age than when they entered as young teens, with society viewing them as adults and expecting them to be experienced at many daily tasks and routines that were not developed within the institution. The program needs to address supporting the youth to develop their independence with the requisite skills to do so.

Project STAY OUT's Service Delivery Model

In the Project STAY OUT'S service delivery model, a TS is the key project staff person. Each TS works directly with the youth and PO to develop a project transition plan that is coupled with the youth's parole plan. Services are provided collaboratively with staff from the three agencies along with community support agencies: 1) a VR or WIA counselor, 2) a treatment manager, 3) a PO, and 4) facility and community education staff. These staff work in partnership with the TS who provides direct services to project participants. The TS is responsible for gaining informed consent from the project participants or their guardians to participate in the project and for data to be collected on participants. The TS also ensures that appropriate sharing of information occurs and that requisite paperwork for various court, educational, and psychological services needed to develop an effective transition plan is signed.

The initial responsibility of the transition specialist is to define each youth's strengths, needs, interests, and life goals in order to develop a transition plan with services aligned to the unique needs and interests of each project participant. Services are not a prescriptive set of activities provided to each youth, but instead rely on the TS's ability to make decisions and connections with each youth based on information and guidance provided by the youth, parole officer, family, and other agency staff. After a youth has been screened and referred into the project, services typically occur in three distinct phases: 1) in-facility services, 2) immediate pre- and post-release activities, and 3) ongoing community support (see Figure 6.1). A training manual for a transition specialist can be found at http://www.sset.uoregon.edu.

Once a youth has been screened into the project, the TS initiates the in-facility activities. The primary purpose of these activities is to develop a positive mentoring relationship with the youth and define the transition needs (e.g., educational status, preemployment skills, ongoing treatment needs) for returning to the community. The TS works with facility staff (e.g., treatment manager and facility education staff) and the youth's parole officer to gather information to develop a project transition plan. After reviewing a youth's records, the TS may find that the youth has a disability that may qualify him or her for VR or WIA services. An individual's evaluation documentation (e.g., mental health records, special education assessments) will be shared with these staff located in the youth's region of exit, and a meeting is scheduled with a counselor to define eligibility for services.

In addition, the TS works individually with the youth to learn more about his or her career interests, aptitudes, education goals, and inde-

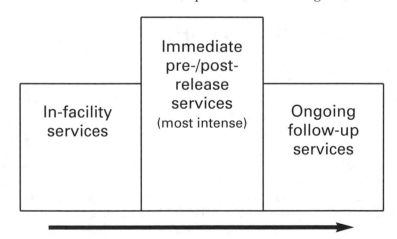

Figure 6.1.   Phases of STAY OUT service delivery.

pendent living skills. These activities include assisting the youth to develop skills to 1) complete accurate job applications; 2) practice job interviews; 3) complete financial aid paperwork to enroll in school; 4) develop skills in budgeting, completing taxes, and opening checking accounts; 5) obtain needed identification cards (e.g., social security, birth certificate); and 6) locate local community resources when the youth exits custody (e.g., mental health treatment, alcohol and other drug treatment).

The most critical phase of the project is immediately prior to and following parole from the youth correctional facility: the immediate pre- and post-release activities. This phase was carefully planned as prior research noted that immediate access to employment and/or school engagement was critical to reducing a youth's risk of recidivism (Bullis et al., 2002). The parole officer and TS work very closely during this phase. Their responsibilities are different but support the community reintegration of the project participant. For example, the parole officer may have specified that the youth obtain a job as part of the parole plan, but it is the TS who works with the youth to accomplish this goal.

While the youth is still in the correctional facility, the TS works closely with the parole officer to begin setting up services that are to be accessed immediately when the youth enters the community. Typically, these activities consist of assisting the youth to secure employment by connecting them with a VR counselor or with WIA offices often located within One-Stop Centers. The transition specialist also provides employability skill development in the community by 1) coaching the youth in job search activities, making employer contact, and completing application processes, 2) reviewing appropriate attire to wear to interviews, and if needed, 3) job coaching to resolve problems between the employer and the youth. Other community-based supports provided by the TS may include 1) assisting the youth to learn how to access public transportation; 2) obtaining housing (e.g., apartment searches, completing rental applications); 3) continuing a youth's education goals (e.g., completing financial aid paperwork, visiting disability services office on community college campuses); 4) navigating the ever-changing health care system (e.g., obtaining a medical card, making appointments, securing needed medications); and 5) locating healthy leisure activities (e.g., sports clubs in the neighborhood.).

Once a youth has stabilized in the community and is positively engaged in work, school, or a combination of the two, the TS's role is to continue collaborating with the PO to support and maintain the youth's engagement within the community. This ongoing community support phase includes maintaining contact with the youth, family, parole officer, and other community agencies. The TS primarily serves as a resource and typically provides assistance in the following issues: 1) continuing to further develop employment or education goals (e.g., get a promotion or higher level position, receive additional employment training), 2) developing higher levels of independent living skills (e.g., completing taxes, obtaining car insurance), and 3) gaining access to services surrounding parenting needs and/or decisions. The TSs are trained to identify signs of a youth returning to former negative habits (e.g., drug use, affiliating with negative peer groups). If these signs of negative behavior occur, the parole officer, TS, and youth address these issues.

Evaluation Results

Both process and outcome data were collected from project initiation to the present. We collected extensive information about the background characteristics of the individuals, what TS activities were completed and what services accessed by clients, and outcome information in the broad transition domains of employment, education, and reduced criminality (recidivism). The process evaluation helped inform us about the program in order for us to examine ways to improve services. We systematically examined the background characteristics that documented types of barriers to transition the youth faced, in order to better forecast the types of activities and services the young adults would need. We also examined the type of transition activities completed by the TS and the types of community services accessed by the youth to see if we needed to expand the capacity of the project or work further to develop relationships with other local service partners. We also examined the outcome data to ensure that the youth were engaged in employment and education opportunities, which was the primary focus of the TS. In this section, we will describe the results from each of these areas for the reader.

Snapshot of STAY OUT Youth

This description of STAY OUT participants provides a profile of young adults with EBD who are involved in the justice system in which services need to be tailored for their unique interests, needs, strengths, and challenges to be addressed through program services. The average age of STAY OUT youth was 17.4 years of age at entry into the project. Because project services to youth began 3–6 months prior to exit from a correctional setting, the youth were approximately the age of 18 upon release into the community, which meant individuals were on the cusp of many social services (i.e., adult corrections, mental health) between child and adult services. Two-thirds of the youth were Caucasian, with the other top three ethnic groups consisting of African American, Hispanic, and Native American youth in order of prevalence of involvement in the project. In Oregon, approximately 13% of the population is composed of individuals from minority groups. Overrepresentation of minorities in the juvenile justice systems is common across states. Slightly more than 80% of all youth involved in STAY OUT were male, which is representative of the 80:20 ratio of males to females incarcerated in Oregon. A total of 87% of all youth had a diagnosable mental health condition as defined by the *Diagnostic and Statistical Manual of Mental Disorders* (American Psychiatric Association, 1994). Surprisingly, only 46.4% had an active individualized education program required for the receipt of special education services. The authors feel that this rate is underrepresentative of participants eligible for special education services. Many systemic issues are suspected to contribute to the underrepresentation; some explanations could include the following:

• The youths' education cumulative files are not transferred to the facility in a timely manner—or at all—to identify the youth for special education services.

• The youth may not have been enrolled in a public school setting for several years prior to being incarcerated, and locating the student's cumulative file may be difficult.

• Students who may be truant or receiving drug and alcohol treatment may be declassified from special education because, at the adolescent level, it may be hard to discern the true impediment to educational progress.

We also collected information on possible barriers to transition or the community adjustment process. A list of 22 barriers to transition was provided on the entry form in the domains of 1) employment (e.g., unable to maintain jobs), 2) education (e.g., reading/math below fifth- to sixth-grade level), 3) living status/residence (e.g., multiple living arrangements), and 4) family or personal issues (e.g., history of abuse/neglect). For the young adults served through Project STAY OUT, the top six barriers to transition (and the percentage of youth reported to experience these) included

• Excessive absenteeism from school: 77.5%

• History of substance abuse: 76.3%

• History of running away from home: 63.6%

- Placement in foster care at the time of incarceration: 61.5%

- Attendance at multiple schools during their education history: Almost 60%

- Anger control problems: Almost 60%

In examining the youth's criminal history background, 41.5% of youth were adjudicated for their first crime at the age of 13 or younger. For youth in the project, 41.6% of the youth were adjudicated for a property crime as their first offense, 40.1% with a person-to-person crime, and 13.0% of youth being adjudicated for a behavioral crime.

Receipt of Transition Specialist Transition Services

In order to better understand the types of activities the TSs were completing with each of the young adults participating in STAY OUT, the TS tracked activities and reported them to the evaluators. A list of 38 activities across the transition domains of 1) employment, 2) education, 3) independent living, and 4) social and family supports was created by the TS to indicate what services they were providing with the young adults on their caseload. We then had the TS report, as part of the data collection process, describing the types of activities completed at each 2-month data collection point. This list reflects only the activities that the TS engaged the youth in and not the services from other agencies with which the youth was connected. Figure 6.2 provides a summary of the number of youth who received specific types of services for each of these activities. The dark black bars depict the percentage of youth who received any one of the domain's transition activities (e.g., any employment-related activity). The gray bars communicate the percentage of youth who received that type of TS activity. This graph illustrates that 91% of participants received employment supports; 71% of young adults received some type of educational support from the TS; 60% of youth received training in various independent living skills; and 66% of youth received support from the TS in relation to the family and the community. Reviewing the list of activities can help readers or future TSs identify which activities were most prevalent with most youth and also the breadth of activities completed with individual youth.

Project STAY OUT Outcomes

We also tracked youth transition-related outcomes on 2-month intervals from the beginning of the project through completion of service delivery. Primary outcomes that were collected included whether the youth was employed and/or enrolled in some type of educational opportunity. An overall outcome of *engaged* was then calculated. A youth

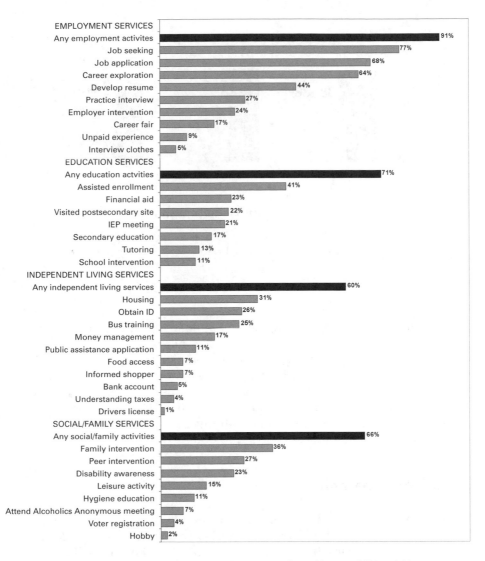

Figure 6.2.   Percentage of young adults receiving types of transition specialist activities.

would be defined as engaged if he or she were actively employed and/ or enrolled and had not recidivated. We then reviewed these outcomes specifically at 2, 4, and 6 months post-release to ensure that youth were positively engaged in activities related to a successful community adjustment process. Figure 6.3 presents the summary of these outcomes for the STAY OUT youth through 6 months post-release. On average, almost two-thirds of youth were engaged in either an employment and/

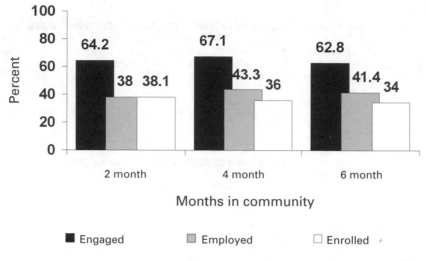

Figure 6.3.   STAY OUT outcomes.

or educational setting during the first 6 months post release. In addition, youth were employed between 38% and 43% and enrolled between 34% and 41%. The overall engagement rate at approximately 60% is promising because an earlier longitudinal study conducted in Oregon reported an engagement rate of 35% 6 months post-release, with an overall recidivism rate of 60% (Bullis et al., 2002). These outcomes speak to the additional difficulty that youth involved in the juvenile justice system face in their trajectory to adulthood.

Lessons Learned

Lessons learned in developing this facility-to-community transition project for youth with EBD who were also involved in the juvenile justice system are many. In this section, we capture lessons that, with hope, can help others implement programs to support positive outcomes for this hard-to-serve population.

Create System Capacity Across Multiple Agencies

This project initially had three primary state partners and expanded to five: The Oregon Youth Authority, Oregon Department of Education, Vocational Rehabilitation, Workforce Investment Boards, and the Oregon's Addiction and Mental Health Services. It is critical that these partners at both the state and local level are at the table when developing the service model. Through the development of localized memoranda of understanding, agreements can be made that may support braided funding strands and allow for assurances to each of the partners that there is no duplication of services and an efficient use of minimal dollars to serve these youth.

Define Common Language and Eligibility Requirements

When developing the local capacity across these agencies, we found that one of the most important tasks was educating each of the agencies about one another. For example, each agency has a myriad of acronyms used within the agency. Breaking them down so that each community player knows what these acronyms are, what services are provided by each agency, and the eligibility requirements for entry into the agency is essential. This knowledge-gaining process will allow the TS to support the youth to gain access to various agencies within the community and navigate the eligibility requirements in a timely manner. The TS can then work with youth correctional facility staff to ensure that various assessments (e.g., psychological, vocational) needed to define eligibility in various agencies may be completed in the facility prior to the youth exiting to the community. Having these assessments in place can facilitate a quicker engagement of the youth into community services.

Develop Cross-Agency Sharing of Information Procedures

Sharing of information across agencies and between various individuals has become very restrictive. It is important that these sharing procedures are discussed across agencies to ensure that all requisite guidelines for each agency are followed. Developing a process of sharing information that follows requisite guidelines is helpful to ensure timely access to community services—specifically, when service initiation is critical immediately upon exiting the youth correctional facility.

The Role of the Transition Specialist Is Key

We found that the role of the TS was invaluable. Even if we developed the capacity of each of the agencies to ensure that services were available and accessible to youth with EBD leaving the correctional system, it was the role of the TS that supported the engagement in each of the agencies. Having one individual that develops a relationship with the youth in the facility and then seamlessly follows the youth into the community allows for tailored services to be provided based on the youth's strengths and needs. The TS does not only help the youth get a job but also, more important, helps the youth maintain it over time. Training and providing ongoing technical assistance to the newly hired TS is critical. One of the hardest tasks in the training is to make sure that the TS really develops the youth's self-determination and self-advocacy skills to ensure that the youth is driving his or her own transition plan. Often, the TS would try to make decisions about type of services, employment, or educational opportunities, but we found that if the youth was not at the center of the plan and driving it him- or herself, then long-term engagement in the prescribed plan would not be achieved. The TS needs to be trained not to enable the youth, even though mistakes are sometimes made by the youth in their decision-making processes. The TS's task of allowing the youth to experience natural consequences while being ready to help the youth problem solve and get back on track is essential to the development process in the transition to adulthood and throughout life.

CONCLUSION

Our intent in this chapter was to provide a framework for why services to youth with EBD involved in the juvenile justice system are so critical, a model for service delivery, a review of our evaluation information, and the hard lessons learned along the way. With this information, we are hopeful that readers will take what has been learned and apply their new knowledge in working with this hard-to-reach population. With your efforts and diligence, we can improve the long-term adult outcomes for young adults with EBD who have been involved in the juvenile justice system.

REFERENCES

Altschuler, D.M., & Armstrong, T.L. (1991). Intensive aftercare for the high-risk juvenile parolee: Issues and approaches in reintegration and community supervision. In T.L. Armstrong (Ed.), *Intensive interventions with high-risk youths: Promising approaches in juvenile probation and parole* (pp. 45–84). Monsey, NY: Criminal Justice Press.

American Psychiatric Association. (1994). *Diagnostic and Statistical Manual of Mental Disorders* (4th ed.) Washington DC: Author.

Aos, S., Miller, M., & Drake, E. (2006). *Evidence-based public policy options to reduce future prison construction, criminal justice costs, and crime rates.* Olympia: Washington State Institute for Public Policy.

Bridgeo, D., Davis, M., & Florida, Y. (2000). Transition coordination: Helping young people to pull it all together. In H.B. Clark & M. Davis (Eds.), *Transition to adulthood: A resource for assisting young people with emotional or behavioral difficulties* (pp. 155–178). Baltimore: Paul H. Brookes Publishing Co.

Bullis, M., & Cheney, D. (1999). Vocational and transition interventions for adolescents and young adults with emotional or behavioral disorders. *Focus on Exceptional Children, 31*(7), 1–29.

Bullis, M., & Fredericks, H.D. (Eds.). (2002). *Providing effective vocational/transition services to adolescents with emotional and behavioral disorders.* Champaign-Urbana, IL: Research Press.

Bullis, M., Yovanoff, P., & Havel, E. (2004). The importance of getting started right: Further examination of the facility-to-community transition of formerly incarcerated youth. *Journal of Special Education, 38,* 80–94.

Bullis, M., Yovanoff, P., Mueller, G., & Havel, E. (2002). Life on the "outs": Examination of the facility-to-community transition of incarcerated adolescents. *Exceptional Children, 69,* 7–22.

Cheney, D., Hagner, D., Malloy, J., Cormier, G., & Bernstein, S. (1998). Transition services for youth and young adults with emotional disturbance: Description and initial results of project RENEW. *Career Development for Exceptional Individuals, 21*(1), 17–32.

Clark, H.B., & Davis, M. (Eds.). (2000). *Transition to adulthood: A resource for assisting young people with emotional or behavioral difficulties.* Baltimore: Paul H. Brookes Publishing Co.

Clark, H.B., Deschênes, N., & Jones, J. (2000). A framework for the development and operation of a transition system. In H.B. Clark & M. Davis (Eds.), *Transition to adulthood: A resource for assisting young people with emotional or behavioral difficulties* (pp. 29–51). Baltimore: Paul H. Brookes Publishing Co.

Cohen, M.A. (1998). The monetary value of saving a high-risk youth. *Journal of Quantitative Criminology, 14,* 5–32.

Leone, P.E., Meisel, S.M., & Drakeford, W. (2002). Special education programs for youth with disabilities in juvenile corrections. *Journal of Correctional Education, 53,* 46–50.

McCord, J. (1992). The Cambridge-Somerville Study: A pioneering longitudinal-experimental study of delinquency prevention. In J. McCord & R. Tremblay (Eds.), *Preventing antisocial behavior* (pp. 196–208). New York: Guilford Press.

Shufelt, J., & Cocozza, J. (2006). *Youth with mental health disorders in the juvenile justice system: Results from a multi-state prevalence study.* Delmar, NY: National Center for Mental Health and Juvenile Justice.

Skowyra, K.R., & Cocozza, J. (2007). *Mental health screening within juvenile justice: The next frontier.* Delmar, NY: National Center for Mental Health and Juvenile Justice.

Snyder, H.N., & Sickmund, M. (2006). *Juvenile offenders and victims: 2006 national report.* Washington, DC: U.S. Department of Justice Programs, Office of Juvenile Justice and Delinquency Prevention.

Unruh, D., & Bullis, M. (2005). Community and self-report of the facility-to-community transition needs for adjudicated youth with disabilities. *Career Development for Exceptional Individuals, 28,* 67–79.

Unruh, D., & Bullis, M. (2005). Female and male juvenile offenders with disabilities: Differences in the barriers to their transition to the community. *Behavioral Disorders, 30,* 105–118.

Unruh, D., Gau, J., & Waintrup, M. (2008). An exploration of factors reducing recidivism rates of formerly incarcerated youth with disabilities participating in a re-entry intervention. *Journal of Child and Family Studies*. DOI 10.1007/s10826-008-9228-8

Unruh, D., Povenmire-Kirk, T., & Yamamoto, S. (in press). Perceived barriers and protective factors for juvenile offenders on their developmental pathway to adulthood. *Journal of Correctional Education*.

Vander Stoep, A., Davis, M., & Collins, D. (2000). Transition: A time of developmental and institutional clashes. In H.B. Clark & M. Davis, (Eds.), *Transition to adulthood: A resource for assisting young people with emotional or behavioral difficulties* (pp. 3–28). Baltimore: Paul H. Brookes Publishing Co.

Waintrup, M., & Unruh, D. (June, 2008). Career development programming strategies for transitioning incarcerated adolescents to the world of work. *Journal of Correctional Education, 59*, 127–144.

More than Friends

Peer Supports for Youth and Young Adults to Promote Discovery and Recovery

Lisa B. Galasso, Amy Arrell, Paul Webb,
Samuel Landsman, David Holmes,
Kimberly Frick, Luke Bradford Knowles,
Crystal Fair-Judson, Rebecca Smith, and
Hewitt B. "Rusty" Clark

"Being a peer support worker has offered me a future to help others and to help myself by learning from my peers."

—Kimberly Frick, PSW

Recovery from mental illness is a concept that is difficult for youth and young adults with emotional and/or behavioral difficulties (EBD) to grasp, especially given that most of these young people are just becoming acquainted with their status as adults with mental health problems. The mental health consumer recovery movement (http://www.samhsa .gov), which is attempting to change the delivery of mental health care around the nation, has recently set its sights on young adults with mental illness. Peer support programs and consumer-run services have been developed to provide a collective voice for those in recovery to infuse hope to those newly diagnosed or just setting out on their journey. The passage from youth to adulthood can be complicated and often unsteady; for those with EBD, there are far more hazards and intensified risks. Peers play an important role in helping young people with major mental illness to navigate not only the journey toward health and wellness but also the transition from adolescence to adulthood.

From the mid 1970s until about 2008, mental health consumer organizations, despite divergent historical origins and philosophies, have

---

We would like to thank Ruth Osterman from the Genesis Club, Inc., for substantial contributions.

shared several overlapping goals: overcoming stigma, preventing dis-
crimination, promoting self-help groups, and promoting recovery from
mental illness. One of these groups' greatest contributions has been the
organization and proliferation of self-help groups and their impact on
the lives of thousands of consumers of mental health services (Surgeon
General, 1999). The New Freedom Commission on Mental Health
(2003) called for a *transformation* of the mental health care system in
which emphasis is placed on recovery as opposed to symptom reduc-
tion. The Massachusetts Department of Mental Health (DMH) has
heeded the call by actively and fully involving consumers and their
families in the delivery of services. One important role in which mental
health consumers can act as transformative agents in Massachusetts is
as peer support workers and peer specialists throughout all types of
DMH funded, operated, and licensed services (residential, clubhouse,
employment, and education) and in all community-based service systems. Young adult mental health consumers have played active roles as
members of a DMH steering committee charged with developing recommendations for peer and family support services. As Rebecca Smith,
one young adult participant noted,

> As a member of the Central Massachusetts DMH Steering Committee,
> I am able to discuss and create new programs to help other young
> people struggling with mental illness. The committee is a collaborative
> team of young adults, staff at various programs who orient toward
> youth issues, and high-level DMH managers. It is both exciting and
> empowering to help shape the direction of DMH transition-age initia-
> tives, knowing that we have the power to greatly improve the wellness
> and success of young people in the present and future.

As a result of the work and recommendations of this DMH Young
Adult Steering Committee, funding was allocated to finance two innovative peer support programs that have been implemented in the central part of Massachusetts that foster recovery throughout the transition
period for young people with EBD. The Transition to Independence
Process (TIP) model (Clark & Davis, 2000; Clark & Foster-Johnson,
1996) was used as a template for establishing best practices for the design and implementation of these programs. The remainder of this chapter will describe these two transition initiatives.

The first program description is focused on the provision of peer
supports to young adults and is operated by The Bridge of Central Massachusetts, which is a community mental health provider agency special-
izing in residential treatment and supported housing services for young
adults with mental health challenges. The second program described
provides peer supports for youth and young adults and is a collabora-

tive initiative between the Bridge and the Genesis Club, which operates a clubhouse and other community supports. The program descriptions address the rationales for their development, the youth and young adults being served, the principles and foundation on which the programs operate, the lessons learned through the implementation of these programs, and the transformational nature of respecting youth voice and choice. The voices of peer support workers and peer support recipients are woven throughout the chapter to illustrate the real impact of these programs on the lives of young people embarking on their simultaneous journeys toward adulthood and recovery from mental illness.

THE BRIDGE PEER SUPPORT PROGRAM

The Bridge Peer Support Program (PSP) is based on the concepts of discovery and recovery to set the occasion for young people to explore and experience the world of relationships, work, career training, and community life in the context of learning to cope and manage their own emotional and behavioral wellbeing. It employs a holistic approach to understanding young adults with EBD, focusing on Wellness Recovery Action Plans (WRAP) (Copeland, 2000) rather than on simply reducing symptoms and managing illnesses. The TIP system guidelines and practices informed the development of the Bridge PSP and the framing of the transition domains of employment and career, educational opportunities, living situation, personal effectiveness and wellbeing, and community-life functioning. The goal of the Bridge PSP, as identified by its young adult stakeholders and included in the program's mission statement, is to "share in both the successes and obstacles that life has to offer while incorporating skills and tools needed to foster healthy relationships and recovery."

Structure and Services of the Bridge Peer Support Program

The Bridge PSP is designed to bring peer support and leadership opportunities to transition-age young adults, ages 18–25, who are part of the transition-age young adult (YA) population already receiving services from this agency (e.g., individual/group therapy, residential treatment, supported housing). The Bridge PSP workforce is recruited from the agency's network of current and former transition-age youth who have disclosed their experience with the mental health system and have shown that they can use this experience in a positive way to help others

"I feel my own personal trials with mental illness have given me a unique tool other providers may not have, first-hand experience. It is good to have a chance to share those experiences in a way that helps people. It gives those struggles a sense of greater purpose."

in their own personal recovery. When a YA expresses interest in becoming a peer support worker (PSW), he or she signs up for orientation training, during which time the ability to apply his or her own recovery experiences to help others is assessed through the development of a WRAP. If program staff determine that a YA needs to be further along in his or her own recovery before assuming a support role, he or she may still qualify as a PSW in training. In this capacity, the YA is mentored by a PSW and given tasks other than support contracts to hone their skills.

Orientation and ongoing training are viewed as fundamental to the PSP because these events not only teach recovery and wellness planning but also prepare YAs to assume help-giving roles by teaching the foundational skills of professional boundaries, standards of conduct, and therapeutic self-disclosure, as well as the core values of helping relationships, all of which will be discussed in more detail.

The PSP uses a team approach, which comprises a program manager and two distinct levels of peer workers: PSWs and peer specialists (PSs). The PSWs are entry-level positions and focus on working directly with YAs on a one-to-one basis and as group facilitators, whereas the PSs coordinate services and perform supervisory duties. The primary distinction between these two roles is the level of education and training received by the YAs. All PSs must be certified through the Massachusetts Certified Peer Specialist Project, which requires a high school diploma or GED, completion of an 8-day intensive training program, and a passing score on a certification examination. A complete description of these two positions is more fully illustrated within Table 7.1. The rigorous certification requirements have proven to be a barrier to recruiting PSs within this program; however, many PSWs have articulated that their professional development goal is to complete the requirements necessary to obtain this PS certification.

A primary function of the PSP team is to screen all referrals, to match PSWs with appropriate referrals, and to develop support contracts. If a referral is received that does not have a suitable PSW match, the program manager and/or PS will conduct a brief intensive training that provides a PSW with the skills needed to effectively carry out the contract assignment. For example, a young person may submit a referral to receive peer support in maintaining sobriety. If there are no PSWs who have the knowledge or skills to work with a peer on relapse prevention, a brief intensive training will be developed and employed that provides the team with substance abuse education and basic relapse

Table 7.1. Differentiation between peer support worker and peer support specialist roles

	Peer support worker (PSW)	Peer specialist (PS)
Qualifications	Primary diagnosis of mental illness	Primary diagnosis of mental illness
	A strong desire to identify self as a person with mental illness	A strong desire to identify self as a person with mental illness
	A current or former user of mental health services	A current or former user of mental health services
		A GED or high school diploma
		Certification through the Massachusetts Certified Peer Specialist Project
Requirements and compensation	Supervised by PS or program manager	Supervised by program manager
	Works full- or part-time	Works full- or part-time
	Earns hourly wage	Earns hourly wage and has employee benefits (e.g., annual leave, sick leave, health coverage)
Range of possible functions filled	Full range of support, education, and advocacy functions, including both group and one-to-one activities	Full range of support, education, and advocacy functions, including both group and one-to-one activities
		May fill supervisory, administrative, and consultative functions
Integration into staff team	Encouraged	Fully integrated into staff; attends staff/treatment team meetings; has usual staff access to records and confidential information
Connection with Transformation Center and recovery learning communities	Encouraged	Has a consistent connection
Continuing education	Optional	Required
Core competencies	Demonstrated progress and commitment to one's own discovery and recovery processes	Demonstrated progress and commitment to one's own discovery and recovery processes
	Ability to utilize personal experience to teach, validate, and motivate others	Ability to utilize personal experience to teach, validate, and motivate others

(*continued*)

Table 7.1. *Continued*

	Peer support worker (PSW)	Peer specialist (PS)
Core compe- tencies (*continued*)	Ability to work with peers in groups and individually	Ability to work with peers in groups and individually
	Understanding of the special needs and developmental issues of transition-age individuals	Understanding of the special needs and developmental issues of transition-age individuals
	Ability to abide by rules of confidentiality and maintain appropriate boundaries and set personal limits	Ability to abide by rules of confidentiality and maintain appropriate boundaries and set personal limits

prevention strategies. Referrals to more traditional or formal treatment providers are also made when contracts are determined to be beyond the scope of the PSP team's capability or expertise. In addition to contract assignments and specialized training, the team also meets weekly to address burnout and boundary issues, monitor job performance concerns, complete contract reviews at the end of each contract, and collect progress/outcome data on program quality indicators. Each member of the PSP team is expected to participate in 1 hour of weekly supervision with the program manager or PS. All supervision is provided in a manner that gives consideration to the PSWs' generic needs as staff members as well as their different experiential base, roles, and minority status within the organization.

Participation by YAs in the Bridge PSP is completely voluntary and they have a choice regarding the PSW from whom they receive support. PSP services are culturally competent and are available in youth-friendly community settings, as mutually decided on by the young person and his or her PSW. Services and supports are delivered with a focus on promoting discovery and recovery, increasing resiliency, and facilitating goal setting and goal achievement. They address the gamut of transition domains outlined by the TIP model, including employment, education, living situation, personal effectiveness and wellbeing, and community-life functioning. PSWs represent and advocate for the needs, preferences, and perspectives of the young adults they serve while having them assume greater roles in self-advocacy, responsibility, and leadership.

In designing the peer support program, one of the most formidable barriers was creating a practical, developmentally appropriate boundary policy that was not only consistent with the discovery and recovery process and with the core values of the program (to be discussed later) but also aligned with the Bridge's highly structured boundary rules and regulations. Many complicated questions needed to be tackled. For instance, how do the boundaries of peer helper relationships differ from the boundaries adhered to by traditional direct-care staff? How is the nature of the peer support relationship fundamentally different from traditional helping relationships? Would YAs have more difficulty maintaining professional boundaries than their adult counterparts? How could we possibly plan for the seemingly endless stream of interpersonal or boundary issues that were likely to arise as part of the work of the PSWs and PSs? Answering these questions forced program administrators and stakeholders to examine their own apprehensions and concerns about creating a peer workforce and resulted in the elucidation of a policy addressing two distinct areas of professionalism: professional standards and boundary expectations. The professional standards consist of nine standards of conduct that include 1) prohibitions against sexual relationships between peers during a peer support contract; 2) no borrowing or lending of money; 3) no making threats against others; 4) abstinence from drugs and/or alcohol while providing peer support; 5) refraining from giving or accepting gifts during a contract; 6) not bringing weapons, drugs, or alcohol to any peer support activity; 7) abstaining from gossiping about anyone involved in the PSP; 8) using one's own support network when experiencing distressing symptoms and not disclosing one's own feelings of distress as a means of gaining emotional, psychological, or social support from individuals using the program; and 9) respecting the dignity, confidentiality, and privacy of all individuals in the program. The grayer areas are seen as the flexible aspects of professional boundaries that are dependent on the PSW and PS's own personal limits, the preferences of the PS recipient, and the environmental or contextual aspects of the PS relationship. As part of their training, PSWs and PSs are guided through the process of exploring, discovering, and articulating their own personal limits and boundaries in order to be able to skillfully navigate the unchartered "gray" waters inherent in all peer helper relationships. A metaphor is used to facilitate this discovery process among the YA workforce:

> Imagine that you are in an airplane looking down on the seashore. You see a stone seawall that never changes. Beyond the wall is a sandy beach that's shape and breadth flows naturally with the tides, seasons, and weather. The professional standards of conduct identified in the code of conduct belong behind the seawall, along with any information that you decide is uncomfortable for you to share. Information that you *may* decide to share is placed thoughtfully and deliberately somewhere along the beach, which represents the boundary expectations that are flexible and vary from person to person.

For this reason, PSWs and PSs are trained to assess the environment, the individual recipients' needs and preferences, and their own roles and motivations when deciding to self-disclose. This assessment and decision-making process begins in orientation and is supported and shaped throughout the tenure of the PSW/PS in supervision and staff meetings. PSWs and PSs are challenged to explore and articulate their comfort in revealing aspects of themselves across a variety of themes such as politics, religion, physical expressions of affection, sexuality, illness, drugs and alcohol, body image, and death and dying. Each individual is guided through the creation of a personal self-disclosure policy to refer to when boundaries become an issue in a peer support role. For instance, if a PSW is asked by a recipient if she has any children, she has already determined how much about herself she is comfortable sharing and can take ownership of her response rather than replying that she cannot answer the question because it violates a boundary policy. Through role play and practicing with their coworkers, PSWs and PSs develop strategies for setting personal limits in a manner that is sensitive to the feelings of others while protecting and supporting their own privacy. Inherent in this process is the understanding that people's limits may change over time, and as such, must be reevaluated on an ongoing basis. By helping YAs to create firm yet flexible individualized boundary frameworks, they are prepared to enter into helping relationships that are safe, genuine, and unambiguous.

Special Program Features of the Bridge PSP

One of the most important features of the Bridge PSP is its complete reliance on the program's core values to guide all decisions, activities, and personal conduct. The mission statement that was developed by the PSP team and documented in the internal program manual reflects the core values of the program:

> Peer support is committed to providing strength-based interventions, creating a culture of hope, educating in self-management, and engaging all program members in meaningful occupation so that each person shall direct his or her own treatment, recovery, and life.

The core values apply to the PSs, PSWs, and the YAs with whom they work.

Strength-Based Focus

The first core value, which is modeled on TIP guideline (described in Chapter 2), ". . . building on strengths to enable young people to pursue their goals," is that all interventions are strength based. The initial step in providing strength-based interventions is for PSs and PSWs to engage in a strength discovery process in which they identify their own interests, needs, talents, abilities, resources within themselves, and potential resources surrounding them (e.g., family members, friends, and other informal and formal key players). For example, one PSW realized through this process that what she considered to be her deficits—her psychiatric symptoms—were in fact also sources of strength for her because she was able to use these experiences as seeds of hope to help others, leading to her recognition that her challenges and recovery process could be an asset. The TIP model dictates that, in addition to being strength based, interventions need to be tailored to be accessible, coordinated, culturally sensitive, and developmentally appropriate to YAs. The PSP program is easily accessible to all YAs served across the array of programs operated by the Bridge of Central Massachusetts; the only referral criteria is that YAs must self-refer and they must be able to identify their own goals at their entry into the program or work with a PSW to develop goals. Coordination of services is accomplished through self-advocacy. Peer support recipients are taught how to advocate for themselves across all transition domains. In stark contrast to formal mental health care services, in which providers tend to act on behalf of consumers by virtue of their "expert" positions, YAs in this program must act as experts in their own lives and as such learn to coordinate their own supports and services based on their own evaluations of their needs, strengths, and goals. Finally, in the spirit of providing support that is tailored to recipients' developmental levels, PSWs and PSs approach all interactions in a nonjudgmental manner and strive to meet their YAs "where they're at." For example, some YAs may need coaching and support for riding the public bus while other YAs may be fully independent and gainfully employed but seek peer support for learning how to improve their interpersonal relationships.

Hope

The second core value of the peer support program is hope—hope that is embodied through shared experiences with others, powerful personal changes, discovery exploration, and the recovery process related to mental illness. This core value is closely related to the TIP guideline of "Engage young people through relationship development, person-centered planning, and a focus on their futures." Relationships inspire hope in both the providers and the recipients of peer support. One PSW described relationships as the vehicle through which she works. Common recovery experiences are the glue that connects the peer support team; they feel that they share elements of a common history, a common

"Being a peer support worker has offered me a future to help others and to help myself by learning from my peers." | purpose, and a common goal. As one PSW commented, "These are the people who understand what I'm going through." The futures of YAs are also affected by the role modeling provided by their PSWs and PSs, where a change in the course or direction of their lives is not uncommon as a result of emulating the helpers who are mentoring them.

In addition to inspiring hope, the relationships that develop among peers in this program are consistent with the TIP guideline of "ensuring a safety net of support by involving a young person's parents, family members, and other informal and formal key players." The PSWs see their role as coaches and cheerleaders to their peers, encouraging them to share information with others in their informal and formal support networks and continuing to nurture and expand their informal support network. For example, one PSW reported that she has frequently persuaded other YAs to share information with their girlfriends or boyfriends, family members, and/or therapists when they have confided in her about personal difficulties and preferences. Notably, this PSW observed that when young people learn how to advocate for themselves with their family members and mental health professionals, they have been able to transfer these self-advocacy skills to other support relationships, improving the quality of these relationships.

Self-Management

The third core value of the Bridge PSP is self-management, which entails that each person must take action to manage his or her own life and recovery. This is different from self-determination, which refers to choosing one's own direction and making one's own decisions. Rather, self-management is associated with taking steps toward personal recovery from mental illness by achieving meaningful life goals. In accordance with the TIP guideline of "Acknowledge and develop personal choice and social responsibility with young people," this core value is seen by the PSWs as especially important in guiding their work with young adults. Any time an individual takes on a helping role, there are ethical principles that must be grappled with. PSWs and PSs must evaluate their personal motivations for sharing their recovery experiences, and they constantly ask themselves, "How much are my actions aimed at benefiting *me* versus the *young people* I'm supporting?" PSWs and PSs recognize that there is a delicate balance that must be achieved when sharing their personal stories and experiences. Interpersonal boundaries and self-disclosure, although powerful tools of the trade, can also have a strong negative impact if they are not exercised thoughtfully and with sensitivity to the welfare of the other. One PSW described how she must constantly balance sharing enough about herself with not sharing too much in order to maintain effectiveness in her PSW role. She is acutely aware of the impact she has on those she works with, which is a valuable lesson about personal choice and social responsibility.

Meaningful Occupation

The fourth core value involves "meaningful occupation," which refers to the notion that involvement in personally meaningful activities is an essential element of discovery and recovery. Identifying the different roles that each young person plays in his or her own life—student, peer, teacher, friend, romantic partner, parent, child, community member, employee—and building on the skills needed to perform each role effectively, are essential goals of the Bridge PSP.

This aim is consistent with the TIP guideline of "Enhance young persons' competencies to assist them in achieving greater self-sufficiency and confidence." Skills training is achieved through both groups and individual contracts, and skills are built through both providing and receiving peer support. PSWs and PSs assist YAs in acquiring relevant skills through individual coaching and group sessions. Some of the groups that have been offered by PSWs and PSs range from practical to philosophical; these include a substance abuse recovery group, Role Players Club (based on the Dungeons and Dragons Game), Philosophy Forum, and a Prevocational Education Group. One PSW made the observation that, in addition to learning leadership skills and practical knowledge about the topics she teaches, she has also learned important organizational and time-management skills. According to PSW David Holmes,

> Peer support has given me an opportunity to test my assertion that I can do as good a job in helping another as has been [done] in helping me. It offered me what I wanted and needed—level opportunity with room for individual attainment and growth. Peer support as a frontier venture offers a job where not only my intellect is challenged but also my creativity, such as in group development—I have created a group called Philosophers Forum to show that philosophy is an everyday part of life and that by identifying one's own philosophy, members can better navigate life. This group helps members learn correspondence skills to discover their root, the point of strength around which to grow and branch off to new experiences.

Peer support recipients learn important skills through their participation in both groups and individual contracts and interactions. Some individual contracts have focused on such activities as gathering some friends to prepare and enjoy a meal together to helping a young woman who was struggling with adequately caring for her pet. Confidence is built throughout this process by setting achievable short-term and long-term goals as well as relying on the relationships that develop among peers to sustain engagement and motivation. PSW Karen Ahearn noted,

> Given the opportunity to teach a prevocational group, I thought to myself, what are the most important skills to teach? I thought that of course it was important to teach the skills needed to write a resumé and cover letter, but there is more than that you need to know to obtain employment. I decided to teach some life skills as well as teach the basics. One of the topics that I thought would be important was a group on decision making. I ran this group with the idea that we would mainly talk about making decisions in the work place. What I received from the group was amazing insight into the support system that exists between each of them. One of the things we did in the group was to go around the room and discuss what an important decision was that we had made in the past. As each person shared a powerful story, the amazing support that they gave to each other was something to be witnessed. I was truly impressed with the level of care that they showed each other. It makes my job worth doing when I see each group member caring for and supporting their peers.

Self-Determination

The final core value that is promoted in the program is self-determination. This value reflects a commitment to the idea that each young person can and should direct his or her own life, recovery, and treatment. This process requires that the young person is ultimately free to decide how to incorporate input from others into a life plan. Embedded in this value is the TIP guideline of "Involve young people, parents, and other community partners in the TIP system at the practice, program, and community levels." At the system level, YAs on the statewide Steering Committee originally identified the need for peer support initiatives, which was the impetus behind the allocation of state funding for this program. YAs from the Bridge PSP continue to be part of this Steering Committee as a means of influencing system governance and stewardship. At the community level, YAs who are consumers of the Bridge of Central Massachusetts have played a key role in shaping the structural and functional operations of this peer support program. At the programmatic level, several PSWs have naturally progressed into self-identified leadership roles and, in conjunction with the program manager, are responsible for the day-to-day operations of the program, including reviewing referrals, developing contracts, planning and implementing group interventions, collecting outcome data, and ensuring that TIP system guidelines and practices are driving their work with young people. The decisions of how to participate in peer support have been made by the YAs themselves, and they have likewise identified their own talents and interests that have guided their participation.

Program Impact of the Bridge PSP

The Bridge PSP has promoted program transformation at many levels within the agency and across other collaborating agencies in the region. Individual PSWs and YA recipients have demonstrated through their behavior and testimonies that this program has influenced their lives in significant ways. For one young woman, the PSW role provided her with the opportunity to experience emotional and behavioral difficulties from a completely different perspective—that of helper, which was profoundly eye opening to her:

> When I was first approached with the idea of peer support I thought, what an amazing chance to see the "other side." I had these visions of sitting in an office, at my desk, and having clients come in and pour their hearts out to me and I would be able to ("poof") fix all their problems. I remember thinking that all my counselors did was to sit at a desk and every now and then I would see them working on something, but in my mind they were just waiting for me to come in with a problem. How amazing that I could be so wrong in so many ways! My visions of fixing clients' problems are almost laughable now. The so-called problems that I wanted so badly to fix are what life is. My job is to help them deal with these problems as they arise. I cannot fix them, but I can be compassionate, listen, and truly do my best to understand in some aspect what my peer is feeling. As far as thinking my counselors have it easy, I truly had no idea the emotion and heart, not to mention the paperwork, that it takes to be amazing at this job. I am lucky that I now have had the chance to see and be part of the "other side." (Kim Ahearn, PSW)

For another young person, the impact of the program has been to foster greater independence and adult responsibility in himself by teaching these skills to others:

> There are few more important words in the vocabulary of transition-age youth than the word *independence*. No such single word carries as much weight for a youth trying to break free from the structure of regulations and restrictions, seemingly unnecessary in their mind. The desire to be free from rules is only the half of it. The other half [is] a

genuine desire to be responsible and to succeed for themselves. But these two thoughts are not nearly as clear cut as half and half. They are more of a balance or sometimes imbalance, always present and sometimes invisible. It is somewhat ironic and somewhat unfeeling logic that I work with transition-age youth today to assist them in becoming more independent. Isn't it ironic that I have mastered my own finances and health systems not more than a year before teaching these skills to others my own age? But in another facet of my job, how logical it is to have young adults and youth teaching their peers these skills and therefore bypassing the negative feelings created by the parent/youth or teacher/youth authority structures. My occupation as a peer support worker thus far has been an experience in independence. Here I am, suddenly brought to responsibility for the education and guidance of those whom I serve. At this time, I'm running a group for young adults with the intention of teaching them the public transportation systems in the city and state. My supervisors began this contract, acknowledging the fact that public transportation is essential knowledge for young adults, most of whom do not have cars. For my journey towards independence, it cannot be understated that giving an individual an opportunity to teach empowers them to add to their own vision of independence and come closer to it. Giving an individual an opportunity to support another makes them support themselves. (Luke Bradford Knowles, PSW)

Lessons Learned

The most essential lesson learned from the implementation of the Bridge PSP initiative is that YAs represent a powerful and influential resource that has been largely untapped in the provision of mental health care among this particular age group. Although there is a need for empirical data supporting the efficacy of peer support interventions among transition-age youth, the anecdotal evidence is clearly favorable. The young adult voices woven throughout this chapter ring loud and clear, collectively singing the praises and value of peer support. It is critical, however, that peer support not be marginalized in the delivery of interventions to this age group, but rather embraced as an integral aspect of successful transitions to independence and interdependence. Through the course of meeting with YAs during the writing of this chapter, it became clear that many of them have a fear that peer support roles run the risk of tokenism; that is, they worry that their roles are in some way illegitimatized by virtue of their emotional or behavioral difficulties. They worry that their work could be discounted as "a job for someone with a mental illness." PSWs and PSs strive for legitimate status within the service delivery system, sharing equally among provider partners to influence decision making at the treatment team level and to have substantive operational input at the program and agency levels. One way to counter the potential pitfall of tokenism is to provide career advancement opportunities for PSWs so that they have well-established roles in the organization with access to full-time employment, raises, promotions, and continuing education, similar to other agency personnel. Another strategy for legitimizing their role is to apply the nontraditional interventions developed by PSWs (e.g., Philosophers Forum and Prevocational Education Group) outside of the realm of the PSP into more traditional mental health services. It is also essential to engage other agency staff in dialogues about their thoughts, feelings, and values related to working shoulder-to-shoulder with PSWs and PSs with mental health challenges. Their concerns must be validated while at the same time their prejudices and assumptions must be challenged. Embracing YAs as partners in the delivery of mental health care requires a dramatic paradigm shift in which all tenets of the concept of discovery and recovery are fully embraced—and this transformation is facilitated greatly by listening to youth voice!

THE TRANSITION AGE SUPPORT INITIATIVE (TASI)

The Transition Age Support Initiative (TASI) program is a collaboration between DMH and two provider agencies with histories of divergent philosophical underpinnings, but with the new common shared vision to serve YAs who are transitioning from the child/adolescent system of care into functioning in adulthood roles. The Genesis Club, which is a clubhouse, and the Bridge of Central Massachusetts have joined forces to create TASI, whose mission is, "To assist and support young people with serious mental illness in the transition process from adolescence to adulthood by facilitating access to resources and skill building opportunities. The foundation of TASI services is grounded in peer support."

Program Structure for TASI

The TASI program serves youth and YAs (16–25 years of age) with serious mental health problems who qualify for state-funded mental health services. The program has two distinct tiers of service. All program participants are referred by DMH and enter into the first tier, which has a capacity to serve up to 15 young people, provides high-intensity services involving numerous one-to-one contacts per week for a 60–90 day period, and is guided by an individualized goal plan. Upon completion of their goals, TASI participants graduate to the second—or low intensity—tier, in which they are welcome to continue to attend all program groups and activities but do not necessarily receive the one-to-one contacts, nor do they have a formalized goal plan that is monitored by TASI staff. Rather, the expectation is that their efforts will be aimed at continuing to develop their formal and informal social support network, including socializing with other graduates from TASI, and expanding upon the goals they completed as intensive participants.

In addition to the two tiers of program participation, TASI also engages in community outreach activities such as speaking at local middle and high schools. The purpose of TASI outreach activities is to educate youngsters about the TASI program, initiate discussions about transitioning from one system of care to the next, as well as issues that arise as one accepts the responsibilities of adulthood. This process works in concert with the DMH's transition-age case management system that coordinates the transition from one system to the next. YAs in TASI also serve as active members on the program's advisory committee as well as other local, regional, and state committees to advance the transition-to-adulthood issues.

> I've been at TASI for almost a year, and I'm already in four different young adult committees and [am a] representative for Genesis Club as a young adult. The young adult committees are 1) DMH Young Adult Committee, 2) Massachusetts State House Advisory Committee, 3) Genesis Young Adult Committee, 4) Statewide Youth Council, and 5) TASI Taskforce. (Patrick [pseudonym], young adult participant)

The role DMH plays in the TASI program is integral to its success. DMH supervisors who oversee transition-age case management participate in all TASI taskforce meetings, discuss all referrals with program stakeholders, and employ one case manager to work exclusively with all TASI participants. The case manager's role is to aid the program in outreach activities, problem-solve how to engage YAs who are resistant to joining the program, and collaborate in the goal planning process with the YAs and program staff. There is a true shared responsibility with DMH for each YA in the program, which is intended to provide a seamless service delivery system for these individuals and their families. The cultivation of this level of collaboration requires a strong commitment and frequent communication among agency stakeholders.

Program Services of TASI

TASI's high-intensity services are future focused and based on the individual needs and goals of the YA members. Once referred to the program, young people are engaged through an initial "meet and greet" by a peer associate/staff team in a youth-friendly community setting (e.g., coffee shop, restaurant, shopping mall) or at their home or apartment.

> Frequently during our initial meeting with the young adults, as the staff, I noticed their eyes begin to glaze over as I attempt to convey to them the supports and services TASI provides. Often the real impact of our initial meeting is provided in the role of the young adult peer associate that accompanies the TASI staff. The immediate connection that naturally occurs with these peer associates facilitates the relationship that I will continue to develop as we support them through the transition period. (Evan, TASI staff member)

If a young person chooses to enter the program, he or she develops a goal plan with a TASI staff member that is person centered, goal driven, and focused on connecting to supports that will be long-term. Goals are individually tailored and can range in focus from education and employment to living situations and community life. Although the assessment of strengths and needs are an integral aspect of the person-centered goal-planning processes, the young person's perspective and wishes dictate the development of the goal plan.

> The good thing about goal planning with the TASI program is that you're able to set your own goals, which makes you more willing to follow through with them. I mean, who else knows you better than you do? You create your goals and TASI gives you the support to put them into action. (Laura [pseudonym], young adult participant)

Once an initial goal plan (or part of a plan) has been developed, the focus of work is directed to guiding the young person to natural supports and/or relevant adult services that are accessible, coordinated, developmentally appropriate, and built on the young person's strengths. The model of service delivery is one of coaching the young person across all transition domains (Chapter 2). There is an expectation of independence and responsibility from the YA, with an understanding that there is a learning curve, therefore TASI provides guidance to build these skills in an environment that leads to natural consequences with room for error. This means that rather than *doing* for the young person peer associates and staff are available to support and guide the young person as he or she works on setting and completing goals.

Transitional employment placements offered through the Genesis Club employment program provide the young person with the opportunity to work quality, supported, part-time jobs for 6–9 months (Bilby, 1999). These are real positions in local businesses that do not initially require experience or an interview but are managed by Genesis Clubhouse staff to train and support the member on-the-job, as well as cover absences as the young person builds job readiness and retention skills. If the person is unable to sustain the position for a full 9 months, they are not penalized but encouraged to take another position with a revised plan of support that focuses on building job readiness and vocational skills, the lack of which led to the individual leaving the last position. In this instance, there is the expectation that trial-and-error learning through natural consequences (e.g., starting a job and quitting after a short interval because it is not a good fit) is a critically important part of exploring the world of work and relationships. However, these youth and YAs are in a discovery mode and need to have the opportunity to try on different work experiences, interactions with supervisors and co-workers, and all the other challenges, demands, and rewards associated with employment and building a possible career.

One young person's priority goal might relate to the postsecondary education or technical/vocational training domain and encompass such tasks or steps as learning to complete applications, connecting with the disabilities office, accessing campus services, securing financial aid, and tapping regular on-campus peer support or tutoring. At school/ training sites, a young person might be supported by a peer associate who can coach in such things as campus life, study skills, or how to obtain tutorial services. In some cases a young person might do well to initially only take one or two courses or audit classes at a particular school before making a decision that requires significant financial and time commitments. Some young people have chosen to bypass this step and have found themselves enrolled in an academic program that's a poor fit; they have then had to take future semesters off to pay for the one they were not able to complete. Of course, this example is a natural consequence and may represent a necessary learning opportunity for some young people. However, coaching can guide young persons to make more informed decisions regarding these matters, which may help to advance their goals more proficiently.

"At Genesis Club there are seven different units to choose from and there are a lot of things to do to keep busy. They teach you the basics to prepare for school, jobs, etc. Right now, they are helping me to find an apartment and school. Those are the two goals that I am working on right now."

Most TASI members (95%) also join the Genesis Clubhouse, which is a member-driven model of discovery and recovery based on strengths and talents and grounded in peer support. The members support each other through significant life and mental health hurdles. These connections may lead to the basis for lifelong friendships. TASI and the Genesis Clubhouse provide a safety net of support from informal and formal key players in the lives of young people. The program promotes and nurtures relationship development between young people and their families through various social, leisure, and other activities. *Family* is defined broadly, meaning that for some young people at one point in time it may be the family of origin or foster mother and for other young people (or at another point in time) it may be a boyfriend and their infant. Personnel and peer associates often assist young people and family members to mediate issues, simultaneously attempting to develop these types of skills within the young person. As necessary, the various psychosocial and educational programs and agencies provide the formal supports. The goal of assisting young people in establishing a safety net of support is to 1) secure necessary supports and services to address current needs and goals; 2) learn to tap necessary formal supports in the future by teaching them to identify relevant services and resources, and how to arrange, advocate, and/or negotiate for them; and 3) build, nurture, and maintain informal supports in family, friends, and other mentors that may become lifetime key players in their lives.

> Through the TASI program I have met a lot of good friends. When I first came to TASI, I was a young and vulnerable teenager, straight out of high school. I had no idea where I was going or what I was going to do with the rest of my life. It's here that I met my two best friends, Mike and Eric. All in all, the best thing about the program is that no matter what, you have people to turn to, and those are the people that will be there forever. One of the great things about my friendships is that through it all, they have given me support, especially through the tough times I've had with the passing of my aunt. My friend offered to go to California with me for her funeral. That's the kind of friendships you encounter through TASI. (Raphael [pseudonym], young adult participant)

Another primary goal of the TASI program is to enhance the competencies of young people across all transition domains, so that they are better prepared to advance their progress on their goals in education, employment and careers, living situations, personal effectiveness and wellbeing, and in their roles within the community. Assistance with these transition areas occurs through individual work with TASI staff and peer associates, obtaining employment and school opportunities,

"TASI is the coolest program because it teaches you to be more comfortable with the community and to be more social, with strangers and friends. It helps you with housing, social problems and personal problems, too."

receiving feedback from peer associates, attending evening skill building groups, and/or being an active part of the Clubhouse community of work, learning, and play.

Relevant skills and competencies are taught on an individual or group basis as the best fit occurs for the young person. Role play is often used, and peer associates and staff also take best advantage of in-situation opportunities to teach the young people (e.g., teaching a young person to deal with a security screening at a government building while going through the screening). There are also group formats using experiential learning techniques such as those developed by Adventure Based Counseling (ABC) (Schoel & Maizell, 2002). ABC is especially useful for teaching YAs how to openly and honestly address interpersonal conflicts among their peers, how to hold themselves and others accountable to interpersonal rules (e.g., honesty and trustworthiness), and how to effectively communicate difficult feelings. For example, one young adult lied to his peers about a significant loss in his family to gain the sympathy of others and was held accountable by his peers to repair his relationships before the group felt comfortable allowing him to return. Two other specific skill areas that have been developed into evening groups that they can choose to attend are 1) Tour of Worcester, through which one learns public transit system and community resource access, and 2) Wellness Group, which educates young people on health and wellness practices as well as provides weekly transportation and memberships to the YMCA. As one participant, Patrick, noted, "In TASI I have accomplished the Wellness and Project Adventure groups, and I graduated but I can still go to the groups and help new members when they come in. I train them to get to know the rules and help them to accomplish their goals."

Whereas the program maintains a future orientation for the young person, there is a similar focus on outcomes. The individualized goal plan is reviewed at least every 3 months after admission to the program to measure progress on goals and to determine whether the young person is ready to graduate or requires more time to accomplish goals. Each program participant is also asked to complete a set of questionnaires at enrollment and, when they graduate, to assess their knowledge of community resources, functional skills, social networks, and program satisfaction. Program level data are also gathered quarterly on 1) engagement in the program (i.e., number of young adults referred and number of these young adults who do not engage with the program over a 3-month period); and 2) progress and outcomes indicators for young adult participants being served (e.g., percentages of participants employed, enrolled in postsecondary education/training programs, living in less restrictive settings). Program administrators analyze these data and prepare summary graphs and tables with brief descriptions of the findings across such factors as the percent of young people making progress or reducing their progress in achieving their own individualized goals, and the number of successful outreach efforts. The TASI program managers, personnel, peer associates, and other stakeholders use these data to assist them in their continuing quality improvement efforts to enhance the program's services and effectiveness.

Special Program Features

Anyone who works with youth and YAs knows that episodes of drama and calamity are frequent events. Historically, adolescence has been described as a period of heightened "storm and stress" (Hall, 1904); Marsha Linehan (1993) described patients with problems of the emotional regulation system as facing a perpetual state of unrelenting crisis. In the TASI program, it is a well recognized fact that many young people with EBD possess these characteristics and are dealing with frequent crises as an accepted part of the work. All crises are seen as teaching opportunities that provide the program staff with a chance to enhance the capabilities of the young person. Program staff support each young person through a crisis, mindfully relinquishing control of the situation to the young person and assuming a coaching role as opposed to directing him or her on what to do. Staff try to maintain a balance between sensitively attending to crises while discouraging them from overshadowing or totally derailing a youth's engagement in activities or his or her goals. A barrier that sometimes reduces program effectiveness in this area is the lack of consistent response to crises across different service providers in the community who are not versed in the TIP model and its strategies in prevention planning (Haber et al., this volume).

Aside from different approaches to crises, the inconsistencies between systems can be very confusing for YAs transitioning from one system of care to the next because the child/adolescent system utilizes a caregiving approach that is in stark contrast to the hands-off approach of adult services. Thus, the rules of the game change with very little preparation or advance notification. TASI attempts to work with young people and parents to help them learn the new rules of the adult system. TASI also advocates and provides reform efforts in an attempt to better align child- and adult-serving agencies to focus on developing greater self-sufficiency and yet remaining more proactive in engaging young people.

Cultural competency is another critical ingredient in the success of the TASI program. In addition to creating an inclusive atmosphere where young peoples' ethnicity, race, culture, and sexual orientation are respected, program stakeholders are aware that YAs share a culture of their own to which older adults are not privy. The YA culture has its own linguistic characteristics, fashion trends, high-tech communication, social hierarchy, values, and norms, as well as exclusive membership. The inclusion of peer associates in all aspects of the program has been an effective way of engaging YAs for the reason that their cultural similarity earns them a foot in the door with their cohorts. Adult program staff are often regarded as outsiders but aspire to achieve cultural competency in their connections with the YAs. They do this by employing a nonjudgmental stance through which they reveal their belief that the YA culture is as valid as any other culture and that YAs as a group are as valued as any other group.

TASI Program Impact

The TASI program, even in its infancy, has already significantly affected the lives of its YA members. Figure 7.1 illustrates some of the functional engagement and progress accomplishments of program participants. These data are based on the 45 YAs who participated in the TASI program for 3–18 months during the first 18 months of program operation. Programmatic impact data such as those in Figure 7.1 can be supplemented by the perspectives of YAs in illustrating the impact of the program from their perspective, as is exemplified here:

> My mind was made up and I wanted nothing to do with the TASI program. I would dodge appointments, not answer phone calls, and sometimes I would even hide and peek out the window until they were gone. I wondered, what possibly could be so good about this place if it's voluntary . . . now I know. They give me the desire to want to work on myself. If I never engaged in this program, I would be a lot less fortunate. It made me better and I'm glad they didn't give up on me. (Laura [pseudonym], young adult participant)

> The TASI program has been essential to me as I made the transition from teen to adult. Before getting involved, I had no direction in my life and relied on others for everything. TASI has taught me independence. I learned to use public transportation, which was important for

Figure 7.1. Percent of engagement and progress outcomes for the 45 young adults who participated in the Transition Age Support Initiative (TASI) program for 3–18 months during the first 18 months of operation. *Note:* Of the 59 referrals during this 18-month period, 14 young adults did not choose to engage in this program.

getting to appointments. Wellness gave me the skills physically to take care of myself, such as how to use exercise equipment. I became more confident in all aspects of my life and was able to get a job helping others. The program taught me how to relate to others and be more understanding and patient. The program has taught me what it means to be an adult and [given me] the resources to become a fully functional one. (Crystal Fair-Judson, young adult participant)

CONCLUSION

The most vital lessons to be learned from this program implementation are the importance of: 1) soliciting and listening to the voice of young people; and 2) collaborating with community partners to create flexible, accessible, supportive services that meet the unique developmental needs of transition-age young people. TASI was created to bridge the gap between service delivery systems as well as to develop, expand, and consolidate existing services for YAs in a way that integrates the TIP guidelines and practices across service entities. An overarching goal of the program is to divert young people with EBD from experiencing many of the negative outcomes for which they are at risk. Peer supports are powerful in reaching, engaging, and coaching youth and YAs on a new trajectory of discovery, recovery, and creating a life.

REFERENCES

Bilby, R. (1999). Transitional employment: The most supported of supported employments. *The Clubhouse Community Journal, 1,* 34–36.

Clark, H.B., & Davis, M. (2000). *Transition to adulthood: A resource for assisting young people with emotional or behavioral difficulties.* Baltimore: Paul H. Brookes Publishing Co.

Clark, H.B., & Foster-Johnson, L. (1996). Serving youth in transition into adulthood. In B.A. Stroul (Ed.), *Children's mental health: Creating systems of care in a changing society* (pp. 533–552). Baltimore: Paul H. Brookes Publishing Co.

Clark, H.B., Deschênes, N., & Jones, J. (2000). *Transition to adulthood: a resource for assisting young people with emotional or behavioral difficulties* (pp. 29–52). Baltimore: Paul H. Brookes Publishing Co.

Copeland, M.E. (2000). *Wellness Recovery Action Plan (WRAP).* Dummerston, VT: Peach Press.

Hall, G.S. (1904). *Adolescence: Its psychology and its relations to physiology, anthropology, sociology, sex, crime, religion, and education.* New York: Appleton.

Linehan, M.M. (1993). *Cognitive behavioral treatment of borderline personality disorder.* New York: Guilford Press.

Mental Health: A Report of the Surgeon General. (1999). Rockville, MD: U.S. Department of Health and Human Services, Substance Abuse and Mental Health Services Administration, Center for Mental Health Services, National Institutes of Health, National Institute of Mental Health. http://www.surgeongeneral.gov/library/mentalhealth/

New Freedom Commission on Mental Health. (2003). *Achieving the promise: Transforming mental health care in America. Final Report.* (DHHS Pub. No. SMA-03-3832.) Rockville, MD: 2003. http://www.mentalhealthcommission.gov/reports/FinalReport/toc.html

Propst, R.N. (1987). Mining our value system. Presented at the 4th International Seminar on the Clubhouse Model, Seattle, WA.

Schoel, J., & Maizell, R. (2002). *Exploring islands of healing. New perspectives on Adventure Based Counseling.* Portland, ME: J. Weston Walch Publishing.

SECTION

III

Improving Practice, System, and Policy

Prevention Planning

Collaborating with Youth and Young Adults to Reduce Risk Behavior and Related Harm

Mason G. Haber, Hewitt B. "Rusty" Clark, and Ryan Parenteau

> *"I feel that if a person is committed, the Prevention Plan is more likely to succeed; someone's not going to do something if they don't want to. They have to be willing to make changes and follow up on the plan to be successful."*
> —Ryan Parenteau, young adult coauthor

The transition to adulthood is a period in life where risk taking becomes increasingly common. Many consider this increased risk taking, including particular types of behaviors leading to increased risk or *risk behaviors,* to be a normative and in some respects necessary aspect of development (Siegel & Scovill, 2000). Despite this, for a variety of reasons, young people with emotional and/or behavioral difficulties (EBD) are extremely vulnerable to harm related to risk behavior. Some have psychiatric diagnoses, including disruptive or substance-abuse disorders, in which risk behavior has an ongoing, pervasive impact on their functioning. Even among those with other types of EBD, however, risk behaviors can lead to temporary setbacks or have more serious consequences with long-term implications. Given these harsh realities, finding ways to address current or potential problems with risk behavior has been a high priority for programs providing support to young people with EBD, such as those using the Transition to Independence Process (TIP) model (Chapter 2).

Although methods for reducing risk behaviors of young people have been written about extensively, little guidance exists on prevention and intervention considerations specific to transitioning young people with EBD. Furthermore, with very few exceptions (Brucculeri, Gogol-Ostrowski, Stewart, Sloan, & Davis, 2000), almost no resources exist to inform such intervention for young people in TIP and similar programs. This chapter discusses unique aspects of risk behavior among young people with EBD and efforts by TIP and similar programs to either prevent risk behavior problems or address emerging ones. A new approach for risk behavior prevention and early intervention designed for these settings, Prevention Planning, is also described. Experiences of the second author as a young adult in a TIP program are shared to highlight important points related to Prevention Planning and other efforts to reduce risk-behavior problems among transition-age youth and young adults with EBD.

UNDERSTANDING RISK BEHAVIORS AMONG YOUNG PEOPLE WITH EBD: A COMMON FRAMEWORK

Types of Risk Behavior

As detailed in national surveys of risk behavior among American youth such as those conducted by the Centers for Disease Control and Prevention (CDC, 2008), specific types of behavior that place youth at risk include

- Use or abuse of cigarettes, alcohol, and/or illicit drugs
- Risky dating and/or sexual behaviors (e.g., early initiation of sexual activity, sex with multiple partners, unprotected sex, sex under the influence of intoxicants, lack of caution in selecting dating and/or sexual partners)
- Illegal and/or delinquent behavior (e.g., vandalism, theft, truancy, participation in gang activities)
- Violent behavior (e.g., physically threatening or fighting with strangers, peers, parents)
- Dangerous thrill-seeking behavior (e.g., risky driving such as street racing)
- Self-harmful behavior (e.g., self-mutilation, suicide attempts, and gestures)

Clearly, these risk behaviors differ from one another in key ways; however, they often occur together, are affected by similar personal and situational influences, and share similar short- and long-term impacts. Thus, for programs seeking to address risk behaviors of young people with EBD, the similarities across risk behaviors may be more important than their differences.

The Role of Common Factors

As noted above, although risk behaviors differ from one another in important ways, a number of personal and situational characteristics are associated with most or all of them. These characteristics or *common factors* help to explain why young people who have problems with one type of risk behavior often develop others either concurrently or later on (Osgood, Johnston, O'Malley, & Bachman, 1988). There are two types of common factors that are important to consider, *risk factors* and *protective factors* (Hawkins, Catalano, & Miller, 1992; Sandler, 2001).

Risk and protective factors influence young people in somewhat different ways, each having a unique relationship to the likelihood of engaging in risk behavior (Ostaszewski & Zimmerman, 2006). Risk factors increase the likelihood of risk behavior problems. They include personal characteristics often found among young people with EBD (e.g., impulsivity, difficulties with planning, social skills deficits, emotional difficulties such as depression and anxiety), and frequent features of their environments, such as poor peer or adult role models. Protective factors decrease risk behavior problems, either by promoting healthy processes, reducing unhealthy processes, or both. For example, involving youth in positive social contexts such as after-school activities, church, or positive youth development programs may increase their self-determination, self-esteem, positive peer connections, and other healthy attributes while reducing unhealthy attributes such as time spent with antisocial peers or poor adult role models. Intervention and prevention strategies for risk behavior can utilize both risk and protective factors to reduce risk behavior among young people with EBD. Some specific risk and protective factors related to risk behavior are identified in Table 8.1.

Because certain types of risk behavior are extremely common among young people, particularly those with EBD, risk and protective factors should be understood as predicting *risk behavior severity* or *risk behavior problems,* rather than risk behaviors in themselves. For example, getting into a shoving match with another youth is a poor way of negotiating conflict, but not an unexpected event for an adolescent or even a young adult. More serious and potentially injurious violence is obvious cause for concern, however. Similarly, experimental drinking and drug use occur relatively frequently among adolescents and young adults (CDC, 2008), but are less of a concern than repeated binge drinking, drinking and driving, and so forth.

How Risk Behaviors Affect Young People with EBD: Common Processes

In addition to being associated with similar common risk and health protective factors, risk behaviors may also affect young people through similar processes, involving progression from factors that predict risk

Table 8.1.   Risk and protective factors related to risk behaviors

Risk Factors		Protective Factors	
Personal	Environmental	Personal	Environmental
• A history of risk behavior	• Poor adult role models	• Goals and aspirations	• Positive adult role models
• Anxiety, depression	• Lack of adult supervision	• High self-esteem	• Adequate supervision
• Impulsivity and planning difficulties	• Sexual or physical victimization	• Scholastic abilities and achievements	• Friends who are productively engaged
• Positive attitudes toward risk behavior	• Friends who engage in deviant or risk behavior	• Endorsing prosocial values (e.g., of hard work)	• Friends who disapprove of risk behavior
• Poor engagement with protective settings (e.g., school, church)	• Friends who are poorly engaged in school and other protective settings	• High participation & sense of belonging in protective settings	• Neighborhood protective factors (availability of extracurricular activities)
• Social skills & problem-solving deficits	• Neighborhood risk factors (e.g., high crime, violence)	• Personal competencies (e.g., problem-solving skills)	• Family and work responsibilities

Sources: Allen, Leadbeater, & Aber (1994); Bachman, Wadsworth, O'Malley, Johnston, & Schulenberg (1997); Beam, Gil-Rivas, Greenberger, & Chen (2002); Fergus & Zimmerman (2005); Greenwald, Pearson, Beery, & Cheedle (2006); Hawkins et al. (1992); Hussong & Chassin (2004); Jessor (1998); Kandel, Simcha-Fagan, & Davis (1986); Leventhal & Brooks-Gunn (2000); Masten, Rosiman, Long, Burt, Obradovic, Riley, et al. (2005); Mounts & Steinberg (1995).

behavior and the likelihood of risk behavior problems (i.e., risk and protective factors), to short-term harmful consequences, or *setbacks,* and finally, to long-term consequences that interfere with transition success or other aspects of health, or *chronic harm.* Although the first two phases of this process do not inevitably lead to long-term poor outcomes, they are cause for concern because they increase the likelihood of long-term consequences. For example, the loss of a job (e.g., due to violence at work or substance-use-related absenteeism) may be unpleasant for a young person but would be expected to have limited impact as an isolated event. However, repeated loss of employment could lead a young person to lose confidence in his or her employability or to fail to establish a record of employment over a prolonged period. The impact of this progression from minor to more serious consequences would be more likely to be enduring. Similarly, infractions related to violent or criminal behavior may in some cases have only limited immediate consequences (e.g., suspended sentences or probation), but these in turn increase the likelihood of more serious charges and a permanent criminal record when the behavior is repeated. Use of alcohol and street drugs can precipitate increased symptoms of depression, psychotic disorders, and other psychiatric problems, leading to dangerous episodes resulting in psychiatric hospitalization, disrupting school, work, and other productive activities, or worse, episodes of violence toward self or others that could cause serious injury or death (Chung, 2008). Fortunately, some young people can also learn from setbacks related to their risk behaviors, building on their strengths to avoid further setbacks or more serious consequences (Bradshaw, Brown, & Hamilton, 2006).

Although the potential for negative escalation of risk behaviors may have relevance to all young people, it may play a particularly important role in determining outcomes for transitioning young people with EBD, both because 1) young people with EBD have greater risk factors and fewer protective factors, increasing the likelihood of setting this progression in motion; and 2) short-term consequences of risk behavior may be more likely to lead to long-term problems among young people with EBD. The term *ensnarement* has been used to describe the process through which increased risk and decreased protective factors lead to setbacks and long-term consequences (Moffitt, 1993). This label well describes the process, because of the high propensity of young people with EBD to move from earlier to later phases, thus ensnaring themselves through behavior that other young people may engage in with impunity. The label is also apt given how the consequences of risk behavior may limit options of young people with EBD for succeeding in developmental tasks concurrently or later in life.

The gray shaded areas in Figure 8.1 depict a conceptual model of the phases through which young people either become ensnared in or escape chronic harm. The figure also lists specific differences between young people with EBD and their peers related to this process. The panel on the far left lists differences between young people with EBD and their peers in their risk and protective factors, with young people with EBD having a greater likelihood of risk factors and a lesser likelihood of protective factors. These disadvantages of young people with EBD increase the likelihood that young people with EBD will escalate to more severe risk behaviors and experience setbacks. The middle panel shows differences between young people with EBD and their peers in their frequency of setbacks, in the types of setbacks they experience, and in the likelihood that these setbacks will lead to a negative outcome rather than a positive one. Possible negative outcomes (e.g., chronic harm), and possible positive outcomes (e.g., learning from experience, thriving) are shown on the far right in the lower and upper squares respectively. The white portions of Figure 8.1 show the variety of ways in which transition support or specialized treatment programs

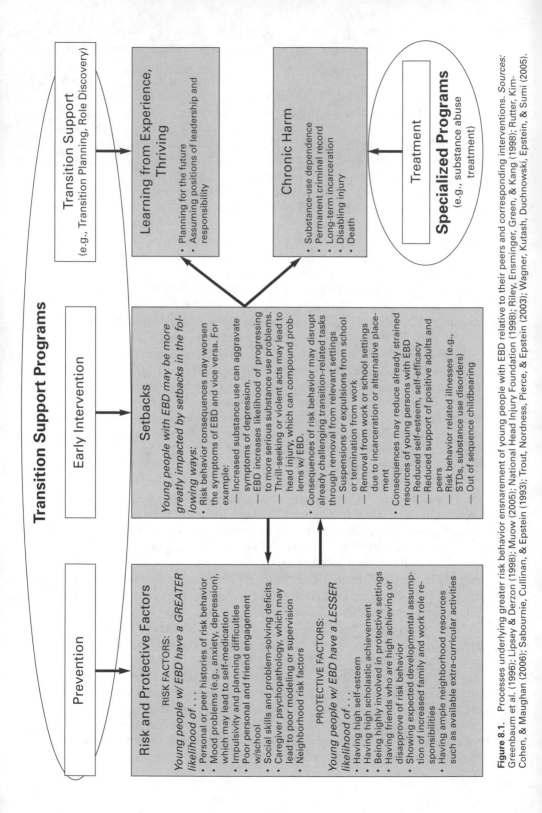

Figure 8.1. Processes underlying greater risk behavior ensnarement of young people with EBD relative to their peers and corresponding interventions. *Sources:* Greenbaum et al. (1996); Lipsey & Derzon (1998); Muow (2005); National Head Injury Foundation (1998); Riley, Ensminger, Green, & Kang (1998); Rutter, Kim-Cohen, & Maughan (2006); Sabournie, Cullinan, & Epstein (1993); Trout, Nordness, Pierce, & Epstein (2003); Wagner, Kutash, Duchnowski, Epstein, & Sumi (2005).

can reduce the differences between young people with EBD and their peers, decreasing their risk factors, increasing their protective factors, decreasing their likelihood of setbacks, and decreasing their vulnerability to long-term and negative outcomes. These strategies are discussed further in the next section.

In interpreting this figure, it is important to avoid generalizing the *more likely* disadvantages in risk and protective factors and in setbacks to all young people with EBD. Though young people with EBD may be at an overall disadvantage relative to their peers in these areas, many have particular strengths that diverge from this pattern. For example, considerable variation in past risk behavior, problem-solving abilities, academic achievement, family environment, and other factors is evident across groups of young people with EBD (Vance, Bowen, Fernandez, & Thompson, 2002). Thus, supportive individuals should attend to the particular ways in which young people with EBD may be more vulnerable, or alternatively may show particular areas of resilience or strength (Epstein, Rudolph, & Epstein, 2000).

As shown by the reverse arrow in Figure 8.1 (i.e., from setbacks to risk and protective factors) setbacks can also affect risk behavior by affecting risk and protective factors. For example, setbacks can decrease young persons' self-esteem, reduce supportiveness of parents or other helpful adults, or confine the young person to a less successful, more deviant peer group (e.g., by alienating more prosocial peers or causing the young person to lose access to prosocial activities such as work due to legal sanctions; Foshee et al., 2007; Pinquart, Silbereisen, & Wiesner, 2004; Stice & Barrera, 1995), all of which would ultimately increase the likelihood of risk behavior and related harm. However, setbacks may also create opportunities for improvement, since they often provide young people with feedback on the destructiveness of their behavior that, if fully considered—possibly through assistance of a supportive adult—could motivate them to change this behavior and avoid long-term negative consequences (Stockwell, Gruenewald, Toumbourou, & Loxley, 2005). Setbacks can also help young people to recognize the importance of risk and protective factors by helping them to see how they set the chain of setbacks and more serious consequences in motion. In turn, they may become open to making positive changes involving risk and protective factors (e.g., seeking additional adult support, associating with more positive peers). Any of these three objectives (i.e., changing risk behavior, avoiding harm related to risk behavior, or altering the risk and protective factors) can be addressed through specific behavioral plans (e.g., the Prevention Plans to be discussed later in the chapter). The challenges and opportunities provided by setbacks in addressing young persons' risk behavior are well illustrated in Ryan's following comments.

I struggle to take my meds every day because I forget. When you make it a habit, it's easy, but I've gotten away from that. I've tried to make a habit of taking them in the morning, for example, but then kind of drifted away from doing that. Sometimes I drink too much and I don't want it interacting with my meds, so I purposely don't take them. Even if I could establish a pattern, that would disrupt it. . . . Last night, I knew I had to work at 9 o'clock in the morning. My friends asked me if I wanted to go to a bar; we went and ended up staying till 1 o'clock . . . we went back to the apartment and had a glass of wine, and by the time I got to bed it was 3 in the morning, so I was 15 minutes late to work and I've been tired all day . . . .

The setback Ryan describes is one that he can get away with once in a while—not taking his medications in order to drink—but interferes with his efforts to develop consistent habits of medication use, habits which in turn might help to prevent more the more serious consequence of being hospitalized. Drinking also compromises Ryan's judgment, leading him to stay out too late and be exhausted at work the next day or drive under the influence. As occasional events, not taking medications, staying out too late, or driving under the influence do not *necessarily* inflict lasting harm (though they may), but as these setbacks accumulate, lasting consequences such as job loss, loss of a driver's license, a return to the psychiatric hospital, or worse become more and more likely. Although these challenges are considerable, Ryan's understanding of links between his risk behavior and setbacks provides a foundation for him to plan ways to avoid more significant harm (e.g., either by avoiding drinking entirely, or by devising ways to drink that are less likely to lead to setbacks).

Given the cumulative short- and long-term impact of risk behavior on transition for young people with EBD, it is no wonder that risk behaviors are among the most prevalent and problematic issues that youth with EBD face (Greenbaum et al., 1996). As illustrated by Ryan's anecdote, programs supporting transition of young people with EBD often find that risk behaviors interfere with transition-related tasks such as keeping jobs, undoing progress of youth and young adults. Tragically, such difficulties with transition-related tasks are among the best predictors of whether young people with EBD develop pervasive, enduring problems with risk behavior over the long term such as substance dependence (Brown, Myers, Mott, & Vik, 1994; Guo, Hawkins, Hill, & Abbott, 2001).

"Sometimes I drink too much and I don't want it interacting with my meds, so I purposely don't take them. Even if I could establish a pattern, that would disrupt it. . . ."

Implications of Common Factors and Processes for Transition Support Programs

The cumulative ways in which risk behaviors affect transition, such that young persons' engagement in risk behavior leads to increased problems over time, suggests that transition support programs may be most effective in reducing risk behavior problems by addressing them early, before or as significant problems begin to emerge. The unshaded portions of Figure 8.1 depict four types of approaches programs can use to address risk behavior and related harm at different points in the ensnarement process. Two "early" types of approaches include *prevention* approaches, designed to reduce risk factors and increase protective factors, and *early intervention* approaches, designed to interrupt the progression to chronic harm, often by helping young adults to recognize and address setbacks. These two "early" types of approaches will often need to be employed within transition support programs. A third type of approach, *treatment,* is suited to addressing problems that are already well established or have resulted in more serious harmful consequences and is perhaps best offered in specialized settings such as specialty mental health and substance abuse programs. Finally, *transition support* approaches, including transition planning or role discovery, are useful in addressing risk behaviors because they help young people to find alternatives to engaging in risk behavior, and because they can help clarify the costs of continued risk behavior problems. Due to their focus on positive outcomes, transition support approaches are shown in the "late" portion of the conceptual model (i.e., following setbacks). Through transition planning, young people can be assisted in creating plans that build on past accomplishments and that help them envision new roles (e.g., as college students or successful members of the workforce; Unger, 1998; Webb et al., 1999). Some transition support programs have also sought to help young people discover new adult roles by entrusting them with positions of leadership and responsibility, either in the transition support program itself, or in its surrounding community (e.g., West, Fetzer, Graham, & Keller, 2000).

Because young persons' patterns of risk behavior and setbacks are likely to change over time, intervention efforts focused on specific types of risk behavior problems could quickly become irrelevant for certain young people. Thus, in selecting interventions to interrupt the ensnarement process, programs should select options that are sufficiently flexible to address a variety of possible risk behavior problems and can be adjusted on a continuing basis as young persons' situations change. Ideally, interventions should also involve ongoing assessment and plan-

ning to increase the likelihood that they remain relevant and responsive. Because autonomy and identity are key developmental issues for
young adults, young people should also be involved as full partners in
this ongoing assessment and planning. Finally, interventions would be
expected to be most optimal where they are well integrated with transition support approaches such as transition planning and role discovery. The last of these criteria may be particularly important, as strategies
to reduce risk behaviors may have little appeal for young people with
EBD unless they are explicitly tied to their efforts to achieve their transition-related goals (Haber, 2008). Conversely, explicit efforts to explore
links between risk behavior and transition-related outcomes can help
demonstrate to young people their stake in avoiding risk behaviors and
preventing risk-behavior related problems.

　Ryan's description of a recent experience with hospitalization illustrates ways in which young people can meaningfully connect risk behavior and goals related to the transition to adulthood—in this case,
working, staying connected to a supportive peer group, and maintaining an independent residence:

> I had a breakdown where I didn't take my meds and wasn't in my
> right mind. It was because of my illness, but the substance abuse
> didn't help. I'm thinking it triggered me. I felt people were coming
> after me; I messed up my apartment . . . it wasn't a pretty scene.
> Patrick, my case manager, calmed me down and suggested that I go
> to the hospital. I was there about a month. I was anxious toward the
> end. I felt that I couldn't be helped anymore, that I needed to get back
> and start my life back up on the outside, find a new job, get help from
> the outpatient program, get back to my apartment. The feeling was al-
> most bad enough to where I want to stay out of the hospital just to
> avoid going through it again. The transition back out, when it hap-
> pened, was tough. You kind of find out who your real friends are. It
> seemed like a lot of my old friends didn't care. The only people who
> were there for me were my parents, aunt, and uncle; that's just about
> it. It's tough to get back to where you were before you went in. I re-
> member when I first got back to my apartment, there were fruit flies
> all over. It took 3 weeks to get rid of them.

ADDRESSING RISK BEHAVIORS
THROUGH PREVENTION PLANNING

Based on the experiences of pioneering programs for facilitating transition of young people with EBD (e.g., Bullis, Morgan, Benz, Todis, &
Johnson, 2002; Clark & Foster-Johnson, 1996; Clark, Pschorr, Wells, Cur-

tis, & Tighe, 2004; Clark, Unger, & Stewart, 1993; Hagner, Cheney, & Malloy, 1999), Clark (2004) designed the TIP model in the mid-1990s, and he and his colleagues have continued to research and refine the model. Recently, the lead author of this chapter undertook research to strengthen Prevention Planning, an important practice element within the TIP model (Haber, Deschênes, & Clark, 2008). This research initially involved surveying TIP model sites, some of which were a part of the Partnerships for Youth Transition (PYT; Clark et al., 2008). The second phase of this research involved conducting focus groups with various stakeholders at a TIP site. Both phases of this effort are described in the section that follows.

Survey on Experiences of PYT sites

Description of Survey

In order to better describe experiences of sites providing transition support to young people with EBD in assessing and addressing risk behaviors, questionnaires were distributed to all five PYT sites as well as several other sites using the TIP model to inform their services. Of the five PYT sites and three other TIP model sites contacted, three PYT sites and one other TIP site responded to open-ended questions regarding ways in which risk behaviors are problematic for young persons with EBD, ways in which their organization assessed and addressed youth risk behavior, barriers to addressing risk behavior, and outside resources that might assist the organizations in better addressing risk behavior.

Survey Results

PYT and TIP sites described particular ways in which risk behaviors are problematic for young people with EBD, including their effects on youths' abilities to achieve their transition plan goals. They indicated difficulties in balancing young persons' needs with larger program considerations in responding to risk behaviors (e.g., concerns about liability). They also shared their strategies for risk behavior prevention and intervention, including both in-house efforts and collaboration with outside experts (e.g., providers of specialized services). In describing these strategies, they particularly stressed the importance of supportive relationships with adults, including relationships with transition facilitators (i.e., intensive case managers in transition support programs), and described the need to train these individuals to increase their knowledge of young persons' risk behavior and how to assist young people in avoiding or reducing problematic risk behavior patterns.

Challenges Related to Risk Behaviors

PYT and TIP sites noted that one of the challenges faced by many young people is that risk behaviors are sometimes modeled or even reinforced by their family members or other adults in their support networks. This was observed to be particularly the case for young people with histories in the child welfare system. A variety of potential adverse effects related to young persons' risk behaviors were noted by PYT and TIP sites; however, sites generally agreed that the most destructive aspect of risk behaviors for young people is their capacity to effectively derail progress toward their transition plan goals (e.g., those related to employment and education).

Efforts to Address Risk Behavior Are Often Not Youth Driven

Programs also noted how responses to risk behavior may sometimes be driven by a variety of considerations other than young adults' needs. These included situations in which interventions are selected based on priorities of a setting (e.g., in a school setting, reducing delinquency), or based on the needs of other young people receiving services (e.g., to be protected from violent behavior). Some sites noted difficulties in engaging youth and young adults in certain types of services that, while more expedient in their delivery, are not individualized in nature (e.g., psychoeducational, psychosocial rehabilitation, or treatment groups).

Needs for Training on Risk Behavior and Greater Knowledge of Community Resources

Sites noted the importance of ensuring that supportive adults have adequate education regarding youth risk behaviors, providing them with training on factors related to risk behavior problems, and providing information on available resources for risk behavior prevention and intervention in the community. All programs mentioned difficulties in identifying, accessing, or using resources to address youth risk behaviors. In particular, programs indicated that they would like to collaborate more extensively with prevention programs in the community (e.g., Planned Parenthood, Victims Against Violent Crimes) and individual experts in the community (e.g., police liaisons, nurses and/or sexual education specialists), but were sometimes unaware of how to do so.

Combining In-House Resources and Outside Expertise

PYT and TIP sites indicated the usefulness of other programs in cases where risk behaviors were beyond their capacity to manage (e.g., young people in need of detoxificaton services). PYT and TIP sites also reported sometimes amplifying their existing expertise by having outside experts train staff or by contracting them to deliver on-site services. Most sites favored using less intensive, general problem-solving strategies such as the Prevention Planning approach described in this chapter as a first-line approach to risk behavior, reserving more specialized, focused techniques for young people with especially severe risk behavior problems. Close, one-on-one relationships with well informed transition facilitators and other supportive adults were described as key to the success of Prevention Planning and similar strategies. Reflecting this point, Ryan describes in the following quote the importance of his relationship with his transition facilitator, Patrick, to his own recovery and his abilities to cope with crises precipitated by his risk behavior:

> Patrick is a one-man crisis hotline. I trust him and can call him when there is no one else to call. When I call him, he responds to me pretty quickly too. . . . When my drinking got bad and I had my breakdown, it was Patrick who calmed me down and suggested that I go to the hospital.

Implications of PYT and TIP Site Experiences

PYT and TIP site experiences suggest that in addressing risk behaviors of young people, cultivating supportive one-on-one relationships with adults is important. The observation that risk behaviors can compromise young persons' transition plans has a clear implication for engaging young persons in addressing risk behavior issues; namely, that they will want to address risk behavior issues if they feel that transition plan goals truly reflect their desires and if supportive adults help them to understand how risk behaviors might undermine these plans. However, the observations of PYT and TIP sites that efforts to address young persons' risk behavior can sometimes be driven by considerations other than young persons' needs suggests that keeping goals of young persons in the forefront can be challenging. In order to be helpful to young people in evaluating and planning responses to actual or potential risk behavior problems, supportive adults need to be knowledgeable about risk behavior and about when it is most likely to cause harm, and which resources are available to help young adults avoid or reduce harm. They should also find ways to approach these issues with youth that are sensitive to young persons' fears about compromising their autonomy to others' agendas (e.g., programs' priorities to reduce risk of harm, if necessary, at the expense of young persons' freedoms). These considerations have helped to inform the ongoing development of the Prevention Planning approach (Haber et al., 2008).

The Prevention Planning Approach to Risk Behavior

Building on an understanding of relationships between different risk behaviors as well as the Transition to Independence Process (TIP) guidelines for providing responsive services to assist transition of youth with EBD (Clark, 2004), the Prevention Planning approach emphasizes collaboration with young people to address risk behavior by helping them, members of their formal support networks (i.e., professionals), and informal support networks (e.g., family members, employers, mentor figures, supportive peers) to 1) identify their risk behaviors and their harmful consequences; 2) ask about the situations and functions that are associated with the behaviors (i.e., recognize the circumstances accompanying or not accompanying risk behaviors and what young people "get" from engaging in them); 3) generate options; 4) specify a Prevention Plan; and 5) follow up on the Prevention Plan. Using this initial framework of steps, Haber (2008) recently conducted a series of focus groups with young people in a TIP program, their family members, transition facilitators, and supervisors in order to further elucidate specific challenges to application of the technique and develop pilot versions of Prevention Planning tools, including trainings, a manual, and an adherence measure. During this project, transition facilitators in the program also piloted Prevention Planning techniques with young people, generating a number of sample plans that were reviewed to garner further insights about Prevention Planning implementation. The present description of Prevention Planning incorporates lessons learned from this project as well as continuing technical assistance efforts centered on Prevention Planning with TIP sites and similar programs.

Theory of Change

Each of the Prevention Planning steps is designed to reduce risk behavior problems individually and by building on prior steps. Although most young people have some awareness of the harmful consequences of risk behavior, they may not have fully considered how these could be relevant to them personally. Assisting youth in linking consequences of risk behavior to their personal goals can be an effective way to help them with this task. Through recognizing circumstances or warning signs that accompany risk behavior and considering its functions, young people can gain insight into how to avoid risk behaviors and related harm. (For examples of how techniques similar to the first two steps of Prevention Planning have been used in addressing substance use risk behaviors; see Baer & Peterson, 2002; Godley et al., 2001; and Sampl & Kadden, 2001.) Generation of options, or "brainstorming," is a very commonly used technique for helping youth to solve problems such as how to avoid unwanted behavior (Wagner, Blasé, & Clark, 2005). Having identified specific behaviors or behavior-related problems to avoid and ways to avoid these behaviors and problems, young people can then be assisted by supportive adults in creating a specific action plans. Such action plans have been shown to increase the likelihood that young people will follow through on strategies to reduce risk behaviors (Godley et al., 2001; Rotheram-Borus et al., 1996). Finally, following up is an important determinant of the success of a risk behavior action plan (Adams & Grieder, 2005; Godley et al., 2001).

Prevention Planning Guidelines

Timing of Prevention Planning

Prevention Planning is designed to be practiced in advance of rather than in response to risk behavior crises, as part of the broader person-centered planning process of care coordination used by wraparound, TIP, and similar programs. Engaging in Prevention Planning early in the working relationship enables facilitators and youth to decide how to handle risk behaviors in advance of their occurrence. This allows for discussion of these issues in a more supportive and less threatening context.

Use of Formal and Informal Supports

Practices to address risk behavior in wraparound and similar programs (e.g., safety planning; Bruns et al., 2004), have often used a team approach in which a group of professional and natural supports (i.e., family and friends) assist youth in planning how to address risk behaviors. Pursuing a team approach may be problematic in Prevention Planning with young people with EBD, however given the developmentally normative needs of these youth for their autonomy to be respected. Across the youth focus groups on Prevention Planning, although there was general agreement that it was important to involve family and friends in planning, strong consensus emerged on wanting to control the pace and extent of this involvement except in very extreme circumstances.

We have found that it is usually easier to respect young persons' desires for autonomy in this regard by initiating Prevention Planning through one-on-one interactions involving a young person and a transition facilitator. Advantages of involving additional supports can still be preserved, based on the young person's willingness and comfort level, by approaching these individuals after the initial Prevention Planning discussion. At that point, additional supports can either help the young person and facilitator to complete the plan (e.g., by suggesting the *other-support* options; see the section on Generating Options that follows) or can agree to carry out aspects of a completed plan with the understanding that it may need to be modified based on experience (see the section on Follow-up). A straightforward way of helping young people to identify additional supports to participate in the plan is to ask them who they think might be helpful in reducing or avoiding a particular type of risk behavior or avoiding a particular harmful consequence related to risk behavior (e.g., "who could you go to for support when tempted to . . . "). Note that the recommendation for effectively engaging young people in Prevention Planning parallels that which is used in TIP futures planning (see Chapter 2).

Content of Prevention Planning

Next, guidelines for each of the five steps of Prevention Planning are briefly described.

1. *Identifying problematic risk behaviors and their consequences:* Simply observing that a young person engages in risk behavior is not sufficient grounds for deciding to address that behavior through Prevention Planning. Because Prevention Planning is designed to be a collaborative process, an important criterion in deciding whether to address risk behavior is the degree to which the individual young person sees the behavior as problematic. Clearly, young people can benefit from information regarding the potential dangers of risk behaviors, and it is incumbent on the transition facilitator and/or others working with youth to provide it. However, if despite this guidance, the problem recognition of the young person is poor, he or she may be unwilling to participate in other aspects of Prevention Planning. Helping young people to recognize links between possible or actual consequences of their risk behaviors for their transition-related goals can be a key part of the process of improving their problem recognition. Participants in our young person, family, and program staff focus groups agreed that a good way to do this was to explicitly relate aspects of the Prevention Plan to goals in their transition of "future plans" (i.e., plans for pursuing transition-related tasks such as those related to employment, education, and independent living).

   An important guideline for the identification step of Prevention Planning relates to the specificity of what is being targeted.

Many young people have multiple risk behaviors that could pose a problem for them. Based on our review of Prevention Plans developed at the focus group and other TIP sites, we believe that a plan should generally focus on a single behavior problem in order to be straightforward enough to be easily comprehended, remembered, and implemented by a young person. However, because different types of risk behavior often share similar precipitating factors, one means for addressing multiple risk behaviors in a single plan is to focus on a risky situation where multiple behaviors might occur. For example, in response to conflict with a romantic partner, a young person might be more likely to become violent, use substances, or both. A plan to address both the violence and the substance use, then, might focus on helping the young person to avoid conflict with the romantic partner.

2. *Asking about situations and functions associated with risk behavior:* The purpose of this step is to increase understanding of circumstances where risk behaviors occur and the functions that they serve. Asking questions about *situations* where risk behavior occurs (or does not occur) helps the youth and transition facilitator to identify places, people, thoughts or emotional states, and so forth, that tend to accompany risk behavior. In turn, this information can assist youth in identifying the situations that they should avoid or where they should take precautionary measures. Some possible specific questions to ask could include the following: Who is with the youth when the youth engages in risk behavior (or is the youth alone)? Where does the risk behavior occur? When does it occur? What happens before it occurs? Are there warning signs that signal when it might become a problem (e.g., emotional distress, withdrawal from supportive others)? When is the behavior *least* likely to occur? Similarly, by appreciating the *functions* of risk behaviors, youth and transition facilitators can better identify other behaviors that might serve as alternatives. Youth with EBD may be motivated to engage in risk behavior as a way of regulating mood, avoiding problems, or feeling more socially accepted. Others may engage in risk behavior due to lack of more constructive activities to keep themselves occupied. Some may engage in risk behavior because it helps them feel more independent, mature, or powerful. Young people can often have helpful insights if asked about the functions of their behavior using concrete, youth-friendly language (e.g., how they benefit or what they "get" out of the behavior). Our focus group participants agreed with this approach and suggested that discussing causes in a broader or more abstract sense was less useful. For ex-

ample, rather than discussing the role of "trauma" in risk behavior, it would be more helpful to focus on how the behavior might help the youth to feel more in control or comfortable in specific situations (from the youth's own perspective, rather than the facilitator's).

3. *Generating options:* This step involves assisting young people in generating possible solutions for reducing or preventing risk behaviors and related harm in a nonjudgmental way. These solutions should emphasize young persons' own strengths and the resources in their natural support networks rather than relying on professional supports (e.g., calling 911 or a crisis line). Solutions do not need to be elaborate but should be sustainable and result in young persons feeling empowered when they are enacted. For example, young people might be encouraged to plan their activities to minimize temptation or opportunity to engage in risk behaviors, a *self-support* strategy, or talk with a peer or mentor figure who they trust in situations where they believe they may be at risk, an *other-support* strategy. Efforts should be made to identify options that help young people to avoid risk behavior problems long before they occur, for example, by avoiding going to places where they drank or used drugs in the past (e.g., a bar) rather than trying to cope at a disadvantage once the risky situation is present. Prevention Plans can also include actions to decrease risk factors and increase protective factors, such as planning for constructive activities (e.g., by structuring a schedule to include these on a regular basis), or increasing exposure to more pro-social, less risk-behavior-prone groups of peers (e.g., by initiating involvement in extracurricular sports activities, church groups, and support groups).

4. *Specifying a Prevention Plan:* The Prevention Plan builds on activities in Steps 1 through 3. If these steps are accomplished optimally, specification involves simply helping young people choose from among the options they have generated in order to arrive at their preferred plan. The Prevention Plan should not be thought of as a contract. Rather, it can be seen as a roadmap or guide for young people, professionals, and informal supports describing preferred ways to avoid or reduce risk behavior problems. In their discussions about what a plan should contain, our focus group participants tended to embrace the idea that both self- and other-support strategies should be incorporated in any plan, with many suggesting that the optimal plan would balance the two, such that, for example, for every self-support strategy an other-support strategy would also be included and vice versa. Once the self- and other-support options to be used in addressing risk behaviors are specified, a document summarizing Steps 1–4 can be prepared.

Plan summaries should be kept as simple and brief as possible, and ideally could be contained on a single page. For example, each of the following plan components could be described in one or two sentences: 1) how the risk behavior problem being targeted affects transition-related goals; 2) the accompanying and/or non-accompanying circumstances and motives; 3) a short list of options that were considered most seriously in the Prevention Planning discussion prior to the plan specification; and 4) two options (a "Plan A" and "Plan B") that were most preferred. In addition to summaries of other aspects of the Prevention Plan, a *back-up plan* is another possible feature to include in a summary. The idea of including a back-up plan—and referring to it in this way, rather than using other language that might imply coercion to some young adults (e.g., "crisis plan" or "safety plan")—was regarded favorably by our focus-group participants and stakeholders at other sites. A back-up plan briefly describes what will happen if the preferred Prevention Plan options fail and the young adult has lost control of the situation (e.g., in situations where the young adult poses immediate risk of harm to self or others). The back-up plan serves the function of a conventional, stand-alone crisis plan; however, including it in the context of a Prevention Plan takes some of the emphasis off of emergency measures, placing it instead on strategies for avoiding crises. A suggested tool to facilitate Prevention Planning containing the elements described above, including fields summarizing each of the steps, is posted on the TIP web site (http://tip.fmhi.usf.edu).

In examining the Prevention Plans created by the young adult focus-group participants and their transition facilitators, we found that self- and other-support options were closely integrated in many cases. One means for integrating self and other support involved using a self-support strategy first, and following this with an other-support strategy in the event that the self-support strategy did not work. For example, a plan to help a young person avoid losing her temper violently at work might involve the young person first taking an allotted 15-minute break (a self-support strategy). Then, in cases in which the young person still feels worried about losing control of her temper, an other-support strategy such as approaching a trusted friend at work or calling the transition facilitator to talk could be used. Another means for integrating self- and other-support options was to use other-support options to help prepare or bolster self-support strategies. For example, various self-support strategies might be used to reduce states of agitation that would otherwise lead to harmful risk behavior. To increase the likelihood that such a self-support strategy would work in the relevant situation, an other-support strategy might be used, such as having the transition facilitator or another trusted adult set up regularly scheduled deep breathing rehearsals with the young person. A third means that was used to integrate self and other supports was to have the young person request (e.g., from parents or other caregivers) the freedom to use a self-support in certain risky situations where they might otherwise be barred from doing so. For example, the young person might request the freedom to leave the house in potential conflict situations, or request transportation to a safe place such as a support group if temptation to use substances is running high.

5. *Following up on the Prevention Plan:* In most cases, effectively addressing the "moving target" of young persons' behavior problems will involve an ongoing assessment of whether plans are successful or need to be modified. Young people, family members, and transition facilitators participating in our focus groups identified this step as being particularly crucial in order for plans to be effective. At minimum, follow-up should involve discussing with young people after an appropriate, mutually agreed period the extent to which the plan was used, whether it was effective in either reducing risk behavior or problems related to risk behavior, and whether adjustment of the plan might be necessary. It is also important to discuss any circumstances related to the risk behavior problem or the plan that may have changed and adjustments these changes might require. Follow-ups might also serve the purpose of reviewing planned practice of the plan. For example, for a plan involving behavior alternatives to substance use such as scheduling outings with non-using friends, the young person might be encouraged to practice the behaviors at times when the temptation to use substances is low in order to develop a habit that can withstand higher levels of temptation. Part of the follow-up in this instance might be to review with the young person whether any attempts to schedule outings with friends have occurred at low-risk as well as at higher risk times. Our focus group participants also suggested that developing ways to remember the plan in high-risk situations might be important (e.g., index cards listing aspects of the plan, acronyms, rhyming mnemonics), and that these should be evaluated and, if necessary, adjusted as part of follow-up as well.

In the following quote, Ryan describes how Prevention Planning was implemented in support of his own recovery:

> I worked on the plan with my transition facilitator. We each contributed what we thought was important. In the beginning, I wasn't

too thrilled about it, but I like the way that it includes things that I would want to do anyway. I don't look at it every day, but when I look back at it, it's helpful and keeps me on track.

Resources to Inform Prevention Planning

Relapse Prevention Planning, Wellness Recovery Action Planning, and Motivational Interviewing

Treatment and rehabilitation strategies created for adults may be helpful in providing ideas for how to generate plans with young people. Relapse prevention, an approach used to help individuals with substance use or violence problems avoid a return or relapse to problematic patterns of behavior (e.g., Carroll, 1998; Gorski & Miller, 1986; Sampl & Kadden, 2001), involves many strategies similar to those used in Prevention Planning. These include avoiding risky situations (i.e., the settings in which risk behaviors occur) and modifying risk and protective factors to decrease the likelihood of risk behavior overall. Similarly, Wellness Recovery Action Planning (WRAP; Copeland, 1997), incorporates techniques for helping individuals with severe mental illnesses to reduce risk prior to relapse or exacerbation of symptoms, as well as a component analogous to the back-up plan described previously. Depending on the young person and situation involved, these strategies could be integrated with the Prevention Plan (e.g., creating a WRAP could serve as a one of the Prevention Plan self-support options, along with other strategies), or used in lieu of Prevention Planning. Motivational interviewing techniques (Baer & Peterson, 2002), can be helpful in ensuring that discussions with youth and young adults about risk behavior are supportive rather than confrontational.

Caveats About Alternative Strategies

Two key issues are important to keep in mind in employing available treatment and rehabilitation resources for adults as part of or as an alternative to Prevention Planning. First, because young people with EBD tend to have emerging patterns of risk behavior that are less clear, developed, and consistent than those of older adults, more careful consideration of the particulars of their situations may be necessary than is typical in treatment and rehabilitation approaches. Second, because young persons' lives change rapidly, plans need to be simple enough that adjusting them frequently is

In the beginning, I wasn't too thrilled about it, but I like the way that it includes things that I would want to do anyway. I don't look at it every day, but when I look back at it, it's helpful and keeps me on track.

not a discouraging process for the transition facilitator and young person. Finally, a key aspect of Prevention Planning's theory of change is the importance of supporting young persons' autonomy in discussing and intervening with risk behavior. Thus, transition facilitators need to consider whether specific structured intervention processes (e.g., relapse prevention or WRAP) would be a good match for a given young adult and his or her coping style. Even more important, transition facilitators should attend to whether the *young person* considers them to be a match or alternatively might prefer to use a different type of approach.

CONCLUDING COMMENT: TOWARD A PERSON-CENTERED UNDERSTANDING OF RISK BEHAVIOR

During the transition to adulthood, risk-taking appears to be a biologically based, culturally accepted norm, one that may in some cases contribute to personal growth and discovery (Hall, 1904; Siegel & Scovill, 2000). In addition, perceived benefits are more predictive of young persons' risk behavior than perceived negative consequences (Steinberg, 2007). Thus, in considering whether and how to address risk behaviors of a young person, it is important to attend to the real or perceived benefits of his or her risk behavior rather than simply the negative consequences involved. Otherwise, young persons may understandably object that efforts to help them address risk behavior, however well intended, are inadequately responsive to their needs and values. In order to be sensitive to the normativeness and functions of the risk behavior and respond accordingly, transition facilitators and other supportive adults should help young people to identify instances where risk behavior patterns are clearly outside the norm (e.g., substance dependency) or are associated with an unacceptably high level of risk (e.g., unprotected sex with multiple partners, use of substances if dangerous interactions with medication are likely), and help them to find alternatives to risk behavior for achieving desired benefits, such as new coping strategies or alternative activities. Certainly an awareness of the normativeness and functions of risk behavior argues against traditional, confrontative strategies for risk behavior management that label youth as pathological or deviant and demand abstinence as the sole acceptable goal.

TIP Guideline 1 specifies, "Engage young people through relationship development, person-centered planning, and a focus on their futures." In addition to being a primary objective of the enterprise of transition support generally (Bridgeo, Davis, & Florida, 2000), engagement of young people, whether with pro-social peers, formal and informal adult supports, or positive settings (e.g., school, church, work), is a central and critical aspect of helping them to manage risk behaviors. As reviewed previously, young people who are engaged with their support networks and broader communities are less likely to participate in risk behaviors. They are also more likely to benefit from risk-behavior-focused treatment, should this become necessary (Thompson, Pomeroy, & Gober, 2005). Broader engagement often begins with one trusted relationship, as our PYT and TIP sites have found, in turn shifting patterns of youth behavior away from risk behavior and into more beneficial activities. In order to be optimally helpful, transition facilitators and other supportive adults need to attend to both sides of this "decreased risk behavior equals increased positive activities" equation, simultaneously assisting youth with both of these objectives and not emphasizing one at the expense of the other. By focusing on risk behavior without adequately attending to young persons' strengths and goals, supportive adults will miss opportunities to help young people find alternatives to risk behavior. Conversely, focusing only on strengths and goals without attending to the potential undermining impact of risk behavior may set young people up for failure. The balance between addressing risk behaviors and supporting strengths and goals can sometimes be difficult to achieve, particularly given the fact that adults and young people differ in how they prioritize pursuing benefits versus avoiding risks (Steinberg, 2007). By using youth-driven, person-centered planning processes such as Prevention Planning in the context of such relationships, our hope is that transition facilitators and young people can better negotiate the sometimes difficult balance between responsibly reducing risk and adequately emphasizing strengths and goals.

Despite significant limitations and often bleak current circumstances, young people with EBD are full of potential. Those who are able to appreciate their potentially bright future—particularly when they are able to taste some of the benefits along the way—are much less likely to take chances with it. Given some assistance in achieving personal goals and perhaps some sensitive, collaborative planning, young people with EBD can begin the process of replacing their risky and destructive behaviors with the more committed, productive activities of a successful adult.

REFERENCES

Adams, N., & Grieder, D.M. (2005). *Treatment planning for person-centered care: The road to mental health and addiction recovery.* Burlington, MA: Elsevier.

Allen, J.P., Leadbeater, B.J., & Aber, J.L. (1994). The development of problem behavior syndromes in at-risk adolescents. *Development and Psychopathology, 6,*
323–342.
Bachman, J.G., Wadsworth, K.N., O'Malley, P.M., Johnston, L.D., & Schulenberg, J.E. (1997). *Smoking, drinking, and drug use in young adulthood: The impact
of new freedoms and new responsibilities.* Mahwah, NJ: Lawrence Erlbaum Associates.
Baer, J.S., & Peterson, P.L. (2002). Motivational interviewing with adolescents and
young adults. In W.R. Miller & S. Rollnick (Eds.), *Motivational interviewing: Preparing people for change* (2nd ed.) (pp. 320–332). New York: Guilford Press.
Beam, M.R., Gil-Rivas, V., Greenberger, E., & Chen, C. (2002). Adolescent problem behavior and depressed mood: Risk and protection within and across social contexts. *Journal of Youth and Adolescence, 31,* 343–357.
Bradshaw, C.P., Brown, J.S., & Hamilton, S.F. (2006). Applying positive youth
development and life-course research to the treatment of adolescents involved with the judicial system. *Journal of Addictions and Offender Counseling,
27,* 2–16.
Bridgeo, D., Davis, M., & Florida, Y. (2000). Transition coordination: Helping
young people pull it all together. In H.B. Clark, & M. Davis (Eds.), *Transition
to adulthood: A resource for assisting young people with emotional or behavioral difficulties* (pp. 155–178). Baltimore: Paul H. Brookes Publishing Co.
Brown, S.A., Myers, M.G., Mott, M.A., & Vik, P.W. (1994). Correlates of success
following treatment for adolescent substance abuse. *Applied and Preventative
Psychology, 3,* 61–73.
Brucculeri, M.A., Gogol-Ostrowski, T., Stewart, D., Sloan, J., & Davis, M. (2000).
Clinical and substance abuse treatment: Applications in the trenches. In H.B.
Clark & M. Davis (Eds.), *Transition to adulthood: A resource for assisting young
people with emotional and behavioral difficulties* (pp. 133–154). Baltimore: Paul H.
Brookes Publishing Co.
Bullis, M., Morgan, T., Benz, M.R., Todis, B., & Johnson, M.D. (2002). Descrip-
tion and evaluation of the ARIES project: Achieving rehabilitation, individu-
alized education, and employment success for adolescents with emotional
disturbance. *Career Development for Exceptional Individuals, 25,* 41–58.
Bruns, E.J., Walker, J.S., VanDenBerg, J.D., Rast, J., Osher, T.Wj., Koroloff, N., et
al. (2004). *Phases and activities of the wraparound process.* Portland, OR: National
Wraparound Initiative, Research & Training Center on Family Support &
Childrenís Mental Health. Portland State University.
Carroll, R.M. (1998). *A cognitive-behavioral approach: Treating cocaine addiction.*
Rockville, MD: U.S. Department of Health and Human Services, Public
Health Services, National Institutes of Health.
Centers for Disease Control and Prevention. (2008). Youth risk behavior surveil-
lance—United States, 2007. *Surveillance Summaries, MMWR, 57*(SS-5).
Chung, T. (2008). Adolescent substance use, abuse, and dependence: Preva-
lence, course, and outcomes. In Y. Kaminer & O.G. Bukstein (Eds.), *Adolescent
substance use, abuse, and dependence: Psychiatric comorbidity and high-risk behaviors* (pp. 29–52). New York: Routledge, Taylor, & Francis.

Clark, H.B. (2004). *TIP system development and operations manual* (rev.). Tampa, FL: Louis de la Parte Florida Mental Health Institute, University of South Florida.

Clark, H.B., Deschênes, N., Sieler, D., Green, M., White, G., & Sondheimer, D. (2008). Services for youth in transition to adulthood in systems of care. In B.A. Stroul & G.M. Blau (Eds.), *The system of care handbook: Transforming mental health services for children, youth, and families.* Baltimore: Paul H. Brookes Publishing Co.

Clark, H., & Foster-Johnson, L. (1996). Serving youth in transition into adulthood. In B.A. Stroul (Ed), *Children's mental health: Creating systems of care in a changing society* (pp. 533–551). Baltimore: Paul H. Brookes Publishing Co.

Clark, H.B., Pschorr, O., Wells, P., Curtis, M., & Tighe, T. (2004). Transition into community roles for TAY w/MHP with emotional/behavioral difficulties: Collaborative systems and program outcomes. In D. Cheney, (Ed.), *Transition issues and strategies for youth and young adults with emotional and/or behavioral difficulties to facilitate movement in to community life* (pp. 201–226). Arlington, VA: The Council for Children with Behavioral Disorders and the Council for Exceptional Children Division of Career Development and Transition.

Clark, H.B., Unger, K.V., & Stewart, E.S. (1993). Transition of youth and young adults with emotional/behavioral disorders into employment, education, and independent living. *Community Alternatives: The International Journal of Family Care, 5,* 19–46.

Copeland, M.E. (1997). *Wellness Recovery Action Plan (WRAP).* West Dummerston, VT: Peach Press.

Epstein, M.H., Rudolph, S., & Epstein, A.A. (2000). Using strength-based assessment in transition planning. *Teaching Exceptional Children, 32,* 50–54.

Fergus, S., & Zimmerman, M. (2005). Adolescent resilience: A framework for understanding healthy development in the face of risk. *Annual Review of Public Health, 26,* 399–419.

Foshee, V.A., Ennett, S.T., Bauman, K.E., Granger, D.A., Benefield, T., Suchindran, C., et al. (2007). A test of biosocial models of adolescent cigarette and alcohol involvement. *Journal of Early Adolescence, 27,* 4–39.

Godley, S.H., Meyers, R.J., Smith, J.E., Karvinen, T., Titus, J.C., Godley, M.D., et al. (2001). *The adolescent community reinforcement approach for adolescent cannabis users, Cannabis Youth Treatment (CYT) series, Volume 4* (DHHS Pub. No. 01-3489). Rockville, MD: Center for Substance Abuse Treatment, Substance Abuse and Mental Health Services Administration.

Gorski, T.T., & Miller, M. (1986). *Staying sober: A guide for relapse prevention.* Sydgaarden, Denmark: Herald House and Independence Press.

Greenbaum, P.E., Dedrick, R.F., Friedman, R., Kutash, K., Brown, E., Lardieri, S., et al. (1996). National adolescent and child treatment study (NACTS): Outcomes for individuals with serious emotional and behavioral disturbance. *Journal of Emotional and Behavioral Disorders, 4,* 130–146.

Greenwald, H.P., Pearson, D., Beery, W.L., & Cheadle, A. (2006). Youth development, community engagement, and risk behavior. *Journal of Primary Prevention, 27,* 3–25.

Guo, J., Hawkins, J., Hill, K.G., & Abbott, R.D. (2001). Childhood and adolescent predictors of alcohol abuse and dependence in young adulthood. *Journal of Studies on Alcohol, 62,* 754–762.

Haber, M.G., Deschênes, N., & Clark, H.B. (2008). *Risk behavior in the transition to adulthood: A common issue.* Tampa, FL: Louis de la Parte Florida Mental Health Institute.

Haber, M.G. (2008). *Prevention Planning: A Feasibility Evaluation.* Final report to the Massachusetts Department of Mental Health. Tampa, FL: Louis de la Parte Florida Mental Health Institute, University of South Florida.

Hagner, D., Cheney, D., & Malloy, J. (1999). Career-related outcomes of a model transition demonstration for young adults with emotional disturbance. *Rehabilitation Counseling Bulletin, 42,* 228–242.

Hawkins, J.D., Catalano, R.F., & Miller, J.Y. (1992). Risk and protective factors for alcohol and other drug problems in adolescence and early adulthood: Implications for substance abuse prevention. *Psychological Bulletin, 112,* 64–105.

Hussong, A.M., & Chassin, L. (2004). Stress and coping among children of alcoholic parents through the young adult transition. *Development and Psychopathology, 16,* 985–1006.

Jessor, R. (1998). *New perspectives on adolescent risk behavior.* New York: Cambridge University Press.

Kandel, D.B., Simcha-Fagan, O., & Davis, M. (1986). Risk factors for delinquency and illicit use from adolescence to young adulthood. *Journal of Drug Issues, 16,* 67–90.

Leventhal, T., & Brooks-Gunn, J. (2000). The neighborhoods they live in: The effects of neighborhood residence on child and adolescent outcomes. *Psychological Bulletin, 126,* 309–337.

Lipsey, M.W., & Derzon, J.H. (1998). Predictors of violent or serious delinquency in adolescence and early adulthood: A synthesis of longitudinal research. In R. Loeber & D.P. Farrington (Eds.), *Risk factors and successful interventions* (pp. 86–105). Thousand Oaks, CA: Sage Publications.

Masten, A., Roisman, G.I., Long, J.D., Burt, K.B., Obradovic, J., Riley, J.R., et al. (2005). Developmental cascades: Linking academic achievement, externalizing and internalizing symptoms over 20 years. *Developmental Psychology, 41,* 733–746.

Moffitt, T.E. (1993). Adolescence-limited versus life-course persistent antisocial behavior: A developmental taxonomy. *Psychological Review, 100,* 674–701.

Mounts, N.S., & Steinberg, L. (1995). An ecological analysis of peer influence on adolescent grade point average and drug use. *Developmental Psychology, 31,* 915–922.

Muow, T. (2005). Sequences of early transitions: A look at variability and consequences. In R.A. Setterstein, F.F. Furstenberg, & R. Rumbaut (Eds.), *On the frontier of adulthood: Theory, research, and public policy.* IL: The University of Chicago Press.

National Head Injury Foundation, Professional Council, Substance Abuse Task Force (1998). *Substance abuse task force white paper.* Washington, DC: Author.

Osgood, D.W., Johnston, L.D., O'Malley, P.M., & Bachman, J.G. (1988). The generality of deviance in late adolescence and early adulthood. *American Sociological Review, 53*, 81–93.

Ostaszewski, K., & Zimmerman, M.A. (2006). The effects of cumulative risks and promotive factors on urban adolescent alcohol and other drug use: A longitudinal study of resiliency. *American Journal of Community Psychology, 38*, 237–249.

Pinquart, M., Silbereisen, R.K., & Wiesner, M. (2004). Changes in discrepancies between desired and present states of developmental tasks in adolescence: A 4-process model. *Journal of Youth and Adolescence, 33*, 467–477.

Riley, A.W., Ensminger, M.E., Green, B., & Kang, M. (1998). Social role functioning by adolescents with psychiatric disorders. *Journal of the American Academy of Child and Adolescent Psychiatry, 37*, 620–628.

Rotheram-Borus, M.J., Piacentini, J., Van Rossem, R., Graae, F., & Cantwell, et al. (1996). Enhancing treatment adherence with a specialized emergency room program for adolescent suicide attempters. *Journal of the American Academy of Child and Adolescent Psychiatry, 35*, 654–663.

Rutter, M., Kim-Cohen, J., & Maughan, B. (2006). Continuities and discontinuities in psychopathology between childhood and adult life. *Journal of Child Psychology and Psychiatry, 47*, 276–295.

Sabournie, E.J., Cullinan, D., & Epstein, M.H. (1993). Patterns and correlates of learning, behavior, and emotional problems of adolescents with and without serious emotional disturbance. *Journal of Child and Family Studies, 2*, 159–175.

Sampl, S., & Kadden, R. (2001). *Motivational enhancement therapy and cognitive behavioral therapy for adolescent cannabis users: 5 sessions, Cannabis Youth Treatment Series, Volume 1.* (DHHS Pub. No. 01-3489). Rockville, MD: Center for Substance Abuse Treatment, Substance Abuse and Mental Health Services Administration.

Sandler, I. (2001). Quality and ecology of adversity as common mechanisms of risk and resilience. *American Journal of Community Psychology, 29*, 19–61.

Siegel, A.W., & Scovill, L.C. (2000). Problem behavior: The double symptom of adolescence. *Development and Psychopathology, 12*, 763–793.

Steinberg, L. (2007). Risk taking in adolescence: New perspectives from brain and behavioral science. *Current Directions in Psychological Science, 16*, 55–59.

Stice, E., & Barrera, M., Jr. (1995). A longitudinal examination of the reciprocal relations between perceived parenting and adolescents' substance use and externalizing behaviors. *Developmental Psychology, 31*, 322–334.

Stockwell, T., Gruenewald, P.J., Toumbourou, J.W., & Loxley, W. (2005). Recommendations for new directions in the prevention of risk substance use and related harms. In T. Stockwell, P.J. Gruenewald, J.W. Toumbourou, & W. Loxley (Eds.), *Preventing harmful substance use: The evidence base for policy and practice* (pp. 443–464). New York: Wiley.

Thompson, S.J., Pomeroy, E.C., & Gober, K. (2005). Family-based treatment models targeting substance use and high risk behaviors among adolescents: A review. In C. Hilarski (Ed.), *Addiction, assessment, and treatment with adolescents, adults, and families* (pp. 207–233). Binghamton, New York: Haworth Social Work Practice Press.

Trout, A.L., Nordness, P.D., Pierce, C.D., & Epstein, M.H. (2003). Research on the academic status of children with emotional and behavioral disorders: A review of the literature from 1961 to 2000. *Journal of Emotional and Behavioral Disorders, 11,* 198–210.

Unger, K.V. (1998). *Handbook on supported education: Providing services for students with psychiatric disabilities.* Baltimore: Paul H. Brookes Publishing Co.

Vance, J., Bowen, N.K., Fernandez, G., & Thompson, S. (2002). Risk and protective factors as predictors of outcome in adolescents with psychiatric disorder and aggression. *Journal of the American Academy of Child and Adolescent Psychiatry, 41,* 36–43.

Wagner, M., Kutash, K., Duchnowski, A.J., Epstein, M.H., & Sumi, W. (2005). The children and youth we serve: A national picture of the characteristics of students with emotional disturbances receiving special education. *Journal of Emotional and Behavioral Disorders, 13,* 79–96.

Wagner, R., Blasé, K., & Clark, H.B. (2005). *Problem-solving/decision-making processes for working with transition-aged youth and young adults: The SODAS framework.* Tampa, FL: Louis de la Parte Florida Mental Health Institute.

Webb, K., Repetto, J., Beutel, A., Perkins, D., Bailey, M., & Schwartz, S.E. (1999). *Dare to Dream: A guide to planning your future.* Gainesville, FL: The Transition Center, University of Florida.

West, T.E., Fetzer, P.M., Graham, C.M., & Keller, J. (2000). Driving the system through young adult involvement and leadership. In H.B. Clark & M. Davis (Eds.), *Transition to adulthood: A resource for assisting young people with emotional and behavioral difficulties* (pp. 195–208). Baltimore: Paul H. Brookes Publishing Co.

Policy, Funding, and Sustainability

Issues and Recommendations for Promoting Effective Transition Systems

Cheri Hoffman, Craig Anne Heflinger,
Michele Athay, and Maryann Davis

> "If people can't understand how critical it is to constantly evaluate and
> improve the various systems and programs that have been established to
> help transition-age youth with emotional and behavioral disorders, they
> should try having their lives and futures literally depend on them, the way
> mine did. I remember the day I realized I had disappeared in the system.
> After yet another transfer to a different facility, I overheard staff discussing
> my case and treatment goals. No one could remember my name. Instead,
> they referred to me as "feeding tube girl." These professionals were in
> charge of my care—they were the ones making significant decisions for me,
> decisions that drastically changed my life. But they couldn't even remember
> my name. I can't even begin to explain how lost and helpless I felt. Where
> did I exist in all of this? Not only did I not have a voice in the process,
> I didn't even have a name."
>
> —Michele Athay, young adult coauthor

Numerous public systems serve the transition-age youth who are the
focus of this book—child mental health, child welfare, education (particularly special education), juvenile justice, and others that may touch
the lives of these youth as they approach adulthood. Vocational rehabilitation, adult mental health, corrections, employment services, substance abuse, housing, state higher education, and others may influence

Funded by NIMH Training Grant for Children's Mental Health Services Research
(T32MH019544-12).

these young adults as they enter adulthood. Each of these systems has its own set of policies and funding mechanisms that affect the services they are able to provide to help prepare youth for impending young adulthood roles. Often, these youth and young adults cross these systems (i.e., a young person with EBD in foster care might receive special education services at school, or voluntarily continue in foster care services as they enter community college). As described in Chapter 1, navigating just one of these various systems with one of its particularities and barriers can be confusing, even daunting at times, much less navigating multiple systems at the same time.

This chapter briefly reviews existing policies that affect transition-age youth and young adults and their families, examines the strengths of existing policies, and makes suggestions for ways to bolster them to facilitate smoother, stronger transitions. The chapter reports on funding and sustainability issues for transition service systems, and finally makes recommendations at the funding and policy level designed to set the occasion for the implementation of effective transition systems for these vulnerable youth and young adults and their families.

MODEL POLICY

The systems with which transition-age youth are most likely to interact are governed by distinct policies that shape what services are available, the manner in which they are provided, and who can gain access to them. In this section we address the policies that affect the primary systems experienced by transition-age youth and young adults. Davis and Koyanogi (2005), after a thorough review of the research and academic literature on the characteristics of the transition-age population with EBD and transition support service models, formulated some basic policy tenets that support the types of services that are needed. Chapter 1 touched on these tenets as related to current gaps in transition services. These tenets are described here more fully, with implications for needed policy reform.

Policy Tenet 1: Provide Continuity of Care from Ages 14 or 16 to Ages 25 or 30

Policies need to support continuation of beneficial services during the transition years, regardless of a young person's chronological age. Age continuity means that a young person's change in age doesn't *mandate* the ending or beginning of a service. *Service ending* includes terminating a given service or maintaining the same kind of service but having to switch providers or settings (e.g., switching from an adolescent to an adult day treatment program). Policies should allow choices about ending services to be based on therapeutic progress or other important treatment considerations, not age.

Policy Tenet 2: Provide Continuous and Coordinated Care Across the Many Systems that Offer Relevant Services

System of care values (Stroul & Friedman, 1986) call for the continuity and coordination of services within and across children's systems. For transition-age youth, this needs to be extended to adult systems, as well. *Coordination* should ensure that there are no redundancies or conflicts in service approaches or foci. Continuity of care in this case refers to bridging any gaps between needed services so that transition-age youth access all needed care. *Continuity* also refers to consistency in service approach; treatment and/or service cultures should be consistent and not in conflict with one another.

Policy Tenet 3: Provide Developmentally Appropriate and Appealing Services

An understanding of what is developmentally appropriate during the transition years has been bolstered by much of the research since the mid-1990s. There is increased awareness of the developmental stage of the transition into adulthood (Settersten, Furstenberg & Rumbaut, 2005), also called *emerging adulthood* (Arnett, 2000), for the general population. Transitioning into adulthood is more prolonged for individuals than in the past, now lasting well into the late 20s. It is a unique period of life that is neither adolescence nor mature adulthood, and services need to reflect this. Recent changes in our society and their impact on the transition to adulthood are well described for the general and other vulnerable populations (Osgood, Foster, Flanagan, & Ruth, 2005; Settersten et al., 2005). Our society has changed in important ways since the Voting Rights Act of 1970 reduced the age of majority to 18. Many policies are based on a legal definition of adulthood starting at age 18 or 21. However, major economic changes make it difficult for young people to function as adults at these ages, particularly within vulnerable populations. Our economy has shifted from a predominantly manufacturing economy to a service and information economy, which requires higher levels of education. There are also proportionately fewer minimum wage jobs, and the minimum wage is worth far less than in the past. Thus, higher levels of education are generally needed to obtain better paying jobs, there are fewer jobs for those with lower education levels, and many of those jobs pay relatively less than they have in the past (dramatically so when adjusted for inflation). In addition, the economy and rising food and fuel costs are affecting even established households let alone those of people just entering the work force. Housing prices have increased well beyond inflation in most areas of the country (see Settersten et al., 2005). Other societal factors, such as the women's rights movement and the development of the birth control pill, have particularly influenced women's transitions into adulthood by providing options for delaying marriage and first childbirth and increasing the time for education and preliminary work experiences (Goldscheider & Waite, 1993).

As a result, there is a prolonged period *after* adolescence before young people complete their education, live financially independently, and start their own families (traditional benchmarks of adulthood). Many young people with EBD are delayed in their psychosocial development relative to peers (reviewed in Davis & Vander Stoep, 1997). Thus, it is important that transition support services address the unique developmental needs of this age group and tailor services to them. Many such developmental considerations are described in the TIP system guidelines in Chapter 2.

Transition support services and developmentally appropriate clinical services are needed in both child- and adult-serving systems because the transition ages (minimally, ages 16–25) span these systems' age boundaries. As described in Chapter 1, those systems are designed for individuals who are younger and older (respectively) than transition-age individuals. Thus, child-serving systems need to prepare youth for the changes that will occur when they enter adulthood and adult-serving systems, and adult-serving systems must tailor their services to the unique needs of *young* adults (e.g., continuing their preparation for mature adulthood, providing services that appeal to this age group). Youth have indicated that discomfort from being lumped together with individuals much older than them in adult mental health services was one of the main reasons they did not pursue those services (Delman & Jones, 2002). This also applies to the corrections system. Adult prisons have been shown to be both unsafe (Campaign for Youth Justice [CYJ], 2007) and ineffective in reducing recidivism for juveniles (Centers for Disease Control [CDC], 2007).

Hand in hand with developmentally appropriate services is the need for *appealing* services. Services can be developmentally appropriate but still unappealing to emerging adults due to cultural or other considerations. Once an individual can legally decline services, it is important to offer appealing services that engage young people's motivation. There is no better way to develop appealing services than to have young people help develop the service and supports—they know best what they need and what will be attractive to their peers.

Policy Tenet 4: Promote a Density of Good Services from Which Individualized Service and Treatment Plans Can Be Constructed

Although natural supports should always be emphasized and given priority, the absence of numerous quality transition support programs can force young people to use suboptimal programs or reject services altogether. In particular, individualizing services requires choice, which requires offering options. Individualized treatments and services are embraced within evidence-based practice (e.g., Multisystemic Therapy; Henggeler et al., 1992), system of care (Stroul & Friedman, 1986), and the TIP system (Clark, Deschênes, & Jones, 2000; Clark & Foster-Johnson, 1996) values.

Policy Tenet 5: Promote Appropriate Involvement of Family

The studies of the changing transition to adulthood within our society (summarized previously) describe an increasingly important family role beyond adolescence to help establish youth in economically stable positions. Families can also provide emotional support to individuals as they struggle to make changes in their lives throughout the transition period. It is clear, however, that the parental role moves from a central position in early adolescence to a more peripheral role as youth mature and develop their own social networks and significant or marital relationships. Policies should provide the freedom for practitioners, young people, and family members to make this decision to best suit their circumstances.

Policy Tenet 6: Promote the Development of Expertise in Professionals Who Work with this Population

Policies need to promote the establishment of evidence-based and evidence-informed practices with this age group. Knowledge about young adults with EBD and how to work effectively with them is still in its infancy. Professionals in the field need to be appropriately trained and able to exchange knowledge with other practitioners working with these youth.

BUILDING ON EXISTING POLICY

The Mental Health System

> I'm not sure what magical thing was supposed to happen at midnight when I turned 18, but I think I must have missed it. I woke up that day with the same needs, fears, problems, and circumstances as I had the day before, but now I was seen as an "adult" and had to figure out a whole new system and navigate a different set of services. I think I cried out of frustration more that year than any other year of my life.

As described in Chapter 1, the mental health system is divided into two systems, child and adult, which are largely guided by state and local policy about which services will be offered, the framework of those services, and who these systems serve. These services are also influenced by federal policies shaping access to additional funds to support those services, including federal block grants, a variety of system improvement grants, and use of Medicaid funding.

Also described in Chapter 1, population policies (those that define either eligibility criteria to access services or the target population for which services are designed) are discrepant between child and adult mental health systems across the country, including the federal government's policies regarding federal block grant funds (Davis & Koroloff, 2006). The first step in building on existing mental health policy is to form a bridge in population policies so that any transition-age individual with EBD can access services provided by state mental health authorities. There are two basic approaches possible for this remedy: 1) extend the broader child system definition further into adulthood (a "grandfathering" approach), or 2) align child and adult policies so that they encompass the same population, thus ensuring a seamless transition into adult services. Several states employ the former approach. Massa-

> "I remember walking out of the treatment facility holding a piece of paper with discharge instructions in one hand and a little paper bag with three-days-worth of medication in the other. 'Three days, I have three days,' I kept thinking. And then I remember saying out loud, 'You've got to be kidding me!' as I walked out the door."

chusetts grandfathers the eligibility of all youths in residential treatment for entry into the adult system so that they do not need to apply
for eligibility for the adult mental health system. Oklahoma more
broadly defines eligibility as continuing until services are no longer
needed, such that if a minor is found eligible that eligibility can extend
as far into adulthood as their need for services (Davis & Koroloff, 2006).

A model for aligning child and adult population policies was described in detail by Davis and Koroloff (2006). This model was based on
the Federal Center for Mental Health Services' definitions of serious
emotional disturbance (SED) and serious mental illness (SMI). Generally, the two policies were in alignment regarding qualifying diagnoses
and only discrepant in their definition of functional impairment. By
adding consideration of development in the SMI definition of functional impairment, the two definitions could be considered aligned.
Thus, Davis and Koroloff offered the following as wording for both the
SED and SMI definition:

> Functional impairment is defined as difficulties that substantially in-
> terfere with or limit an individual from achieving or maintaining one
> or more developmentally appropriate social, behavioral, cognitive,
> communicative, or adaptive skills, or functioning in social, family, and
> vocational/educational contexts. Adaptive skills include self-care,
> home living, community use, self-direction, health and safety, func-
> tional academics, and work. (2006, p. 64)

The type and density of transition support services should also be
a focus of policy. Many states have policies embracing Stroul and Friedman's (1986) principles of a system of care for children with SED (Davis,
Yelton, Katz-Leavy, & Lourie, 1995). These types of policies provide at
least broad guidelines for specifying the nature of services. Similar policies could define the need for and nature of services during the transition years. Although assessment of state policies regarding transition-
age youth are somewhat dated (Davis & Hunt, 2005), as of 2005, no state
had embraced a broad guideline such as the TIP system (Clark et al.,
2000, Chapter 2) in state policy. However, taking the example set by
policies that embrace the Stroul and Friedman principles, states could
easily provide similar language, using Clark's system, for transition-
age youth and young adults. There is much overlap in the two sets of
principles, and the language could be streamlined to include additional
or replacement guidelines for the transition-age population. For example, whereas Stroul and Friedman articulate the need for partnering
with families, transition-age youth guidelines would overlay partnering with families in a developmentally appropriate manner that increasingly puts the young person at the helm of setting goals, aspira-

tions, and actions for their services and supports. In addition, the Stroul and Friedman guidelines call for smooth transitions to adult systems. While assessment of states that embraced these principles have not been updated recently, as of 1994 a significant proportion of the states that had written these principles into policy included this element (Davis et al., 1995). The transition agenda could be advanced greatly by federal and state policies that embrace this element of the system-of-care values, adopt the TIP model guidelines, and expand the definition of *transition* so that it refers to *transition to adulthood* rather than transition into the adult mental health system.

Connecticut currently has some of the most explicit language surrounding the provision of continuing services for transition-age youth. They have a consolidated child agency that includes mental health, child welfare, and juvenile justice. The policy defines how youth from the child agency will be transitioned to the adult system and how services will be paid for, as well as having established young adult programs within adult mental health (see Davis & Hunt, 2005).

At the federal level, some steps have been taken. In 2005, transition to adulthood was included as a priority in SAMHSA's *Transforming Mental Health Care in America: Federal Action Agenda* (2005). Action steps from this document include "Promote the transition of youth with serious emotional disturbances from school to post-secondary opportunities and/or employment" (p. 42) and "Assist youth with serious emotional disturbances who are involved with the juvenile justice system to transition into employment" (p. 43).

The United States General Accounting Office of the federal government recently released a report (USGAO, 2008) on the transition challenges faced by young adults with serious mental illness in response to a request by Representative Pete Stark (D-CA) and former Senator Gordon Smith (R-OR). Although some aspects of the report are disappointing to advocates for transition-age youth, including the report's failure to address the issue discussed previously of differing definitions between SED and SMI and underestimating the number of young adults with serious mental illness, it represents a significant step forward in prioritizing the needs of this population at a federal level. In fact, following the release of the USGAO report, Representative Stark, Senator Smith, and Senator Chris Dodd (D-CT), introduced the Healthy Transition Act of 2008 (H.R. 6375 and S. 3195) to help youth with serious mental illness receive needed services and successfully transition to adulthood. This legislation would provide planning and implementation grants to states to develop statewide coordination plans. States would be urged to target specific populations, including but not limited to those involved with the child protection and juvenile justice systems.

The legislation would establish a federal committee to coordinate service programs helping young adults with mental illness, and provide technical assistance to states.

This increased awareness of the issues of transition-age youth on a federal level is promising, and the legislative push toward systems coordination is key. Taken together with promising state practices, it is apparent that there are numerous building blocks from within and outside mental health agencies from which stronger transition support policies can be built.

The Child Welfare System

Although state child welfare policies have not been examined for their relevance to the transition needs of their sizeable population with EBD, federal policies have taken a strong stance around transition-to-independence needs for the foster care population in general. The child welfare system has provided independent living services to youth aging out of the system since 1985. The original policy was reorganized and expanded under the Foster Care Independence Act of 1999 (FCIA, PL 106-169), which established the John H. Chafee Foster Care Independent Living Program. FCIA doubled the funding for independent living services to $140 million and offers services to youth still in foster care or who have aged out of foster care up to the age of 21 regardless of their Title IV-E status. "Chafee dollars," as they are known, can be directed at the discretion of the states, with up to 30% of program funds eligible to be spent on room and board. The monies can also be used to support educational opportunities, vocational training, counseling, support services, life skills training, family planning, parenting classes, and youth advisory boards (Foster & Gifford, 2005). The legislation also gives states the option to extend Medicaid eligibility for former foster youth up to age 21, although only 13 states had taken advantage of that option as of 2007 (Oldmixon, 2007). Although the list of services allowable under Chafee dollars is extensive and can be helpful to youth as they age out of child welfare, limitations on the amount of available federal funding means that states have had difficulty providing a comprehensive array of services and has led to a "chaotic blend of programming with little theory base or evaluation" across the states (Collins, 2004, p. 1056).

The Promoting Safe and Stable Families Act of 2001 (PL 107-133) amended FCIA and authorized the Educational and Training Voucher (ETV) program for foster youth. This helps states pay for postsecondary education and training and related costs for youth who were eligible under the Chafee program, up to $5,000 a year. Students who have participated in the ETV program prior to turning 21 are eligible to receive support up to their 23rd birthday (Oldmixon, 2007).

Many states also have policies in place to assist foster youth with the transition to adulthood. For example, in 2005, California enacted a law that allows foster youth to remain in their existing placement after their 18th birthday if they are pursuing the completion of their high school degree (National Center for Youth Law [NCYL], 2007). This law minimizes school disruption as a result of placement changes and allows foster youth the freedom to complete their high school education. It also provides for assistance in gaining access to federal disability benefits, such as Social Security Income (SSI), for which a number of foster youth with physical or mental disabilities are eligible but do not receive, either because they are not aware of their eligibility or the application process is too daunting. This California law established a work group to consider the issues of how best to ensure that those young people eligible for the SSI funds receive them, how to inform young people of the availability of the funds, and how to oversee the management of the federal funds by the counties responsible for administering them. The goal is to see that each emancipating foster youth has at least $2,000 to help make the transition to independent living (NCYL, 2007).

A number of states have also enacted policies to assist with higher education for former foster youth. Tuition waivers allow emancipated youth to attend state institutions of higher learning without paying the cost of tuition, and in some cases, room and board. The National Child Welfare Resources Center for Youth Development (NCWRCYD; 2007) reported that 17 states currently offer this option in some form, with varying requirements and statutes regarding what costs are covered.

Federal policies could be strengthened for the transitioning population with EBD by offering states incentives to embrace the policy in general (since a minority of states do so), and specifically to embrace the extension of Medicaid benefits to age 21, which can pay

"Despite all the doctors, counselors, case managers and social workers I was working with, the person who informed me about the possibility of being qualified for SSI was a roommate in a residential treatment facility who also received these benefits. I am not sure where I would be had I not pursued and been granted that assistance. Of course it was not an easy road to navigate. I consider myself very intellectually capable (I am currently pursuing my doctoral degree) but I had great difficulty with all of the paperwork, red tape, and complicated explanation of benefits. I still wonder how people wade through that system and if more could be done to ensure that those who qualify receive it and that they are able to fully utilize it."

for many mental health services. Furthermore, youth with EBD are particularly prone to dropping out of school. Currently, in order to take advantage of the voluntary foster care independent living services after age 18, a youth must be enrolled in school. Thus, these policies would be more beneficial to foster youth with EBD if the requirement to be a student were removed from voluntary independent living supports. While incentives to remain in school are important, punishing those who drop out only punishes those who are more vulnerable during the transition years.

Landmark legislation addressing a number of issues within the child welfare system was signed into law on October 7, 2008. The Fostering Connections Act (PL 110-351) provides a number of significant benefits to children in foster care, but specific to transition-age youth it allows states to extend foster care up to the age of 21 and extends adoption assistance and/or guardianship payments on behalf of youth up to the age of 21. These benefits are available as long as youth are in school or employed. The legislation also requires child welfare agencies to help youth develop detailed and specific transition plans prior to exiting from care (Child Welfare League of America [CWLA], 2008). It is hoped that this legislation sets a precedent for implementing the recommendations in this chapter specific to youth with EBD.

The Special Education System and Postsecondary Education

The primary policy governing special education and mandating transition services for students is the Individuals with Disabilities Education Act (IDEA; 1990; PL 101-476) (USDOE, 2007). This originated in 1975 with the Education for All Handicapped Children Act (PL 94-142), which was the first legislation to guarantee access to education in the least restrictive environment for all children with disabilities. This legislation became known as IDEA in 1990, and revisions in 1997 (PL 105-17) required that the individualized educational program (IEP) include transition planning to prepare youth for further vocational/technical training, postsecondary education, and employment (Levine & Wagner, 2005).

Recent changes took effect in 2005 as a result of a reauthorization of IDEA (2004; PL 108-446). Many of these changes came about to bring the policy in line with the No Child Left Behind Act (2001; PL 107-110) (USDOE, 2007), which is the second major current policy affecting transition-age youth. According to the current legislation, transition services are defined as a coordinated set of activities for a child with a disability that

- Is designed to be within a results-oriented process, that is, focused on improving the academic and functional achievement of the child with a disability to facilitate the child's movement from school to post-school activities, including postsecondary education, vocational education, integrated employment (including supported employment), continuing and adult education, adult services, independent living, or community participation

- Is based on the individual child's needs, taking into account the child's strengths, preferences, and interests

- Includes instruction, related services, community experiences, the development of employment and other post-school adult living objectives, and, if appropriate, acquisition of daily living skills and functional vocational evaluation. (USDOE, 2007, p. 1)

IDEA mandates that IEPs contain "appropriate measurable postsecondary goals based upon age-appropriate transition assessments related to training, education, employment and, where appropriate, independent living skills; and the transition services (including courses of study) needed to assist the child in reaching those goals" (USDOE, 2007, p. 2). The young person must be invited to the IEP meetings where these transition-related goals are discussed, as should any agencies that might be paying for or providing the transition services (e.g., vocational rehabilitation). Transition planning is to begin no later than the first IEP after the student's 16th birthday, and can begin as early as age 14 with the approval of the IEP team. In fact, some states have maintained their requirements that transition planning begin at age 14 because of the need for additional time to prepare students for independent adulthood. Special education services can continue for young people through the age of 21 in order to support them obtaining a diploma. This is one potential area for cross-systems linkage, as a young person who chooses to remain in custody of the child welfare system beyond the age of 18 can receive special education services to assist him or her in receiving a high school diploma.

Of course, the existence of the policy does not in itself solve the issues of the target population—it has to be implemented and found to be effective. As described in Chapter 1, two studies have examined transition practices and found that their implementation in general is often less than needed (Geneen & Powers, 2006), or specifically unsuited for students with EBD (Wagner & Davis, 2006). Although IDEA is a fairly comprehensive mandate, because it addresses needs of students with any disability it cannot address specific needs for particular disabilities.

Thus, for youth with EBD, this policy would be strengthened by mandating more frequent transition planning meetings and a planning approach centered on the youth (Clark et al., 2000). Building a better federal policy for special education students with EBD could stem from funding from CMHS/SAMHSA that provides states with resources for more frequent transition planning meetings and incentives for embracing person-centered planning or TIP-system planning processes that include the mental health system. Additional state-level multiagency collaboration could include partnerships between vocational rehabilitation and secondary/postsecondary schools as described in Chapter 4. Such a policy should also encourage states to identify fiscal resources that can support a more robust transition planning and provision process, and provide some federal funding that can be used to leverage other funding. Finally, evidence-based supported employment programs in adult mental health all indicate that the best practices need the ability to continue over a long period of time to allow for the fluctuations in success that individuals with serious mental health conditions experience. Given the fluctuations in success that are typical of young employees in general, this is particularly true for the transition-age population. A bridge between the initial transition from school to work to more sustained support of working life should also be built into policies that emanate from IDEA.

Research shows that youth with EBD have the lowest high school completion rate (56%) out of all youth with disabilities and significantly less than peers without any disabilities (National Longitudinal Transition Study-2, 2005). The good news is that many youth (60%) who drop out of high school do eventually pursue completion of their secondary education, either through a diploma program or a GED certificate, and many of those (59%) go on to enroll in some type of postsecondary education option; however, only 10% of all dropouts who complete their high school credentials and subsequently enroll in college are able to earn a degree (Almeida, Johnson & Steinberg, 2006). This speaks to the fact that the challenges these youth face multiply when they attempt to make the shift to postsecondary education. Newman (2005) explained that the differing legal framework governing secondary and postsecondary education can contribute to these challenges: Whereas in high school it was the education system's responsibility to provide all necessary services to the student, in college, that burden shifts to the student him- or herself. Partially due to this factor, only about 21% of youth with EBD are pursuing postsecondary education options, compared with approximately 40% of their peers without disabilities.

Federal policy support for improving the transition to postsecondary education came about in 2008 with the Higher Education Opportunity Act (PL 110-315), which was a long-awaited reauthorization of the Higher Education Act of 1965 (PL 89-329). This act expands student aid and authorizes several pilot programs specifically aimed at overcoming key challenges faced by low-income adults and older youth who are pursuing postsecondary education and training (Duke-Benfield & Strawn, 2008). For example, Student Success Grants offset the costs of colleges providing services that research has shown to be effective in helping at-risk youth (including those with EBD) stay in school, such as intensive advising and counseling, work study, learning communities, tutoring, child care, and transportation assistance. Bridges from Jobs to Careers grants will provide colleges with resources to serve the more than 60% of community college students who need remedial coursework in reading, writing, or math by customizing these basic skills curricula to specific occupational programs, resulting in increased access to and completion of occupational certificates. It is hoped that appropriations for these initiatives are sufficient and that comprehensive evaluations of the pilot programs are done to show what elements are successful in improving the transition to postsecondary education.

The Juvenile and Criminal Justice Systems

Few state policies focus on the transition needs of youth and young adults in juvenile or criminal justice systems, with or without EBD. As described in Chapter 1, the transition to adulthood in this population is most affected by policies that have swung heavily toward punishment and away from rehabilitation, making the transition to adulthood even more difficult by adding the consequences and stigma of incarceration and a record to the conditions that led to the criminal behavior in the first place.

A successful transition from incarceration has several of the same prerequisites for a successful transition to adulthood: literacy, employability, independent living, and maintenance of stable and positive relationships. Policies that would strengthen the likelihood of desistance would also enhance the likelihood of a more successful community adjustment from incarceration and transition into adulthood. Moreover, since most evidence of the efficacy of the more punitive treatment of juveniles indicates a failure of these policies to reduce crime (CDC, 2007), new policies that focus on helping youth to attain the elements for success would benefit society as well as these youth and their families.

The primary piece of legislation that governs the juvenile justice system, the Juvenile Justice and Delinquency Prevention Act of 1974 (JJDPA), was up for Congressional reauthorization in 2008. Late in 2007, the first Senate hearings on juvenile justice issues in 8 years were held on Capitol Hill (testimony available at http://judiciary.senate.gov/hearing.cfm?id=3043). During this hearing, much of the aforementioned information about the ineffectiveness of trying youth as adults was presented to members of the Senate Judiciary Committee, along with examples from successful programs across the country that are reducing the recidivism rate among juvenile offenders (e.g., Small, Reynolds, Conner, & Cooney, 2005). Many of their recommendations focus on systemic integration, particularly for mental health and juvenile justice systems. It is clear that the systems must work together better to protect the vulnerable youth of our nation. Chapter 6 provides an example of a program with cross agency collaboration for young offenders. Policies supporting access to appropriate mental health care for young offenders with EBD during incarceration and ensuring linkage and supports post release would also help this particular population during their transition years. Finally, there are innovative ideas and community-based treatment models that can divert appropriate juveniles from the juvenile justice system to the mental health system for treatment rather than detention (Cocozza & Skowyra, 2000; Cocozza et al., 2005). One such program, the Post-Arrest Diversion (PAD) program for first-time nonviolent juvenile offenders in Miami-Dade County in Florida, is a 60-day diversion program that provides detailed screening and assessment of youthful offenders, as well as services including individualized case planning, case management, substance abuse and/or mental health treatment, and restitution to victims (Cocozza et al., 2005). Research has shown that these types of programs reduce system inefficiencies and prevent further penetration of youth into the justice system, and those programs that provided intensive services and supports within the community setting showed reduced recidivism (Whitehead & Lab, 2001). Policies allowing for treatment of these youth in community without introducing them into the justice system may prevent long-term and costly interventions by the adult corrections system. Senator Patrick Leahy (D-VT) sponsored legislation (S. 3155) that incorporated many of these recommendations. The bill was approved by voice vote in the Senate Judiciary Committee on July 21, 2008, but was not voted on by the full Senate during the 110th Congressional Session, and as of 2009 had not yet been reintroduced.

Bringing It Together

There were several years where most of my energy and the energy of my treatment team was devoted to learning how to navigate through the mental health system. There were new policies to understand, various transfers between institutions to document and keep up with, insurance and SSI benefits to understand and apply for, and different programs that had their own specific requirements and rules that needed to be followed. Although I became much better at this navigation over time, I remember thinking that we were losing sight of the real goal: Not to learn how to exist in these systems, but rather to use them to learn how to live independently outside of the system!

Transition is a challenging time for any young person, with a myriad of issues to face and hurdles to overcome to be independent and successful in adult roles. For young people who face the additional transition between child- and adult-serving systems, too often there is a lack of accountability at the point of transfer between those systems. That is where the proverbial "ball"—in this case, a young person with potential and promise—is "dropped" and neither system takes responsibility for the outcome of the young adult. The result is that young people, who with developmentally appropriate supports could make a successful transition to adulthood, fall through the cracks and are in effect forced to deteriorate to a point where an adult system, whether that be an adult mental health facility, corrections, or other system, steps in to try to repair what could have been prevented. This system disconnect is harmful to young people and stands in opposition to the focused recovery framework for mental health issues that is grounded in the public health approach (Cooper, 2006; Stroul & Blau, 2008). This is one more example of the "significant mismatches that exist between the emerging and varied pathways now taken into adulthood and the institutions, policies and programs that affect young people" (Settersten et al., 2005, p. 536). Young people, parent advocates, program administrators, researchers, and policymakers need to determine ways to establish funding and policies that promote transition practices and systems that will improve the long-term outcomes for youth and young adults across the transition domains of employment and career, educational opportunities, living situation, personal effectiveness and well-being, and community-life functioning (Clark & Foster-Johnson, 1996; see Chapter 2).

FUNDING AND SUSTAINABILITY

A major challenge in providing seamless access to services across the transition to adulthood, as it is with most needed services, is funding to support implementation of effective services and supports. In all likelihood, a comprehensive approach to meeting the mental health needs of youth and young adults in transition will require a creative combination of federal, state, local, and private dollars, as well as the establishment of new links across systems to allow young people and their families to access developmentally appropriate services and supports.

Federal Support

Numerous sources are available for funding programs and services related to transition-age youth and young adults. The Bazelon Center for Mental Health Law (2005) released a report entitled *Moving On,* which analyzed federal programs funding services for transition-age youth. This report listed 57 sources of funding, each with unique purposes, requirements, and restrictions. Some sources are specific to the population of transition-age youth and young adults, and other sources might be used at state or agency discretion to help fund services relevant to transition-age youth and young adults. The programs described include mental health programs, health services, substance abuse programs, basic supports (i.e., food stamps), educational services, independent living programs, housing supports, vocational training, social services, and prevention programs.

In spite of what would seem to be a wealth of funding options, the actual securing of funding for relevant transition services remains devastatingly difficult for young people, families, and providers alike. The patchwork nature of these programs and their differing rules of eligibility and funding mechanisms make it very confusing to navigate through and across them. Each program also has a different definition of *youth* and might serve an entirely different age range than another that also offers services needed by the same youth. The same applies to income requirements, where a youth whose family income makes him or her eligible for service from one program does not necessarily make him or her eligible for another.

In the long run, there is an extremely limited pot of money that is being distributed among all these programs. Some are just too small with too limited a range to influence a significant number of individuals, whereas others are too specific in their eligibility guidelines to reach the young people in need. The categorical and inflexible funding requirements of these separate funding systems result in *turf struggles* (Davis, 2001). Even if developmentally appropriate services were available, unfortunately, because transition-age young people are considered a 'specialty' population and not a priority, significant new funds would be needed to support delivering services to them. In an economic environment in which new funds are extremely hard to come by, this is not a likely scenario.

For example, the establishment of the Chafee Independent Living Program was a big step forward for transition services to foster care youth aging out of the system. However, the funding level makes it difficult to make a considerable impact on any one youth. Considering the number of youth and young adults eligible in the system for these services at any one time—not counting those who have already aged out—a maximum of about $1,400 would be available to any given eligible youth in a year. The comprehensive array of services allowed in the legislation can hardly be provided on that amount of money. Furthermore, if states spent the maximum-allowed 30% of funds for housing assistance on the 60,000 youth who have aged out and are eligible for assistance with housing, then that would amount to a total of $700 per youth. This is clearly not sufficient to provide adequate housing for more than a brief period of time (Courtney & Heuring, 2005).

Medicaid is the single most important funding stream affecting the lives of transition-age youth and young adults, particularly those interacting with these systems. Medicaid has become the largest health insurance program in the country (Weil, 2003), and it is the primary health insurer and most widespread public system in the U.S. for adolescents' health needs (Schneider, Fennel, & Long, 1998). Nationally, Medicaid covers roughly one out of every four U.S. children (Kaiser Commission on Medicaid and the Uninsured, 2007). Almost all youth in foster care are eligible for Medicaid through the Title IV-E provisions (Kaiser Commission on Medicaid and the Uninsured, 1998). As an example of the primacy of Medicaid coverage for transition-age youth with EBD, in the state of Tennessee in 2003, 42% of all children were covered by Medicaid, and approximately one quarter of 14- to 17-year-old youth were either diagnosed with EBD and in contact with the public mental health system and/or involved with the child welfare agency (Heflinger & Hoffman, 2008).

Youth involved in the public sector have been reliant on Medicaid to a large degree to pay for health and mental health services throughout their childhood, but as they approach the critical transition-to-adulthood time period in most cases they are cut from the Medicaid rolls and left without coverage and with few opportunities to regain it. The federal mandatory Medicaid eligibility coverage goes up to the 19th birthday, with state options to expand coverage to the 21st birthday (Department of Health & Human Services [DHHS], 2005). However, as youth make the transition out of the child welfare system, they lose Title IV-E eligibility, and it is up to state and local processes and personnel to help them shift to another category of eligibility. Likewise, young people who are incarcerated lose Medicaid eligibility, and states may or may not have mechanisms in place to ensure a smooth transition back into this coverage upon discharge from these institutions.

Even if young people retain Medicaid coverage, the benefits package and the criteria for medical necessity are out of alignment with many of the needs of these transition-age youth and young adults. Medicaid is based on a medical model that does not truly recognize the multisystemic factors that influence mental illness, does not emphasize prevention or early intervention, and has not fully caught up with evidence-based practice. Coverage for community-based services through Medicaid is spotty at best, as is coverage of school-based services, although reaching these youth through the schools would be the single best point of access for necessary services, including prevention and early intervention activities that could result in more youth with mental health issues being identified and appropriately treated (Cooper, 2006).

Unique Approaches

The Jim Casey Youth Opportunity Initiative (JCYOI) developed a program for former foster youth known as the Opportunity Passport, designed to assist youth leaving care with organizing resources. A primary component of this program is an Individual Development Account (IDA), which is a matched savings account that can be used for specific approved purchases of assets such as education expenses, transportation needs, and housing payments (JCYOI, 2008). This innovative program is an example of partnering private funds with personal responsibility by youth and young adults in order to simultaneously teach sustainable economic skills and provide necessary financial assistance (Clark & Crosland, 2008).

The New York State Office of Temporary Disability Assistance (OTDA) announced new funding in March of 2007 for the Supported Housing for Young Adults program. Families and young adults eligible for Temporary Assistance for Needy Families (TANF), including youth aging out of foster care and other young adults who might otherwise find themselves homeless, can receive services such as employability enhancement and employment retention, pregnancy prevention, parenting skills, self-sufficiency enhancement, and service coordination. The original $2.5 million appropriation for this program support was increased to $5 million (OTDA, 2007). A forthcoming study for the National Center for Children in Poverty found that states such as New York, California, Oregon, Arizona, and Washington are investing state resources heavily in promoting and in some cases mandating the use of evidence-based practices for services to transition-age youth (Cooper,

2007). The same study reported that a number of states are finding ways to invest state funds in agencies that utilize youth and family members in service provision roles.

Sustainability

Federal and state funding sources are significant but not sufficient sources of funding for programs aimed at transition-age youth and young adults. They are subject to budget cuts and changes in political will. For example, although Medicaid is the largest health insurance program in the country, there is also a large group of U.S. children who lack any type of medical insurance to pay for needed health and behavioral health care. An estimated 9.4 million U.S. children were uninsured in 2006 (Kaiser Commission, 2007). Of these cases some are eligible for Medicaid but have not enrolled (Dubay, Holahan, & Cook, 2007); however, most are children of working families who do not meet the requirements for Medicaid. The revamped Children's Health Insurance Program (CHIP), which was signed into law in February 2009, is designed to include some of these youth. However, recent tenuous debate over CHIP funding (e.g., Wayne, 2007), including a presidential veto of reauthorization legislation in 2007, has highlighted the uncertainty of this and other federal resources.

Building sustainable programs without over-reliance on federal sources of funding takes creative energy. One example of harnessing that kind of energy is The Finance Project (http://www.financeproject .org), a specialized nonprofit firm dedicated to helping finance and sustain initiatives that positively affect children, their families, and their communities. They have recently launched a Youth Transitions Resource Center providing links to sources of private funding and other resources that can build a network of supports and services for youth who transition out of foster care.

Two recent sources provide very encouraging guidance regarding the sustainability of transition programs. A report titled *Pioneering Transition Programs* presented a study of some of the factors that may have contributed to the development and sustainability of tenured transition programs (Davis, 2008). A second source is a chapter that described the five community sites that participated in the Partnerships for Youth Transition initiative (Clark et al., 2008). This chapter illustrates strategies that were used in the planning, development, and implementation of the community transition systems—and the role of early efforts and planning for sustaining the transition system. Of the five community sites, four continue to operate most, if not all, of their array of services and supports across the transition domains of employment and career, education, living situation, personal effectiveness and well-being, and community-life functioning. The chapter also provided the preliminary findings from a cross-site study that shows improved outcomes for the youth and young adults across transition domains (Clark et al., 2008; see Chapters 2 and 3 in this volume).

RECOMMENDATIONS

A comprehensive approach to policy and funding reform is necessary to enable states and communities to develop and implement transition systems that will improve the real-life outcomes for youth and young adults with EBD. The identification of the young people who need assistance is possible, and the number of them who need assistance in this category is manageable. Laudable efforts have been made in the recent past, but they are piecemeal and insufficient. The broad issues facing these young people will not be overcome with single efforts that place a band-aid on one area without addressing the wider issues they face in transition to adulthood roles in our society. "Policies that promote systemic reform are needed to encourage the multiple agencies that have responsibility for these children and their families to come together with a shared vision that is focused on the students and their families" (Wagner, Kutash, Duchnowski, Epstein, & Sumi, 2005, p. 93).

Recommendations for improving the transition across child- and adult-serving systems include the following:

Redefining Adulthood

Policy makers need to change the way adolescence and the transition to adulthood is viewed. It is clear from research that the life course has been altered in recent decades. Adulthood is no longer achieved at the age of 18 in today's economy, and probably not until at least the age of 25 for the average young person (Settersten et al., 2005). Given this reality, the policies that govern access to mental health care for our most vulnerable populations cannot continue to expect adult behavior at this young age. Policy shifts such as mandating the extension of Medicaid coverage beyond the age of 18 for young people facing transition challenges due to mental health issues or aging out of foster care, and expanding other support services (e.g., education, employment, social support, independent living skills) that improve young adult outcomes, are examples of changes this kind of redefinition might allow.

Coordinating Transition Planning Across Service Systems

Collaborative and coordinated transition planning is necessary to ensure continuity of care from age 14 through age 25. Adult service systems into which these young people will eventually transfer, such as the public mental health system, must be included. Coordination at this level demands a type of flexibility and individualization that has not historically been a part of bureaucratic service systems. However, the population being served has changed dramatically and the systems must keep pace with the change in order to continue being effective at any level.

One example of this kind of coordinated planning is the Transition Service Integration Model (Certo et al., 2003; Luecking & Certo, 2003), which integrates the resources and expertise of public schools, vocational rehabilitation, and the developmental disability systems to serve individuals with developmental disabilities. A partnership between school districts and private nonprofit adult-serving agencies that provide job training and inclusive community activities facilitates a seamless transition to adulthood that results in higher employment outcomes for young adults with mental retardation or autism. This model could be applied to the mental health issue and others specific to transition-age youth. Chapters 4 and 6 also provide models for programs that blend funding across agencies in serving transition-age youth.

Highlighting the Voice of Youth, Young Adults, Parents, and Advocates

Youth input regarding transition services and their experiences in crossing the divide from youth- to adult-serving systems is crucial to developing appealing and accessible services (Clark et al., 2008). Youth advisory boards or youth councils have been developed in many agencies and on state levels that have empowered young people to speak out about the issues affecting them, allowed them the opportunity to share their ideas for change, and resulted in more appropriate service environments for young people. Including parents and advocates "at the table" for policy and programming discussions is an important step to ensuring that young people receive the services they need to make a successful transition to adulthood and that families are guided and supported in this process.

Targeting Supports to the Crucial Time Period of Transition

The current "no-man's land" between reaching the age cutoff for services and becoming a young adult with enough serious problems to warrant intervention by an adult-serving system must be filled with supportive services that target the outcomes young people need to achieve for success. This includes educational programs that focus on helping youth with EBD complete high school, vocational training, and community college programs, job training programs that focus on the social and job skills necessary for success, independent living preparation programs, affordable housing supports to avoid homelessness and the range of additional problems that it creates, and the development of social support networks that can provide lifelong connections for youth (Clark & Crosland, 2008).

The challenges in developing a comprehensive system that assists young people in a successful transition to adulthood are many and real. However, the benefits, not only to these young people and their families but also to society as a whole are equally numerous and important. Young people who have the coordinated supports they need to become healthy, productive adults also have the foundation to build strong families and contribute to their communities in the future.

REFERENCES

Almeida, C., Johnson, C., & Steinberg, A. (2006). *Making good on a promise: What policymakers can do to support the educational persistence of dropouts.* Boston: Jobs for the Future.

Arnett, J.J. (2000). Emerging adulthood. A theory of development from the late teens through the twenties. *American Psychologist, 55*(5), 469–480.

Bazelon Center for Mental Health Law. (2005). *Moving on: Analysis of federal programs funding services to assist transition-age youth with serious mental health conditions.* Washington, DC: Author. Retrieved March 24, 2008, from http://www.bazelon.org/publications/movingon/

Campaign for Youth Justice. (CYJ). (2007). *Jailing juveniles: The dangers of incarcerating youth in adult jails in America.* Washington, DC: Author. Retrieved January 23, 2008, from http://www.campaignforyouthjustice.org/Downloads/NationalReportsArticles/CFYJ-Jailing_Juveniles_Report_2007-11-15.pdf

Centers for Disease Control. (CDC). (2007). *Morbidity and mortality weekly report—Recommendations and reports: Effects on violence of laws and policies facilitating the transfer of youth from the juvenile to the adult justice system.* Atlanta, GA: Author. Retrieved January 23, 2008, from: http://www.cdc.gov/mmwr/pdf/rr/rr5609.pdf

Certo, N.J., Mautz, D., Pumpain, I., Sax, C., Smalley, K., Wade, H.A., et al. (2003). A review and discussion of a model for seamless transition to adulthood. *Education and Training in Developmental Disabilities, 38*(1), 3–17.

Child Welfare League of America. (CWLA). (2008). *Summary of fostering connections to success and increasing adoptions act, H.R. 6893.* Washington, DC: Author. Retrieved October 13, 2008, from http://www.cwla.org/advocacy/adoption hr6893summary.htm.

Clark, H.B., & Crosland, K. (2008). Social and life skills development: Preparing and facilitating youth for transition into young adult roles. In B. Kerman, A.N. Maluccio, & M. Freundlich (Eds.), *Achieving permanence for older children and youth in foster care.* New York: Columbia University Press.

Clark, H., Deschênes, N., & Jones, J. (2000). A framework for the development and operation of a transition system. In H.B. Clark & M. Davis (Eds.), *Transition to adulthood: A resource for assisting young people with emotional or behavioral difficulties* (pp. 29–52). Baltimore: Paul H. Brookes Publishing Co.

Clark, H.B., Deschênes, N., Sieler, D., Green, M.E., White, G., & Sondheimer, D.L. (2008). Services for youth in transition to adulthood in systems of care. In B.A. Stroul & G.M. Blau (Eds.). *The system of care handbook: Transforming mental health services for children, youth, and families* (pp. 517–544). Baltimore: Paul H. Brookes Publishing Co.

Clark, H.B., & Foster-Johnson, L. (1996). Serving youth in transition into adulthood. In B.A. Stroul (Ed.), *Children's mental health: Creating systems of care in a changing society* (pp. 533–552). Baltimore: Paul H. Brookes Publishing Co.

Cocozza, J.J., & Skowyra, K.R. (2000). Youth with mental health disorders: Issues and emerging responses. *Juvenile Justice, 7*(1), 3–13.

Cocozza, J.J., Veysey, B.M., Chapin, D.A., Dembo, R., Walters, W., & Farina, S. (2005). Diversion from the juvenile justice system: The Miami-Dade Juvenile Assessment Center Post Arrest Diversion program. *Substance Use and Misuse, 40*(7), 935–951.

Collins, M.E. (2004). Enhancing services to youths leaving foster care: Analysis of recent legislation and its potential impact. *Children and Youth Services Review, 26*(11), 1051–1065.

Cooper, J. (2007). *Children's mental health: Key challenges, strategies, and effective solutions.* Testimony at Congressional Briefing, October 10, 2007.

Cooper, J. (2006). *Establishing a universal and consistent approach to transition-age youth with mental health problems.* Memo to Jane Knitzer, National Center for Children in Poverty. Received October 25, 2007, from Janice Cooper.

Courtney, M.E., & Heuring, D.H. (2005). The transition to adulthood for youth "aging out" of the foster care system. In D.W. Osgood, E.M. Foster, C. Flanagan, & G.R. Ruth (Eds.), *On your own without a net: The transition to adulthood for vulnerable populations.* Chicago: University of Chicago Press.

Davis, M. (2008). *Pioneering transition programs: The establishment of programs that span the ages served by child and adult mental health.* Rockville, MD: Substance Abuse and Mental Health Services Administration, Center for Mental Health Services.

Davis, M. (2001). *State efforts to expand transition supports for adolescents receiving public mental health services.* Alexandria, VA: National Association of State Mental Health Program Directors.

Davis, M., Yelton, S., Katz-Leavy, J., & Lourie, I. (1995). "Unclaimed children" revisited: The status of state children's mental health service systems. *Journal of Mental Health Administration, 22*, 147–166.

Davis, M., & Hunt, B. (2005). *State adult mental health systems' efforts to address the needs of young adults in transition to adulthood.* Rockville, MD: U.S. Substance

Abuse and Mental Health Services Administration, Center for Mental Health Services.

Davis, M., & Koroloff, N. (2006). The great divide: How public mental health policy fails young adults. In W.H. Fisher (Ed.), *Community based mental health services for children and adolescents* (pp. 53–74) (Vol. 14). Oxford, UK: Elsevier Sciences.

Davis, M., & Koyanagi, C. (2005). *Summary of Center for Mental Health Services Youth Transition policy meeting; National experts panel.* Rockville, MD: U.S. Substance Abuse and Mental Health Services Administration, Center for Mental Health Services.

Davis, M., & Vander Stoep, A. (1997). The transition to adulthood for youth who have serious emotional disturbances: Developmental transition and young adult outcomes. *Journal of Mental Health Administration, 24*(2), 400–427.

Delman, J., & Jones, A. (2002). *Voices of youth in transition: The experience of aging out of the adolescent public mental health system in Massachusetts: Policy implications and recommendations.* Dorchester, MA: Consumer Quality Initiatives, Inc.

Department of Health and Human Services. (DHHS). (2005). *Medicaid at a glance, 2005: A Medicaid information source.* Washington, DC: Center for Medicare and Medicaid Services. Retrieved December 13, 2007 from http://www.cms.hhs .gov/MedicaidEligibility/Downloads/MedicaidataGlance05.pdf

Dubay, L., Holahan, J., & Cook, A. (2007). MarketWatch: The uninsured and the affordability of health insurance coverage. *Health Affairs, 26*(1), published online November 30, 2006, 10.1377/hlthaff.26.1.w22.

Duke-Benfield, A.E., & Strawn, J. (2008). *Congress expands student aid and supports innovation in student success, basic skills, and workforce partnerships.* Washington, DC: Center for Law and Social Policy. Retrieved October 13, 2008, from http://www.clasp.org/publications/hea_expandsstudentaid.pdf

Education for All Handicapped Children Act of 1975, PL 94-142, 20 U.S.C. §§ 1400 *et seq.*

Foster, E.M., & Gifford, E.J. (2005). The transition to adulthood for youth leaving public systems: Challenges to policies and research. In R.A. Setterson, F.F. Furstenberg, & R.G. Rumbaut (Eds.), *On the frontier of adulthood: Theory, research, and public policy.* IL: University of Chicago Press.

Foster Care Independence Act of 1999, PL 106-169, 42 U.S.C §§ 677.

Fostering Connections Act (2008) (PL 110-351). 42 U.S.C §§ 1305.

Geenen, S.J., & Powers, L.E. (2006). Transition planning for foster youth. *Journal for Vocational Special Needs Education, 28*(2), 4–15.

Goldscheider, F., & Waite, L.J. (1993). *New families, no families: The transformation of the American home.* Berkeley, CA: University of California Press.

Henggeler, S.W., Melton, G.B., & Smith, L.A. (1992). Family preservation using multisystemic therapy: An effective alternative to incarcerating serious juvenile offenders. *Journal of Consulting & Clinical Psychology, 60*(6), 953–961.

Heflinger, C.A. & Hoffman, C. (2008). Transition age youth with SED in publicly-funded systems: Identifying high risk youth for policy planning. *Journal of Behavioral Health Services and Research, 35*(4), 390–401.

Higher Education Act of 1965 PL 89-329, 20 U.S.C §§ 1070 *et seq.*

Higher Education Opportunity Act PL 110-315, 20 U.S.C §§ 10111 *et seq.*

Individuals with Disabilities Education Act (IDEA) of 1990, PL 101-476, 20 U.S.C. §§ 1400 *et seq.*

Individuals with Disabilities Education Act Amendments (IDEA) of 1997, PL 105-17, 20 U.S.C. §§ 1400 *et seq.*

Individuals with Disabilities Education Improvement Act (IDEA) of 2004, PL 108-446, 20 U.S.C. §§ 1400 *et seq.*

Jim Casey Youth Opportunities Initiative. (2008). *Opportunity passport.* Retrieved March 28, 2008, at http://www.jimcaseyyouth.org/opportunitypassport.htm

Juvenile Justice and Delinquency Prevention Act (JJDPA) of 1974, PL 93-415, 42 U.S.C. §§ 5601 *et seq.*

Kaiser Commission on Medicaid and the Uninsured. (2007, September). *Health coverage of children: The role of Medicaid and S-CHIP.* Washington, DC: Author. Retrieved December 13, 2007, from http://www.kff.org/uninsured/7698 .cfm

Kaiser Commission on Medicaid and the Uninsured. (1998, September). *Medicaid eligibility for families and children.* Washington, DC: Author. Retrieved December 13, 2007, from http://www.kff.org/medicaid/2106-eligibility.cfm

Levine, P., & Wagner, M. (2005). Transition for young adults who received special education services as adolescents: A time of challenge and change. In D.W. Osgood, E.M. Foster, C. Flanagan, & G.R. Ruth (Eds.), *On your own without a net: The transition to adulthood for vulnerable populations.* Chicago: University of Chicago Press.

Luecking, R.G., & Certo, N.J. (2003). Integrating service systems at the point of transition for youth with significant support needs: A model that works. *American Rehabilitation, 27*(1), 2–10.

National Center for Youth Law (NCYL). (2007). *NCYL's AB 1633: Helping Foster Youth Leaving Care.* Retrieved November 11, 2007, from http://www.youth law.org/policy/advocacy/california_legislative_update/1/. Washington, DC: Author.

National Child Welfare Resource Center for Youth Development (NCWRCYD). (2007). *State by state search results: Tuition waivers.* Retrieved November 11, 2007, from http://www.nrcys.ou.edu/yd/state_pages/search.php?search_ option=tuition_waiver. Tulsa, OK: Author.

National Longitudinal Transition Study-2. (2005, November). *Facts from NLTS-2: High school completion by youth with disabilities.* Menlo Park, CA: SRI International. Retrieved October 13, 2008, from: www.nlts2.org/fact_sheets/nlts2 _fact_sheet_2005_11.pdf

Newman, L. (2005). Postsecondary education participation of youth with disabilities. In *After high school: A first look at the postschool experiences of youth with disabilities.* Washington, DC: National Longitudinal Transitional Study-2. Retrieved October 13, 2008, from: http://www.nlts2.org/reports/2005_04/ nlts2_report_2005_04_ch4.pdf

No Child Left Behind Act of 2001, PL 107-110, 115 Stat. 1425, 20 U.S.C. §§ 6301 *et seq.*

Oldmixon, S. (2007). *Issue brief: State policies to help youth transition out of foster care.* Washington, DC: National Governor's Association for Best Practices. Retrieved November 11, 2007, at http://www.nga.org/Files/pdf/0701YOUTH .PDF

Osgood, D.W., Foster, E.M., Flanagan, C., & Ruth, G.R. (Eds.). (2005). *On your own without a net: the transition to adulthood for vulnerable populations.* IL: University of Chicago Press.

Office of Temporary and Disability Assistance (OTDA). (2007). Funding for Young Adult Housing Programs Announced. Retrieved February 21, 2009 at http://www.otda.state.ny.us/main/news/2007/2007-03-20.asp

Promoting Safe and Stable Families Act of 2001, PL 107-133, 42 U.S.C. §§ 629.

Schneider, A., Fennel, K., & Long, P. (1998). *Medicaid eligibility for families and children.* Washington, DC: Kaiser Commission on Medicaid and the Uninsured.

Setterstein, R.A., Furstenberg, F.F., & Rumbaut, R.G. (Eds.). (2005). *On the frontier of adulthood: Theory, research and public policy.* Chicago: The University of Chicago Press.

Small, S.A., Reynolds, A.J., O'Connor, C., & Cooney, S.M. (2005). *What works, Wisconsin? What science tells us about cost-effective programs for juvenile delinquency prevention.* Madison, WI: University of Wisconsin-Madison.

Stroul, B.A., & Blau, G.M. (Eds.). (2008). *The system of care handbook: Transforming mental health services for children, youth, and families.* Baltimore: Paul H. Brookes Publishing Co.

Stroul, B., & Friedman, R. (1986). *A system of care for severely emotionally disturbed children and youth.* Washington, DC: CASSP Technical Assistance Center.

Substance Abuse and Mental Health Services Administration, U.S. Department of Health and Human Services. (2005). *Transforming mental health care in America. Federal action agenda: First steps* (DHHS Pub. No. SMA-05-4060.) Rockville, MD: Author.

U.S. Department of Education. (USDOE). (2007). *IDEA Regulations: Secondary Transition.* Retrieved November 11, 2007, at http://idea.ed.gov/explore/view/p/%2Croot%2Cdynamic%2CTopicalBrief%2C17%2C. Washington, DC: Author.

U.S. General Accounting Office. (USGAO). (2008). *Young adults with serious mental illness: Some states and federal agencies are taking steps to address their transition challenges.* Washington, DC: Author. Retrieved August 6, 2008, at http://www.gao.gov/new.items/d08678.pdf

Wagner, M., & Davis, M. (2006). How are we preparing students with emotional disturbances for the transition to young adulthood? Findings from the National Longitudinal Transition Study-2. *Journal of Emotional and Behavioral Disorders, 14,* 86–98.

Wagner, M., Kutash, K., Duchnowski, A.J., Epstein, M.H., & Sumi, W.C. (2005). The children and youth we serve: A national picture of the characteristics of students with emotional disturbances receiving special education. *Journal of Emotional and Behavioral Disorders, 13*(2), 79–96.

Wayne, A. (2007, October). House passes new children's health bill despite GOP protests. *Washington Health Policy Week in Review* (October 29, 2007). Retrieved December 13, 2007 from http://www.commonwealthfund.org/healthpolicy week/healthpolicyweek_show.htm?doc_id=566863&#doc566865

Weil, A. (2003). There is something about Medicaid. *Health Affairs, 22*(1), 13–30.

Whitehead, J.T., & Lab, S.P. (2001). *Juvenile Justice: An Introduction.* Cincinnati, OH: Anderson Publication Company.

Collaborative Approach to Improving Quality in Process, Progress, and Outcomes

CHAPTER

10

Sustaining a Responsive and Effective Transition System

Karyn L. Dresser, Peter J. Zucker, Robin A. Orlando, Alexandra A. Krynski, Gwendolyn White, Arun Karpur, Nicole Deschênes, and Deanne K. Unruh

"I want to grow up and feel like I'm not always being evaluated—but the system is!"

—Young man from Alameda County, California

Imagine that young adults with emotional and behavioral disorders served in a community-based transition program report to staff the many barriers they face when trying to find independent, safe, and affordable housing. Imagine that the staff work with them, one by one, by helping to budget for the steep costs of rental deposits; negotiating with landlords; supporting age-appropriate claims to freedom at home; or showing up during crisis. "Running interference" around housing becomes a normal part of case management as staff readily perceive the destabilizing affect that a lack or loss of housing will have on the young adults, and the desire some have to move on from living with family. Now, imagine staff comparing notes and discussing with their manager the patterns they see regarding the various housing challenges of the young people. The manager elicits the help of the agency's quality assurance or evaluation staff, who design a survey to systematically study the young adults' housing experiences. Clients and staff are asked for input on the survey tool to make sure that the questions are clear and the most important ones are asked. The survey explores young adult perceptions on 24 different topics related to housing, and discovers that the most problematic ones relate to landlords being positive about renting to young people; neighborhoods being crime and drug free; wanting to have someone to talk to at home; wanting to have someone to help when needed; and being able to contribute to how things are done. The results express both the young persons' fears and realities and their budding developmental priorities, with variations in emphases between those in the housing market and those still living at home.

Based on this groundwork, the agency's leadership sponsors a quality improvement team (QIT) of the program's manager, representative staff and young adult clients, and the evaluator. This team meets over a few sessions to discuss the housing situation of its current clients, the survey results, and the small network of contacts they have with local apartment managers, room and board providers, and board and care operators. The staff decide to embark on a quality improvement initiative to formalize and strengthen relationships in this housing network as well as to increase the size of the network to include more operators. The QIT goals are to improve the experience of young adults with emotional and behavioral disorders in the housing market and in their homes, and to pave the way for good housing arrangements for those seeking to leave home and live independently. Initially, the networking activity involves the program manager in making personal contact with each housing operator to explain the transition program, the young persons' general human and developmental needs and objectives (without disclosure of personal information about any particular client) and the availability of staff to provide support when needed. The manager listens closely to the operators' worries about extending housing to young adults and addresses these concerns as best he or she can. The manager also arranges for agency staff to visit the housing settings and assess how each functions based on the housing survey objectives and the housing management's willingness to work on a collaborative basis with the program. As a result, the staff elect to "screen out" some housing providers while increasing their outreach and contacts with others whom they believe offer the best living environments. The team "works" this network on behalf of the young adults in the program, building a strong set of relationships over the course of a couple of years that yields multiple housing options—where the normative expectation is ongoing support and problem solving around issues that may arise. The QIT's success is demonstrated by both the practical solutions to housing that the team now has at hand and by a re-administration of the housing survey. The survey results show marked increases in clients' positive perceptions on 67% of the surveyed topics, including the initial lowest scoring ones, with the remainder holding steady (no statistically significant downturns) (Dresser, 2007).

This particular QIT may be over, but the continuous quality improvement (CQI) process is embedded within the agency and is never completed. What relatively low-scoring housing issues remain? How will a sufficient pool of affordable and quality housing providers be sustained by the program over time, particularly in an increasingly competitive housing market? What about the other domains of life of the transitioning young adults: education, work, relationships, health, symptom management, and community involvement? Continuous quality improvement is the ongoing system through which such questions can be addressed.

RATIONALE FOR A CONTINUOUS QUALITY IMPROVEMENT SYSTEM

Any team, group, department, organization, or community will face at any time any number of challenges, from relatively simple to multi-faceted to extremely thorny and seemingly intractable. Having problems is a normal part of the human condition. Thankfully, being stuck in solving problems rarely works well for anybody or for very long; thus, the motivation arises to open out (invite others to help) and innovate (try something different). CQI is one process through which people can self-organize to recognize needs and challenges, envision alternatives, build on strengths, and create desirable changes.

As any study of innovation will show, many of the values of CQI are long held in human history, but the formal discipline of the process as a cross-functional team effort with a strong integration of data evolved out of the business industry (Deming, 1986; Gabor, 1992), with many popular applications and contributions[1] from the primary health care industry (e.g., Hospital Corporation of America, 1989). In many ways, CQI is a historical adjustment away from Taylorism and assembly line production, in which work became divided into so many discrete parts that no one but upper management could see the overall picture. These models had serious consequences for product quality, as well as worker morale and quality of work life (Gluckman & Reynolds-Roome, 1990).

A good articulation of the basic concepts of CQI applied to the human services field can be found in a number of books and articles (e.g., Fetterman, Kaftarian & Wandersman; 1996; Gabor, & Grinnell, 1994; Patton, 1997; Pecora, Seelig, Zirps & Davis, 1996), including those that focus on the *internal quality management* of the human participants (e.g., Childre & Cryer, 2000).

CQI Values and Principles

As depicted in the opening scenario, CQI embraces the following values and principles:

1. CQI is an organized process through which stakeholders come together to identify challenges, analyze contributing factors, recommend alternative approaches, and implement strategies to enhance performance and quality.

2. CQI involves participatory decision making during which all relevant stakeholders are engaged and the process is facilitated to maximize the sharing and cross-fertilization of ideas toward knowledge and excellence.

3. CQI is data driven. Data are tracked on either an ongoing or ad hoc basis to monitor quality indicators, stimulate action, and explore and understand issues.

4. CQI is results oriented and iterative until desired results are achieved. If data tracking does not show desired results, stakeholders revisit the challenge and try another strategy to produce changes toward an overall mission.

5. Done well, CQI is hopeful and affirmative. Even when data are discouraging, the focus is not on blame or fault finding, but rather on what can be done to move forward and create change for improved outcomes.

6. CQI encourages, stimulates, and models the sharing of power and influence in an organization and the transparent flow of information between various levels of the organization, facilitating distributed gains in practice knowledge.

7. CQI is a bridge between the agency mission and best-practice standards, the related quality objectives, and the operational mechanics of achieving these, particularly through incremental steps and process improvements.[2]

Continuous Quality Improvement with TAY Involvement

This chapter is written as a primer on how youth transition services, programs, and systems of care can move forward to design and implement a CQI process that includes youth and young adult involvement. First, we describe the critical components of CQI, and second we describe specific, concrete strategies for young adult involvement in the process. The chapter represents a wedding of CQI to developing systems that support transition age youth (TAY) development (Clark, 1995; Clark & Davis, 2000; Koroloff, 1990) consistent with best practices in both literatures. CQI is profoundly significant for working with TAY, as the CQI model of fostering ongoing service and organizational improvements mirrors key expectations we have as a society for youth's emergence into adulthood—that there be voice, mindfulness, a striving to improve, a taking stock of resources, an ability to base life decisions on good information and thinking skills, a sense of making a contribution, and the experience of living within a healthy and collaborative interdependent community.

What is asked of TAY is also asked of the programs and organizations that serve them. When young people learn how to collaboratively review and unpack complex problems that span multiple systems, such as safe housing (e.g., availability and locations of housing; operators and managers of housing; fire, police, and other emergency services; recreation and transportation links; family, neighbors and community relationships), they learn techniques that resemble the skills taught in therapeutic and rehabilitative programs that emphasize problem solving and solution building. Worth noting, CQI adds the specific cultural value of power sharing among participants, which is fully consistent with the highest aims of TAY programs and with young adults' successful engagement in everyday civil society. The remainder of this chapter is devoted to describing the features of quality improvement systems and strategies for engaging young adults in the improvement process. Young people have unique histories, perspectives, and expertise to contribute to the improvement of human service programs, and a vital TAY-CQI process builds on this foundation of youth strength.

FEATURES OF CQI SYSTEMS

A "system" for quality improvement implies that a degree of organization is brought to the planning, implementation, operation, and evaluation of change, whether of a group, department, program, agency, or community. Such a system needs to be scaled to the size, budget, and resources of the entity, yet all CQI systems offer solutions to common planning questions:

1. Who are the stakeholders?

2. How will information and communication flow?

3. What resources are needed to effect and sustain quality changes?

4. What facilitative processes are best used to plan, monitor, and evaluate?

5. What types of data, information systems, and analyses are needed?

Stakeholders

One of the most important planning steps for developing a quality improvement process is balancing the value of inclusiveness with the practical need to achieve one or more goals efficiently. It might seem that the fewer the number of people involved, the more efficient the process, but this is not necessarily the case for the actual and eventual success of implementation (Fixsen, Naoom, Blasé, Friedman, & Wallace, 2005; Helgesen, 1995). Who the stakeholders are may be obvious, because their vested interests often shape the decision to pursue quality improvements. Yet good planning involves reflection on the stakeholder question, in particular, consideration of two types of possibly hidden stakeholders: individuals who had little or insufficient voice in decision making related to the topic, and individuals who are in a position of power or influence to block the implementation, maintenance, and success of an initiative. Those who have not had sufficient voice in the past, such as TAY, as well as those with critical and otherwise overlooked political or operational roles (e.g., the housing managers in the opening scenario), will have important and unique perspectives about what is needed, what is achievable, and what will make a difference. Identifying and eliciting the early participation of hidden stakeholders in the CQI process is essential because not doing so may undermine a project or create long-term inefficiencies in engaging relevant stakeholders who can provide critical information for resolving a problem.

Example of Stakeholder Process

A recent large-scale example of making planning choices regarding stakeholders is the California Mental Health Services Act (MHSA), through which voters ushered in a new funding mechanism for the transformation of mental health services to various populations. Some of these services are programs called Full Service Partnerships for TAY. In implementing the voter's intentions, the California State Department of Mental Health (DMH) required submission of initial planning proposals to conform to the state's planning guidelines. These guidelines, widely vetted throughout California, emphasized the need for each county to develop mechanisms to engage a diverse array of community stakeholders in the MHSA planning process (California Department of Mental Health, 2005). Counties that submitted proposals lacking in comprehensive stakeholder involvement were delayed and had to resubmit a better plan.

Usually, there are not mandated consequences to ignoring stakeholder groups in quality improvement processes—yet often there are unplanned social consequences for not including all stakeholder groups in the process, as well as repercussions for data quality. The legislature's and mental health department's wisdom in the previous example expresses a fundamental truth about the importance of stakeholders in decision making. Ensuring accessible, high-quality, and effective human services implies that the people most affected, and especially consumers and family members, have a voice in the process of prioritizing and designing those services. For example, in California's Alameda County, community services and supports for TAY took a major step forward when the MHSA community stakeholder process engaged a number of young adults on the planning committee. Their voice helped expand the age range for accessing these services up through age 25 from the prior cap of age 23, with the expanded range more aligned with national standards and the length of time that transition to adulthood normatively takes for most youth (Clark & Davis, 2000). In this case, stakeholder input ensured a fuller measure of the construct (i.e., the transitional age range), which led to better decisions (Messick, 1995).

Stakeholder Participation and Cultural Competency

An important component of stakeholder participation that needs to be activated but often is neglected in planning decisions is cultural competency—a guiding principle of systems of care since the 1990s (Cross, Bazron, Dennis, & Isaacs, 1989; Stroul & Friedman, 1994). The "dynamics of difference" (Cross et al., 1989) between providers and consumers may have an impact on consumers' access to services as well as the quality and outcomes of those services—the contributions of both parties needs to be considered to create positive change at the levels of service intervention, program approach, and agency system (Cauce et al., 2002; U.S. Department of Health and Human Services, 2001). This is also true of the relationship between evaluators and cultural communities in the conduct of participatory research (Cronbach & Associates, 1980; U.S. Department of Health and Human Services, 1992).

In sum, when planning stakeholder involvement in CQI, consider the following:

- Consumers and family members who represent a diverse experience base related to needs, challenges, and solutions

- Providers and other staff with unique insights or expertise for addressing and resolving challenges

- Leadership, decision makers, or agency positions needed to embrace, implement, and sustain changes

- Agency partners and community members who may provide balance and a broad view of needs, risks, benefits, resources, and innovations

- Quality assurance staff and/or evaluators with technical skills needed to measure, track, and report quality indicators and results

Stakeholder Creation of Theory-Based Logic Models for Transition Systems

Sponsoring agencies, funders, and policy makers at all levels require increasingly sophisticated, evidence-based documentation. It is therefore important to demonstrate that transition efforts have meaningful impact on youth, their families, and the community. The creation of a theory-based logic model will help a community meet this need by generating a shared, overall conceptual framework for how a program functions to achieve desirable outcomes.

The process of developing a logic model is an extremely valuable exercise because it encourages community stakeholders in a dialogue that results in a deep understanding of each element of the initiative by everyone concerned. Logic models provide the foundation for all site activities, framing the community's goals and objectives for the selected approaches to service delivery. In the process of defining their theory-based logic model, stakeholders are invited to clearly identify the focus of their transition efforts; the guiding values, goals, and objectives; the population of concern; strengths and resources; barriers and challenges, and strategies for achieving goals and objectives including intended short and long-term outcomes. The logic model helps ensure that activities are outlined for each level of intended impact—system, organization, and practice (Hernandez & Hodges, 2003).

A well-defined, theory-based logic model can also serve as a framework for ongoing monitoring and CQI. Indicators for elements that will need to be assessed—both process and outcomes—can be identified throughout the logic model. All defined elements of the logic model can be measured as benchmarks for success. Once a logic model is put into action, CQI efforts can provide stakeholders with information as to whether the logic model is working, and if not, help to identify areas where adaptations and/or training may be necessary.

The Logic Model Team at the University of South Florida (USF) has worked with several communities to craft logic models that reflect their unique context and theories of change—incorporating evidence-based practices and evidence-supported practices as appropriate (e.g., TIP model). The USF Logic Model Team's web site (http://logicmodel .fmhi.usf.edu) provides examples of theory-based logic models; a tutorial on developing logic models; and other resource materials including an English versioni and the Spanish translation of a monograph on developing logic models for community systems of care.. Specifically related to the develometn and use of transition system logic models, the Clark, Deschenes, Sielr, and colleagues (2008) article may be helpful. Examples of transition system logic models are also available through the NNYT and TIP web sites (httep://nnyt.fmhi.usf.edu; http://tip.fmhi.usf.edu).

Information and Communication Flow

An important planning question is about *how, when, where,* and *with whom* to communicate and share information about quality improvement. Specific care needs to be given to carefully define the audiences for *how* and *what* information to disseminate. For example, there may be a conflict between the value of distributing information widely, so that all stakeholders are knowledgeable and can learn from the results, and the potential proprietary nature of quality improvement activities. Staff or leadership may be uncomfortable at times with sharing data that expose problems, or may seek to protect valuable information about the results of quality improvement activities from competitors.

It is also the case that although quality improvement is essentially a hopeful and positive process (it implies that change for the better is possible), it is not always or necessarily experienced that way. The impetus to change may imply that something is not sufficient or is less than optimal, or perhaps that someone (or some group, team, department, or agency) is not doing a good job. Therefore, how quality improvement projects are framed and described *is very important* and may trigger anxiety, defensiveness, and resistance—or with hope, will pave the way for collaborative joining of stakeholders with the process (Cooperrider & Srivasta, 1987; Hammond & Royal, 2001). The good news from organizational development theory is that the more a program engages in quality improvement using affirmative principles, the easier it becomes to do so, as the overall culture shifts toward embracing change as a learning organization (Argyris & Schon, 1978; Senge, 2006).

Structured Routines

A sound approach to building and maintaining a quality improvement system over time ensures that discrete quality improvement projects continuously occur, each of modest scope. Structural decisions related to communication and information flow then become a matter of establishing and using routines. The structure includes the role of an organizational "holder" of the CQI system, which may be a manager, department, or oversight committee (e.g., an administrator, evaluator, and consumer may comprise a simple oversight group). This group becomes responsible for clarifying decision rules about projects such as the nature, scope, aims, expected length, use of staff and other resources, and how final choices about QI interventions will be made. They do this by facilitating agency sponsors and managing information content and flow, including providing project descriptions at varying levels of detail to those directly involved and to other staff, managers, agency executives, governance boards, regulators, consumers, and the community. Details of CQI deliberations, including data that stimulate a need for change, are shared only among those directly involved and are treated as proprietary information, with minutes and related documents gathered back up before the meeting is adjourned.

The CQI system allows for general sharing and knowledge gain, which can occur through use of electronic technologies such as secure intranet or web-based postings of summary information. At the same time, the oversight function ensures the privacy and confidentiality of participants and the organization, creating internal freedom to ask tough questions, reveal difficult information, and entertain novel solutions. In this system, the people directly reviewing data and steering a quality improvement project are *peer reviewers* and their activities are most likely not discoverable in a court of law, which greatly facilitates leadership's willingness to sponsor quality improvement. Policies or bylaws about the quality improvement system in agency governance documents are important to develop and should include a written description about the mission, scope, and focus of the CQI system, so these are bona fide agency procedures.

Resources

The third planning question is about the resources available to support continuous quality improvement. Unfortunately, human service organizations, and particularly provider agencies, are often thinly budgeted and are staffed primarily to deliver an array of direct services. These services must be fully accounted for, and—in the case of publicly funded mental health services—will be audited, with resources taken back by the government if audit results fail to meet established standards, down to the *minute* that all services are provided. At the same time, there is little or no administrative cost coverage for functions such as evaluation, quality assurance, and program improvement even though governmental regulators often require performance-based contracting.

Coping with Unfunded Mandates

Evaluation and quality management are included in a new generation of *unfunded mandates*. Consumers and providers are natural allies in advocacy to improve the quality of human services and cost coverage. Meanwhile, larger organizations can create economies of scale and creatively target a few people to carry out these functions, but smaller agencies typically find it necessary to assign CQI responsibilities to staff that already have other full-time duties or near full-time duties. This adds to the leadership challenge of transforming "have to" into "want to" responsibilities among agency staff, which must be accompanied by reasonable CQI productivity expectations. One strategy that supports the evolution of a CQI system is to add a general line to all position descriptions that staff "will participate in and contribute to agency quality improvement activities." Staff are then prepared in advance to contribute to and participate in quality improvement projects, optimally when their CQI activities are matched to their interests, knowledge, and availability. External consultants may be used on an ad hoc basis to provide technical assistance (i.e., data collection and analyses).

Data Yields from External Mandates

External mandates often create pressure to move forward with quality improvement with little or no funding, though these mandates usually contribute other types of resources to the process, specifically data and benchmarks for gauging performance to standards. For example, quality improvement data targeting educational transition can be acquired from local school districts and state Departments of Education. These data are made possible through the Individuals with Disabilities Act (IDEA) reauthorization in 2004 (Individuals with Disabilities Education Improvement Act; PL 108-446). One of the purposes of the Act is that, "all children with disabilities have available to them a free appropriate public education that emphasizes special education and related services designed to meet their unique needs and prepare them for *further education, employment, and independent living* [italics added]." To achieve this purpose, the U.S. Office of Special Education Programs requires states to report on 20 accountability indicators. The purpose of these indicators are twofold. First, states must report data on these indicators to the federal government as a measure of accountability that transition services aligned with the IDEA law are targeted to youth with disabilities. Second, the intent of these indicators is to support both state and local systems change initiatives for data based program improvement to ultimately improve outcomes of youth with disabilities. Four of the 20 indicators relate to transition age youth (http://idea.ed.gov):

- *Indicator 1:* Percent of youth with individualized education programs (IEPs) graduating from high school with a regular diploma (20 U.S.C. 1416 (a)(3)(A))

- *Indicator 2:* Percent of youth with IEPs dropping out of high school. (20 U.S.C. 1416 (a)(3)(A))

- *Indicator 13:* Percent of youth with IEPs ages 16 and above with an IEP that includes appropriate measurable postsecondary goals that are annually updated and based upon an age-appropriate transition assessment, transition services, including courses of study that will reasonably enable the student to meet those postsecondary goals, and annual IEP goals related to the student's transition services needs. There also must be evidence that the student was invited to the IEP Team meeting where transition services are to be discussed and evidence that, if appropriate, a representative of any participating agency was invited to the IEP Team meeting with the prior consent of the parent or student who has reached the age of majority (20 U.S.C. 1416 (a)(3)(B)).

- *Indicator 14:* Percent of youth who are no longer in secondary school, had IEPs in effect at the time they left school, and were

   A. Enrolled in higher education within 1 year of leaving high school

   B. Enrolled in higher education or competitively employed within 1 year of leaving high school

   C. Enrolled in higher education or in some other postsecondary education or training program; or competitively employed or in some other employment within 1 year of leaving high school. (20 U.S.C. 1416(a)(3)(B))

If educational and/or human service programs (e.g., a non–public school with community day treatment) receive state school funds to educate clients, then these programs are expected to be included in state-level data collection and reporting on students receiving special education services. State departments of education are required to publicly report these data and should provide districts with technical assistance to use the data locally for program improvement. School districts may request that service programs help collect the data, and programs may in turn work with their school districts to provide comparison data. These data will then be accessible to districts, schools, and individual programs for use within their program improvement activities.

Facilitation

The fourth planning question at the heart of CQI is appropriate facilitation strategies. What are the committee, team, group, and meeting processes that best support CQI? There is an art to staging, managing, and facilitating the quality improvement dialogue that can be mastered by anyone with intelligence, organization, perseverance, and good people skills—higher degrees are not required. For example, sharing and rotating meeting facilitation or co-facilitation among youth participants is a good way to mentor youth leadership. Staff members' agility with facilitation, in turn, furthers youth mastery because the youth then have opportunities to observe and learn skills related to collaboration, thinking, and problem solving. Shared facilitation also makes the prospect of youth involvement with quality improvement exciting and rewarding for the young people, helping them develop tangible skills that are applicable to all kinds of life and employment opportunities.

Practical Mechanics of Continuous Quality Improvement

The art of CQI is built on practical mechanics that can be acquired through training, use, and feedback (CQI on CQI). Building feedback about facilitation, project progress, and fidelity to best-practice standards simply and directly into the CQI process itself ensures that no one can get too far off track while a practice is being integrated into an agency's normal operating procedures or maintained thereafter.

One very practical component of facilitation is running effective meetings. This includes 1) communicating in advance, 2) having an agenda, 3) starting and ending on time, 4) limiting the number of main topics, 5) staging interactive opportunities, 6) discouraging side conversations, and, 7) distributing minutes for follow-up. There are multitudes of resources about running meetings, and most have very similar guidelines (e.g., Doyle & Strauss, 1993; Iacafano, 2001; Kelsey & Plumb, 2004).

Participatory Decision Making

Other key components of facilitation involve both the fundamental and advanced practices of participatory decision making (e.g., Cohen, 1994; Cohen & Bailey, 1997; Gastil, 1993; Issacs, 1999; Kahane, 2004), including formalized models of teamwork in the human services field now being subjected to systematic evaluation. For example, formal models include *team decision making* (e.g., Alaska Department of Health and Human Services, 2007; Iowa Department of Human Services, 2007), *family conferencing* (Merkel-Holguin, Nixon, & Burford, 2003; Pennell & Burford, 1999; Shore, Wirth, Cahn, Yancey, & Gunderson, 2001; Thomas,

Berzin, & Cohen, 2005), and *child and family teams* in wraparound (Bruns et al., 2004; Burchard, Bruns & Burchard, 2002; Walker & Shutte, 2004; Walker, 2008). The Stars Behavioral Health Group (SBHG) in California has trained staff across affiliated programs using the *Facilitator's Guide to Participatory Decision-Making* (Kaner, Lind, Toldi, Fisk & Berger, 2007). This interactive curriculum is based on the experiences and applied examples of people working in the human services field and provides a wealth of practical insights, tools, and techniques, which can be readily mastered by a diverse array of managers, staff, consumers, youth, and advocates.

Commitment and Follow-Through

A primary theme throughout the facilitation literature is how to initiate creating clarity, commitment, and follow-through among participants so that agreements are sustained until outcomes are achieved. Most everyone has experienced attending a meeting or participating on a committee only to discover afterwards that there were as many interpretations about decisions made, next steps, and designated responsibilities as there were attendees present. To succeed, quality improvement initiatives must prevail both through the normal human confusion, puzzlements, and politicking of group process, and the potentially numerous barriers to project success that can occur during implementation (e.g., mission drift and the press on every one of the team members' usual obligations). Success strategies include the tips for handling meeting processes described in prior mentioned references; accurate note-taking, disseminating information or decisions, and checking of minutes; and, the overall steps described in this chapter for gaining project sponsorship, participant commitment, and tracking and reporting progress over time.

When recruiting stakeholders into a CQI or QIT process, it is important to communicate the value of specific behavioral norms. These include being thoughtful, creative, and flexible; a willingness to consider differences of opinion as healthy; persisting through completion; and following the evidence toward success. One strategy to support success is inviting those members, such as youth or family members who are unfamiliar with this kind of work, to do preparatory orientation and training about the process. The orientation might address the stages and time commitment of the QIT; participant roles and responsibilities; participatory values and skills (e.g., active listening, which is a good brief training focus during such an orientation); who the team members will be; what kinds of things the facilitator will do (e.g., open up discussions to involve everybody) and will not do (e.g., take sides on a proposal); and how results will be monitored and evaluated. An abbreviated version of the orientation training can be repeated at the beginning of the first QIT session.

Discrete Steps of CQI

Quality improvement teams best move through discrete steps, diagrammed in Figure 10.1, which experienced facilitators know not to skip or rush.

The number of QIT sessions needed and at what interval, over what span of time, varies based on the nature of the issue being examined and the ease with which good data are available for use by the team. The team needs to pause and celebrate successes when they occur because doing so reinforces the value of the QI process in the organization and builds positive morale.

Data Systems

The last planning question is about the types and kinds of data to be collected, measured, and analyzed in a quality improvement program. The objectives of quality data systems include 1) applying or developing clear and unambiguous fidelity and quality indicators and data definitions, 2) implementing standardized measurement tools and benchmarks, 3) using robust sampling and research designs, 4) applying sta-

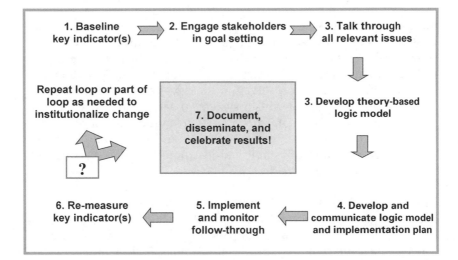

Figure 10.1.   Quality improvement team steps.

tistical analyses that match the sophistication level of the data and questions of interest, and, 5) making sense of data through logic models and interpretative theories (Hernandez & Hodges, 2003; Mayeske & Lambur, 2001; Weiss, 1995; also refer to the previous section titled, "Stakeholder Creation of Theory-Based Logic Models for Transition Systems". Often, in the face of such a list of objectives, agencies are overwhelmed with where to start!

Getting Started on Performance Indicators

One good place to start is with performance indicators in agency and/or funding contracts, regulations, or accreditation and certification standards. For example, the special education IDEA standards applicable to TAY presented earlier are to be collected by states in a reliable and valid manner. States are required to report the demographic representation in the data by age, gender, ethnicity, and disability type. This process allows states and school districts to examine the indicator rates across each of these demographic categories, such as for adolescents diagnosed through special education services with ED. Programs can use these data to set benchmarks and compare the performance of their young adults with that of students at local and state levels, and to monitor performance across time.

Standardized TAY Data Systems

Another sound strategy is to adopt a standardized tracking system designed by university-based researchers who have already worked through the complexities of making reliable and valid psychometric measurements. Such adoption usually requires a formal contract and possibly some procurement costs and/or de-identified data submissions. The benefits include having confidence that the indicators are important and are derived from expert knowledge of empirical literature and that attention has been given to the development of the tool kit. Typically, adopting standardized systems means there are already instruction manuals and data dictionaries to guide staff. Ideally, such measurement systems are built with youth and young adult involvement. Three examples of established instruments tailored specifically for transition programs are described next.

Young Adult Needs and Strengths Assessment

The Child and Adolescent Needs and Strengths Assessment (CANS; Lyons, 1999) is an assessment and planning tool that has been adopted widely for use with children, youth, and families. In the summer of 2003, the Allegheny County, Pennsylvania, System of Care Initiative (SOCI), a recipient of a federal Partnerships for Youth Transition (PYT) grant,[3] began adapting the CANS into what is now known as the Adult Needs and Strengths Assessment—Transition Version (ANSA–T). This development effort was done in collaboration with young people and parents. Once developed, the PYT-SOCI program began administering the assessment at intake and every 6 months to collect information on youth needs, strengths, and culture. Transition personnel used ANSA-T data to assist in planning services and supports at the appropriate intensity in a way that builds on individual strengths and culture—encouraging a youth-driven, individualized, and strength-based approach to service delivery. The ANSA-T data are also analyzed in aggregate across the service population to examine these service features for CQI, thereby ensuring that young people's strengths, needs, and culture are driving the work of PYT-SOCI. The ANSA-T is available through the Praed Foundation web site (http://www.praedfoundation.org). Another version of the CANS applicable for transition-age young people is the Adult Needs and Strength Assessment (ANSA)–Indiana version, available through the Indiana Behavioral Health web site (http://ibhas.in.gov.maindocuments.aspx).

Transition to Adulthood Program Information System

The Transition to Adulthood Program Information System (TAPIS) has been developed by the National Network on Youth Transition for Behavioral Health (NNYT)[4] (Clark, Karpur, Haber, Deschênes & Knab, 2007). The purpose of TAPIS is to assist young people and transition personnel in tracking the progress or difficulty that youth and young adults (ages 14–29 years) are having in progressing toward assuming adulthood roles. The two major components of the TAPIS are the Goal Achiever and the Progress Tracker. These are displayed across the top of Figure 10.2 and are briefly described below.

The first major component of TAPIS is the *TAPIS Goal Achiever*, which is designed as a transition plan for use with young people in assisting them in setting and tracking their own individualized goals. For each goal, there may be several measurable objectives, and these may be broken into discrete steps to accomplish the objective and advance toward goal achievement. In addition, the transition plan may include other features such as person responsible and target date for each goal.

The second major component of TAPIS is the *TAPIS Progress Tracker*. The purpose of the progress tracker is to assess and track, on a quarterly basis, a young person's progress and/or difficulty in transition across five transition domains: employment and career, education, living situation, personal effectiveness and wellbeing, and community-life functioning. The personal effectiveness and wellbeing domain is composed of four sub-domains: interpersonal relationships, emotional and behavioral wellbeing, physical health and wellbeing, and parenting (Clark & Davis, 2000; Clark & Foster-Johnson 1996). The initial

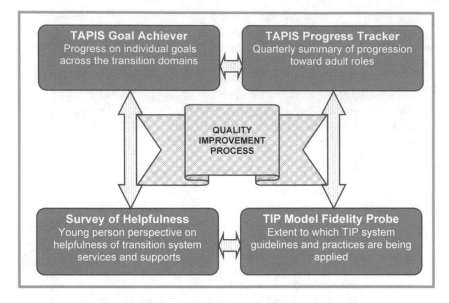

Figure 10.2. Transition to Adulthood Program Information System (TAPIS) overview. The components of the TAPIS provide an organized way to identify and track the goals and progress of young people over time, as well as their perceptions of the services and supports provided by a program, and the extent to which the services and supports are consistent with desirable program standards.

TAPIS Progress Tracker assessment is used to establish a baseline prior to entry to the transition program and provides information to assist in the development of the initial transition plan.

The TAPIS Progress Tracker is completed by a transition facilitator or other person most knowledgeable about the young person's recent experiences based on all of the sources of information available, including the youth, parents, foster parents, various agency records, school reports, and other informal and formal key players in the young person's life. The TAPIS Progress Tracker is conducted every 90 days and provides a visual display of the progress and/or difficulty across each of the transition domains over time and enables continuing system improvement through the provision of both individualized and aggregate data.

The TAPIS Goal Achiever and TAPIS Progress Tracker have been computerized by the Mosaic Network, Inc., into an integrated system so that personnel can access relevant data reports for their direct service delivery work, supervisory responsibilities, program management decisions, and evaluation activities. For example, a program manager might want to query the TAPIS Progress Tracker data set to answer a question such as, "What percentage of young people who have been in the program at least 9 months are employed and/or attending school or a vocational/technical training program?" Figure 10.2 also illustrates other data sources such as a Survey of Helpfulness and the TIP Model Fidelity Probes. These are described more fully in the following paragraphs of this chapter. For more information regarding the TAPIS, please refer to the NNYT and Mosaic Network web sites (http://tip.fmhi.usf.edu; http://www.mosaic-network.com).

The NNYT team has also developed the Transition Program Fidelity Assessment Protocol (Deschênes, Herrygers, & Clark, 2008) to assess the adequacy of implementation of transition practices within a transition system. The 57-item fidelity assessment scale measures adherence to critical components of the transition system. The scale developed for Transition Program Fidelity Assessment Protocol was operationally defined through an expert consensus process. It measures the seven TIP system guidelines and various organizational and structure elements deemed essentials to improved outcomes. Each item of this instrument is rated on an objective 5-point anchored scale.

The fidelity scale measures behavior and activities of transition program personnel involved in a transition initiative. Data is collected through multiple approaches to collect the best and most reliable information (e.g., interviews, document reviews, focus groups, surveys and observation). Sources of information include: young people who are receiving transition facilitation services through the system, documents relating to the administration of the system as well as charts of young people who are receiving transition facilitation services, transition program personnel who assist these young people and their families during the transition process, formal and informal key players such as family members, friends, service providers or others who assist the young person in his or her transition and administrators of the transition system. Such a multimodal approach—which can include both quantitative and qualitative measures—is more likely to accurately capture the full range of implementation. The information gathered is then used by reviewers to complete the fidelity rating sheet.

Because it is important that the ratings be made objectively, there should be at least two reviewers who have experience and training in interviewing and collecting data who are independent yet familiar with the agency/organization, and who understand the essential ingredients of the transition system. The program fidelity assessment can, therefore, be conducted by a trained on-site evaluator (e.g., as a quality improvement activity) who can then, either independently or with the assistance of an external reviewer, conduct follow-up assessments, assist in the development of action plans and monitor progress.

Integrating fidelity assessment and more traditional process evaluation measures with outcome evaluation can provide critical information about what really works in bringing about sustained improvements for youth in transition. It also allows the agency to determine and test the relevance of its theory-based logic model. For more information regarding the Transition Program Fidelity Assessment Protocol, please visit the NNYT web site (http://nnyt.fmhi.usf.edu).

Building and Refining Quality Monitoring Systems

A third strategy for using data systems is to incrementally build and refine measurement procedures over time, in tandem with the development of the overall quality improvement program. This strategy has been used successfully at SBHG, which now (10 years after its inception) provides affiliated agencies with a comprehensive approach to quality management known as the SBHG Total Quality Management (TQM) program. The program embraces multiple sources of information from an array of specific tools that have been created, piloted, and improved upon with staff and consumer input. For example, the TAY housing survey described at the beginning of this chapter was initially designed for a specific quality improvement project but is now used annually to monitor young adults' housing experiences. A TAY-focused Strengths-Discovery Inventory is another SBHG tool designed to support ongoing care planning in transition-age youth programs.

Stars Behavioral Health Group Total Quality Management
The SBHG TQM program features these components:

- *Key indicators.* Routine tracking of operational functioning related to quality, such as referrals, intakes, census, missed appointments, high-risk behaviors, incidents, accidents and complaints, crisis and hospitalizations, and discharge level of care.

- *Quality checklists.* Brief checklists called *probes* are keyed to regulations, evidence-based practices, professional standards, and/or agency policies and procedures. Over time, SBHG has developed more than 100 specific probes tailored to each program, depending on the types of services and target population (e.g., children, youth, young adult, adult). Each program's probes are organized into a quarterly schedule and administered or completed by different departmental staff, with results verified by corporate quality assurance staff annually. Probes for SBHG's TAY programs are in alignment with the TIP model and include probes such as TAY Program Essentials and TAY Engagement Across Relevant Transition Domains. These probes are available through the NNYT web site: http://nnyt.fmhi.usf.edu.

- *Quality assurance reviews.* Utilization, quality assurance, and peer reviews include chart audits of basic service documentation (i.e., required paperwork completed and signed), service billing (as relevant, e.g., for Medi-Cal mental health services), and quality reviews (e.g., thorough assessment, services provided per the service plan, client/family engagement and response to interventions, ongoing need for services).

- *Satisfaction surveys.* Satisfaction surveys collected in SBHG programs include semiannually mandated performance tools and SBHG-designed satisfaction surveys gathered from clients, families, and agency partners annually. These surveys collect consumer and stakeholder input on a wide range of topics: including access to relevant supports and services; helpfulness of supports and services; and cultural competency of service provision, service process, quality, and outcomes.

- *Outcome tracking.* Client and family outcome tracking is focused primarily on four key domains: 1) Are clients living safely in a home or family-like setting? 2) Are clients attending and progressing in school and/or vocationally? 3) Are they improving in their health and mental health, including decreasing reliance on alcohol and other substances? and 4) Are they staying out of trouble with the law? Standardized assessments, including purchased, proprietary tools, are applied as appropriate to each program to provide specific measures within and across these domains.

Avoiding Data Rich, Information Poor

Now, having presented five key planning questions for creating a quality improvement system relevant for transition-age youth and young adults, an important warning is to avoid *DRIP* (Data Rich, Information Poor). Data gathering is important, but the most critical processes for quality improvement are transforming these data into information and knowledge useful for program decision making that culminates in desirable, tangible results. Engagement, teamwork, and collaboration are essential in this process because it is the collective rumination over what the data and information mean to stakeholders in light of their theory-based program logic model that eventually translates into actions toward quality improvement through facilitative program management methods. The actions or processes of quality improvement work in human services are almost always improvements to program practices, policies, and procedures, necessarily coupled with staff training and development. Using youth and consumer input provides the framework for improvements that are meaningful and relevant to program quality. Moreover, young persons' direct participation furthers program aims of coaching life skills, such as transforming complaints into solutions, collaborative teamwork, rational decision making, and perseverance toward goal obtainment.

STRATEGIES TO ENGAGE TAY IN QUALITY IMPROVEMENT

In this chapter we have discussed the importance of and approaches to increase quality assurance and quality improvement methods within human services organizations. An essential component is the participation of varied stakeholders in the process. This next section will further provide concrete strategies to engage youth and young adults in quality improvement. Increasingly, youth-serving organizations have identified youth engagement as a key component of participation in care, leading to a shift in service-delivery structures toward individualized, youth-driven services and supports (e.g., California Collaborative for Youth Development, 2004; Henrich & Gyamfi, 2006). Furthering this thought, some progressive organizations embrace consumer voice and choice as a fundamental service value, having concluded that youth involvement in systems or programmatic work is fundamental for meeting the needs of youth, young adults, and families. This level of consumer involvement surpasses common practices such as complaint or grievance procedures that allow consumers to seek redress for specific complaints, which may improve service quality. Comprehensive youth engagement is strategic in that young people are deliberately involved in all levels and phases of program development, service delivery, and evaluation, and their involvement is characterized by an equal partnership with professionals.

Example of Youth Engagement

For example, as a mentioned previously, the Allegheny County, Pennsylvania PYT-SOCI staff worked closely with transition-age young people to inform the overall planning and implementation of a community-based transition system. Youth contributions included the creation of a paid position for a consumer/family evaluator (in addition to the grant-funded youth coordinator role); the use of focus groups in planning and implementation; a Community Evaluation Team (youth "think tank") that reviews and develops assessments and surveys; and consistent youth leadership at evaluation-focused meetings and conferences.

In the SOCI-PYT experience, the young people were an incredible resource. They brought clarity to the organization's mission and vision; ushered in the inclusion of diverse, multicultural groups in decision making; and stimulated the commitment, creativity, and energy of other program staff. Youth involvement also served to increase interest and enrollment in the program, particularly of young people who had been underrepresented in the mental health system. Today, youth involvement continues to be an essential part of SOCI-PYT, with great significance to their CQI work.

Methods of Youth Engagement

Organizations have nothing to lose and much to gain when it comes to developing or revising plans to involve consumers throughout the system of care, agency, or program, but the question remains: Where to start? This section will discuss a variety of methods (not an exhaustive list) for involving youth in the continuous quality improvement of human services. Engagement methods include young adult participation through 1) membership on professional services teams (paid positions), 2) involvement in focus groups or QITs, 3) membership on committees or quality review councils, 4) input through surveys and questionnaires, and 5) participation as active co-evaluators.

Paid Positions

Creating paid positions for young adult consumers on administrative and direct-service teams is a strategy that guarantees a partnership relationship between young people and professionals. Professional roles for young adults who have personal experience in the mental health system ensure that the youth perspective will be a strong and valid voice in the system. Many organizations accomplish paid positions through the creation of youth-coordinator or peer-advocate roles (Henrick & Gyamfi, 2006). For example, a Google search on "paid youth peer advocates," will result in more than 100,000 entries. Valuing the youth coordinator or peer advocate as an integral member of the professional team reflects a high level of organizational commitment to authentic youth involvement.

Successful youth coordinators are emerging leaders who have the desire and ability to use their personal experiences in youth-serving systems in a creative and proactive way for system-level impact. Youth coordinators take on many roles. They may act as coaches for youth, oversee efforts to ensure meaningful youth involvement at every level,

Valuing the youth coordinator or peer advocate as an integral member of the professional team reflects a high level of organizational commitment to authentic youth involvement.

and educate others on the importance of youth involvement. They may also provide training and support to youth who currently

receive services and work to engage youth from the community in informal activities and groups as well as formal services.

Youth coordinators and others in paid consumer–professional roles can play an integral part in quality improvement efforts. As experts on authentic youth involvement and engagement efforts, youth coordinators can participate in the development of standards for programs in these areas. They can also function as a part of the review team and review service-delivery documents, including service plans, notes, and correspondence for evidence of youth-friendly practices. Following a structured review, youth coordinators can develop and provide technical assistance to programs in their area of expertise. Youth coordinators or peer advocates can be essential to the success of youth and young adult involvement in quality improvement, and have an important, facilitative, and complementary role in each of the following methods of youth involvement.

Focus Groups and Quality Improvement Teams

Focus groups and QITs are qualitative techniques for ensuring consumer involvement in the quality assurance of service delivery and program operations. A focus group is a small-group process (e.g., five to eight people) for gathering information, using a semi-structured format, such as the use of specific questions or prompts to initiate and guide the discovery of participants' views and input on a topic or related set of topics. In contrast, a QIT is a small-group process for generating specific ideas and strategies for addressing an identified quality concern and for monitoring the implementation and results of quality initiatives across time.

In a program's developmental stage, focus-group participants might provide data, such as a needs assessment, to support the design of services that young people define as welcoming, accessible, respectful of their unique culture, and capable of meeting their diverse needs. Continuing the periodic use of focus groups once the program is operational is one strategy to gauge the success of services from the youth perspective and to recognize areas in which improvements are needed. Youth involvement on a QIT is an excellent strategy to ensure that youth are involved in the problem-solving process and are creating and monitoring quality-improvement efforts. As described earlier, training young people in these procedures is critical prior to initiating the process.

Use Open-Ended Facilitation Approaches

In either a focus group or QIT context, an open-ended facilitative approach to youth involvement is best; it provides young people with the opportunity to disclose what they are comfortable with sharing and to interact with one another, often resulting in rich discussions providing growth for all involved. Young people are the experts on their own lives and experiences, and many will share a wealth of valuable information that may be relatively inaccessible to professionals. The best facilitators are those with whom the participants are most comfortable. Selecting and training a facilitator capable of connecting with the youth group on their level; for example, considering age and cultural match, is critical to the success of valuable young person involvement.

Compensate Young People for Their Contributions

Compensation is important because it clearly signals an organization's valuing of youth input. Compensation might include a small stipend, a thoughtfully selected gift card, and/or youth-friendly practices such as providing food and assistance with transportation or child care during a QIT meeting or focus group. Meetings held in community settings familiar to the participants will help make them feel more at home during the process. Youth can be polled to find the most convenient times to meet. For example, youth may be more able and willing to participate in late afternoon or evening groups than those held in early morning.

Example of Youth Focus Groups

Allegheny County's preparation for implementation of the SOCI-PYT grant provides an example of youth involvement in the program development phase. The focus groups gathered information about youths' life experiences to build a system of care capable of meeting their diverse needs. Twelve focus groups, composed of 85 young adults ages 18–24, were conducted in June and July of 2003. Data were gathered from participants on their goals and thoughts about the future, stressors encountered in daily life, definition of family, the role of trust in the service process, and what their ideal system of care would look like. The SOCI-PYT team partnered with organizations and communities that had relationships with the young adults who they wanted to engage to solicit their participation. The participants represented a varied population that included geographic diversity; homeless and runaway youth; youth receiving intensive mental health treatment; and gay, lesbian, and bisexual youth. Separate groups were held in various community settings, including different groups for males and females, so that participants would feel comfortable, and to increase the likelihood of similar experiences emerging for discussion purposes. Based on the information shared, a decision was made to collect additional data that captured many of their life experiences, including commitment to future aspirations, exposure to violence, education and employment functioning, and hopefulness. A strong presence of resiliency was evident as many expressed hopeful life views amidst their expression of need for resources and support to attain their goals.

Quality Committees or Councils

Standing quality assurance committees or councils are an ongoing practice of many agencies in which quality indicators and related data are reviewed to detect trends across time—both positive and negative—that can inform quality improvement efforts. As a result, these committees may direct, initiate, or sponsor a QIT targeting a specific issue. Youth involvement on a standing committee might be challenging to recruit and maintain. A youth coordinator or peer advocate in a paid position may be the most appropriate choice for such membership because he or she will be better oriented to the agency, program, or service and easier to prepare for this function, which will involve reviewing potentially sensitive, confidential, and proprietary information. Having the youth/young adult coordinator spend time with other committee members one-to-one and apart from the meeting may be useful in helping the young person understand the organizational roles and functions in the agency.

Example of Youth Participation in a Continuous Quality Improvement Council

Agencies affiliated with SBHG hold quarterly quality improvement councils with invited community stakeholders, including youth consumers and family members. In this forum, one role of the young participants is to provide insight and narrative input and feedback as to what makes services work and what does not; this is usually done in tandem with the agency's presentation of outcome data and provides a nicely textured, qualitative counterpoint to quantified outcomes. The quality council forum is fairly formal, and community participants, especially youth, are coached and guided through the process by their staff person and/or unit supervisor. The presentations are often very moving as well as informative to all participants, especially staff, with much pride evident in the young person's ability to come forward in such a well attended, auspicious environment.

Satisfaction Surveys

Consumer satisfaction surveys are a vital component of quality and outcome data and are relatively easy to use on a consistent basis given their general low cost and minor time constraints. Satisfaction surveys may be designed to correspond with specific events in the service-delivery process and/or may be geared toward gauging overall satisfaction with services received. Survey design and administration can be tailored to ensure that survey forms are youth-friendly, with non-English translations made available, as well as comfortably keyed assistance to young people with literacy limitations. Often young people can help in the development and piloting of a survey, providing input on item content, language use, and how best to administer a survey. A program's CQI process provides the mechanism through which collected data are meaningfully presented back to consumers and staff, understood, and applied to programmatic decisions for quality improvement.

Co-Evaluation

Focus groups and surveys may take place in or apart from a group that is frequently referred to as a community evaluation team. All stakeholders, including consumers, families, community members, and professionals can play a part on such a team, which may evolve into a standing quality committee once a system, program, or service is fully operating. Activities of a community evaluation team might include prioritizing and monitoring what type of data is collected and the method for doing so, providing feedback on services received, or discussing personal stories in a way that augments or contrasts with available data, analyzing outcomes, and brainstorming ways to improve service quality. In Allegheny County, the SOCI-PYT community evaluation team became the essential part of the CQI-feedback loop for reporting and discussing data and then integrating data into program operations. Recruitment of youth and others into such a team, or into any of the other venues of participation in quality improvement discussed in this chapter, is often most successful when the invitation to participate comes from someone the young person already knows and trusts.

SUMMARY

There are myriad ways to engage and organize youth and young adult involvement in the quality oversight of a program, agency, or system of care. This chapter explored some of these strategies and the multiple compelling reasons and benefits of such involvement from the vantage point of established practices regarding continuous quality improvement—as these echo the mission and objectives of transition-age youth programs focused on fostering youth and young adult development and supporting achievement of successful adult outcomes.

REFERENCES

Alaska Department of Health and Human Services. (2007). *Team decision making survey.* Anchorage: Publication of the Alaska Department of Health and Human Services, Office of Children's Services.

Argyris, C., & Schon, D. (1978). *Organizational learning.* Boston: Addison-Wesley.

Bruns, E.J., Walker, J.S., Adams, J., Miles, P., Osher, T.W., Rast, J., VanDenBerg, J.D., & National Wraparound Initiative Advisory Group. (2004). Ten principles of the wraparound process. Portland, OR: National Wraparound Initiative, Research and Training Center on Family Support and Children's Mental Health, Portland State University.

Burchard, J.D., Bruns, E.J., & Burchard, S.N. (2002). The Wraparound Approach. In Burns, B., and Hoagwood, K. (Eds.), *Community treatment for youth: Evidence-based treatment for severe emotional and behavioral disorders.* Oxford: Oxford University Press.

California Collaborative for Youth Development. (May, 2004). Youth development principles for policymakers—a checklist. Retrieved April 1, 2009, from: http://www.ccyouthdev.org/Policymakers.pdf

California Department of Mental Health. (2005). *County funding request for Mental Health Services Act (MHSA) community program planning.* Implementation of MHSA Welfare and Institutions Code 5847, 5845 and 5892. (DMH Letter No. 05-01.) Retrieved April 3, 2009, from http://www.dmh.ca.gov

Cauce, A.M., Domenech-Rodriquez, M., Paradise, M., Cochran, B.N., Shea, J.M., Srebnik, D., et al. (2002). Cultural and contextual influences in mental health help-seeking: A focus on ethnic minority youth. *Journal of Counseling and Clinical Psychology, 70,* 44–55.

Childre, D., & Cryer, B. (2000). *From chaos to coherence: The power to change performance.* Boulder Creek, CA: Institute of HeartMath.

Clark, H.B. (1995). *Operating procedures for a transition to independence process system.* Tampa, FL: University of South Florida, Florida Mental Health Institute.

Clark, H.B., & Davis, M. (2000). *Transition to adulthood: A resource for assisting young people with emotional and behavioral difficulties.* Baltimore: Paul H. Brookes Publishing Co.

Clark, H.B., Deschênes, N., Sieler, D., Green, M., White, G., & Sondheimer, D. (2008). Services for youth in transition to adulthood in systems of care. In B.A. Stroul & G.M. Blau (Eds.), *The system of care handbook: Transforming mental health services for children, youth, and families* (pp. 517–544). Baltimore: Paul H. Brookes Publishing Co.

Clark, H.B., & Foster-Johnson, L. (1996). Serving youth in transition to adulthood. In B.A. Stroul (Ed.), *Children's mental health: Creating systems of care in a changing society* (pp. 533–551). Baltimore: Paul H. Brookes Publishing Co.

Clark, H.B., Karpur, A., Haber, M.G., Deschênes, N., & Knab, J. (2005) *TAPIS Progress Tracker: Domain Indicators & Progress Assessment.* Tampa, FL: University of South Florida, Louis de la Parte Florida Mental Health Institute, National Center on Youth Transition. See NCYT website.

Cohen, S.G. (1994). "Designing effective self-managing work teams." In Byerlein, M. (Ed.), *Advances in interdisciplinary studies of work teams* (Vol. 1, pp. 67–102). Greenwich, CT: JAI Press.

Cohen, S.G., & Bailey, D.E. (1997.) What makes teams work: Group effectiveness research from the shop floor to the executive suite. *Journal of Management,* 23(3): 239–290.

Cooperrider, D., & Srivasta, S. (1987). Appreciative inquiry into organizational life. In R. Woodman & W. Pasmore (Eds.), *Research in organizational change and development* (Vol. 1) (pp. 129–169). Greenwich, CT: JAI Press, Inc.

Cronbach, L.J., and Associates (1980). *Toward reform of program evaluation: Aims, methods, and institutional arrangements.* San Francisco: Jossey-Bass.

Cross, T.L., Bazron, B.J., Dennis, K.W., & Isaacs, M.R. (1989). *Toward a culturally competent system of care,* Vol. I. A monograph on effective services for minority children who are severely emotionally disturbed. Washington, DC: Georgetown University Childhood. Development Center, CASSP Technical Assistance Center.

Deming, W.E. (1986). *Out of the crisis.* Cambridge, MA: MIT Press.

Dresser, K. (2007), *STARS CS Quarterly CQI Council Proceedings.* Oakland, CA: Stars Behavioral Health Group.

Doyle, M., & Strauss, D. (1993). *How to make meetings work.* New York: Berkley Books.

Fetterman, D.M., Kaftarian, A.J., & Wandersman, A. (Eds.). (1996). *Empowerment evaluation: Knowledge and tools for self-assessment and accountability.* Thousand Oaks, CA: Sage.

Gabor, A. (1992). *The man who discovered quality: How W. Edwards Deming brought the quality revolution to America.* New York: Penguin.

Gabor, A., & Grinnell, R. (1994). *Evaluation and quality improvement in the human services.* Boston: Allyn & Bacon.

Gastil, J. (1993). *Democracy in small groups: Participation, decision-making, and communication.* Philadelphia: New Society Publishers.

Ginavan, R., & Jozwiak, T. (1993). *Self determination: A critical element in transition planning.* In R. Fry & W. Garner (Eds.), Sixth national forum on issues in vocational assessment (pp. 292–320). New York: NY University Press.

Gluckman, P., & Reynolds-Roome, D. (March 1990). *Everyday heroes: From Taylor to Deming: The journey to higher productivity.* Knoxville, TN: SPC Press, Inc.

Fixsen, D.L., Naoom, S.F., Blasé, K., Friedman, R.M., & Wallace, F. (2005). *Implementation research: A synthesis of the literature.* Tampa, FL: University of South Florida, Louis de la Parte Florida Mental Health Institute, The National Implementation Research Network (FMHI Publication #231).

Hammer, M., & Champy, J.A. (1993). *Reengineering the corporation: A manifesto for business revolution.* New York: Harper.

Hammond, S.A., & Royal, C. (Eds.). (2001). *Lessons from the field: Applying appreciative inquiry.* Plano, TX: Thin Books Publishing Co.

Helgesen, S. (1995). *The web of inclusion.* New York: Doubleday.

Henrich, N., & Gyamfi, P. (2006). *Youth involvement in systems of care: Youth and youth coordinator's perspectives.* 18th Annual Conference Proceedings—A System of Care for Children's Mental Health: Expanding the Research Base. Research and Training Center for Children's Mental Health, Tampa, Florida.

Hernandez, M., & Hodges, S. (2003). *Crafting logic models for systems of care: Ideas into action: Vol. 1. Making children's mental health services successful series.* Tampa,

FL: University of South Florida, Louis de la Parte Florida Mental Health Institute, Department of Child and Family Studies.

Hospital Corporation of America. *Hospitalwide quality improvement process, strategy for improvement: FOCUS-PDCA.* Nashville: Hospital Corporation of America, 1989.

Iacafono, D. (2001) *Meetings of the minds: A guide to successful meeting facilitation.* Berkeley, CA: MIG Communications.

Iowa Department of Human Services. (2007). *Family team decision making: Evaluation handbook.* DesMoines: Publication of the Iowa Department of Human Services.

Individuals with Disabilities Education Improvement Act (IDEA) of 2004, PL 108-446, 20 U.S.C. §§ 1400 *et seq.*

Isaacs, W. (1999). *Dialogue and the art of thinking together.* New York: Doubleday.

Kahane, A. (2004). *Solving tough problems: An open way of talking, listening and creating new realities.* San Francisco: Berrett-Koehler Publishers, Inc.

Kaner, S., Lind, L., Toldi, C., Fisk, S., & Berger, D. (2007) *Facilitator's guide to participatory decision-making.* San Francisco: Jossey-Bass.

Kelsey, D., & Plumb, P. (2004). *Great meetings! Great results.* Portland, ME: Great Meetings, Inc.

Koroloff, N.M. (1990). Moving out: Transition policies for youth with serious emotional disabilities. *Journal of Mental Health Administration, 17*(1), 78–86.

Lyons, J. (1999). *Child and adolescent needs and strengths: An information integration tool for children and adolescents with mental health challenges.* Winnetka, IL: Buddin Praed Foundation.

Mayeske, G.W., & Lambur, M.T. (2001). *How to design better programs: A staff centered stakeholder approach to program logic modeling.* Crofton, MD: The Program Design Institute.

Merkel-Holguin, L., Nixon, P., & Burford, G. (2003). Learning with families: A synopses of FGDM research and evaluation in child welfare. *Protecting Children, 18*(1&2), 2, 11.

Messick, S. (1995). Validity of psychological assessment: Validation of inferences from persons' responses and performances as scientific inquiry into score meaning. *American Psychologist, 50*(9), 741–749.

Patton, M.Q. (1997). *Utilization focused evaluation: The new century text.* Thousand Oaks, CA: Sage.

Pecora, P.J., Seelig, W.R., William, R., Zirps, F.A., & Davis, S.M. (1996). *Quality improvement and evaluation in child and family services: Managing into the next century.* Washington, DC: CWLA Press.

Pennell, J., & Burford, G. (1999). *Family group decision making: Outcome report and summary.* Englewood, CO: American Humane Association.

Senge, P. (2006). *The fifth discipline: The art and practice of the learning organization.* New York: Doubleday.

Shore, N., Wirth, J., Cahn, K., Yancey, B., & Gunderson, K. (2001). *Long term and immediate outcomes of family group conferencing in Washington state.* Bethlehem, PA: International Institute for Restorative Practices.

Stroul, B.A., & Friedman, R.M. (1994). *A system of care for children and youth with severe emotional disturbances* (Rev. ed.). Washington, DC: Georgetown University Childhood Development Center, CASSP Technical Assistance Center.

Thomas, K.L., Berzin, S.C., & Cohen, E. (2005). Fidelity of family group decision making: A Content analyses of family conference and case plans in a randomized treatment study. *Protecting Children, 19*, 4.

U.S. Department of Health and Human Services. (1992). *The challenge of participatory research: Preventing alcohol-related problems in ethnic communities.* Rockville, MD: U.S. Department of Health and Human Services, Substance Abuse and Mental Health Services Administration, Center for Substance Abuse Prevention.

U.S. Department of Health and Human Services. (2001). *Mental health: Culture, race, and ethnicity—A supplement to mental health: A report of the Surgeon General.* Rockville, MD: U.S. Department of Health and Human Services, Substance Abuse and Mental Health Services Administration, Center for Mental Health Services.

Walker, J.S. (2008). *How and why does wraparound work: A theory of change.* Portland, OR: National Wraparound Initiative, Portland State University.

Walker, J.S., & Shutte, K.M. (2004). Practice and process in wraparound teamwork. *Journal of Emotional and Behavioral Disorders, 12*(3), 182–192.

Weiss, C.H. (1995). Nothing as practical as good theory: Exploring theory-based evaluation for comprehensive community initiatives. In J.P. Connell, A.C. Kubisch, L.B. Schorr, & C.H. Weiss, (Eds.), *New approaches to evaluating community initiatives.* New York: Aspin Institute.

ENDNOTES

[1] These include FOCUS for Find a process to improve, Organize to improve a process, Clarify what is known, Understand variation, and Select a process improvement; PDCA for Plan, Do, Check, Act; and, SWOT for Strengths, Weaknesses, Opportunities and Threat analyses.

[2] In contrast to widget-making, in the human service field, the radical re-engineering framework (Hammer & Champy, 1993) is not always or fully applicable because the field 1) values the benefits of building on existing strengths; 2) must manage within considerable financial constraints; and, 3) does not emphasize efficiency and productivity for profit.

[3] From the Center for Mental Health Services, Division of Service and Systems Improvement, Child, Adolescent, and Family Branch of the Substance Abuse and Mental Health Services Administration of the U.S. Department of Health and Human Services.

[4] The National Network on Youth Transition for Behavioral Health (NNYT) is focused on improving the outcomes of transition-age youth and young adults through system development, program implementation, and research. For more information, please visit the NNYT web site (http://lnnyt.fmhi.usf.edu) and the TIP system web site (http://tip.fmhi.usf.edu)

Future Focus
Advancing the Transition Agenda

Future Focus

Practice, Program, System, Policy, and Research

Deanne K. Unruh and Hewitt B. "Rusty" Clark

"My involvement as the Youth Coordinator at the Options Transition Program has been just as therapeutic for me as it has for the youth in the program. I've been given the opportunity to take the most negative things in my life and turn them into something positive for other young people. I used to sit around and wonder what I should do with my time and with my life. Now I don't have time to wonder—I'm too busy sorting through all of the opportunities that have developed for me. I have purpose in my life— I'm finally alive again."

—Melanie Green, Mental Health Recovery Coordinator,
Vancouver Washington

Our programmatic and research efforts on transition to adulthood issues have been inspired greatly by the youth and young adults we have met and interacted with along their and our journeys. We have learned from their voices and experiences—helping to inform our perspectives as well as our programmatic and research efforts. As we developed this handbook, we again turned to young adults and parents to join us in communicating our efforts to the field; thus, the chapters are co-authored by one or more of these key players. Their voices ensure that the service gaps, highlighted programs, and recommendations included in this handbook are not only grounded in best practices and research but also in the reality of the experiences and lives of young people and families. Their voices and footprints throughout have highlighted that their interests, dreams, and goals are typical of most young people and families, yet they are wrestling with largely invisible disabilities as they navigate through a treacherous obstacle course in an attempt to secure needed services and supports.

The time period between adolescence and adulthood is ever-changing and is reflective of our society as whole. Over the past two decades, the economy and social infrastructure of this nation have shifted and the age at which young people in general are becoming economically independent has increased to well into their twenties (Arnett, 2000; Settersten, Furstenberg, & Rumbaut, 2005). Unfortunately, policies and services targeting youth and young adults with emotional and/or behavioral difficulties (EBD) are not aligned with these new realities. This handbook reflects on these demographic shifts and provides current recommendations for programmatic, systemic, and policy change. It is our goal that the content of this handbook is providing the impetus for thoughtful decision making at the practitioner, program, system, and policy levels that will advance the availability and access of relevant and effective services and supports for youth and young adults with EBD and their families, ultimately improving their life outcomes.

We designed this handbook for readers to gain a new perspective on transition-age youth and young adults with EBD in several broad areas including

- Descriptions of service challenges that these young people and their families face—and the barriers that hinder the effectiveness of practitioners and educators in the provision of transition-related services and supports

- Knowledge of evidence-supported practices that have been demonstrated to improve the progress and outcomes of these young people through developmentally appropriate and appealing services and supports that are tailored to the individual's strengths, interests, needs, and goals

- Understanding that effective transition systems require an approach that supports youth and young adults in more of a *discovery* process than that of a *recovery* process, and that supports and services need to function across all relevant transition domains of employment/career, education, living situation, personal effectiveness and wellbeing, and community-life functioning

- Numerous examples of program applications that illustrate the evidence-supported practices as adopted and adapted to community settings by child/adult mental health, education, juvenile justice, and/or vocational rehabilitation

- Information and recommendations on planning, implementing, and sustaining transition systems along with the types of policies that will facilitate and support these community systems

In this chapter we provide an overall synthesis of the broad themes in each of the handbook's sections and then present recommendations for future programmatic, systemic, research, and policy action. We offer concrete suggestions, some of which can be acted on immediately and easily and others that may be long-term policy issues that will take multiple policy makers, consumers, advocates, researchers, and program leaders to shape into reality.

UNDERSTANDING THE SERVICE CHALLENGES FOR YOUTH AND YOUNG ADULTS WITH EBD

Service challenges for this population are a product of the often multi-faceted needs of these youth and young adults and are then further complicated by the service fragmentation within and across agencies—specifically the fragmentation between the child- and adult-serving agencies. As illustrated in the introduction, the employment, education, and community-life functioning outcomes for young adults with EBD are far worse than their peers with other types of disabilities and their peers in the general population. On the positive side, when comparing the first and second National Longitudinal Transition Studies (NLTS), improvements in outcomes across a decade were noted in youth identified with the special education diagnosis of *emotional disturbance*. Unfortunately, these outcomes still lag behind those outcomes of their peers with other disability categories (NLTS-2, 2005; Wagner et al., 1993).

In Chapter 1, Maryann Davis, Melanie Green, and Cheri Hoffman describe the service gaps within and across multiple categorical service systems that provide challenges for young people with EBD striving to achieve successful adult outcomes. The multiple categorical systems have varying eligibility requirements, inconsistent age restrictions for service receipt, and varying service philosophies and agency cultures often leading to developmentally inappropriate or unappealing services for these young people on the cusp between childhood and adulthood. The lack of a seamless, coordinated set of services makes it difficult for young people and families to navigate between the fragmented service systems to address the unique needs of each individual and their families.

Designing and Implementing Effective Transition Systems

In Chapter 2, Hewitt B. "Rusty" Clark and Karen Hart provide an up-to-date description on the Transition to Independence Process (TIP) model. This model is now an evidence-supported practice that has six published studies that demonstrate improvements in real-life outcomes across the transition domains of employment and career, education, living situation, personal effectiveness and well being, and community-life functioning. The TIP system is driven by seven guidelines and the associated practices for effectively engaging youth and young adults in a process that increases their self-sufficiency and accomplishment of short-term and long-term goals. The guidelines and practices that are used by the transition facilitators in coaching the young people are designed to help them 1) build protective factors through their engagement in productive arenas related to their interests, and 2) build social connections that assist in achieving productive engagement and, nuturing and strenthening relationships with some supportive people for life. These coaching and teaching processes assist young people in understanding the reciprocal nature of relationships and the benefits to them for building and maintaining a broad network of enduring social supports (e.g., friends, family members, intimate relationships). The transition facilitators are focused on assisting young people in "getting a life" that relates to the developmental markers of our society (e.g., dating, working, friends, career-related schooling, and their own sense of family) and supporting this trajectory with tailored services and supports that meet their needs, interests, and goals. The extent to which a network of connections are developed that increases both the social and economic growth of the youth as they move into adulthood determines how likely young adults are to experience positive long-term adult outcomes (Clark & Crosland, 2008).

Section II of this handbook highlights multiple community initiatives exemplifying transition services aligned with the principles of the TIP model. We selected these program examples to provide practical, yet tested methods to improve the progress and outcomes of youth and young adults with EBD. Each of the highlighted programs in these chapters used a transition facilitator or transition specialist either employed by local mental health providers, child welfare, school systems, or vocational rehabilitation. All programs were youth-centered and targeted the relevant needs and goals of youth and young adults across the transition domains. Each program's model was inclusive of the TIP guidelines, yet each chapter provided a unique application of particular guidelines within a local context.

An illustration of how youth and stakeholder participation was used in the planning and implementation of a community transition model is provided in Chapter 3 by DeDe Sieler, Spencer Orso, and Deanne K. Unruh. This program was initiated by a local mental health provider and uses a continuous improvement assessment process focusing on youth and program progress indicators to align the transition system to the service needs of the young people.

K. Brigid Flannery, Lauren Lindstrom, and Michael Torricellas provide two examples of model programs in Chapter 4 demonstrating how these transition strategies can be applied in high school and post-secondary community college settings through unique collaborations between schools and vocational rehabilitation. These two programs provide examples for how multiple agencies can work together to blend resources and funding yet not duplicate services, to support both high school and postsecondary students with EBD with a transition program targeting their goals in employment, education, and career.

The application of the TIP guidelines in working with young adults with serious mental health challenges is illustrated in Chapter 5. Marc A. Fagan and Wayne Munchel highlight tailored services that are accessible, appealing, and developmentally appropriate and that focus on a young adult's achievement of self-sufficiency based on their two separate and unique programs.

Chapter 6 focuses on strategies to engage youth involved in the juvenile system by developing problem-solving and social responsibility skills for their successful community adjustment after leaving a youth correctional setting. In this chapter, Deanne Unruh, Miriam G. Waintrup, and Tim Canter provide the lessons learned for developing collaborative transition-related services across multiple agencies that include the juvenile justice system, local education providers both high school and postsecondary, workforce investment boards, vocational rehabilitation, and finally addiction and mental health services.

The voices of young adults were the impetus for developing two consumer-focused programs described in Chapter 7. Lisa Galasso, along with other program supervisors and five young adults, co-authored this chapter, which highlights how peer mentoring programs can assist young people in learning new skills, setting and achieving goals, gaining greater self-sufficiency, establishing solid friendships, and learning leadership roles.

Practice, System, Quality Improvement, and Policy Issues

By providing specific examples of transition programs aligned with the TIP model, it was our hope to encourage community and state stakeholders to explore specific actions they could initiate to advance the development and implementation of transition systems in their communities. Unfortunately, such evidence-supported practices cannot be developed, implemented, and sustained in a vacuum. Transition systems require aligned policies and quality improvement evaluative processes to support the long-term sustainability of these programs and ensure their effectiveness.

The purpose of Section III of this handbook is to provide information on additional implementation issues, sustainability strategies, and finally, policy-related recommendations. As we have discussed in this Handbook, all transition-age youth and young adults are in a mode of discovery. They are experimenting with different appearances for individuation; different ways of relating to their peers, parents, and authority figures; different identities as to who they are; and exploring a variety of experiences and thrills. Youth and young adults with EBD are trying to navigate this same treacherous curvy road, and often place themselves in riskier situations or engage in even riskier behaviors than their peers without disabilities—who may be better equipped to assess and manage their level of risk exposure. In Chapter 8, Mason G. Haber, Hewitt B. "Rusty" Clark, and Ryan Parenteau presented a conceptual framework and procedures for conducting "prevention planning" to assist young people with EBD in avoiding or minimizing the negative impact of risk situations and behaviors.

Cheri Hoffman, Craig Anne, Heflinger, Michelle Athay, and Maryann Davis, in Chapter 9, tackle the complexities of current policies and funding systems across the multiple agencies of child welfare, mental health, juvenile and criminal justice systems, secondary schools, and postsecondary technical training and education. They recommend a policy with six tenets designed to improve access to the multiple systems that transition-age youth and young adults and their families must often negotiate.

A primary strategy for making certain services target the ever-changing needs of local communities is to implement a quality improvement process embedded in the operating practices of the program and local community. Karyn Dresser took the lead in writing Chapter 10, which provides practical suggestions for how to develop and embed quality assurance procedures within program initiatives to ensure that data-based decision making drives program improvement.

FUTURES FOCUS

What Can You Do to Advance Transition Systems?

Our goal for this handbook was to provide information, motivation, and solutions for improving the services and outcomes for transition-age youth and young adults with EBD. We have provided a framework of an evidence-supported transition model along with a host of program implementation examples from which readers can learn. We have shared strategies for implementation of programs, quality improvement, and policy reform. In this section we provide a set of concrete actions that each stakeholder group can use separately, and also collaboratively to advance the transition agenda. Some activities are simple, some complex; some can be accomplished in the short term, and some will take careful maneuvering across competing bureaucratic systems; yet we hope that each of you will choose to act. Without your individual and collective actions, improving practices, systems, and policies for transition-age youth and young adults will not advance and outcomes in general will remain unchanged. Your help is needed for the development of a seamless, coordinated transition system that addresses the myriad needs of transition-age youth and young people approaching this unique juncture into adulthood.

Several broad themes to improve transition service systems have emerged from these chapters. Advancing these themes will require efforts at the local, state, and federal levels to facilitate the development and sustainability of transition systems for improved outcomes for young people with EBD and their families. These system/funding/policy themes are

- Continuity of services and funding by redefining the age of transition from ages 14 or 16 through ages 25 or 29

- Access and coordination of child and adult services to promote progress across all transition domains

- Provision of developmentally appropriate, culturally competent, and appealing services that are individually tailored to the needs, interests, and goals of the young person

- Appropriate services, supports, and education for family members

- Emphasis on promoting "connections for life" and building economic capital with young people

- The need to build workforce capacity for personnel with expertise in working effectively with this population—including provisions for hiring young adults and parents in community transition systems

- Local, state, and federal support of evaluation and research to advance the development, implementation, and sustainability of effective and cost-efficient transition practices and systems

These themes emerged from prior work of Davis and Koyanagi (2005) and expanded for presentation here are based on more recent programmatic and policy knowledge and research. As validation of these same policy themes utility, policy recommendations from other organizations, federal agencies, and advocacy groups have reported many of these same policy reform themes. We then urge local, state, and federal entities to begin their work of implementing these recommendations to initiate the development of sustainable transition systems.

Policy Recommendations by Related Agencies

Here, we briefly share recommendations from several agencies and advocacy groups focused on transition-age youth and young adults. It is interesting to note that most of the core recommendations proposed by these parties are aligned with those that we listed above. In the National Council on Disability for Youth (NCD, 2008) report on the Rehabilitation Act and Outcomes for Transition-Age Youth, 11 recommendations were made to congress for implementation by the Rehabilitation Services and related agencies. Of these 11 recommendations many specific to the agency, 4 recommendations are directly aligned with our recommendations: 1) ensuring transition services were expanded to the age span of transition-age young people, 2) mandating the development and implementation of coordinated service-delivery approaches that would include the blending of funds across agencies serving transition-age youth, 3) conducting rigorous evaluation and research focused on the characteristic and programmatic service needs of transition-age young people, and finally, 4) increasing the workforce capacity of individuals serving transition-age young people (NCD, 2008).

Another recent NCWD-sponsored report by Woolsey and Katz-Leavey (2008) provides an overview of some transition programs that have been sustained and describes features that may contribute to their tenure and sustainability.

The Office of Disability and Employment Programs, a division of the U.S. Department of Labor, and the National Collaborative on Workforce and Disability for Youth, provided a guide for practitioners and policy makers for serving youth and young adults with mental health needs (Podmostko, 2007). Their aligned recommendations included the need for continuity of services across the transition-age group that provides for extended services with no interruptions in services across agencies. These coordinated sets of services also need to target the specific needs of the youth and include service options across the various transition domains (e.g., employment, education). The report also recommended that mental health and related services for young people needs to be expanded to as high as the age of 30 (Podmostko, 2007). Another recent NCWD-sponsored report by Woolsey and Katz-Leavey (2008) provides an overview of some transition programs that have been sustained and describes features that may contribute to their tenure and sustainability.

The National Center for Mental Health and Juvenile Justice has also weighed in with recommendations for serving youth with mental health needs involved in the juvenile justice system. Although their recommendations were more specific to the identification, diversion, and treatment of youth involved in the juvenile justice system, several of their recommendations parallel those in this handbook: 1) the alignment of services to the unique needs of the young person, 2) the need for provision of evidence-based programs, 3) increased collaboration across agencies, and 4) the critical need to evaluate programs and increase research targeting transition-age youth in their community adjustment process (Skowyra & Cocozza, 2007).

More recently, the Substance Abuse Mental Health Services Administration (SAMHSA) has released a grant program referred to as the *Healthy Transitions Initiative*. The purpose of this grant program is to set the occasion for seven states or tribes to examine ways for enhancing their policy and funding infrastructure for supporting and sustaining transition systems for youth and young adults with EBD and their families in their communities. Each state forms a partnership with at least one of its communities (e.g., several rural counties, an urban setting) for the development of a local transition system. This demonstration should serve to inform the state as to what aspects of the community/state/federal infrastructure is facilitative of services and supports for transition-age youth and which need reform. SAMHSA also conducts a *Policy Academy on Transition* that will assist the states in identifying and formulating recommendations for the types of policy and funding infrastructure that will be needed to facilitate and sustain community transition programs to improve the outcomes for youth and young adults with EBD and their families.

Calls for Action

To move our recommendations for improving transition systems and policies to reality, we provide concrete "calls for action" across the multiple stakeholder groups connected to transition-age youth and young adults and their families. Calls to actions to address each of our recommendations themes are embedded across the stakeholder groups described in the material that follows. Although we are providing examples of particular actions that various stakeholders can take, most of these actions will require collaborative efforts within and across stakeholder groups to achieve an improved transition service system and, ultimately, the life outcomes of young adults with EBD.

Policy-Related Decision Makers
at Local, State, and Federal Levels

Multiple actions are necessary to improve the policies that affect transition-age youth and young adults with EBD. First and foremost, policy makers must initiate policies that support continuity of services and blended funding streams across ages for transition-age youth and young adults. Redefining the age of adulthood can support the provision of a seamless service delivery system from ages 14 or 16 through the age of 25 or even 29 (Chapter 1, 2, & 9). As described throughout this handbook, the age of adulthood is measured in large part by the ability for individuals to be economically independent. Policies must reflect the new reality that economic independence is typically not occurring until individuals reach at least their mid-20s in today's society (Arnett, 2000; Settersten et al., 2005), and services should be aligned to this demographic shift.

Second, a focus on access and coordination between and across the multiple child- and adult-serving entities needs to be implemented to ensure access to relevant services across various transition domains. One strategy for states is to require Memoranda of Understandings (MOUs) between state agencies such as child welfare, state departments of education, child and adult mental health systems, and vocational rehabilitation or workforce investment boards (Podmostko, 2007; Unruh & Bullis, 2005). Components of the MOU could include strategies for defining each agency's service responsibility in order to blend resources and funds without duplicating services. Other components to the MOU could include strategies for aligning definitions for services, refining and aligning eligibility requirements, defining a common method for sharing of information meeting current state and federal guidelines, and strategies for increasing access of services across the various agencies (Goldman, Stroul, Huang, & Koyanagi, 2008; Unruh, Waintrup, & Canter, in press).

Federal, state, and local level policy makers can promote the initiation of appropriate transition-age services and supports by requiring and funding evaluations of the impact of services conducted by their relative agencies. To foster sustainability and embed program improvement strategies, local or state contracts targeting transition-age young people can require that 10%–15% of the contract be dedicated solely to quality assurance and evaluation activities. In addition, states and programs should be encouraged to conduct cost-benefit analyses of the implementation of transition systems and report findings to legislators to ensure continued evidence to sustain funding for transition-age youth and young adults with EBD and their families.

Personnel development is needed to train and coach staff members in the provision of evidence-supported transition practices and systems (e.g., supported employment, TIP model). Professional development will increase the workforce capacity of providing quality services. Policy makers can work with existing agencies and institutions of higher education to increase the level of preservice and in-service professional development for individuals currently or planning to work with transition-age young people (Dodge & Huang, 2008).

Policies need to address building supportive connections for life and encouraging greater economic self-sufficiency for young adults with EBD (Clark & Crosland, 2008). An essential feature of effective work with these youth and young adults is to assist them in building social and economic capital. As the TIP model emphasizes, a focus must be on facilitating young people's interpersonal skills and connections with others in ways that build a social network that will endure across time. Economic capital can be built through young people being supported in the development of funds that position them for pursuing goals, such as enrolling in a vocational/technical training program, securing the tools for working in a trade, going to college, or gaining access to affordable housing. A young adult's "nest egg" could be built through the aid of such strategies as individual development accounts (see Chapter 9) and scholarships for community college or vocational/technical training. Similarly, supports and services targeting job and career development (e.g., work apprenticeships, vocational rehabilitation funding of tuition/books or required job tools) prepare young adults for improved short-term and long-term economic independence (Waintrup & Unruh, 2008).

Program Managers/Administrators

Program managers/administrators must serve as champions and lead advocates for their young people and program personnel. One of the primary responsibilities of a program administrator is to ensure that evidence-supported practices, such as the TIP model, are being implemented with fidelity for transition-age young people to achieve improved progress and outcomes. Program administrators must value, support, and conduct quality assurance and evaluation activities in their programs to make certain that 1) evidence-supported services are being implemented as intended, 2) the transition system is meeting the needs of the young people and families being served, and 3) they target program improvement for sustaining high-quality services across time. Quality assurance and continuous improvement activities as described in Chapter 10 must be infused into all elements of the program and involve program personnel, youth served by the program, and parents and advocates in the quality assurance process. To promote the longevity and continuity of services, sustainability strategies need to be implemented early in program development (Clark, Deschênes, et al., 2008; Sailor, Wolf, Hoon Choi, & Roger, 2008; Woolsey & Katz-Leavy, 2008). Often, these sustainability activities will include partnering with the other agencies requisite in providing services in one or more the transition domains relevant in supporting youth's advancement to adulthood (Unruh, Waintrup, & Canter, in press). It is particularly significant when an agencies' services and supports span seamlessly from child-serving (e.g., child welfare, children's mental health, special education, juvenile justice) to adult-serving (e.g., adult mental health, vocational rehabilitation, postsecondary education, housing).

Program managers/administrators are directly responsible for the program personnel who provide direct service to the transition-age young people. Personnel should be hired based on their commitment to transition-age young people and professionalism (e.g., willingness to learn new practices; not personalizing everything that young people say; maintaining appropriate boundaries; comfortable working with youth- and family-friendly settings in the community). Position descriptions need to provide clear expectations of the level of youth-focused services provided to youth and young adults as part of the program's service delivery model. These personnel also need to have the benefit of supervisors who are competent and have time to provide ongoing training and coaching to ensure that program personnel are using developmentally appropriate and appealing practices and services with their youth and young adults on their caseload (e.g., Case-Based Reviews; periodic field-based coaching; see Chapter 2 and Rotto, McIntyre, & Serkin, 2008). Committed personnel need adequate compensation in order to maintain these staff and increase the longevity of highly trained staff within the program—since continuity of personnel is integral to a well-operating and sustaining program, and to serving youth and young adults effectively.

Program administrators must also be committed to providing culturally appropriate and gender specific services. Several programmatic strategies supportive of this initiative can include 1) actively recruiting and retaining multiethnic, multiracial, multi-linguistic staff representative of the community and young people in the program community, 2) providing ongoing staff training to support the development of cultural competence, and 3) including measures of cultural competence in the quality assurance process (Chapter 10; Hernandez & Isaacs, 1998; Podmostko, 2007).

A commitment to youth voice and choice is also imperative to the development, implementation, and sustaining of transition systems.

Program administrators and other transition program personnel should solicit and value the input from youth and young adults as well as parents and parent advocates. Soliciting involvement from parents and young adults in the quality assurance process is important. In addition, appointing parents or young people to serve specific roles on program boards and committees can help ensure that all voices and perspectives in the community are heard. The hiring of young adults as peer mentors or peer counselors and parents as family support specialists can advance one's program immeasurably. Participation of these individuals should be culturally and gender reflective of the diversity of consumers served within the program (Clark, Deschênes et al., 2008, Chapter 7).

Program administrators must also serve as primary lobbyists to local and state policy makers for the creation of transition systems. Administrators can serve as the catalysts to inform policy makers by identifying the local barriers to service provision to transition-age youth and young adults. Administrators can additionally provide strategies for efficient service collaboration across and within multiple agencies. Advocacy efforts are advanced most significantly by having a strategic plan and efforts being undertaken collaboratively by young people, parents, program supervisors, and administrators (Chapters 2 and 10).

Transition Program Personnel and Partnering Agency Personnel

Program personnel working directly with transition-age youth and young adults are essential to the engagement and outcomes for the young people that they serve. Most important, program personnel need to embrace the program model being adopted for the transition system, and they need to be willing to learn and apply the associated practices. Balancing the role of facilitating the success of young people while ensuring that these young people are in charge of their transition plans is a juggling act—but one that pays high dividends. Youth and young adults are more in a discovery mode, than a recovery mode. The discovery mode can cross all transition domains of employment/career, education, living situation, personal effectiveness and wellbeing, and community-life functioning. Transition program personnel and their partners at other agencies need to be able to provide exploration and services/supports across the transition domains that are relevant to a young person at a particular point in time.

Transition personnel must also be advocates for and actively participate in the system's quality assurance and evaluation activities. These evaluative activities may include assessments of service needs, service utilization, periodic assessments of personnel activities, tracking progress and outcomes of young people, and measures of program fidelity. As described in Chapter 10, participation and support of continuing quality improvement efforts is not feasible without a commitment to professionalism among all transition program personnel and the other stakeholders.

Parents, Family Members, and Family Advocates

The role of parents and other family members is to provide support as key players in young people's transition process. For young people with EBD, family may be defined quite broadly and include extended family members, foster care, friends of the family, and other key persons who provide positive support for the young person. Involvement in the transition planning and implementation process is critical; yet family members and advocates must honor the need and voice of the young adult to build and practice independence to achieve greater self-sufficiency.

Parents and other advocates do not need to limit their involvement with their specific young person but can also become involved in the quality assurance and evaluation activities of the local transition system. They can also bring authentic value to personnel training and technical assistance—and help in expanding the base of community stakeholders to ensure cultural representation within and across these groups. Parents, family members, and other advocates can also lobby local, state, and federal policy makers to ensure that these decision makers maintain transition-age young people as a priority.

Youth and Young Adults

Youth and young adults with EBD are the central focus of the entire transition process (Matarese, Carpenter, Huffine, Lane, & Paulson, 2008). Young people need to be encouraged and skills developed to take charge of their own transition plans. As young adults progress through their transition process, they can become role models, and through peer mentoring provide first-account information to other young people just starting the transition pathway (Chapter 2–7). Youth and young adults can also actively participate in the continuous quality improvement efforts in their program (Chapter 10). It is their voice and experiences that provide the authenticity of service provision—helping to ensure that relevant services and supports are accessible, developmentally appropriate, appealing, and effective.

Program Evaluators and Researchers

Research on transition issues and on effective services and policies that provide improved adult outcomes is needed. Through 2009, research funding and research publication on these transition topics has been limited. However, some progress is being made. In a special issue of the

Journal of Behavioral Health Services and Research, several significant research articles on the transition to adulthood were presented and contribute to our knowledge base regarding service utilization across different age groupings, strategies for building social support networks, interventions for special populations, and progress and outcome findings related to transition systems (Clark, Koroloff, Geller, & Sondheimer, 2008), The guest editors of this special issue also recommended four areas of research requisite in advancing the knowledge-base of the field. This taxonomy of types of studies deserves to be revisited here and includes

1. Studies of population characteristics, service utilization, and developmental trajectories of youth and young adults with EBD

2. Research on the development and adaptation of components of service

3. Research on the impact of a service system

4. Research on the implementation of effective program components or transition service systems (Clark, Koroloff, et al., 2008)

With these types of studies, we can further understand the unique developmental process for youth and young adults with EBD as they transition to adulthood. It is critical to further create and test various service components targeting this developmental process on the cusp between adolescence and adulthood. Impact studies are needed to measure the efficacy of programs and also on shifting implementation of effective transition models to scale with fidelity.

All of these studies and evaluation efforts speak to the need for more systematic attention to the development and validation of process, fidelity, and outcome instrumentation. In this handbook, we described the Adult Needs and Strength Assessment (ANSA)–Transition Version as an assessment instrument, the Transition System Fidelity Protocol or probes to determine the integrity to which a program model is being implemented, and the Transition to Adulthood Program Information System (TAPIS) Progress Tracker for tracking the progress or difficulty that youth and young adults are making across the transition domains over time (refer to Chapters 2 & 10). Related to progress and outcome tracking instruments, it is important that we examine information on developmentally relevant indicators of career exploration such as job shadowing, work practicum, and coursework at the community college. We also need to better understand the typical progression of progress and outcomes across the transition period. For example, what are the typical series of job entrances/exits, arrest rates, postsecondary education experienced by youth and young adults without disability (Wagner & Davis, 2006). Clearly, these efforts are going to require state, federal, and foundation funding of additional evaluation/research efforts to advance these transition-related efforts.

Program evaluators and researchers also are needed to collaborate with local and state agencies to participate in systematic evaluations of service systems to test program efficacy with these youth and young adults. Evaluators can support various service sectors' process evaluations and quality assurance practices to help measure the fidelity of implementation of various programs, but also to assist in the program improvement process. In addition, researchers can participate as external evaluators to ensure that objective third-party assessments are completed on developing and sustaining transition programs (Friedman & Israel, 2008).

Evaluators and researchers also can guide and participate in the personnel development process to ensure the knowledge and competencies necessary for working with youth and young adults with EBD are based on the evidence-supported practices driven by the current research base. Competency-based professional development is needed in preservice arenas (e.g., community colleges and universities) responsible for training future personnel and also for current transition-age service personnel already in the field.

Finally, evaluators and researchers can contribute greatly to advocate for continued policy and service development grounded in field-based research. It is only through this new evidence that ongoing gaps in service structures and the developmental needs of this population can be met. However, data alone are not the only powerful advocacy tool. A researcher's testimony can be strengthened enormously by having a parent and/or young adult co-present. A youth and parent can add authenticity to the issue. A parent advocate can also state that she represents "x" number of families in the state or "y" number of families nationally.

CONCLUSION

We fully realize that many of these calls for action will require substantial reform at the federal, state, and local levels. However, these actions are grounded in the fact that it is more cost effective to facilitate a young person's transition into a productive, self-sufficient adulthood than to bear the long-term economic and societal costs related to a lifetime of involvement with adult service systems and other types of public support (Clark, Pschorr, Wells, Curtis, & Tighe, 2004). By addressing the needs and goals of these young people during their transition period, these individuals can be positioned to be productively engaged in employment and community; contribute to local, state, and federal tax bases; and function with an appropriate balance between independence and interdependence.

We are hopeful that this handbook contributes to your understanding of and efforts to advance the planning, development, implementation, and sustainability of effective transition systems for youth and young adults with EBD and their families. Improved real life outcomes can be achieved with these young people—enabling them to live beyond their emotional and behavioral challenges and to navigate their own pathways in work, relationships, family, career, and community involvement. After all, is this not the hope for all our citizenry?

REFERENCES

Arnett, J.J. (2000). Emerging adulthood. A theory of development from the late teens through the twenties. *American Psychologist, 55*(5), 469–480.

Clark, H.B., & Crosland, K. (2008). Social and life skills development: Preparing and facilitating youth for transition into young adult roles. In B. Kerman, A.N. Maluccio, & M. Freundlich (Eds.), *Achieving permanence for older children and youth in foster care* (pp. 313–336). New York: Columbia University Press.

Clark, H.B., Deschênes, N., Sieler, D., Green, M., White, G., & Sondheimer, D. (2008). Services for youth in transition to adulthood in systems of care. In B.A. Stroul & R.M. Friedman (series Eds.) & B.A. Stroul & G.M. Blau (Vol. Eds.), *Systems of care in children's mental health: Vol. 9. The system of care handbook: Transforming mental health services for children, youth, and families* (pp. 517–544). Baltimore: Paul H. Brookes Publishing Co.

Clark, H.B., Koroloff, N., Geller, J., & Sondheimer, D.L. (2008). Research on transition to adulthood: Building the evidence base to inform services and supports for youth and young adults with serious mental health disorders. *Journal of Behavioral Health Services and Research, 35*(4), 365–372.

Clark, H.B., Pschorr, O., Wells, P., Curtis, M., & Tighe, T. (2004). Transition into community roles for young people with emotional behavioral difficulties: Collaborative systems and program outcomes. In D. Cheney (Ed.), *Transition of secondary approaches for positive outcomes* (pp. 201–226). Arlington, VA: The Council for Children with Behavioral Disorders and the Division of Career Development and Transition, Divisions of the Council for Exceptional Children.

Davis, M., & Koyanagi, C. (2005). *Summary of Center for Mental Health Services Youth Transition policy meeting; National experts panel*. Rockville, MD: U.S. Substance Abuse and Mental Health Services Administration, Center for Mental Health Services.

Dodge, J.M., & Huang, L.N. (2008). Workforce implications: Issues and strategies for workforce development. In B.A. Stroul & G.M. Blau (Eds.), *The system of care handbook: Transforming mental health services for children, youth, and families* (pp. 643–662). Baltimore: Paul H. Brookes Publishing Co.

Friedman, R.M. & Israel, N. (2008). Research and evaluation implications: Using research and evaluation to strengthen systems of care. In B.A. Stroul & G.M. Blau (Eds.), *The system of care handbook: Transforming mental health services for children, youth, and families* (pp. 689–705). Baltimore: Paul H. Brookes Publishing Co.

Goldman, S.K., Stroul, B.A., Huang, L.N., & Koyanagi, C. (2008). Policy implications: New directions in child and adolescent mental health. In B.A. Stroul & G.M. Blau (Eds.), *The system of care handbook: Transforming mental health services for children, youth, and families* (pp. 663–688). Baltimore: Paul H. Brookes Publishing Co.

Hernandez, M., & Isaacs, M.R. (1998). *Promoting cultural competence in children's mental health services*. Baltimore: Paul H. Brookes Publishing Co.

Materese, M., Carpenter, M., Huffine, C., Lane, S., & Paulson, K. (2008). Partnerships with youth for youth-guided systems of care. In B.A. Stroul & G.M. Blau (Eds.), *The system of care handbook: Transforming mental health services for children, youth, and families* (pp. 275–300). Baltimore: Paul H. Brookes Publishing Co.

National Council on Disability. (NCD). (2008, October). *The Rehabilitation Act: The outcomes of transition-age youth*. Washington DC: National Council on Disability.

National Longitudinal Transition Study-2 (2005). Wave 3—Parent/Youth Survey [Online data table]. Retrieved August 6, 2008, from http://www.nlts2.org/data_tables/tables/12/np3U5_Anyfrm.html

Podmostko, M. (2007). *Tunnels and cliffs: A guide for workforce development practitioners and policymakers serving youth with mental health needs*. Washington, DC: National Collaborative on Workforce and Disability for Youth, Institute for Educational Leadership.

Rotto, K., McIntyre, J.S., & Serkin, C. (2008). Strengths-based, individualized services in systems of care. In B.A. Stroul & G.M. Blau (Eds.), *The system of care handbook: Transforming mental health services for children, youth, and families* (pp. 401–435). Baltimore: Paul H. Brookes Publishing Co.

Sailor, W., Wolf, N., Hoon Choi, J., & Roger, B. (2008). Sustaining positive behavior support in a context of comprehensive school reform. In W. Sailor, G. Dunlap, G. Sugai, & R. Horner (Eds.), *Handbook of positive behavior support* (pp. 633–669). New York: Springer.

Settersten, R.A., Furstenberg, F.F., & Rumbaut, R.G. (Eds.). (2005). *On the frontier of adulthood: Theory, research and public policy*. Chicago: University of Chicago Press.

Skowyra, K., & Cocozza, J. (2007). *Blueprint for change: A comprehensive model for the identification and treatment of youth with mental health needs in contact with the juvenile justice system*. Delmar, NY: National Center for Mental Health & Juvenile Justice, Policy Research Associates, Inc.

Unruh, D., & Bullis, M. (2005). Community and self-report of the facility-to-community transition needs for adjudicated youth with disabilities. *Career Development for Exceptional Individuals, 28*, 67–79.

Unruh, D., Waintrup, M., & Canter, T. (in press). Project STAY OUT: A transition project of formerly incarcerated adolescents with special education and mental health disorders. In D. Cheney (Ed.), *Transition of students with emotional or behavioral disabilities from school to community: Current approaches for positive outcomes* (2nd ed). Arlington, VA: Council for Exceptional Children, Division of Career Development and Transition.

Wagner, M., Blackorby, J., Cameto, R., Hebbeler, K., & Newman, L. (1993, December). *The transition experiences of young people with disabilities: A summary of findings from the National Longitudinal Transition Study of special education students*. Menlo Park, CA: SRI.

Wagner, M. & Davis, M. (2006). How are we preparing students with emotional disturbance for the transition to adulthood: Findings from the National Longitudinal Transition Study-2. *Journal of Emotional and Behavior Disorders, 14,* 86–98.

Waintrup, M., & Unruh, D. (2008, June). Career development programming strategies for transitioning incarcerated adolescents to the world of work. *Journal of Correctional Education, 59,* 127–144.

Index

Page numbers followed by *f* indicate figures; those followed by *t* indicate tables; and those followed by *n* indicate notes.

Abuse and neglect, 173
Adjudicated/incarcerated juveniles
  characteristics of, 189–190, 200–202
  gender differences, 191
  number of, 189
  outcomes data, 12, 14*t*–15*t*, 190
  recidivism, 190, 191
  service provision challenges,
    190–191
  Thresholds Young Adult Program,
    168
  Transition-Age Youth program, 168
  transition to adulthood and, 38–39,
    201–202
  see also Juvenile Justice system;
    Project STAY OUT
Administrators, recommendations
  for, 335–337
Adult Needs and Strength
  Assessment–Indiana
  (ANSA-Indiana), 72, 307
Adult Needs and Strength
  Assessment–Transition Version (ANSA-T), 72, 307, 339
Adventure Based Counseling (ABC),
  228
Advocacy, importance of, 77, 85, 98,
  338
Age-based policies, 29–32, 37*t*,
  264–265, 283

Aggression Replacement Therapy
  (ART), 51, 106
Allegheny County, Pennsylvania,
  System of Care Initiative,
  306–307, 312–313, 315–316,
  317
Ansell-Casey Life Skills Assessments
  (ACLSA), 72, 81
Appealing services, need for, 27,
  39–42, 48, 61, 62, 107, 265–267
  see also Engaging young people
Assessment
  functional assessment, 51, 59, 70,
    106
  Options program, 123–124
  strength-discovery assessment,
    52–53, 70–73
  traditional and standardized
    assessments, 71
  Transition to Independence
    Process, 70–73
  see also Program evaluation

Bazelon Center for Mental Health
  Law, 279
Behavior analysis, 51, 59, 70, 106
Behavioral difficulties, *see* Emotional
  and/or behavioral difficulties;
  Risk behavior

Bipolar disorders, 172
Bridge of Central Massachusetts,
    211–212, 223
Bridge Peer Support Program (PSP)
    barriers, 214–215
    lessons learned, 222–223
    peer specialists and peer support
        workers, 212, 213t–214t,
        215–216, 222–223
    principles and values, 211, 216–221
    program features, 216–221
    program impact, 221–222
    structure and services, 211–212,
        214–216
Bridges from Jobs to Careers grants,
    276

California, foster youth transition to
    adulthood, 272
CANS, see Child and Adolescent
    Needs and Strengths
Career-track training, as transition
    domain, 61f, 99f, 100
Career Workforce Skills Training
    (CWST)
    Occupational Skills Training
        Program, 147, 148
    outcomes, 152, 152t
    overview, 146–147
    participants, 147
    services provided, 147–150
    successful program features,
        153–155, 156t, 157
Case-Based Reviews, 81–82, 111
Casey Family Programs, 72
    see also Jim Casey Youth Opportu-
        nity Initiative
Catholic Community Services (Clark
    County, Washington), 119
Cellular technology, as prompting
    strategy, 74
Center for Mental Health Services of
    the Substance Abuse and Men-
    tal Health Services Adminis-
    tration (CMHS/SAMHSA),
    see Substance Abuse and Men-
    tal Health Services Adminis-
    tration
Centers for Disease Control and Pre-
    vention (CDC), 236
Chafee Assessment, 72, 81

Chafee Foster Care Independent Liv-
    ing Program, 271, 280
Checklists/probes, in quality man-
    agement, 310
Child and Adolescent Needs and
    Strengths (CANS), 72, 306
Child welfare system, 271–273
Children in Community Study
    (CICS), 9, 14t–15t
Children's Health Insurance Program
    (CHIP), 282
CICS, see Children in Community
    Study (CICS)
Clark County, Washington, 33, 118,
    119
    see also Options program
CMHS/SAMHSA, see Center for
    Mental Health Services of the
    Substance Abuse and Mental
    Health Services Administra-
    tion; Substance Abuse and
    Mental Health Services
    Administration
Co-morbidity of diagnoses
    incarcerated juveniles, 189–190
    mental illness and, 51, 86, 172
    outcomes data, 12, 14t–15t
    in Thresholds YAP and Village TAY
        Academy programs, 168
Coaching
    axioms for, 67, 177–178
    levels of in Transition to Indepen-
        dence Process, 110–111
Columbia River Mental Health
    Services, 118
Communication among agencies,
    see Coordinated services
Community-based learning, 74
Community colleges
    short-term training programs,
        142–143
    see also Career Workforce Skills
        Training; Postsecondary
        education
Community evaluation teams, 317
Community-life functioning
    goal examples, 80t
    mental illness and, 184–186
    as TIP transition domain, 61f, 99f,
        103
Community Mental Health Service
    Block Grants, 35

Community partnerships, Options program, 127
Competencies, *see* Skills development
Connecticut, services for transition-age youth, 270
Connections program (Clark County, Washington), 119
Contextual fit of interventions, 62
Continuity of services, need for, 27, 37*t*, 63, 256–257, 334
see also Coordinated services
Continuous quality improvement (CQI)
    data collection, 305–312
    engaging youth in, 312–317
    example, 291–293
    facilitation, 303–305
    information and communication flow, 299–300
    legislative mandates, 301–302, 334
    quality improvement teams, 292, 314–315
    rationale for, 293, 294–295
    resources, 300–302
    stakeholders, identifying and eliciting participation, 296–299
    system features, 295
    team steps, 305*f*
    Transition to Independence Process
        process and outcome measures, 81–83
        responsiveness and effectiveness, 78–83, 112
    values and principles, 293–294
Coordinated services
    as basic policy tenet, 27, 265
    case example, 35–36
    consequences of lack of, 4, 36–38, 278
    discontinuity among systems, 37*t*
    Memoranda of Understanding, 334
    need for, 33–34, 35–39, 62–64, 142
    recommendations, 61–65, 284, 332–333
    see also Continuity of services, need for
CQI, *see* Continuous quality improvement
Criminal involvement, *see* Arrested/incarcerated juveniles

Cultural differences
    between children and adult mental health services, 33–34
    youth cultures, 60, 179, 230
Culturally appropriate practices
    with juvenile offenders, 191
    Options program, 125–126, 134, 137–138
    recommendation for, 336
    Transition Age Support Initiative (TASI) program, 230
    transition facilitators, cultural competence of, 60
CWST, *see* Career Workforce Skills Training

Data collection systems
    avoiding Data Rich, Information Poor (DRIP), 311–312
    objectives of, 305–306
    performance indicator analysis, 306
    standardized tracking systems, 306–310
Demographic trends, 10–11, 265–266, 326, 334
Descriptive Outline of a Transition-Age Young Person, 82
Developmentally appropriate services, need for, 27, 34, 39–42, 61–62, 265–267
Discovery mode of young people, 54, 60, 174, 326, 330, 337
Diversity, *see* Culturally appropriate practices
DRIP (Data Rich, Information Poor), avoiding, 311–312
Drug use, *see* Prevention planning, Substance abuse

Early parenting, 12
    see also Pregnancy
EBD, *see* Emotional and/or behavioral difficulties
Economic independence, increased age of, 265–266, 326, 334
Education
    goal examples, 79*t*
    juvenile offenders, 191
    Project STAY OUT, 192–193, 195–196, 203*f*, 204*f*

Education—*continued*
  Transition Age Support Initiative
    program, 226
  as TIP transition domain, 61*f*, 99*f*,
    100
  see also Postsecondary education
Education for All Handicapped Chil-
    dren Act of 1975 (PL 94-142),
    273
Educational and Training Voucher
    (ETV) program, 271–272
Emerging adulthood, 265
Emotional and/or behavioral diffi-
    culties (EBD)
  case examples, 26–27, 29, 32,
    35–36, 39–40
  historical perspective, 25–26
  risk behavior vulnerability and,
    235, 237–239, 240*f*, 241–242
  terminology, 7–8
  see also Mental illness
Employment
  goal examples, 79*t*
  juvenile offenders, 191
  Options program, 123–124
  outcomes data, 10, 14*t*–15*t*
  Project STAY OUT, 195, 203*f*, 204*f*
  Thresholds Young Adult Program,
    168
  Transition Age Support Initiative
    program, 226
  Transition-Age Youth program, 168
  as TIP transition domain, 61*f*, 99*f*,
    100
  see also Vocational rehabilitation
Employment specialists, 84–85
  see also Professional roles
Engaging young people
  appealing services, need for, 27,
    39–42, 265–267
  mental illness, individuals with,
    175–179
  Options program, 120–121,
    129–130
  in quality improvement process,
    312–317
  risk behavior management,
    256–257
  Transition to Independence
    Process, 51–60, 95
Ensnarement process, 239, 240*f*

Evidence-supported practice
  evidence-supported handbook,
    purpose, 12
  Transition to Independence Process
    (TIP) model 13, 48, 86

*Facilitator's Guide to Participatory
    Decision-Making* (Kaner et al.),
    304
Families
  involvement of, 28, 33, 267, 338
  participation in Transition to Inde-
    pendence Process, 48, 56, 58,
    68, 83, 85
  terminology, 7–8
  young adults living with, 11,
    14*t*–15*t*
  see also Parents
FCIA, *see* Foster Care Independence
    Act of 1999
Federal Center for Mental Health Ser-
    vices, 269
Federal policies
  age and eligibility rules, 30–31
  child welfare, 271–273
  funding for programs, 279–281
  mental health services, 270–271
  quality improvement of programs,
    301–302
  recommendations and calls to
    action, 334
  special education, 273–276
Fidelity, 82–83, 308f, 309–310, 339
  see Transition Program Fidelity
    Assessment Protocol
Formal key players 52, 65t
  See Informal key players, Key
    players
Foster care, transition from, 271–273
Foster Care Independence Act of
    1999 (FCIA; PL 106-169), 271
Fostering Connections Act (PL
    110-351), 273
Function of behavior, 59, 248–249
Functional assessment, 51, 59, 70, 106
Funding considerations
  Career Workforce Skills Training,
    153–154
  federal support, 279–281
  Options program, 134

Project STAY OUT, 192–193
state support, 281–282
sustainability of programs,
    282–283
Transition to Independence
    Process, 112–113
unfunded quality improvement
    mandates, 301
Youth Transition Program,
    153–154
see also Policy
Futures planning, 48, 50, 52, 54–58,
    65, 67, 69, 95, 104–105
Planning partners and necessary
    connections 56–57, 105–106
See TIP core practices

Gender differences
adjudicated/incarcerated juve-
    niles, 191
recommendation for gender-
    specific services, 336
Genesis Club, 211, 223
Goals, setting and achieving
futures planning, 54–58
Options program, 124
outcome focus of TIP, 77–78,
    79*t*–80*t*, 80–83
Project STAY OUT, 194
Transition Age Support Initiative
    program, 225
Graduation from school
outcomes data, 10, 14*t*–15*t*
Thresholds Young Adult Program,
    168, 169*f*

Health insurance
Children's Health Insurance Pro-
    gram, 282
Medicaid, 30, 32, 34–35, 280–281
quality improvement applications,
    293, 321*n*1
uninsured children, 282
Healthy Transitions Act of 2008 (H.R.
    6375 and S. 3195), 270–271
Healthy Transitions Initiative, 333
High school graduation, *see* Gradua-
    tion from school
Higher Education Act of 1965 (PL
    89-329), 276

Higher Education Opportunity Act
    (PL 110-315), 275–276
Hospitalization, Thresholds Young
    Adult Program, 168–169, 170*f*,
    172
Housing, *see* Living situations
H.R. Bill 6375, *see* Healthy Transitions
    Act of 2008

IDEA, *see* Individuals with Disabili-
    ties Education Act Amend-
    ments of 1997; Individuals
    with Disabilities Education
    Act of 1990; Individuals with
    Disabilities Education Im-
    provement Act of 2004
Illinois Department of Child and
    Family Services (DCFs), 185
In-vivo teaching strategies, 50, 67,
    73–77, 97, 104
See TIP Core Practices
Independence, development of, 49
Independent living, *see* Living situa-
    tions
Independent living services
for foster care youth, 271
Project STAY OUT, 203*f*
Indiana Behavioral Health web site,
    307
Individual Development Accounts
    (IDAs), 281, 335
Individualized education programs
    (IEPs), need for transition
    goals, 38, 274
Individualized services, need for, 28,
    267
Individuals with Disabilities Educa-
    tion Act (IDEA) Amendments
    of 1997 (PL 105-17), 141–142,
    273
Individuals with Disabilities Educa-
    tion Act (IDEA) of 1990 (PL
    101-476), 273
Individuals with Disabilities Educa-
    tion Improvement Act (IDEA)
    of 2004 (PL 108-446), 38, 273,
    274, 301
Informal key players 52, 65*t*
See Formal key players, Key
    players

Interdependence, development of, 49
Interventions
    contextual fit, 62
    efficacy of for transition-age youth,
        41–42
    risk behavior, addressing, 240*f*,
        243–244
    targeted clinical interventions, 51,
        106
    see also specific programs

Jim Casey Youth Opportunity Initia-
        tive (JCYOI), 281
John H. Chafee Foster Care Indepen-
        dent Living Program, 271, 280
*Journal of Behavioral Health Services
        and Research*, 339
Juvenile Justice and Delinquency Pre-
        vention Act of 1974 (JJDPA),
        276–277
Juvenile Justice system
    effect on transition to adulthood,
        38–39
    policy considerations, 276–277
    see also Adjudicated/incarcerated
        juveniles
Juvenile Offenders, *see*
        Adjudicated/incarcerated
        juveniles

Key players 52, 65t
    see also informal key players,
        formal key players

Learned helplessness, 176
Living situations
    case example, 185–186
    goal examples, 79*t*
    mental illness and, 181, 183–186
    outcomes data, 11, 14*t*–15*t*
    residential facilities, 181, 183
    as TIP transition domain, 61*f*, 99*f*,
        100
Logic Model Team, University of
        South Florida, 298–299
Logic models, 298–299

Massachusetts, transition from child
        to adult mental health ser-
        vices, 268–269

Massachusetts Department of Mental
        Health (DMH), 210, 224
    see also Bridge Peer Support Pro-
        gram (PSP); Transition Age
        Support Initiative program
McGraw Center Study, 9, 14*t*–15*t*
Mediating differences, 50, 68–69, 96
Mediation with young people and
        other key players, 50
    See TIP core practices
Medicaid
    age-based eligibility rules, 30, 32,
        34–35, 280–281
    funding for transition-age youth,
        280–281
Medications, age-appropriate pre-
        scriptions, 40
Meetings, effective, 303
Memoranda of Understanding
        (MOUs), 334
Mental Health Block Grants, 30
Mental health system
    differences in adult and child
        systems, 32–35, 268
    policy considerations, 268–271
    recommendations for, 333
Mental illness
    case examples, 170, 171, 175–176,
        180, 185–186
    denial of, 174
    diagnostic considerations,
        172–173
    engagement, facilitating, 175–179
    incarcerated juveniles, 189–190,
        201
    prevalence, 172
    service delivery considerations,
        179–182, 209–210
    see also Emotional and/or behav-
        ioral difficulties
Mentors
    Options program, 125
    Transition to Independence
        Process, 83–85, 97–98
    see also Peer mentors
Miami-Dade County study, 9,
        14*t*–15*t*
Mosaic Network, 81, 308, 309
Motivation, *see* Engaging young
        people
Motivational Interviewing, 51, 106,
        255

Moving On (Bazelon Center for Mental Health Law), 279
Multiple diagnoses, *see* Comorbidity of diagnoses

National Adolescent and Child Treatment Study (NACTS), 9, 14*t*–15*t*
National Alliance on Mental Illness, 86
National Center for Children in Poverty, 281–282
National Center for Mental Health and Juvenile Justice, 333
National Child Welfare Resources Center for Youth Development (NCWRCYD), 272
National Collaborative on Workforce and Disability for Youth, 332
National Council on Disability for Youth (NCD), 332
National Federation of Families for Children's Mental Health, 86
National Institute of Mental Health (NIMH), 41
National Longitudinal Transition Studies (NLTS/NLTS-2), 9, 9*n*3, 10, 11, 14*t*–15*t*, 151, 151*t*, 327
National Network on Youth Transition for Behavioral Health (NNYT), 48, 64, 86, 131, 307, 321*n*4
  NNYT as purveyor of the TIP model, 86
  NNYT web site, 86
NCD, *see* National Council on Disability for Youth
NCWRCYD, *see* National Child Welfare Resources Center for Youth Development
Necessary connections, 56–57, 105–106
  see also Futures planning
New Freedom Commission on Mental Health, 210
New York, Office of Temporary Disability Assistance (OTDA), 281
NIMH, *see* National Institute of Mental Health

NLTS/NLTS-2, *see* National Longitudinal Transition Studies
NNYT, *see* National Network on Youth Transition for Behavioral Health
No Child Left Behind Act of 2001 (PL 107-110), 273–274
Nonstigmatizing services and supports in the TIP system, 61–64

Office of Disability and Employment Programs, 332
Office of Juvenile Justice and Delinquency Prevention, 194
Office of Vocational Rehabilitation Services (OVRS; Oregon), 144
Oklahoma, transition from child to adult mental health services, 269
One-Stop Centers, 199
Opportunity Passport, 281
Options program (Clark County, Washington)
  community partnerships, 127
  culturally appropriate practices, 125–126, 134, 137–138
  discharge criteria, 120, 121, 134
  engagement of youth, 120–121, 129–130
  evaluation of program impact, 131–132, 137
  identification and enrollment, 119–120
  intervention examples, 123–125
  lessons learned, 132–138
  mission and overview, 117–118
  operations manual, 128
  personal account, 121–123, 126–127, 129, 130–131, 133–134, 136–137, 139–139
  personnel roles, 127–129, 136
  population served, 118–119
  support sources, 132
  Youth House, 129–130
  see also TIP model
Oregon
  Career Workforce Skills Training, 146–150, 152, 152*t*, 153–155, 156*t*, 157

Oregon—*continued*
　Youth Transition Program,
　　144–146, 151, 151*t*, 153–155,
　　156*t*, 157
　see also Project STAY OUT; Project
　　SUPPORT
Oregon Department of Education
　(ODE), 191, 193–194
Oregon Youth Authority (OYA), 191,
　194
Outcome findings
　Poor outcomes for youth and
　　young adults with EBD, 8,
　　10–12, Table I.1
Outcome tracking, 311

Parents
　as advocates, 85
　as family support specialists, 337
　involvement of, 28, 33, 267, 338
　parenting components, 102
　participation in TIP, 56, 58, 68, 85
　support services for, 68
Partnerships for Youth Transition
　(PYT), 118, 131–132, 245–247,
　282
　see also Options program
Peer mentors
　Options program, 125
　paid positions, 313–314
　professional standards and
　　boundary expectations,
　　215–216
　recommendation for, 337
　Transition to Independence
　　Process, 83–84, 97
　willingness of, 186–187
　see also Bridge Peer Support Pro-
　　gram; Transition Age Support
　　Initiative program
Peer reviews, 300, 310–311
Peer support groups, 83–84
Performance indicators, tracking,
　301–302, 306, 310
Person-centered planning
　risk behavior management,
　　256–257
　TIP futures planning, 55–58
　traditional approach, 54–55
Personal effectiveness and well-
　being
　goal examples, 79*t*–80*t*

　as TIP transition domain, 61*f*, 99*f*,
　　101–102
Pioneering Transition Programs
　(Davis), 282
PL 89-329, *see* Higher Education Act
　of 1965
PL 94-142, *see* Education for All Hand-
　icapped Children Act of 1975
PL 101-476, *see* Individuals with Dis-
　abilities Education Act of 1990
PL 105-17, *see* Individuals with Dis-
　abilities Education Act
　Amendments of 1997
PL 105-220, *see* Rehabilitation Act
　Amendments
PL 106-169, *see* Foster Care Indepen-
　dence Act of 1999
PL 107-110, *see* No Child Left Behind
　Act of 2001
PL 107-133, *see* Promoting Safe and
　Stable Families Act of 2001
PL 108-446, *see* Individuals with Dis-
　abilities Education Improve-
　ment Act of 2004
PL 110-315, *see* Higher Education Op-
　portunity Act (PL 110-315)
PL 110-351, *see* Fostering Connections
　Act
Planning partners, 56–57, 105
　see also Futures planning
Policy
　age limits and eligibility issues,
　　29–32
　agency recommendations, 332–333
　basic tenets, 27–28, 264–268
　calls for action, 333–340
　federal policies, 30–31, 270–271
　recommendations, 331
　reform recommendations, 283–285
　state policies, 31–32, 268–270
　see also Funding considerations
Post-Arrest Diversion (PAD)
　program, 277
Postsecondary education
　benefits of, 142
　community college short-term
　　training programs, 142–143
　economic considerations, 335
　emotional and/or behavioral diffi-
　　culties, youth with, 275–276
　federal policy support, 275–276
　for foster youth, 272
　goal examples, 79*t*

lack of planning for, 38, 275
outcomes data, 10–11, 14*t*–15*t*
Transition Age Support Initiative
    program, 226
see also Vocational rehabilitation
Poverty levels, Medicaid criteria,
    34–35
Praed Foundation, 307
Pregnancy, 12, 14*t*–15*t*
Prevention Planning
    basis for, 244–245
    function of behavior, 59, 248–249
    guidelines, 250–255
    steps and techniques, 248–249
    supports, use of, 249–250
    survey of sites providing transition
        support, 245–247
    timing considerations, 249
    TIP core practices, 50, 59
    treatment and rehabilitation strate-
        gies, 255–256
Probes, in quality management, 310
Problem solving, development of,
    66–67, 66*f*
Professional roles
    Bridge Peer Support Program, 212,
        213*t*–214*t*, 215–216, 222–223
    Career Workforce Skills Training,
        153, 154
    consultants, 72
    desired characteristics, 336
    employment specialists, 84–85
    Options program, 127–129, 136
    paid youth peer advocates,
        313–314
    parole officers, 193, 198, 199
    program managers/administra-
        tors, 335–337
    Project STAY OUT, 193, 197–200,
        205–206
    recommendations for, 337–338
    training recommendations, 28, 53,
        66–67, 69, 77, 267–268, 335
    Transition Age Support Initiative
        program, 225
    transition facilitators, 50, 51, 61–62,
        64–65, 74–75, 109–110, 178
    youth coordinators, 313–314
    Youth Transition Program, 153, 154
    see also Peer mentors
Program evaluation
    Career Workforce Skills Training,
        154, 155, 156*t*

community evaluation teams, 317
Options program, 125, 131–132,
    137
recommendations, 338–340
Transition to Adulthood Program
    Information System, 78, 80–81
Transition to Independence
    Process, 78, 80–81
Youth Transition Program, 154,
    155, 156*t*
see also Continuous quality
    improvement
Program managers/administrators,
    recommendations for, 335–337
Project STAY OUT
    administration and governance,
        192–193
    barriers to transition, 201–202
    lessons learned, 204–206
    outcomes, 202–204, 204*f*
    process evaluation, 199–202
    service delivery model, 193–200,
        198*f*
    services received by participants,
        202, 203*f*
    transition specialists, 193, 197–200,
        205–206
    youth profile, 200–202
Project SUPPORT, 192, 193–194
Promoting Safe and Stable Families
    Act of 2001 (PL 107-133),
    271–272
Protective factors, 236–237, 238*t*
PSP, *see* Bridge Peer Support Program
    (PSP)
Psychopharmacology, *see* Medica-
    tions
Purveyor of the TIP Model, NNYT
    as, 86

Quality assurance committees, 316
Quality improvement process, *see*
    Continuous quality improve-
    ment
Quality improvement teams (QITs),
    292, 314–315

Rationale statements, 75–77, 76*f*
    see also TIP core practices
Rehabilitation Act Amendments
    (PL 105-220), 141–142
Relapse prevention, 255

Relationship development, 53–54,
    217–218
Research studies
    methodological concerns, 8–9
    need for, 42–43
    overview, 9–12, 14*t*–15*t*
    recommendations for, 338–340
    successful interventions for
        transition-age youth, 41–42
Residential facilities, 181, 183
Residential status, *see* Living situa-
    tions
Risk behavior
    as behavioral norm, 256
    challenges and issues, 246–247
    effects of, 237–239, 240*f*, 241–242
    ensnarement process, 239, 240*f*
    intervention approaches, 240*f*,
        243–244
    person-centered approach, 256–257
    Prevention Planning approach,
        248–255
    risk and protective factors,
        236–237, 238*t*
    setbacks and, 240*f*, 241–242
    types of, 236
    vulnerability of young people with
        emotional/behavioral difficul-
        ties, 235
    see also Prevention Planning

SAMHSA, *see* Substance Abuse and
    Mental Health Services
    Administration
Satisfaction surveys, 311, 316–317
School completion, *see* Graduation
    from school
SED, *see* Serious emotional distur-
    bance
Self-advocacy, development of, 77,
    206, 218
    see also Youth voice
Self-determination
    Bridge Peer Support Program,
        220–221
    components of, 101–102
    development of, 77
    Project STAY OUT, 194–195, 206
Self-help groups, 210
Self-management, Bridge Peer Sup-
    port Program, 218–219

Senate Bill 3195, *see* Healthy Transi-
    tions Act of 2008
Serious emotional disturbance (SED),
    30–31, 269
Serious mental illness (SMI), 30–31,
    269
    see also Mental illness
Service delivery considerations
    age limits and eligibility require-
        ments, 29–32, 264–265, 283
    appeal of services, 27, 39–42,
        265–267
    case examples, 26–27, 28, 29, 32,
        35–36, 39–40
    child welfare system, 271–273
    culturally appropriate practices, 60,
        125–126, 134, 137–138, 191,
        230
    developmentally appropriate
        approaches, 27, 34, 39–42,
        265–267
    historical perspective, 25–26
    justice system, 38–39, 276–277
    mental health services, 32–35,
        179–182
    recommendations and calls for
        action, 330–340
    special education, 271–273
    see also Coordinated services;
        Funding considerations
Skills development
    Bridge Peer Support Program,
        219–220
    Options program, 125
    rationale statements, 75–77, 76*f*
    Transition Age Support Initiative,
        227–228
    Transition to Independence
        Process, 69–77, 97
SMI, *see* Serious mental illness
Social/family services, Project STAY
    OUT, 203*f*
Social problem solving, 50
    see also TIP core practices,
        SODAS
Social responsibility, developing,
    65–67, 96
Social skills instruction
    Project STAY OUT, 196
    recommendation for, 335
SODAS problem-solving method, 50,
    66–67, 66*f*

Special education
    federal policies, 273–276
    lack of transition planning for
        students, 38
SSI, *see* Supplemental Security Income
Stakeholders
    cultural competency and, 297–298
    including in quality improvement
        process, 296–299
    theory-based logic models,
        298–299
    in TIP system, 86
    see also Engaging young people
Stars Behavior Health Group (SBHG)
    staff training, 304
    Total Quality Management pro-
        gram, 310–311
    youth participation in quality
        improvement, 316
State policies
    age and eligibility rules, 31–32
    child welfare, 272
    funding sources, 34–35
    mental health services, 268–270
    quality improvement of programs,
        301–302
    recommendations and calls to
        action, 334
Stigma, *see* Nonstigmatizing services
        and supports
Strategic planning, Options program,
    138
Strength-based approach, 52–53,
    216–217
Strength-discovery and needs assess-
    ment, 50, 52–53
    see also TIP core practices
Structured Psychotherapy for Ado-
    lescents Responding to
    Chronic Stress (SPARCS/
    DBT), 51, 106
Student Success Grants, 276
Substance abuse, 12, 14*t*–15*t*
    see also Co-morbidity, Prevention
        Planning, Risk behavior
Substance Abuse and Mental Health
    Services Administration
    (SAMHSA)
    Center for Mental Health Services,
        25
    Community Mental Health Service
        Block Grants, 35

Healthy Transitions Initiative, 333
    Partnerships for Youth Transition,
        118
    *Transforming Mental Health Care in
        America,* 270
    web site, 172
Supplemental Security Income (SSI),
    30, 32
Support networks, developing
    Bridge Peer Support Program, 218
    Project STAY OUT, 196–197
    recommendation for, 335
    Transition Age Support Initiative,
        227
    Transition to Independence Pro-
        cess, 67–69, 96
Supported Housing for Young Adults
    program (New York), 281
Supports and services for youth
    access, 63–64
    appropriateness of, 62–65, 95–96,
        180–181
    Career Workforce Skills Training,
        147–150, 155, 157
    continuity of, 63, 264–265
    informal and formal key players,
        65*t*
    Options program, 124–125
    peer support groups, 83–84
    policy needs and calls for action,
        330–340
    Transition to Independence
        Process, 61–65, 95–96
    Youth Transition Program,
        145–146, 155, 157
    see also specific programs
Sustainability of programs, 86,
    282–283, 336
    effectiveness, 78–81

TANF, *see* Temporary Assistance for
    Needy Families
TAPIS, *see* Transition to Adulthood
    Program Information
    System
    continuous system improvement,
        81–83
    TAPIS Goal Achiever. 78, 80–81,
        307–310, 308*f,* 339
    TAPIS Progress Tracker, 78, 80–81,
        307–310, 308*f,* 339

TASI, *see* Transition Age Support Initiative program
TAY, *see* Village Transition-Age Youth Academy
Teaching
    axioms for, 177–178
    enhance young person's competencies, 69–77
    in-vivo teaching strategies, 73–77
    by transition facilitators, 50, 74–75
Temporary Assistance for Needy Families (TANF), 281
Tennessee, Medicaid coverage for youth, 280
Texting, as prompting strategy, 74
Theory-based logic models, 298–299
Thresholds Young Adult Program (YAP)
    breakdown of mental illness diagnoses, 173*f*
    case examples, 171, 175–176, 185–186
    characteristics and comparison to Transition-Age Youth programs, 165–168, 166*t*
    community-living skills, building, 184–185
    intake data, 165*f*
    overview, 163, 164
    progress and outcomes, 168–169, 169*f*, 170*f*
    reinforcement strategies, 182
    supports and services, tailoring, 180–181
    target population, 167–168
    see also TIP model
TIP core practices, 50, 104–105
    Transition facilitators, provided competency training in 50,
    see also Essential elements of the TIP model
TIP guidelines 49t, 51–86, 95–98t, 104
TIP model
    definition of, 48–51
    core practices 50, 104–105
    effectiveness, 78–81
    continuing system improvement, 81–83
    essential element of 104–106
    essential organizational features of 107–113

evidence-supported practice 86
    guidelines and associated elements 49t, 51–86, 95–98t 104
    transition domains 61–62, 61*f*, 99–103, 99*f*, 105
    see also Transition to Independence Process
TIP system, see TIP model, Transition to Independence Process
TIP transition domains
    see also Transition domains
Transforming Mental Health Care in America (SAMHSA), 270
Transition Age Support Initiative (TASI) program
    community outreach, 224
    Genesis Clubhouse, 227
    lessons learned, 231
    mission and principles, 223
    peer associates, 225
    program features, 229–230
    program impact and outcomes, 230–231, 231*f*
    structure and services, 223–229
Transition-Age Youth Academy, *see* Village Transition-Age Youth Academy
Transition domains, 61–62, 61*f*, 99–103, 99*f*, 105
Transition facilitators
    as coaches, 61–62
    core practices, use of, 50
    cultural competence, 60
    qualifications and characteristics, 108–109
    roles of, 50, 51, 64–65, 109–110, 178
    supports for, 111
    as teachers, 74–75
    training, 50, 53
Transition Follow-Along Checklist, 81
Transition Planning Inventory, 70
Transition Program Fidelity Assessment Protocol, 82–83, 308*f*, 309–310, 339
Transition Service Integration Model, 284
Transition services
    defined, 274
    legal mandates, 141–142, 273–274
    see also specific programs
Transition specialists, *see* Professional roles

Transition to Adulthood Program
    Information System (TAPIS),
    78, 80–81, 307–310, 308f, 339
Transition to Independence Process
    (TIP)
    assessment, 70–73, 97
    case examples, 57–58
    engaging young people, 51–60,
        95
    essential practice elements,
        104–106
    futures planning, 54–58, 69, 95,
        105–106
    guidelines, 49t, 95–98
    historical perspective, 25–26
    mentors and partnerships, 83–86,
        97–98
    organizational features, 107–113
    outcome focus, 77–78, 79t–80t,
        80–83, 97
    overview, 48–51, 86, 327–328
    quality improvement process,
        81–83, 112
    relationship development, 53–54
    services and supports, tailoring,
        61–65, 95–96
    skills development, 73–77, 97
    social responsibility, developing,
        65–67, 96
    strength-based approach, 52–53
    support network, developing,
        67–69, 96 97–98
    web site, 58, 64, 83, 132
    see also TIP model, TIP system

Unconditional commitments, facili-
    tating, 69
University of Oregon, 144, 155, 156t,
    191, 194
University of South Florida Logic
    Model Team, 298–299
U.S. Department of Justice, Office of
    Juvenile Justice and Delin-
    quency Prevention, 194
U.S. Department of Labor, Office of
    Disability and Employment
    Programs, 332
U.S. General Accounting Office,
    270
U.S. Office of Special Education
    Programs, 301

Village Transition-Age Youth Acad-
    emy (TAY)
    case example, 170
    characteristics and comparison to
        Young Adult Program,
        165–168, 166t
    community-living skills, building,
        184
    overview, 163, 164–165
    progress and outcomes, 168–169
    reinforcement strategies, 182
    target population, 167–168
Vocational and Transition Services for
    Adolescents with Emotional and
    Behavioral Disorders (Bullis and
    Fredericks), 73
Vocational rehabilitation, 143
    see also Career Workforce Skills
        Training; Youth Transition
        Program
Voice mail, as prompting strategy, 74

Wellness Recovery Action Plans
    (WRAP), 51, 106, 211, 255
Wraparound process, 55

YAP, see Thresholds Young Adult
    Program (YAP)
Youth coordinators, 313–314
Youth cultures, 60, 179, 230
Youth House (Options program),
    129–130
Youth M.O.V.E., 85–86
Youth Transition Program (YTP)
    case example, 157–159
    outcomes, 151, 151t
    overview, 144
    participants, 144
    services provided, 145–146
    successful program features,
        153–155, 156t, 157
Youth Transitions Resource Center,
    282
Youth voice
    importance of, 42, 85–86, 186–187
    need for, 284
    Options program, 133–134
    strategies for encouraging, 110,
        336–337, 338
    Youth M.O.V.E., 85–86
YTP, see Youth Transition Program